CW00530670

OXFORD ENGLISH MONOGRAPHS

General Editors

CHRISTOPHER BUTLER   VINCENT GILLESPIE

DOUGLAS GRAY   EMRYS JONES

ROGER LONSDALE   FIONA STAFFORD

In memory of

NATHAN RICHARD RAWLINSON (1966–1987)

GUY RICHARD RAWLINSON (1930–1994)

British Writing
of the
Second World War

MARK RAWLINSON

CLARENDON PRESS · OXFORD

OXFORD
UNIVERSITY PRESS

Great Clarendon Street, Oxford OX2 6DP

Oxford University Press is a department of the University of Oxford
and furthers the University's aim of excellence in research, scholarship,
and education by publishing worldwide in

Oxford New York

Athens Auckland Bangkok Bogotá Buenos Aires Calcutta
Cape Town Chennai Dar es Salaam Delhi Florence Hong Kong Istanbul
Karachi Kuala Lumpur Madrid Melbourne Mexico City Mumbai
Nairobi Paris São Paulo Singapore Taipei Tokyo Toronto Warsaw

with associated companies in Berlin Ibadan

Oxford is a trade mark of Oxford University Press
in the UK and in certain other countries

Published in the United States
by Oxford University Press Inc., New York

© Mark Rawlinson 2000

The moral rights of the author have been asserted
Database right Oxford University Press (maker)

First published 2000

All rights reserved. No part of this publication may be reproduced,
stored in a retrieval system, or transmitted, in any form or by any means,
without the prior permission in writing of Oxford University Press.
or as expressly permitted by law, or under terms agreed with the appropriate
reprographics rights organizations. Enquiries concerning reproduction
outside the scope of the above should be sent to the Rights Department.
Oxford University Press, at the address above

You must not circulate this book in any other binding or cover
and you must impose this same condition on any acquirer

British Library Cataloguing in Publication Data

Data available

Library of Congress Cataloging in Publication Data

Data available

ISBN 0–19–818456–5

1 3 5 7 9 10 8 6 4 2

Typeset in Sabon MT
by Alliance Phototypesetters, Pondicherry, India
Printed in Great Britain
on acid-free paper by
T. J. International Ltd,
Padstow, Cornwall

Acknowledgements

I COULD not have written this book without the help of many people. I would like to say thank you to: Jon Stallworthy, who supervised my D. Phil. thesis; Desmond Graham and Valentine Cunningham who examined it; my friends who have been generous with their encouragement and criticism, especially the late Jeremy Beadle, Bill Brewer, Simon Carnell, Mario Domenichelli, Nick Everett, David Hesmondhalgh, Tristram Hooley, Piotr Khuhivchak, Rod Mengham, Sharon Ouditt, David Pascoe, Ian Patterson, Simon Port, Felicity Rosslyn, Philip Shaw, Helen Steward, and Rowley Wymer; Adam Piettte and Martin Stannard who read the typescript in its entirety and made incisive and face-saving suggestions; Michael Rice, Greg Williams, and Glenn Black who made all this possible many years ago; the students of literature and war in Leicester and Cambridge who have helped me to change my mind on numerous occasions; my heads of department at Leicester, Bill Myers and Vince Newey; the staffs of the Bodleian Library, the archive of Trinity College, the library of Rhodes House, the English Faculty Library, and the History Faculty Library in Oxford, Leicester University Library, New York Public Library, and the British Library. The British Academy and the department of English and the Research Board of the Faculty of Arts at the University of Leicester have generously supported this research. My greatest debt is to my family, especially to William (sorry there are no pictures), to Gabriel, who arrived as the book went to press, and to my wife Julian who has been my best critic for the duration.

M. R.

University of Leicester
June 1999

Contents

ABBREVIATIONS   viii

INTRODUCTION   I

1. RECONNAISSANCE: VIOLENCE,
   REPRESENTATION, AND BRITAIN'S
   SECOND WORLD WAR   6

2. THE FIGURE OF THE AIRMAN   39

3. 'WHAT TARGETS FOR A BOMB': SPECTACLE,
   RECONSTRUCTION AND
   THE LONDON BLITZ   68

4. SIDE SHOW OR SECOND FRONT?:
   THE LEGIBILITY OF BATTLE IN
   NORTH AFRICA   110

5. WAR AIMS AND OUTCOMES   139

6. 'WE'RE ALL PRISONERS OF WAR'   167

CONCLUSION   205

BIBLIOGRAPHY   210

INDEX   235

Abbreviations

CEJL   George Orwell, *The Collected Essays, Journalism and Letters*, ed. Sonia Orwell and Ian Angus, 4 vols. (Secker and Warburg, 1968)

PNW   *Penguin New Writing*

MOI   Ministry of Information

RHP   Richard Hillary Papers, Archives of Trinity College, Oxford

Introduction

> Above all I am not concerned with Poetry.
> My subject is war, and the pity of War.
> The Poetry is in the pity.
>
> Wilfred Owen.[1]

> Despite Churchill's rhetoric, the war was fought in prose, even prosaically.
>
> A. J. P. Taylor.[2]

OWEN'S apology for writing about war is, paradoxically, a fundamental source of critical uncertainty about the value of the literature of a 'good war' (good both morally and socially, for individuals, for institutions like the BBC and the Labour Party, and for the global community of states).[3] But it is not only within literary institutions that it is assumed that 'hell cannot be let loose twice', that the Second World War fails to live up to the First.[4] 'The popular memory of World War II', writes John Ellis, 'owes more to fond allusions to foreign climes, sunshine, good health and periodic binges than to any real conception of conditions at the front. For only a minority of men ever knew what these could be like—what had been the common experience on the Western Front between 1914 and 1918, was the exception to the rule in most of the theatres of the last war.'[5] Such comparisons reveal more about our own readings of historical events than about the meanings that could be ascribed to them by participants.

---

[1] Wilfred Owen's draft preface for a collection of war poems to be published in 1919, *The Complete Poems and Fragments of Wilfred Owen*, ed. Jon Stallworthy, 2 vols. (Chatto and Windus, Hogarth Press, and Oxford University Press, 1983), ii. 535.

[2] A. J. P. Taylor, *English History 1914–1945* (Oxford: Oxford University Press, 1965), 647.

[3] Peter Clarke, *Hope and Glory: Britain 1900–1990* (Harmondsworth: Allen Lane / The Penguin Press, 1996), 207.

[4] Keith Douglas, 'Poets in This War', *A Prose Miscellany*, ed. Desmond Graham (Manchester: Carcanet, 1985), 119.

[5] John Ellis, *The Sharp End of War: The Fighting Man in World War II* (Newton Abbot: David & Charles, 1980), 53.

The Second World War was fought with an eye on posterity's memory. Prime Minister Winston Churchill and novelist J. B. Priestley ('Is he now the second or third most powerful man in the country?' asked Louis MacNeice) spoke directly to millions of radio listeners. Both interpreted present crisis by imagining the meanings that future generations would discover in their past.[6] Churchill's conservativism borrowed Hitler's millennial rhetoric: 'if the British Empire and its Commonwealth last for a thousand years, men will say, "This was their finest hour." '[7] Priestley's socialist vision rested on the same trope. On 5 June 1940, the day after the Germans took Dunkirk (and after Churchill's 'never surrender' speech), the significance of the defeat of the British Expeditionary Force was, his address implied, conditional on the evacuation being reimagined by 'great grand children, when they learn how we began this War by snatching glory out of defeat, and then swept on to victory'.[8] A crucial component of this victory in the contest of states was the idea of fighting for a better world at home, though Priestley's promotion of this war aim led to his being taken off the air. But the rival broadcasters invoked the same images of 'liberated grandchildren' with which, according to Benjamin, social democracies silence the memories of 'enslaved ancestors' in which the historical experience of economic and political injustice are figured.[9]

The construction of the national memory of a state whose sovereignty was endangered was just one move in mobilizing the manpower and morale on which the defence of that sovereignty depended. But it gives us a good purchase on the structure and functions of the symbolic dimension of warfare. The idea of war's political instrumentality requires that somehow the destruction of persons (killing for and dying for your country) be articulated with conceptions of the future internal and external relations of states. War presupposes the efficacy of a symbolic exchange which overcomes both the reluctance of the individual to surrender control of his body and the as-yet immateriality of the goals in the name of which that surrender is required. This is usually viewed as the province of state-controlled persuasion, but a top-down perspective underplays the importance

---

[6] Louis MacNeice, *Selected Prose*, ed. Alan Heuser (Oxford: Oxford University Press, 1990), 115.
[7] Winston S. Churchill, *The War Speeches of Winston Churchill*, ed. Charles Eade, 3 vols. (Cassell, 1951–2), i. 207.
[8] J. B. Priestley, *Postscripts* (Heinemann, 1940), 4.
[9] Walter Benjamin, *Illuminations*, ed. Hannah Arendt (1970. Fontana, 1973), 262.

of values and symbols disseminated in civil culture to the prosecution of war. It is in relation to both official and private persuasion that this study sets out to read imaginative, memorial, documentary, and critical literature of the war years.

The central issues are the representation of military violence and the ways in which violence is legitimated as the means to some desirable or necessary end. Wartime literature is both critical of the content and vehicles of that legitimation, and fully implicated in the reproduction and invention of alternative justifications of violence. In this regard, much writing produced between 1939 and 1945 disappoints the desire for a reprise of the literature of 'the pity of War'. The bulk of the texts cited are works of prose rather than verse, often ephemeral ones at that (though more verse of the kind that fits modern definitions of war poetry was written in the Second World War than in the First, and the editor M. J. Tambimuttu was unusually judicious in observing, in 1944, that 'there are more interesting poets writing to-day in war-time than last time').[10] Where possible I discuss writing that circulated widely in wartime culture, which engaged with the most salient and equivocal themes of official and popular discourse, and which can be contextualized historically in terms of a contemporary reception. Exceptions to this model of investigation occur where conditions (for instance confinement in POW camps in central Europe) precluded wartime publication of material written wholly or in part during the war.

This study does not seek to literalize A. J. P. Taylor's metaphor of a prosaic war by inferring the relative literary merit of its corpus (the values which this literature codified are another matter) or by debunking the legends that have arisen around Britain's Second World War. Rather, it sets out to say something about the way the war was understood by those who fought it, and to address the division of war and literature which Owen sought to cancel with a denial of the literary.

Chapter one addresses questions about war and representation, and assesses the assumptions that underpin extant literary critical appraisal of writing about war. It challenges the coherence of the opposition of war literature to discourses identified with the prosecution of war, and it proposes a reading of wartime culture whose

---

[10] M. J. Tambimuttu, 'In Memory of Keith Douglas', *Poetry London* X (Editions Poetry London, 1944). The obituary of Douglas, killed during the D-day landings, is an unpaginated, and presumably last-minute insertion in this number.

fundamental premise is that the material events of military conflict, notably lethal wounding, require symbolization and discursive mediation if war is to function as an instrument of political policy. Following Elaine Scarry, manifold verbal representations of violence are interpreted as redescriptions: the destruction of human flesh and consciousness is rationalised and occluded by a logic that substitutes ends for means. This model makes possible a less stratified understanding of the function of representations of violence in a society at war, and permits an analysis which is responsive to the contradictory values invested in state-legitimated killing.

The bulk of the book focuses on significant theatres of war and the concepts through which the events that occurred in them were articulated with more general wartime exigencies and ideals. Chapter two is a study of themes of individualism and social cohesion in the light of the career and posthumous reception of fighter pilot and writer Richard Hillary. Contemporary thinking about heroism, selfhood, and nation is explored in the broader context of wartime developments in writing about military aviation. Chapter three investigates the process by which the Luftwaffe's attacks on the United Kingdom cohered into an event known as the Blitz. The new social and psychological geography of the metropolis revises our thinking about urban representation. The absence of the human body from aestheticizing descriptions of ruined cityscapes is fundamental to the reinvention of London as an emblem of positive wartime outcomes in both the military and political spheres. Interactions of architectonic space and subjectivity in fictional and documentary texts, in graphic art, and in architectural and travel writing, are discussed with particular emphasis on the work of Vera Brittain, Elizabeth Bowen, Henry Green, and William Sansom. Chapter four takes the desert of North Africa as the site of its inquiry into how the battlefield signified in different genres of official and literary writing. Keith Douglas's visceral poetry and prose reveal paradoxical parallels to military redescription. Readings of the New Zealander Dan Davin's wartime fiction and post-war official military history demonstrate the extent to which the battlefield, the scene of killing, is also a verbal and iconic construct. Chapter five is concerned with the enunciation of war aims, and the ways in which military service and civilian sacrifice were connected with the emergent concepts of domestic social reconstruction. The career of Alun Lewis, the war's non-combatant war poet, is read in the context of contemporary formulations of both progressive and bellicose ideals. Dan Billany's fiction provides a counterweight to the sentiment of socialism which facilitated an alternative rationalization of violence in the guise of the 'People's War'. The final chapter examines the critical perspectives on the insularity of Britain at war which were achieved in wartime writings by and about prisoners of war in Europe. Stories of daring escape, rather than re-educative confinement, were predominant in immediately post-war culture, but it is argued that the forms of remembrance were determined in part by wartime symbols and concepts.

This is necessarily a selective approach to wartime print culture: there is not space for sustained attention to the war in the Pacific and the prisoners of the Japanese, to production and industrial relations, to conscientioius objectors, to the medical and administrative treatment of the dead and wounded, or to writing from the senior service. But the already vast corpus of texts discussed confronts us with contemporary responses to a substantial and representative range of technologies, social formations and relationships to the war's casualties. From this vantage, it is possible not only to begin to account for the literature written about the war, but to assess the roles that it played in representing the war to those whose lives were overtaken by it.

Reconnaissance: Violence, Representation, and Britain's Second World War

Reconnaissance: **1.** *Mil* **a.** An examination or survey . . . to discover the nature of the ground or resources . . . before making an advance.[1]

LANGUAGE AND WAR

KEITH Douglas's 'Vergissmeinnicht' (1943) was one of the most striking poems to come out of a North African campaign theatre brimming with poets (though not all of them soldiers). It is a survivor's song with a difference, for the not-to-be-forgotten is not a fallen compatriot but an enemy gunner, and the poet's meditations on mortality are qualified by the traces of an exhilaration at the looting of the battlefield among the signs of the victor's superiority of arms. It is also a reconfiguration of the relations between friend and foe in Wilfred Owen's 'Strange Meeting', though not so as to make Douglas's poem 'tautological' (the fate he feared for the belated poets of this war).[2] In Owen's poem, the Englishman, who has escaped from battle (presumed dead) is recognized by his German counterpart among the 'encumbered sleepers'.[3] The roused corpse aspires to a reconciliation transforming the grip of hand-to-hand combat (suggesting Clausewitz's trope of armies as wrestlers) into a

---

[1] *Oxford English Dictionary*, 2nd edn. (Oxford: Oxford University Press, 1989).

[2] Keith Douglas, *Complete Poems*, ed. Desmond Graham (Oxford: Oxford University Press, 1979), 111; *Miscellany*, 119.

[3] Wilfred Owen, *The Complete Poems and Fragments of Wilfred Owen*, ed. Jon Stallworthy, 2 vols. (Chatto and Windus, Hogarth Press, and Oxford University Press, 1983), i. 148.

sensual embrace of death. But in 'Vergissmeinnicht' the dead German is silent meat, and the killer must piece out the significance of the scene for himself, reading both altered flesh and text, the movement of 'swart flies' over a 'paper eye' and the 'copybook gothic script' inscribed on a photograph of the vanquished man's girl. The poem loops Owen's German soldier's prophecy of civilization's forgetfulness—'men will go content with what we spoiled'—back to the scene of combat and to the ('almost') 'content' experienced gazing on 'gunpit spoil' (which is both trophy and war's waste or by-product). Dismounted from his tank to probe the wounds in his opponent's more-and-less vulnerable flesh, the victor in Douglas's poem has his own unmanning by war revealed in the ironies of the scene of victimization; he is metallized (to borrow Marinetti's term) out of his humanity.[4] 'The soldier male', writes Klaus Theweleit, 'is forced to turn the periphery of his body into a cage for the beast within. In so doing, he deprives it of its function as a surface for social contact. His contact surface becomes an insulated shield, and he loses the capacity to perceive the social corpus within which his insulated body moves.'[5] The military inadequacy of the unarmoured German is spelled out with a sexual pun—'mocked at by his equipment / that's hard and good'—but this is a differential that returns to haunt the victor. The concluding stanza, which plays on the contradictions of the enemy's role in the contrasted realms of domesticity and battle, troubles the vital distinction between the survivor and the corpse, the quick and the dead:

> For here the lover and killer are mingled
> who had one body and one heart.
> And death who had the soldier singled
> has done the lover mortal hurt.

If the former has been 'singled' by death, marked out, cut off, so too has the onlooker, who has been reduced to the status of killer, not only by his role in the death of the lover, but in the larger context of the disciplining of his personality, instanced in his gaze on the victim. What I have called an unmanning, but which might equally be identified as the assumption of a bellicose-masculine ethos, is a symptom of the displacement of the human by strategic, administrative, or economic imperatives:

4 Marinetti's manifesto on the Ethiopian colonial war is quoted in Walter Benjamin, *Illuminations*, ed. Hannah Arendt (1970. Fontana, 1973), 243.

5 Klaus Theweleit, *Male Fantasies*, 2 vols. (1977–8. Cambridge: Polity, 1987–9), ii. 22.

> We see him almost with content,
> abased, and seeming to have paid. . . .

In its intermingling of abomination and fascination, the engaged and the detached, the individual and the disciplined mass, the poem is an emblem of the structure of war, in which material and embodied acts of injuring are always yoked with perspectives that transvalue that destruction. The poem is at once unflinching in its representation of war and, because it does not flinch, exemplary of a way of dealing with the broken bodies of persons upon which the turning of means into ends in war is reliant. Construing this poem is a more straightforward matter than unpacking Owen's meditation on violence and creativity; it is explicitly located amongst the material facts of combat. Readers who readily identify anti-bellicose sentiments in 'Strange Meeting' are often troubled in a more unsettling way by 'Vergissmeinnicht', finding it coolly, even callously, detached because it negates the reflex of revulsion. Auden noted in 1964 that the soldiers of 1916 shared 'a simple emotion of compassion' because they lacked a reason to fight. But in 1939

> it was obvious that the German Reich had fallen into the hands of very wicked men who offered the rest of Europe only the alternative of war or capitulation. The compassion which an English or American soldier might feel for his German fellow-sufferer was complicated by his conviction that the latter was suffering in an evil cause. It would have been impossible to write such a poem as Owen's 'Strange Meeting'.

'Complicated' attitudes are offered as a 'possible reason' for the supposed lesser literary merit of Second World War writing, a judgement that Auden, like many other commentators, does not substantiate in literary terms.[6] But the juxtaposition of necessity and sentiment also complicates later readers' responses, which are powerfully circumscribed by the conventions of Great War memorialization (instanced in Auden's own unhistorical—and very literary—generalization about 1916). The myth that the Great War was, and was widely perceived to be, a war fought despite the absence of issues dividing the antagonists (Henry Williamson's 1950s *roman fleuve* backdates the undeceiving moment to the Christmas truce of 1914 when Phillip Maddison learns 'they are fighting for civilization just as we are!') has determined a literary conception of warfare which in its emphasis on the subjective and somatic horrors has

---

[6] W. H. Auden, 'Private Poet', review of Lincoln Kirstein, *Rhymes of a Pfc*, in *Forewords and Afterwords* (Faber, 1973), 420–1.

nevertheless helped us to forget the cultural and social matrices in which those events are produced and have meaning.[7]

Attempts to outlaw aggressive war in the first half of the twentieth century can be correlated with the waning of 'a fatalistic attitude to war' at the end of the nineteenth, together with the dissemination of the ideas of 'war as exceptional and peace as both normal and morally superior'.[8] Notwithstanding the post-Napoleonic European novel of war (Tolstoy, Stendhal, Thackeray, Hugo, Zola), it is a commonplace that a cadre of English Great War poets and memoirists helped redefine attitudes to war by altering the way it was described in literature. Viewing the poetry of disenchantment as a cultural watershed in the representation of war thus superposes emergent moral and rhetorical distinctions. But rather than clarifying the connections between war and verbal culture, the prominence of this writing has tended to polarize violence and discourse. The association of the putative realism of Great War poetry with a demystified truth about war is forged in the perception of the poets' secession from the precedents of ennobling rhetoric, but it also rests on a correspondence model of representation. Great War writers were made by war experience and were, in a sense, another of war's byproducts. Yeats's conviction that the war poet is a passive victim is shared by many who revile his aesthetic judgement against Owen.[9] In practice, war writing as documentary and as witness is qualified by acknowledgements of war's resistance to representation. On one argument, the resources of culture lag behind innovative technologies of destruction. Paul Fussell draws on modern war writing's rhetoric of disillusionment when he presents the optimistic inadequacy of contemporaneous images of war as an inverse index of war's abhorrent character. War and culture are posited as antithetical.

These views of the correspondence, or the lack of it, between art and violence involve a conception of war as a state of affairs which, even though it may escape attempts to represent it, can nevertheless be posited as the cause of that failure. Samuel Hynes, detecting the sense of an ending in Europe in the Autumn of 1914, suggests that apocalypse was registered in the perceived failure of the available

---

[7] Henry Williamson, *A Fox Under my Cloak* (Macdonald, 1955), 57.

[8] Martin Ceadel, *Thinking About Peace and War* (1987. Oxford: Oxford University Press, 1989), 11–12.

[9] W. B. Yeats (ed.), *The Oxford Book of Modern Verse* (Oxford University Press, 1936), p. xxxiv.

cultural forms to express it.[10] Only experience can reinstate art's witness when war opens a gap between the world and representations of that world: the trench poets 'arrived at the aesthetic of direct experience *through* direct experience'.[11] Vernon Scannell, veteran of the North African campaigns of the early 1940s, affirmed war's unmediated imprint on culture: the soldier-poet in the Second World War 'finds that it is experience which is seeking him out and demanding from him the ability to transcribe it'.[12] The idea that war produces the kind of art which its occurrence proves to be wanting lies behind the claim by G. S. Fraser (poet, critic, and serviceman, though he ended up working for the MOI (Ministry of Information) in Cairo) that the superiority of Keith Douglas over Robert Graves was due to 'the changing technique, not of poetry, but of war'.[13]

But under these descriptions, war paradoxically comes to function as an agent of cultural regeneration. In this respect literary criticism reproduces what Pick calls the 'Manichaean views' by which the nineteenth century figured war alternately as a machine running out of control or the engine of civilization.[14] Desmond Graham notes that war restructures language, 'shifts the meaning of the simplest and commonest words, awakens to new and generally vicious life, dead metaphors and clichés and has the ability to disturb and redefine the whole relationship between what is metaphorical and what literal'.[15] A publisher's blurb from 1942 announced that violence 'create[s] a new style, so that from the destruction of war something of lasting value emerges'.[16] War is knowable as that which, lying beyond the reach of conventional formulations, determines its own representation. In the midst of the war-books boom, *Songs and Slang of the British Soldier* (1930) reported the view that 'the War brought about a great slackening of the inhibitions of speech'.[17]

[10] Samuel Hynes, *A War Imagined: The First World War and English Culture* (Bodley Head, 1990), 3–24.   [11] Ibid. 167.

[12] Vernon Scannell, *Not Without Glory: Poets of the Second World War* (Woburn Press, 1976), 29.

[13] G. S. Fraser, *Vision and Rhetoric: Studies in Modern Poetry* (Faber, 1959), 141–2.

[14] Daniel Pick, *War Machine: The Rationalisation of Slaughter in the Modern Age* (New Haven: Yale University Press, 1993), 4.

[15] Desmond Graham, *The Truth of War: Owen, Blunden, and Rosenberg* (Manchester: Carcanet, 1984), 24.

[16] *War Pictures by British Artists*, no. 2, *Blitz*, introduced by J. B. Morton (Oxford University Press, 1942), dust-wrapper.

[17] John Brophy and Eric Partridge (eds.), *Songs and Slang of the British Soldier: 1914–1918* (Scholartis Press, 1930), 16.

Lexicographical surveys of Second World War service argot decoded the informal lexicon of conscripts while they were still fighting, a priority reflected in Fussell's study of the Anglo-American experience of 1939–45, *Wartime*, in which the glossing of the uncensored speech habits of the inarticulate is preferred to analysis of a euphemistic print culture.[18]

The human subject of twentieth-century war literature is not a hero but a witness, and its archetypal narrative pattern is the exposure of illusions rather than the celebration of deeds of arms. This subject is not exemplary of his culture, but alien to it (though that outsider status became representative). The opposition of war and culture reflects not only the formation of moral distinctions between war and peace, but also reifies the topoi of oft-told stories about crossing boundaries between the polite world of civilization and the barbaric scene of combat. But as a critique of the assimilation or falsification of military violence in heroic genres, and epic or historical narratives, this model may go too far in the other direction, conceptualizing war as the touchstone of a material reality which can be accessed simply by achieving distance from literary culture's rhetorical embellishments or occlusions of violence.

Twentieth-century canons of war literature privilege the perspective of the combatant soldier who is engaged in war's central activity of injuring and killing persons. Hynes argues that war should properly (that is morally) remain external to the analogical operations of language: 'war is not like anything except itself.'[19] Such strictures have been more powerfully articulated by fictions like Remarque's *Im Westen Nichts Neues* (*All Quiet on the Western Front*) which deal with soldiers who have, as Walter Benjamin put it, 'grown silent— not richer, but poorer, in communicable experience'.[20] Henceforth, the more authoritative answers to the question 'what is war like' have been those which take 'like' to mean not what does war resemble, but 'how it is' for the persons who experience war.[21] Writing which rejects 'the old lie' and the obscenity of 'abstract words' in order to show war as it is for those engaged in it acquires the double

---

[18] See J. L. Hunt and A. G. Pringle (eds.), *Service Slang: A First Selection* (Faber, 1943), 18–19, coyly representing 'bullshit' with asterisks, and Eric Partridge (ed.), *A Dictionary of R.A.F. Slang* (Michael Joseph, 1945). Partridge worked for the Public Relations department of the Air Ministry.

[19] Hynes, *A War Imagined*, 95.   [20] Benjamin, *Illuminations*, 84.

[21] See Thomas Nagel, 'What is it like to be a bat?', *Mortal Questions* (1979. Cambridge: Cambridge University Press, 1991), 169.

guarantee of a refusal of outmoded rhetoric and of proximity to the physical and psychological shocks of combat.[22] The conscript-victim's pain or moral dislocation is a reality which normally gets closeted in the idea of dying (or killing) for one's country, or of transcendence through struggle ('only death gives life its meaning').[23] But the evasion of euphemism or bellicose rhetoric, in projecting an essence of war which is always physical and psychological, not metaphysical or ideological, is itself ideological.

Emphasis on the incommunicable experience of individuals excludes other meanings, particularly those connecting violence to policy. George Orwell noted the consequences of such omissions: written from 'a passive, negative angle', the classic books of the 1914–18 war 'are the records of something completely meaningless, a nightmare happening in a void. That was not actually the truth about the war, but it was the truth about the individual reaction.'[24] What is left out of the picture is the matrix of ideological, social and political factors which precipitate and sustain wars, together with the concepts and conventions by which destructive agency is mediated culturally.

Daniel Pick reads William James's dismantling of the distinction between war and peace in 'The Moral Equivalent of War' (1910) as pointing the way to a reconception of the 'relationship between language and military deeds': 'Words, ideas, images constitute the discursive support for military conflict; they should be understood not as though they are a mere froth without consequences, but as crucial aspects of the destructive reality of violent conflict itself.'[25] While the ideal of the war poet depends on the notion that weasel words initiate and sustain conflict—the war poet conducts a campaign against heroic and diplomatic registers—the discourses which rationalize war are all too readily assumed to be compromised by the literature of protest. It is necessary to complicate the idea of an essence of war cut free from fatally false tropes and descriptions, and urge recognition of war's irreducibly symbolic dimension. The view that war is nothing other than material events of bodily alteration is prematurely reductive.

---

[22] Wilfred Owen, 'Dulce et decorum est', *Complete Poems*, i. 140; Ernest Hemingway, *A Farewell to Arms* (Jonathan Cape, 1929), 195.

[23] These words are Ludwig Wittgenstein's, written while a volunteer on the Russian Front in 1916, see Ray Monk, *Wittgenstein: The Duty of Genius* (1990. Vintage, 1991), 139.

[24] Orwell, 'Inside the Whale', *CEJL* i. 523.   [25] Pick, *War Machine*, 14.

In this respect, the intellectual career of Carl von Clausewitz, the early nineteenth-century German theorist of war, may be taken as emblematic. Clausewitz contested the rules and rationalizations of Enlightenment military thought by locating 'the lasting spirit of war' in violent force: 'The nature of war is fighting.'[26] But a universal theory of war itself risked disembodied abstraction: 'when it must omit the living matter in order to hold to the dead form, which is of course the easiest to abstract, it would be in the end a dry skeleton of dull truths squeezed into a doctrine' (192–3). The living matter for Clausewitz was killing, 'massive concentration of forces and aggressive conduct' (199). But in the writing of *On War*, Clausewitz's insistence on 'particularity and local circumstances' confronted him with the fact that all wars do not correspond to the theoretical ideal of totalized violence. His post-1827 definition of war as a continuation of policy by other means introduced a profound tension into his theory. Just as absolute or true war is in practice confounded—policy 'converts the overwhelmingly destructive element of war into a mere instrument'—so the theory of the maximization of violent force (means) is contradicted by the account of the ends to which that violence is shaped: 'War is only a branch of political activity . . . it is in no sense autonomous' (221). Jacqueline Rose, emphasizing the theoretical ambitions of Clausewitz's unfinished work, observes that 'war seems to figure as the violent repressed of its own rationalization'.[27] But read another way, *On War* reveals that the desire to isolate absolute war in its element is always a futile attempt to bracket the social and symbolic contexts of fighting. Like the Kantian aesthetic, Clausewitz's concept of the lasting spirit of war is troubled by both the material and semiotic contexts of its embodiment.

War literature and its reception have been shaped by a series of heuristically useful oppositions, though their value and organization require some unpacking if their full significance is to be apprehended. In the influential figure of the war poet as it has been constructed since 1914, cultural and moral authority is founded in an agent-centred and engaged perspective on combat. The war poet, as opposed to the jingo-versifier, has, crucially, participated in the contest of injuring (though the war poet as injurer is a factor which the

[26] Quoted in Azar Gat, *The Origins of Military Thought: From the Enlightenment to Clausewitz* (Oxford: Clarendon Press, 1989), 191, 199.
[27] Jacqueline Rose, *Why War?—Psychoanalysis, Politics and the Return to Melanie Klein* (Oxford: Blackwell, 1993), 23.

popular reception is largely silent about). The authority of his witness is proportional to its dissociation from administrative objectification and from an aesthetics of detachment. What makes this writing morally compelling is in part the correlation of the opposition of engagement and detachment with the differences between subjective and objective accounts of the value of a person: the difference between the view from inside a sensate body (embodied self-reflection), and the view of that body as just one thing among many in the universe, even an invisible component of one of the big battalions that are salient in the General Staff's appreciations of a battlefield. There is an additional and significant homology with the structure and categories of military command, in particular the relationship between tactics ('the use of military forces in the engagement') and strategy (the 'use of individual engagements to achieve the aim of the war').[28] In Montgomery's expression of the distinction between 'what is strategically desirable' and 'that which is tactically possible', idealized abstractions (detached) and practical contingencies (engaged and agent-centred) are counterpointed.[29] But the linkage of the handling of forces in the immediate presence of the enemy (tactics, the scene of injuring) with the projection and direction of large military movements and operations (Montgomery's 'strategic' desire, the abstract realm of policy and the imaginary), presupposes the primacy of detachment over engagement, the objective over the agent-centred picture. The aesthetic and experiential markers by which we identify the war poet are bound up both with the categories which shape our ethical attitudes to war and with the verbal and conceptual translations upon which the function of war as an instrument of policy depends.

The more obvious point to be made here, echoing Orwell's recognition of the limitations of the truth about the individual reaction, is that the suppression of one term in any of these oppositions, particularly that of violence and politics, commits us to a partial apprehension of the contexts of both military experience and representations of war. But once this is recognized, the way is opened to a more exacting, powerful, and in some ways controversial appreciation of the structure of the events we call war. This involves a full recognition of the intersection of the material and the symbolic. An acknowledgement of the weightiness of verbal and other signs in the prosecution

---

[28] Clausewitz, 'Strategie' (1804), quoted in Gat, *The Origins of Military Thought*, 204.
[29] Field Marshal The Viscount Montgomery, *Memoirs* (Collins, 1958), 87.

of war, and in particular in the exchange of ends for means, permits an approach to war literature that situates it not in remote opposition to the social processes of warfare (the sphere colonized by propagandists), but squarely in the midst of signifying mechanisms which permit conflict to function politically. In the context of Britain's Second World War, the relations between literary writing which makes the suffering caused by military violence resonate, and the descriptions which circulate in the general conversation which seamlessly justifies means in terms of ends, are additionally complicated. To proceed on the assumption that these discourses are opposed (on the basis of their association with, respectively, the conscripted subject and the militarized mass), is to foreclose the question of how each stands with respect to the inflections of the categories of the individual and of the collective which inform wartime self-representation and commentary. This is a particularly complex question in relation to the Home Front and the overtly social dimensions of the British war effort. Manifold reflex and elaborated interpretations of wartime experience address the claims of individualism and collectivism. The manner in which the symbols of private and public life are set to work in descriptions of military violence makes the forms and meanings of those descriptions all the more labile or referentially unstable. This is not only a problem for the student of wartime culture, but a condition which impinged on anyone who sought to intervene in the symbolic economy of wartime Britain.

The writing of combatants has emerged as the most plangent disavowal of bellicose values, and of the official discourses which legitimate military conduct. But the perceived cultural work of this literature (in particular its apparent confirmation of late twentieth-century scepticism about the rationality of war as an instrument of political agency) has effaced more reflexive consideration of the contexts and efficacy of that critique. Owen's 'Strange Meeting' challenges national ideologies of enmity by dramatizing a rapprochement between victim and killer away from the clash of nation states. But the pathos of the poem lies not so much in the discovery of a common humanity, as in the conviction that it will lie buried from sight. The lessons of the war will be forgotten in the peace. The implications of this pessimism are apparent only when the largest contexts of the activity of war are grasped, in particular the way culture functions in the rationalization of war. Critiques of war by non-combatants remain culturally marginal to the extent that they do not themselves reproduce the quasi-sublime fascination of violence.[30] Lynne Hanley notes that the literature of disenchantment is not as '"profoundly unbellicose" as it might appear': the persistent re-cycling of 'the story of the soldier's tragic discovery on the battlefield that what he is a part of is killing' is evidence of an innocence sus-tained despite the dissemination of stories about the disillusioned and the undeceived.[31] The idea that war is an extra-cultural locus of authenticity, reflected in the supposedly unrhetorical aesthetic of war poetry, is actually a source of resistance to anti-bellicose sentiments founded either in reason or repugnance. It helps distract us from the fact that military violence functions and signifies with respect to a cultural frame of reference. *Homage to Catalonia* (1938) had much to say about the struggle over the meanings of the Spanish Civil War, but it was Orwell's difficulties in getting the book published, or read, that demonstrate most forcibly that wars are fought with presses and microphones, as well as with ordinance and aeroplanes. This aspect of warfare takes more prosaic, as well as more insidious forms. Paul de Man has observed that '[w]hat we call ideology is precisely the confusion of linguistic with natural reality'. Conflation of 'the materiality of the signifier with the materiality of what it signifies' is fundamental to the operations whereby the destruction of persons is spoken of as if it were something else, for instance the construction of the political ideals of a new world order.[32]

Grasping the polyvalence of war involves a reconsideration of the opposition of the individual and the mass (and the strategic abstrac-tion of the mass) which underpins the privileging of the 'truth about the individual reaction' over historical, governmental or military descriptions and definitions of war. Thomas Nagel has written ex-tensively on the problem of combining 'the perspective of a particu-lar person inside the world with an objective view of that same world, the person and his viewpoint included'.[33] In 'War and Massacre', he proposes a dialogue between subjective and strategic perspectives on war, perspectives which he represents with the contrast between

[30] See e.g. Sharon Ouditt, *Fighting Forces: Writing Women: Identity and Ideology in the First World War* (Routledge, 1994).

[31] Lynne Hanley, *Writing War: Fiction, Gender, and Memory* (Amherst, Mass.: University of Massachusetts Press, 1991), 27, 29.

[32] Paul de Man, 'The Resistance to Theory', *The Resistance to Theory* (Manchester: Manchester University Press, 1986), 11.

[33] Thomas Nagel, *The View from Nowhere* (1986. New York: Oxford University Press, 1989), 3.

absolutist and consequentialist ethical theories. Absolutism, concerned with what a person is doing (to other people), involves 'a view of oneself as a small being *interacting* with others in a large world' (my emphasis), a view like that of the soldier-victim of Owen's 'Strange Meeting'. Consequentialist theories, such as utilitarianism, are concerned with outcomes, and a perspective which is analogous to the strategic, the outlook of Sassoon's General (who 'did for them . . . by his plan of attack') or Shakespeare's Henry V in the eyes of the soldier Williams.[34] Absolutism has to do with persons as agents, utilitarianism with numbers: there is no room in the latter account for individual agency, or the boundaries between individuals.[35] The justifications of utilitarianism, Nagel notes, 'are primarily administrative': human beings are reduced to utilities, statistics, tropes.[36] To stem the technologically-facilitated erosion of sanctions against certain kinds of violence in wartime, argues Nagel, the targets of that violence should be invested with subjectivity:

whatever one does to another person intentionally must be aimed at him as a subject, with the intention that he receive it as a subject. It should manifest an attitude to *him* rather than just to the situation. . . . Hostile treatment . . . is already addressed *to* a person, and does not take its interpersonal meaning from a wider context. . . . When . . . hostile or aggressive behaviour can no longer be intended for the reception of the victim as a subject . . . it takes on the character of a purely bureaucratic operation.[37]

But the description in the last sentence is accurate enough to shake our faith in the preceding prescriptions, because we inhabit networks of bureaucratic operations. Zygmunt Bauman's argument that 'the very idea of the *Endlösung* [Final Solution] was an outcome of the bureaucratic culture' captures the cancellation of moral responsibility by the command networks of modern society.[38] Nagel's attempt at an examined and punctual combination of the subjective and objective perspectives initially separates values which are, in the social practice of warfare, inseparably dispersed throughout the warring populations. The language in which war is described transforms the subject of one perspective into the statistics of the other. The

---

[34] Siegfried Sassoon, 'The General', *The War Poems*, ed. Rupert Hart-Davis (Faber, 1983), 78; William Shakespeare, *Henry V*, ed. Gary Taylor (Oxford: Oxford University Press, 1982), 212–13.

[35] See Martha Nussbaum, *Poetic Justice: The Literary Imagination and Public Life* (Boston, Mass.: Beacon Press, 1995), 15.

[36] Nagel, 'War and Massacre', *Mortal Questions*, 68. [37] Ibid. 66–7.

[38] Zygmunt Bauman, *Modernity and the Holocaust* (Cambridge: Polity, 1989), 15.

opposition invoked by Nagel models what goes on in war: the label war does not apply to states of affairs in which violence is not already understood to be at one end of a bureaucratic chain of agency. The opposed perspectives may be conceived as occupying the poles of a spectrum of interests and justifications, but in war this spectrum is a channel along which value is transferred (and the flow is in the opposite direction to that promoted by Nagel). This channel connects the individual and an administrative structure: the individual gives his life (dying for his country) and the state legitimizes the individual's actions (killing for his country). Elizabeth Bowen, writing at the end of the Second World War, noted the way this dichotomy was registered in consciousness: 'Outwardly, we accepted that at this time individual destiny had to count for nothing: inwardly, individual destiny became an obsession in every heart.'[39]

Without surrendering the possibility of intuiting and acting on knowledge that war is 'the infliction of human suffering through violence', it is desirable to hold both the material and the symbolic dimensions of warfare in mind simultaneously.[40] Discourses which render violence in war morally unambiguous are determinants of belief and action, however falsifiable they might appear in retrospect. As Christopher Prendergast notes, the distinction between discourse and referent is frequently 'artificial, in so far as the symbolic is also part of what was the case; it too belongs to the history in the direct and active sense of helping to produce it'.[41] War is always more than killing by and of persons: otherwise these activities could not be sustained against the perpetual embodied resistance of the participants' inertia and self-interest, or indeed their humanity.

The best way to 'keep to the element of the thing itself' wrote Clausewitz, is to anthropomorphize strategy:

War is nothing but a duel on a larger scale. Countless duels go to make up war, but a picture of it as a whole can be formed by imagining a pair of wrestlers. Each tries through physical force to compel the other to do his will; his immediate aim is to *throw* his opponent in order to make him incapable of further resistance.[42]

[39] Elizabeth Bowen, *The Demon Lover and Other Stories*, uniform edition (Jonathan Cape, 1952), 220.

[40] John Keegan, *The Face of Battle* (Jonathan Cape, 1976), 30.

[41] Christopher Prendergast, *Paris and the Nineteenth Century* (Oxford: Blackwell, 1992), 16.

[42] Carl von Clausewitz, *On War*, ed. Michael Howard and Peter Paret (Princeton: Princeton University Press, 1976), 75.

As so often, it is sport that naturalizes modern warfare, which has at once little and everything of the Olympic ethos about it. Clausewitz's wrestlers are a rationalization of complex, diffuse and convoluted activity: at the moment he makes war's true content visible, it becomes invisible. Rhetorical figures like these wrestlers occlude the myriad instances of physical hurt that bring about a result to such a contest. The 'rhetoric of battle history' is not simply a case of euphemism, but the displacement of what may already be a euphemistic description of injury with a description of something else, for instance, an outcome, which then stands in place of the injuring event.[43] According to Elaine Scarry, this 'redescription' is not part of a conspiracy, it is conventional:

The convention expresses the fact that the fate of the overall army or overall population, and not the fate of single individuals, will determine the outcome; it also has the virtue of bestowing visibility on events which, because of their scale, are wholly outside visual experience. It is, however, a convention which assists the disappearance of the human body from accounts of the very event that is the most radically embodying event in which human beings ever collectively participate.[44]

Virginia Woolf observed in 1918 that 'the reason why it is easy to kill another person must be that one's imagination is too sluggish to conceive what his life means to him'.[45] This imaginative failure is compounded by linguistic behaviour which mediates violence in the direction of strategy and policy.

War is a collective political activity directed at shaping the future, and is dependent on far-reaching patterns of signification. Because of, not despite, the ethical imperatives to keep the human body firmly before our gaze, it is necessary to recognize that war is a discursive, as well as a material, activity. Only then can we describe how a person's predicament in war is brought about and sustained. 'Because we deploy signs,' writes Terry Eagleton, pointing up the intersection of the real and the symbolic, 'we can overreach our bodies to the point where we can undo them.'[46] The destructiveness of war takes place in 'a complex of legal and political conditions':

---

[43] Keegan, *The Face of Battle*, 36.

[44] Elaine Scarry, *The Body in Pain: The Making and Unmaking of the World* (New York: Oxford University Press, 1985), 71.

[45] Virginia Woolf, *The Diary of Virginia Woolf*, ed. Anne Oliver Bell, 5 vols. (Hogarth Press, 1977–84), i. 186.

[46] Terry Eagleton, *The Significance of Theory* (Oxford: Blackwell, 1990), 25.

'The idea of war itself is a major factor in the way in which it is waged.'[47]

The complexity and necessity of the verbal and rhetorical dimension of modern warfare is evident once it is seen to consist of more than a conspiracy or a politically expedient 'masking' of the real.[48] In the inter-war period, propaganda ('the systematic propagation of information or ideas by an interested party') came to be associated more narrowly with the dissemination of falsehoods.[49] This negative definition feeds into the modern reflex of suspicion concerning discourses promoting war. But, additionally, the character of propaganda as an intentional act of agents or agencies lends it an ironic visibility. One can uncover, or imagine, the site of its production and the dispositions to action which are its intended product. This visibility makes propaganda available as a category by which to aggregate all advocacy of war. The general circulation of martial imagery and values is comparatively much less visible, harder to conceptualize, and, most importantly, resistant to personification. For Adam Piette, poetry and fiction not only camouflage propaganda, they 'constitute it'. But he is right to remark the tendency to 'falsely suspicious and cynically knowing' readings that result from the identification of wartime words with propaganda, that is with the intention to persuade or mislead.[50] As Scarry notes, irrespective of the motives involved, 'the structure of war itself will require that injuring be partially eclipsed from view': 'conventional war entails the participation of a massive number of people, only a small fraction of whom are engaged in the active verbal advocacy of either the elimination or the perpetuation of war; and if injuring disappears, it is its absence in their informal conversation that is perhaps most important.[51] Historical and imaginative writing had a significant role in mediating and rationalizing violence, but one which could only be misrepresented if the category of propaganda ('active verbal advocacy') is the only one in play. The ascription of propagandist functions to a text threatens

---

[47] Ian Clark, *Waging War: A Philosophical Introduction* (Oxford: Clarendon Press, 1988), 2, 11.

[48] G. L. Mosse, *Fallen Soldiers: Reshaping the Memory of the World Wars* (New York: Oxford University Press, 1990), 77. Lt. Brooks in John Del Vecchio's Vietnam novel, *The 13th Valley* (1982. Sphere, 1988), 501, thinks it is possible to ' "restructure human languages to eradicate war" '.

[49] *Oxford English Dictionary* .

[50] Adam Piette, *Imagination at War* (Macmillan, 1995), 155, 160–1.

[51] Scarry, *The Body in Pain*, 65–6.

to incarnate Barthes' hypothetical 'Author-God', licensing the interlinear-reading of a 'single "theological" meaning'.[52] Instead we should recall the plurality of discourses in which war experience is symbolized and note that official agencies of information, no less than creative writers, must wrestle with both the history and the currency of particular symbols to make their meanings. Centrally planned propaganda was only one dimension of verbal war work. The 'production of official history, as of other commodities' was itself a strategic effort, governed by 'the quantity and quality of the available manpower': 'it would have seemed an impossible ... [labour], had it not been accepted in the first place as a necessary war task.'[53] Official, academic, and commercial histories both document and interpret, providing confirmation of the course of war, reasons for its outbreak, and the nature and meaning of its outcome.

'The ultimate purpose of this war', wrote H. G. Wells in 1914, 'is propaganda, the destruction of certain beliefs, and the creation of others.'[54] The introduction to a 1941 pamphlet in the series 'The Democratic Order' maintained 'this is a war of ideas'.[55] On both views, alterations wreaked by physical violence are the means to bring about ideological changes, changes to maps, political systems, and conceptions of reality.[56] Clausewitz drew out the verbal complement of violence when he asked: 'Is not war just another expression of ... thoughts, another form of speech or writing?'[57] But this is not a pre-vision of a post-Saussurean conventionalism which draws the teeth of conflict in what Foucault has argued is a semiological reduction to 'the calm Platonic form of language and dialogue':

one's point of reference should not be to the great model of language (*langue*) and signs, but to that of war and battle. The history which bears

52 Roland Barthes, 'The Death of the Author', in *The Rustle of Language*, trans. Richard Howard (Berkeley and Los Angeles: University of California Press, 1989), 52.

53 W. K. Hancock and M. M. Gowing, preface to *British War Economy* (HMSO and Longmans, Green and Co., 1949), p. x. An indication of the costliness of this aspect of war administration is the fact that HMSO had to take over publication of the official history of the Great War from a commercial house when production trailed into the 1930s. It was still incomplete at the outbreak of the Second World War.

54 Quoted in Peter Buitenhuis, *The Great War of Words: Literature as Propaganda 1914–18 and After* (Batsford, 1989), 21.

55 Francis Williams, introduction to Ritchie Calder, *Start Planning Britain Now: A Policy for Reconstruction* (Kegan Paul, 1941), p. v.

56 See e.g. Denis Wood, *The Power of Maps* (Routledge, 1993), 8.

57 Clausewitz, *On War*, 605.

and determines us has the form of a war rather than that of a language: relations of power, not relations of meaning . . . it is intelligible and should be susceptible to analysis down to the smallest detail—but this in accordance with the intelligibility of struggles, of strategies and tactics.[58]

Jean Baudrillard's contention that the Gulf War didn't take place (or did so virtually, in informational space) would come to represent the irresponsible extreme in the substitution of the image for embodied power and/or suffering (thus usurping the function of abhorred propaganda), and more generally of the collapsing of reality into the means of its representation.[59] But, on another reading, 'La Guerre du Golfe n'a pas en lieu' is a 'specific ontological claim about social reality'.[60] John Searle, who we would expect to be less accommodating to this ontology than Foucault, makes the same point about the role of representation in war (but Searle's 'collective intentionality' is not reducible to the agency of capital): 'part of being a war is being thought to be a war. This is a remarkable feature of social facts; it has no analogue among physical facts.'[61]

It is with the intersection of the brute fact of the spilled and ruptured bowels of a young man in uniform and the institutional fact of the 'steadfastness of purpose that ha[s] brought us from Dunkirk to the very vitals of the German Reich' that this book is concerned: 'the burst stomach like a cave' in Douglas's 'Vergissmeinnicht' is just one of myriad instances where these relations between matter and symbol are mediated in literature.[62] This book confines itself to the war years—another book must be written about post-war writing and about the bowels of Snowdon (Joseph Heller's version of Randall Jarrell's ball-turret gunner)—and it seeks to keep open to question both the form of war and the forms of language.

[58] Michel Foucault, 'Truth and Power', *The Foucault Reader*, ed. Paul Rabinow (1984. Harmondsworth: Penguin, 1986), 56.

[59] Christopher Norris, *Uncritical Theory: Postmodernism, Intellectuals and the Gulf War* (Lawrence and Wishart, 1992), 11, 192–6.

[60] Paul Patton, 'This is Not a War', in Nicholas Zurbrugg, *Jean Baudrillard: Art and Artefact* (Sage, 1997), 128.

[61] John Searle, *The Construction of Social Reality* (1995. Harmondsworth: Penguin, 1996), 34.

[62] 'Brute facts exist independently of any human institutions. . . . Institutional facts . . . require special human institutions for their very existence. Language is one such institution', ibid. 27. The quotation comes from *Current Affairs*, the journal of the Army Bureau of Current Affairs, quoted in Correlli Barnett, *The Audit of War: The Illusion and Reality of Britain as a Great Nation* (Macmillan, 1986), 36.

WRITING AND THE WOUNDED BODY

> Strategy differs materially from tactic, the latter belonging only
> to the mechanical movement of bodies, set in motion by the
> former.[63]

In terms of the desire to visualize conflict, Total War might seem to
make Clausewitz's wrestlers obsolete. If the iconography of the
Western Front of 1914–18 still permits us to envisage the spatial and
demographic demarcations of a battlefield, the global extent of the
Second World War—in which seemingly everyone was both a target
and a belligerent producer—overwhelms the habits of cognitive
mapping based on traditional figures for the contest of arms. The
events of 1939–45, both in their geopolitical and social aspects,
are more readily conceived strategically, in terms of the management of resources. Particular campaigns—for instance, the Battle of
Britain—achieved salience as turning points or 'decisive battles', but
the war eluded narrative forms.[64] In the news media's daily tabula-
tion of RAF and Luftwaffe losses in that most elite and duellistic
phase of hostilities, the deeds of highly individuated aces acquired
their most pressing significance as numerical aggregates. Statistical
representation, crucial to the centralized management of the war effort, underlined the logic of a contest which, when Britain had survived long enough to fight alongside the United States and the Soviet
Union, must be won by the productive might of the Allies.[65]

The strategic vision necessitated by global war is reinforced by the
images with which Britain's war has been turned to account, in particular the mechanisms of state direction which organized popular
participation into a force that would win first the war, then, relocat-
ing Clausewitz's figure to the field of domestic social policy, overcome the 'five giants on the road to reconstruction' identified in
Beveridge's report, *Social Insurance and Allied Services* (1942).[66] But

---

[63] *Oxford English Dictionary.*

[64] See Keegan, *The Face of Battle*, 57–62, on the 19th-cent. historiographical model of
the decisive battle as a legitimation of war.

[65] 'It can be asserted without fear of contradiction that Herr Hitler's powers over the
Reich citizen cannot be greater than those at the disposal of the British War Cabinet',
Stephen King-Hall, *Total Victory* (Faber, 1941), 37. I owe this reference to Tristram
Hooley.

[66] Nicholas Timmins, *The Five Giants: A Biography of the Welfare State* (1995.
Fontana, 1996), 23. The Five Giants were Want, Disease, Ignorance, Squalor, and Idleness.

there is another factor behind the abstractions of strategic organization, and the alienation of violence from the persons who inflicted and suffered it, one that partakes of the fundamental character of war rather than those specificities which are so hard to organize into a picture of the Second World War. This is the cultural work by which violence in war comes to signify politically, morally, and psychologically. In the interests of investigating just how participants conceived of the events they were making, we might think of this as the management or administration of the signs of violence, a network of verbal activities by which the brute facts of killing and being killed are represented and interpreted for purposes ranging from psychological defence to *Realpolitik*. The most charged of these activities is the redescription of violence, which performs the substitution of abstract or strategic forces for the tactical exposure of bodies to violence. Under this view, there is something about the way violence in war is available for inscription which prefigures the form of the particular constructions with which participants tried, to borrow a resonant locution from Army Intelligence, to put themselves in the picture.

It has been claimed that 'the wounds which are the most visible in war feature relatively little in women's fiction.'[67] But we must ask, where do they feature? *The Next of Kin* (1942), a military training film on careless talk which 'sobered the troops who saw it, and sickened many of the civilians', was exceptional in showing the corpses of British servicemen massacred by a forewarned enemy. This explicitness was a deviation from the policy of avoiding the filming of casualties, or of representing them at a remove, as in Noel Coward's *In Which We Serve* (1942).[68] War 'is an abstract concept, which can only be understood through other abstractions such as nationality, honour and duty': however often we assert that its constituent events are the destruction of persons we risk forgetting that even tacitly designating them as war relegates killing in relation to political and military concepts.[69] Elaine Scarry, in her modelling of 'the structural logic of an event in which alterations in human tissue can come to be the freedom or ideological autonomy or moral legitimacy of a

[67] Jenny Hartley, *Millions Like Us: British Women's Fiction of the Second World War* (Virago, 1997), 168.

[68] Clive Coultass, 'British Cinema and the Reality of War', in Philip M. Taylor (ed.), *Britain and the Cinema in the Second World War* (Macmillan, 1988), 84.

[69] Nicholas Hiley, review of Stuart Sillars, *Art and Survival in First World War Britain*, *Times Literary Supplement*, 4,459 (16–22 Sept. 1988), 1,023.

country' has striven to keep the visceral in view.[70] But as her own strained locutions—'alterations in human tissue'—suggest, this effort is confounded by the limitations and the conventions of linguistic description. Keith Douglas, a determinedly visceral writer, ran into this problem with the illustrations for *Alamein to Zem Zem*, his 'Anatomy of Battle':

Whatever these may seem to you to lack, as pictures, they give an accurate idea of the appearance of things, with one exception. In the case of the man burning to death I have had to retain all the features, to give the chap some expression, although of course they're expressionless, as their faces swell up like pumpkins. But I've got the effect I wanted, of pain. Or I think I have.[71]

It is less significant that this pictorial effect rests on a misrepresentation than that the 'appearance of things' prompts a flight from the wounded body to the iconography of culturally recognisable pain behaviour or of vegetable form. As Elaine Scarry has argued, it is the nature of pain—'an intentional state without an intentional object'—that it is so inexpressible verbally that any other phenomenon in the same environment (and this environment may be semiotic) will draw attention away from it.[72] But, as the artist Keith Vaughan recognized, in war this inexpressibility is abetted by the regimented mind's omission of pain from the activity of wounding:

When a tank meets a tank both fire guns, objectives are hit, and men are burnt to death; but between the penultimate and ultimate stages there is no willed connection. The desired purpose is achieved when the objective is hit. Anyone meeting a tank and knowing it to be dangerous would fire at it in self protection, but few people would burn to death three total strangers in a steel coffin. And it is precisely in order to isolate the reality of this final phase, in order to depersonalise it and disguise it as something other than it is, that every ingenuity of language and psychological conditioning has to be constantly employed in order that human beings may be made into efficient soldiers.[73]

Far from being visible, the wounded body is always liable to disappear.

Of Sir William Napier's account of the Penninsular War battle of Albuera, John Keegan observes, 'the dead and the wounded

[70] Scarry, *The Body in Pain*, 81.

[71] Keith Douglas, letter to M. J. Tambimuttu, 30 Jan. 1944, *Miscellany*, 146–7.

[72] Scarry, *The Body in Pain*, 12, 164.

[73] Keith Vaughan, *Journal and Drawings 1939–1965* (Alan Ross, 1966), 87.

apparently dematerialize as soon as struck down'.[74] On the basis of the fugitive character of the wound in representations of conflict, Scarry has proposed that it is the logic of war to make and unmake the wound:

> war entails a . . . structure of physical and perceptual events: it requires both the reciprocal infliction of massive injury and the eventual disowning of the injury so that its attributes can be transferred elsewhere, as they cannot if they are permitted to cling to the original site of the wound, the human body.[75]

The destinations of these attributes are the doctrines or ideologies which are asserted by the regimes contesting a 'reality duel', a phrase which aptly extends conventional ideas of the role of propaganda in war by which 'each side set out to establish its own credibility and to destroy that of the enemy'.[76] War does not bring about desired but as yet imaginary states of affairs by destroying all resistance: the outcome does not contain 'the power of its own enforcement'.[77] The predominantly civilian casualties in twentieth-century wars puts this observation under some stress. The *Encyclopedia Britannica* speculated in 1911: 'Civilised warfare, so the textbooks tell us, is confined, as far as is possible, to disablement of the armed forces of the enemy; otherwise war would continue till one of the parties was exterminated.'[78] Attempted extermination might appear the pattern of twentieth-century Total War. But on Scarry's model, nevertheless, war produces an outcome in one kind of activity, injuring, which is then translated into a wholly different vocabulary, and 'the winning issue or ideology achieves for a time the force and status of material "fact" by the sheer material weight of the multitudes of damaged and opened human bodies'.[79]

Injuring has two functions, first to decide the outcome of the military contest, second to substantiate it. In the second case, the hurt body's reference is fluid, legitimating issues irrespective of which side it died or killed for. War cemeteries and the empty sleeves of veterans are memorials which confirm that war occurred, and that it had an outcome: as Owen put it, 'bodies, the product of aeons of Natural

---

[74] Keegan, *The Face of Battle*, 40.   [75] Scarry, *The Body in Pain*, 64.
[76] Michael Balfour, *Propaganda in War 1939–1945* (Routledge & Kegan Paul, 1979), 427.   [77] Scarry, *The Body in Pain*, 98.
[78] Quoted in Eric Hobsbawm, *Age of Extremes: The Short Twentieth Century 1914–1991* (Michael Joseph, 1994), 14.   [79] Scarry, *The Body in Pain*, 62.

Selection, melted down to pay for political statues'.[80] Benedict Anderson writes that no nation needs to specify the nationality of the absent occupants of empty tombs of unknown soldiers—'who else could they be *but* Germans, Americans, Argentinians?'[81] But this certainty rests on the capacity of the dead, whoever they are, to substantiate the idea of the nation. The veteran Henry Williamson, contemplating the military cemeteries of Flanders, observed that 'in war-time friend and foe were often buried together. But not in peace-time—that time when nations (or those minding the business of other people) practise war, and invent new ways of death.'[82] Archi-tectonic symbols of the return of the fallen (for the majority of the dead had no known or accessible grave) do not represent a 'demobil-ization of the dead' but their rhetorical remobilization to signify that a war had taken place.[83] The capacity of injuring to conjoin the inside and outside of war depends on processes that permit 'extreme attributes of the body to be translated into another language, to be broken away from the body and relocated elsewhere at the very moment that the body itself is disowned'.[84] The human mind 'flees' from the opened human body, assigning its reality to 'a disembodied idea that has no basis in the material world' (125–6).

The most common linguistic route for the disappearance of the hurt body is the omission of the purpose—'to alter (to burn, to blast, to shell, to cut) human tissue'—of the events described. These omissions arise both from 'an active desire to misrepresent the cen-tral content of war's activity', and 'the sense that this activity is too self-evident to require articulation' (64). Injury is also made invisible by 'redescription', a rhetorical substitution for a somatic referent of a higher order and more abstract or general one (69–70). These tropes are conventions in a genre of historiography Scarry calls 'strategy writing', the output of General Staffs and regimental and

---

[80] Wilfred Owen, *Collected Letters*, ed. Harold Owen and John Bell (Oxford: The Clarendon Press, 1967), 282. Compare Tony Harrison, 'Summer Garden', *Selected Poems* (Harmondsworth: Penguin, 1984), 57, 'their menfolk melted down to monuments', and see also Harrison, 'The Gaze of the Gorgon', *The Gaze of the Gorgon* (Newcastle upon Tyne: Bloodaxe, 1992), 63.

[81] Benedict Anderson: *Imagined Communities: Reflections on the Origin and Spread of Nationalism*, rev. edn. (Verso, 1991), 10.

[82] Henry Williamson, *The Wet Flanders Plain* (The Beaumont Press, 1929), 83.

[83] Jay M. Winter, *Sites of Memory, Sites of Mourning: The Great War in European Cultural History* (Cambridge: Cambridge University Press, 1996), 26.

[84] Scarry, *The Body in Pain*, 124, 128.

military historians, but they are also ubiquitous in imaginative writing and journalism, and in the records of wartime dialogue and self-reflection, such as minutes, correspondence, and diaries. In instances of redescription, violence against persons is represented in language which is not 'morally resonant', for instance 'disarming' for 'injuring'. A complex of psychological and ideological factors means that when 'the populations of two nations consent to devote themselves to damaging each other, the dissolution of their language may not be itself morally disastrous; it may be perceived as inevitable and perhaps even "necessary"' (67). Likewise, the tropes characteristic of strategy writing arise not only out of a desire to 'obscure human hurt but out of purposes appropriate to those writings', to describe how the fate of whole armies and not individuals determines the outcome (71). But the 'maimed colossus' invoked by anthropomorphic descriptions of armies, as in Clausewitz's wrestler trope, 'typically require[s] neither our sympathy nor our anger nor our shame' (72). Richard Aldington, in *Death of a Hero* (1929), momentarily returns redescriptive figures to their visceral origins—'George ... wasn't going to be a bit of any damned Empire's backbone, still less part of its kicked backside'—but more commonly they go unobserved as commonplaces.[85] Similar redescriptions operate at the level of the state, further displacing the embodied injury: 'In the literature of international relations, nation-states are often treated as "actors"—as "agents" rather than structures.'[86]

The relegation of injury to a marginal position is another important redescriptive trope. As a by-product, means to a goal, cost, or prolongation of some benign occurrence, injury is less visible. An MOI circular from 1941, blending deception with the gratification of retaliatory impulses, reveals the logic of designating injuring as a side-effect: 'For a number of reasons it does not pay us to adopt indiscriminate bombing ... Some of the targets ... are, in fact, situated in thickly populated towns and districts ... and, consequently, the enemy civilian population has by no means gone unscathed.'[87] Vera Brittain's anti-area-bombing pamphlet *Seed of Chaos* explicitly tackled propagandist redescription, but much writing about the

---

[85] Richard Aldington, *Death of a Hero* (Chatto and Windus, 1929), 87.

[86] Anthony Giddens, *Modernity and Self-Identity: Self and Society in the Late Modern Age* (Cambridge: Polity, 1991), 15.

[87] Quoted in Ian McLaine, *Ministry of Morale: Home Front Morale and the Ministry of Information in World War II* (George Allen and Unwin, 1979), 160.

bombing of Britain collaborates in the disappearing act performed on the body.[88]

No one person necessarily rehearses the series of redescriptions whereby injury has, as a cost, a smaller and smaller place 'but . . . a population as a whole, in their separate murmurings, keep articulating back and forth across their entirety the full series as though to keep the words in the air, to keep them from landing where they can be seen and assessed'.[89] As Keith Vaughan noted in 1944, '[t]he tragedy today is that everyone has now come to accept the destruction in this war as a natural way of life. . . . Instead of being themselves enlarged by it they reduce its conception until it fits with routine habits.'[90] The rhetorical displacements by which injury substantiates a civil project are highly relevant to wartime discourse about a fight for a better social system. The fiction (i.e. imaginary vision) of a new society, whether in governmental or oppositional contexts, diminishes the reality of drowned merchant seamen and burned bomber crews as it seems to redeem them. Ian McLaine's argument that the Beveridge report 'sanctified the nation's sacrifices . . . gave meaning to the war beyond a struggle for survival' recapitulates the transfer of reality from victim to an impersonal, and contingent, political structure.[91]

Rex Warner's allegory *Why Was I Killed?* (1943) poses a difficult question in this connection: 'To some, no doubt, this question of mine may appear unnecessary, already answered, or merely selfish. . . . "Who am I to make a fuss, an anonymous drop in the ocean of so much destruction?"'[92] Warner ventriloquizes the perspective, from the state towards the person, that legitimizes violence, because, rhetorically, the larger unit will always justify the cost of the smaller in a series of transactions. The massive aggregate of destruction substantiates the issues on behalf of which it has been brought about, and stands for the outcome of the contest. It is with this perspective that Nicholas Monsarrat concluded his Battle of the Atlantic novel, *The Cruel Sea* (1951): 'no anti-climax, no quiet end, could obscure the triumph and the pride inherent in this victory, with its huge cost—30,000 seamen killed, 3,000 ships sent to the bottom in this

---

[88] Vera Brittain, *Seed of Chaos: What Mass Bombing Really Means* (New Vision, for The Bombing Restriction Committee, 1944), 6–7.

[89] Scarry, *The Body in Pain*, 76.   [90] Vaughan, *Journal*, 84.

[91] McLaine, *Ministry of Morale*, 182.

[92] Rex Warner, *Why Was I Killed?: A Dramatic Dialogue* (John Lane, 1943), 12.

one ocean—and its huge toll of 780 U-boats sunk, to even the balance.'[93] The contrasting view articulated by Warner inverts the series and undoes the argument that mass death guarantees the reality of the issues contested: 'I am perfectly aware of my own insignificance in history. It is when I think of my own case as multiplied by a million and by ten million that it begins to appear a matter of some importance.'[94] Although it resolves on a reconstructionist note (the future deployment of wartime collectivity or comradeship for peaceful purposes, the Second World War's version of Milton's 'peace hath her victories / No less renowned than war'), the book complicates its own alternative naturalization of violence by asserting the value of the individual. By itself, the promotion of the claims of individuality could not reverse the logic of redescription, or of war. But, turning from abstract to historical considerations, it is evident that the individual flourished as an ideological category implicated both in opposition to, and in attempts to redirect, regimentations imposed by the state and the state's legitimation of violence.

INDIVIDUALS AND THE COLLECTIVE

From my mother's sleep I fell into the State

Randall Jarrell[95]

Much has been written about the war's reinforcement of the global trend to collectivism. By contrast, surprisingly little has been said about the opposite effect: its strengthening and legitimation of a highly privatised and unstructured psychological individualism—an individualism that was explicitly opposed to Fascism, but that also presented definite boundaries to collectivism of all kinds.

Jose Harris[96]

Among the probable reasons for the omission noted by Harris we can count the pressures to recuperate the costs of the war by demoting them to conditions for a social revolution which created what Britons

---

[93] Nicholas Monsarrat, *The Cruel Sea* (Cassell, 1951), 505. In Charles Frend's film of the novel, 'the only villain is the sea'.   [94] Warner, *Why Was I Killed?*, 12.

[95] Randall Jarrell, 'The Death of the Ball Turret Gunner', *The Complete Poems* (New York: The Noonday Press, 1969), 144.

[96] Jose Harris, 'War and Social History: Britain and the Home Front during the Second World War', *Contemporary European History*, 1/1 (March 1992), 31.

like to think of as a unique welfare state. But we might also note the
way the Home Front has entered folklore: if Heath's three-day week
of 1973 was accounted a success, Peter Clarke has written, this was in
large part because of 'the national cult of reliving the hardships of
1940 in safely miniaturized form; out came the candles, and the
wartime lore, showing that Britain could take it'.[97] However, Vera
Brittain recalled that '"Taking it", now universally extolled as a
major virtue . . . meant submitting our standards, our consciences,
and our capacity for thought to progressive brutalisation.'[98] The
competing claims of individualism and collectivity can only be
understood in relation to the complex interaction of compulsion,
voluntarism and belief that characterized the situation of the individual in wartime:

That the adult human cannot ordinarily without his consent be physically
'altered' by the verbal imposition of any new political philosophy makes all
the more remarkable . . . the fact that he sometimes agrees to go to war,
agrees to permit this radical self-alteration to his body.[99]

The construction of claims on the minds and bodies of subjects was
a significant dimension of the war effort, setting out the state's self-
description in the contest of reality claims, not only with its enemy,
but with its own population. 'The whole of the warring nations are
engaged, not only soldiers, but the entire population, men, women
and children', Churchill told parliament on 20 August 1940: 'The
fronts are everywhere.'[100] The symbolic dimension of that mobilization, such as the idea of a 'People's War', not only contributed to consensus, but determined the forms taken by the perception of, and
resistance to, coercion. It is not a paradox that the same measures
were held to contribute to social cohesion and to have a radical
edge.[101] The anarchist George Woodcock claimed that the 'nature
and objects' of the war could 'be understood only as a conflict between rulers and their subjects'; but cognizance of this opposition
was not confined to political radicals.[102]

---

[97] Peter Clarke, *Hope and Glory: Britain 1900–1990* (Harmondsworth: Allen Lane/
The Penguin Press, 1996), 338.
[98] Vera Brittain, *Testament of Experience: An Autobiographical Study of the Years
1925–1950* (Gollancz, 1957), 274–5.
[99] Scarry, *The Body in Pain*, 112.   [100] Churchill, *War Speeches*, i. 235.
[101] Steven Fielding, Peter Thompson, and Nick Tiratsoo, *'England Arise!': The Labour
Party and Popular Politics in 1940s Britain* (Manchester: Manchester University Press,
1995), 19.
[102] George Woodcock, 'The Dark Night of the Intellect', *Now*, NS 2 (1944), 2.

Writers' investments in the category of the self were also shaped by conceptions of resistance to the state's directives. Some of the most important consequences of this discursive struggle are to be found in the way that debates over conditions in wartime Britain helped render critical culture impotent in its reactions to the war experienced in Europe under Nazi rule. Elizabeth Bowen drew on the example of Continental anti-Nazi resistance to explain the predicament of the individual in Britain:

> Literature of the Resistance has been steadily coming in from France. I wonder whether in a sense all wartime writing is not resistance writing? But personal life here, too, put up its own resistance to the annihilation that was threatening it—war.[103]

This statement appeared in a postscript to the first US Edition of *The Demon Lover* (1945), and is dated October 1944. Another version of this text, dated 1945, and printed in *Collected Impressions* (1950), cancelled the implied identification signified by 'too', and added the following rider between the second and third sentences: 'In no way dare we who were in Britain compare ourselves with the French.'[104] The scrupulous but belated revision underlines the earlier failure of perspective, and gives us a hint of the consequences of a mode of self-consciousness in which symbols of the imagined war in Europe were employed to conceptualize the predicament of the private individual in wartime Britain.

But announcements of the demise of this liberal category were premature. Of the war years Karl Miller has written that 'a dynamic of privacy took hold—a privacy which . . . may have been seen as avidly subversive and as an aspect of the freedoms for which the war was being fought'.[105] 'May' turns out to be a big qualification. Stephen Spender's 'September Journal', opening *Horizon*'s second number in February 1940, promoted personal identity as the justification of an uneasy choice for 'the Chamberlain system' of appeasement: 'I hate the idea of being regimented and losing my personal freedom of action. I carry this feeling too far, in fact, I must admit I carry it to the point of hysteria—i.e. the point where I would really fight.'[106] Spender takes up arms, imaginatively, not in response to

---

103 Bowen, *The Demon Lover* (1952), 220.
104 Elizabeth Bowen, *Collected Impressions* (Longmans, Green and Co., 1950), 50.
105 Karl Miller, *Authors* (1989. Oxford: Oxford University Press, 1990), 166.
106 Stephen Spender, 'September Journal', *Horizon*, 1/2 (Feb. 1940), 104.

Nazi ideology, brutality, or territorial ambition, but in recalling that 'you allowed the other boys to take your possessions from you, but finally there was something which you fought for blindly—the possibility of being alone.'[107] With practical resistance limited to flight, or safe jobs in media or government organizations, it remained to writers to publicize the fear that the survival of private life demanded its surrender, a double-bind neatly expressed in Alun Lewis's self-judgement: 'Acceptance seems so spiritless, protest so vain'.[108]

The disciplines of service were registered most frequently by those whose identity was founded on their consciousness of having an identity to lose. In *World Within World* Spender recalled that, while he surrendered the integrity of his self, for the working man, conditions were 'too close to his peace-time existence . . . not to appear at times simply a change for the worse'. Indeed, for a 'toff' like himself, the war was experienced as a supplement: 'his temporary war-time personality seemed added to his peace-time picture of himself.'[109] The waged, women, and the unemployed in the inter-war period lived lives which were, in many ways, more profoundly constricted by economic and ideological forces than in wartime: 'the possibility of having a private life was a class privilege.'[110] The intellectual print culture of the Second World War, even though it manifested a variety of affiliations with official and unofficial populist ideology, was predominantly middle class, and its administration was increasingly centralized.[111] Paul Fussell has noted the 'eloquence problem' which makes the majority with first-hand experience of war, but little

[107] Ibid. 105.

[108] Quoted by Robert Graves, foreword to Alun Lewis, *Ha! Ha! Among the Trumpets: Poems in Transit* (George Allen and Unwin, 1945), 12.

[109] Stephen Spender, *World Within World* (Hamish Hamilton, 1951), 266.

[110] Antoine Prost and Gérard Vincent (eds.), *Riddles of Identity in Modern Times* (Cambridge, Mass.: Belknap Press, 1991), 7.

[111] Cinema and radio had a greater demographic reach, see e.g. Anthony Aldgate and Jeffrey Richards, *Britain Can Take It: The British Cinema in the Second World War*, 2nd edn. (Edinburgh: Edinburgh University Press, 1994), 4. But it is important to note the effects of existing film censorship (the most comprehensive system outside the totalitarian world) and the different audiences of commercial cinema and newsreels and of MOI-sponsored documentaries created by left-wing members of the Documentary Film Movement and on non-theatrical distribution. See Nicholas Pronay, ' "The Land of Promise": The Projection of Peace Aims in Britain', in K. R. M. Short (ed.), *Film and Radio Propaganda in World War II* (Croom Helm, 1983), 51–77, and Helen Forman, 'The Non-Theatrical Distribution of Films by the Ministry of Information', in Nicholas Pronay and D. W. Spring, (eds.), *Propaganda, Politics and Film* (Macmillan, 1982), 232.

education, 'silent about what they know'. The experience of the mass of those who were the targets of the 'sentimentality and moral primitivism' of home propaganda remains equally inarticulate.[112] This is true even with respect to Mass Observation, whose monitoring of public opinion fuelled reconstruction debates as well as prompting governmental surveillance of morale: its investigators and diarists were drawn largely from the middle class.[113] Accounts of class and culture in the Second World War present a confusing picture. Andy Croft has argued that the heirs to the Popular Front culture of the 1930s dominated 'serious writing about the war' throughout the 1940s.[114] Ken Worpole, also writing from the left, counters this optimism with the claim that a 'selective tradition' of writing about the Second World War has suppressed working-class perspectives.[115] Alan Sinfield has provided a more subtle analysis: a '"levelling" tendency of the war' was contained by the propagation of 'a distinctive *ideology* of welfare-capitalism' which 'constituted an unprecedentedly ambitious project of state legitimation'.[116] The hopes of the left were appropriated as potent symbols in the state's mobilization of its human resources, but these symbols caused alarm on the right. Bowen's *The Heat of the Day* is analysed accordingly as entertaining 'the thought that vulgarity dwells with the democratic victors of 1945, and civilization with fascism'.[117]

Sinfield equates Bowen's writing about private life with forces of reaction which, he claims, have betrayed the radical energies emergent in the British experience of the Second World War. But his critique is grounded in the very ideals promulgated by an ambiguous wartime rhetoric of reconstruction: 'The war (though not without contest) exemplified a pattern of state intervention and popular co-operation to organize production for a common purpose. And its successful conclusion afforded a rare opportunity to recast British society.'[118] But the inference that the contested ideals of social reconstruction had already been realized as a by-product of military

---

[112] Paul Fussell, *Killing in Verse and Prose and Other Essays* (Bellew Publishing, 1990), 15, 73.

[113] Jim McGuigan, *Cultural Populism* (Routledge, 1992), 22.

[114] Andy Croft, *Red Letter Days: British Fiction in the 1930s* (Lawrence and Wishart, 1990), 336.

[115] Ken Worpole, *Dockers and Detectives: Popular Reading: Popular Writing* (Verso, 1983), 49.

[116] Alan Sinfield, *Literature, Politics and Culture in Postwar Britain* (Oxford: Blackwell, 1989), 16   [117] Ibid. 17–18.   [118] Ibid. 1.

struggle mistakes symbol for reality, reproducing, not interpreting, the predicament of wartime writers with respect to the imaginary status of outcomes to the war.

During the bombing of London, according to Bowen, 'I hardly knew where I stopped and everyone else began.'[119] War created a crisis of identity: 'life, mechanized by the controls of war-time, and emotionally torn and impoverished by changes, had to complete itself in *some* way.'[120] Anna Kavan, novelist and assistant editor at *Horizon*, promoted neurosis as a form of resistance to 'the fate of the individual in the machine' of the war-state.[121] 'What', she asked, 'will the bright metallic dawn be like when we break into that orderly new realm, that mechanized realm in which individualism will have vanished completely—because life itself will have become one vast omnipotent machine?'[122] However, to read either statement as subversion of 'production for a common purpose' is to privilege one wartime discourse, that of planning, welfare, and reconstruction, over its contexts of personal and political exigencies, material necessities, and symbolic investments.

Symbols of individuality were not monopolized by the intelligentsia of a middle class 'still not mentally at war'.[123] Propaganda presented Britons as 'individualists' intolerant of totalitarian controls (72). The pamphlet *Personality in Wartime* (October 1940) proposed that Germans, because they could not 'credit the individual as such with dignity and worth . . . tried to acquire [those virtues] by huddling into rigid hierarchies and disciplined formations, by reverencing rank and drill' (153). In Britain, by contrast, even before the outbreak of war, 'a patriotism of private life was being felt and expressed'.[124]

The circulation of ideas about social reconstruction was a symptom, not a cause, of the course of the war. The prominence of the theme of the individual likewise emerged from the effort to comprehend and engage in both the material and symbolic processes of wartime. The collective and the individual, categories frequently invoked and contested in wartime culture, were not exclusively rallying

[119] Bowen, *The Demon Lover* (1952), 216.   [120] Ibid. 219.
[121] 'Comment', *Horizon*, 9/50 (Feb. 1944), 78.
[122] Anna Kavan, 'The Case of Bill Williams (i)', ibid. 99.
[123] The phrase was used in a 1940 MOI Policy Committee paper, quoted in McLaine, *Ministry of Morale*, 145.
[124] Alison Light, *Forever England: Femininity, Literature and Conservatism Between the Wars* (Routledge, 1991), 154.

cries of the left and the right respectively. Their opposition is never solely an index of national social organization: these categories are fundamental to the translation of values in discourse about the war. But representations of the self as battened down against external discipline and violence were liable to distort not only the identity being defended, but also an understanding of the political structures and conditions which threatened it.

The contradictions relating to the categories of the individual and the collective are prefigured in texts about post-Munich Europe and the inevitability of war by the journalist and later POW-novelist Michael Burn and by the poet Alun Lewis. In *The Labyrinth of Europe*, published in April 1939, Burn argued that preparedness for war should involve an 'equal and mutual obligation . . . between individual and State', and not the 'unfair balance asked of the individual' in totalitarian regimes.[125] This prognosis anticipates the competition, in discourse about reconstruction, between opposition to totalitarianism and positive social programmes. Reflecting on political prisoners he had seen in Dachau, and on unemployment in Yorkshire, Burn asked whether one should join a crusading war against a regime deemed guilty of atrocities while impotent to 'eradicate evils at your door'.[126] That Burn could not, in 1939, imagine that the demands of an international crusade would produce social change at home is a measure of the extent to which reconstructionist thought shaped understanding of the war. During his incarceration in Colditz, he would write a Marxist-inspired fictional critique of the failure to direct the war to precisely those social ends. Post-Munich, his solution to structural contradictions in British society was to propose the importation of Nazi labour camps as an apparatus of class-levelling: notwithstanding the fact that the German model was 'excessive' and 'too military', 'the effect . . . is as good as the idea'.[127] His contention that equating compulsion with totalitarianism was a superficial reflex, not a rational response, is, however, worth keeping in mind in relation to wartime claims that military opposition to Nazism was turning Britain totalitarian. The vocabulary employed in the critique of regimentation, and the illiberality of wartime governmental institutions, too readily confused universal mobilization with Nazi rule and occupation.

---

[125] Michael Burn, *The Labyrinth of Europe* (Methuen, 1939), 286.
[126] Ibid. 298.   [127] Ibid. 299.

Scepticism also characterized Alun Lewis's response, in his local newspaper, to the events of 1938. Mass regimentation was antithetical to the prerogatives of the individual, and was a greater threat than the ideology and expansionism of the likely enemy. The *levée en masse* of post-Revolution France was not, for Lewis, a people's army struggling for freedom, but a model of total war taken to the extreme of dictatorship: 'Democracy is more likely to perish than survive in a European war.'[128] These pre-war texts both conceive of a yet undeclared war in terms of a threat to the private sphere. The public memorialization of the Great War lies behind Lewis's diagnosis that the state's self-description as the embodiment of democracy and freedom is not incontrovertible. Burn, like Lewis, is more troubled by the individual's responsibilities in a military enterprise, than about the nature of Nazism. But, as Martin Gilbert has reminded us, Britain did not go to war 'to destroy Nazism'; the idea of a war to prevent 'the Jewish persecutions' and change Germany's government 'was unthinkable'.[129] In the culture of the war years, the nature of Nazism remains, by and large, a minor component of discourse about the experience and meaning of the war. Wartime British responses to genocide confirm that this was not because Nazism, and its consequences, were too familiar, too obvious to be repeated in the general conversation about the war. When the concept of totalitarianism enters British discourse during the war, it often forms the imaginary component of a rhetorical diagnosis of the tyranny of wartime Britain. In a war fought in the defence of liberty, the most compelling instances of the self's vulnerability were the most immediate, the constraints on the autonomy of Britons at war, even if this had the effect of dissolving rather than clarifying the difference between the warring ideologies.

The ensuing chapters argue that literary culture is implicated in a network of representations which mediate the semantic operations crucial to the function of war. From this perspective, it is possible to reassess questions about literature's consensual or oppositional character. The capacity of wartime writing to resist the inscription of injury as a political sign was conditional on its handling of a host of concepts—for instance individualism, freedom, discipline, and radicalism—which were also ubiquitous components in official

---

[128] Alun Lewis, *Alun Lewis: A Miscellany of his Writings*, ed. John Pikoulis (Bridgend: Poetry Wales Press, 1982), 84.

[129] Martin Gilbert, *Britain and Germany Between the Wars* (Longmans, 1964), 70.

mediations of violence and policy to the population at war. The extreme difficulties of achieving distance from the social and cultural expressions of political and military expedience militated against a consistent critical recovery of the lethal acts perpetrated on and by bodies at war.

2

The Figure of the Airman

THE LAST ENEMY, THE BATTLE OF BRITAIN, AND THE GOOD OF WAR

INTER-WAR policy neglected fighter defence of the UK. When the RAF came to fight what Churchill dubbed, *in anticipation*, the Battle of Britain (for Hitler the battle never got under way), it did so with recently-acquired technology, but short of manpower. Watson-Watt's radar (trialled as recently as 1935) gave vital early warnings, and the Supermarine Spitfire and Hawker Siddeley Hurricane were being supplied in good numbers under the direction of the newspaper magnate Lord Beaverbrook's new ministry of aircraft production.[1] But, the Prime Minister noted, 'it will indeed be lamentable if we have machines standing idle for want of pilots to fly them'. The 'personnel side' was crucial.[2] The diversion of the Luftwaffe from attacks on air defences to London, from 6 September 1940, gave respite to depleted fighter squadrons which had survived *Adlertag*, Eagle Day, the pre-invasion assault of the previous month.

Richard Hillary, a RAFVR pilot, was shot down on 3 September: he stands out amongst Churchill's 'few' (the first of many wartime invocations of Henry V's band of brothers) because he became 'one of the symbolic names of the war'.[3] Heroic individualism was at once defined against, and dependent upon, industrial technology and national administration. The progenitor of the few was, in Leslie Howard's 1942 film *The First of the Few*, the aero-engineer R. J. Mitchell, whose lone struggle to get the prototypes of the Spitfire built is presented in the mid-air-raid flashbacks of David Niven's fighter pilot. Howard died in a passenger plane shot down over the

---

[1] I. C. B. Dear (ed.), *The Oxford Companion to the Second World War* (Oxford: Oxford University Press, 1995), 158, 919.
[2] Quoted in Chester Wilmot, *The Struggle for Europe* (1951. Wordsworth Editions, 1997), 40.
[3] Arthur Koestler, 'The Birth of a Myth: In Memory of Richard Hillary', *Horizon*, 7/40 (April 1943), 227.

Bay of Biscay in 1943, but Niven, returned from Hollywood to serve in a commando, went on to star in *A Matter of Life and Death* (1946), Powell and Pressburger's allegory of individualism's resistance to the planner's dream of uninterrupted administration (represented as celestial accountancy).

Hillary's fame rested on *The Last Enemy* (1942), a book about dog fights and reasons for fighting the war which was read as a testament of doubt. Early in 1943, when decisive Allied victories appeared to have turned the course of the war, he was killed in a training accident trying to return to active service. The reception of his book by contemporary writers and servicemen is itself a significant episode in wartime discourse about the means and ends of the war. As a projection of a culture's response to conflict, Hillary was the Rupert Brooke of the 1940s.

The Last Enemy is not a reflexively subtle work of autobiography, but its construction resists its author's designs. His gesture at closure, contested by those who read Hillary's death as the book's true completion, is formally vertiginous, appropriately so for a narrative about aviation and the self's orientation. Flight is an escape, but it puts body and mind at risk from a dangerous groundlessness. By concluding with the determination to write himself back into relation with the dead, and with the living in their struggle against the political enemy, Hillary turns a linear conversion into a cyclical alternation between egotism and a collectively-oriented self. Swallowing its tail, the book mimes the fighter pilot's re-enactment, in take-off and landing, of a division between selfhood and the social, a solipsistic version of the Conradian dualism of sublime suspension above the deep, and loss of definition on the swarming earth.

The non-linearity of the book's beginning introduces a more obvious, and repressible, irony. A 'proem' describes bailing out of a burning Spitfire into the North Sea. Hillary's hands are so badly burned that he cannot put an end to pain and the fear of death by detaching his buoyant parachute and drowning. *The Last Enemy* foregrounds injury as the destination of the deluded airman, and as the sign which will precipitate reorientation. In its prefigurations of the disowning of egotism, the narrative makes the wound highly visible, but ultimately turns it into a trope for an abstraction. The book and its reception reproduce the logic of strategic redescription as they wrestle with its implications. This convergence will be unfolded in a reading of *The Last Enemy*, an analysis of the way the book was read and rewritten by Hillary's contemporaries, and a broader interpretation of contemporary representations of the airman and the RAF in relation to wartime discourses of the individual and of the collective.

The question behind *The Last Enemy* is why and how one consents to expose one's body to the dangers of war. The book could be read as propaganda for the war effort because Hillary transcends his personal propaganda (getting what he can out of the war). As a member of the Oxford University Air Squadron in the days before Munich, Hillary enthuses about a fighter pilot's 'exciting . . . individual, and . . . disinterested' role in warfare.[4] War is not a legal relation between belligerent states, a contest of ideologies, or the slaughter of the 'seed of Europe', but an 'opportunity to demonstrate in action our dislike of organized emotion and patriotism', and to prove 'we were a match for Hitler's dogma-fed youth' (35). The enemy are not the agents of a regime which threatens all values, and all lives, but the coevals of the drilled automatons who are beaten by a 'hopelessly casual' Oxford crew in the Goering Prize Fours at a 1938 regatta (27–8). (In the same year of crisis, a Football Association England team defeated a German eleven, vengeance after a poor national performance at the Berlin Olympics.)[5] Hillary's refusal of regimentation—'We had joined the Air Force to fly, and not to parade around like Boy Scouts'—is also a refusal of an instrumental rationalization of war as 'a crusade for humanity, or a life-and-death struggle of civilization' (38, 65).

Hillary believes, as did writers as different as Rosenberg and Hemingway before him, that war will accelerate his literary development: 'war groups the maximum of material and speeds up the action and brings out all sorts of stuff that normally you have to wait a lifetime to get.'[6] While he can turn war to his own account, fellow airmen are inarticulate conscripts to the concept of the 'nation's hero' and want only to 'get back to that closed language which is Air Force slang' (61–2). 'Embryo pilots' are incubated on air stations into 'something bigger than themselves . . . the composite figure that is the Air Force Pilot' (60–1), acquiring in the air, and in the face of death, an insight that matures them. They neither read about the

---

[4] Richard Hillary, *The Last Enemy* (1942. Macmillan, 1950), 21.

[5] Ross McKibbin, *Classes and Cultures: England 1918–1951* (Oxford: Oxford University Press, 1998), 345.

[6] Hemingway to Fitzgerald, quoted in Jeffrey Meyers, *Hemingway: A Biography* (Macmillan, 1986), 22.

war, or talk about it, needing 'their minds clear, their nerves in order' (62).[7] Flying for aesthetic reasons, Hillary reserves his belligerence for the British people waking up in the summer of 1940 to 'their war', and to bait his friend Peter Pease about his reasons for fighting. From Hillary's side, their debate about war aims is an anticipation of the cool, detached performance of the airman-duellist: he waits for the chance to shoot down the arguments of an opponent who 'clouds the issue' with religion and politics. Self-realization is the only coherent war aim. Pease can't deflect this egotism with his reasons—to rid the world of fear, and to see a better world come out of the war—but he predicts that Hillary will be altered:

Something bigger than you and me is coming out of this, and as it grows you'll grow with it. Your preconceived notions won't last long. You are entirely unfeeling, Richard. I'm sure it needs only some psychological shock, some affront to your sensibility, to arouse your pity or your anger sufficiently to make you forget yourself (128–9).

What is at stake is the identity of that 'something bigger', and the individual's relation to it. For Hillary it is the RAF, which makes him 'free from outside interference' (119). But while Pease's crusade to stamp out the Nazis who 'stamp out the divine spark in Man' is immune from his sense of sin, Hillary's sense of invulnerability as a 'duellist—cool, precise, impersonal . . . privileged to kill well' betrays him early on in his Battle of Britain (122, 125).

The 'great sea of pain' Hillary experiences in hospital is a condensation of the hours floating in the North Sea contemplating suicide, and anticipates the ritual agony of the saline-bath treatment for his burns (158). Under anaesthetic, the still-blinded Hillary 'saw Peter Pease killed': news of his death comes two days later (163). The role of antagonist is transferred to Pease's fiancée Denise, who scorns his studied aloofness from the living and the dead as he watches his 'sensibility absorb experience like a photographic plate, so that you may store it away to use for your own self-development' (189–90). But Hillary's skin is imprinted with marks that will catalyse the change that Pease prophesied. The protracted remodelling of his hands and

---

[7] The phrase recalls Owen, letter to Sassoon (10 Oct. 1918), *Collected Letters*, ed. Harold Owen and John Bell (Oxford: Clarendon Press, 1967), 581, 'my nerves are in perfect order', and 'Hands in perfect order' at the pre-arranged hour, the last line of 'Journal of an Airman' in Auden's *The Orators: An English Study* (1932) in *The English Auden: Poems, Essays and Dramatic Writings 1927–1939*, ed. Edward Mendelson (Faber, 1977), 94.

face by the enterprising plastic surgeon Archibald McIndoe is not a restoration of the Richard Hillary constructed in flying training and militarist-subversion. Unerasable traces of violence on his altered and re-altered skin are the grounds of a reformation of personality. During an air-raid, the downed airman is recognized as a fellow victim—'"I see they got you too"'—by a dying woman he helps drag from a bombed house (246).[8] Self-possession—'I had not been injured in their war'—is shouldered-out by her gaze, and his gaze on her broken body, leaving him with 'weak inadequate words' for the enormity of a shattered human being, 'the very essence of anti-life no words could convey' (236, 246). This reversal is the occasion of the book, dedicated to 'that despised Humanity', and written to justify his

right to fellowship with my dead, and to the friendship of those . . . who would go on fighting until the ideals for which their comrades had died were stamped for ever on the future of civilization (253).

As the testimony of 'the last of the long-haired boys', lone survivor of a gang of defiantly sceptical, 'aesthetic' flyers, *The Last Enemy* belongs to the tradition of survivor's songs, the solitary returning to tell of the deeds of the dead (231). But as the realization of that avowal, the book can only replay a debate that is concluded 'beyond the range of thought' (246). Its circularity registers the suspicion that such gestures evade not only the grasp of concepts, but also the tenacity of the self.

The Last Enemy's terminal disciplining of the self to 'their war' and its conditional 'stamping' of ideals on the future cannot disguise the author's efforts to disown the public image of the airman. *Everybody's Weekly* dignified his defeat and wounding as a species of retirement, reprising the treatment of Dunkirk 'almost as a victory' (74), and turning injury into a sign of an outcome: 'His flying days are over, but the memory of a job well done remains.'[9] But Hillary's mood of 'satisfaction at a job adequately done' is conditional on the contrast between the fate of his first 'kill' and his own immunity (137). Once a victim himself, he is prey to conscription: 'the "honourable" scars of a battle that was not mine' draw looks of pity

---

[8] In Robert Harris's novel *Enigma* (Hutchinson, 1995), 46, the phrase turns up in a description of cryptanalysts unwillingly assembled at Bletchley Park: 'they got you too' is what 'their faces said'.

[9] G. J. Poke, 'Story of a Hero', *Everybody's Weekly* (28 Sept. 1940), RHP, file 6.

to which there is no riposte: 'I could not explain that I had not been injured in their war' (238, 236). This refusal to be interpellated ultimately gives way to the gaze of the Blitz-victim, but is not erased.

The Last Enemy was, the novelist Storm Jameson told the author, 'the best book of this war or the last war—and so, I suppose, of any war'.[10] Her exorbitant valuation suggests that she read the memoir as paralleling her own conversion from pacifism (she had been a sponsor of the Peace Pledge Union) to resistance to Nazism: 'The way of reasoning together is not open to us. What is open to us is submission, the concentration camp, the death of our humblest with our best, the forcing of our children's minds into an evil mould.'[11] *The Last Enemy* is, like many memoirs of the Great War, a story of disenchantment, and the lasting imprint of combat on mind and flesh. But it inverts earlier fables of disillusionment with bellicosity by negating the individualist perspective. Hillary is disabused of an illusion of the egoist's separate peace, and the war's destruction of persons itself becomes sufficient justification of the destruction of the enemy. Commitment to a cause flows from the author's recognition of his own wounds as a sign of the issues at stake.

John Strachey, co-founder of the Left Book Club and, after recanting his communism, 'a public relations officer for the war effort' in the RAF (later Under Secretary of State for Air in Attlee's government, and then Secretary of State for War), thought that the way Hillary played-down the 'air fighting' made his book a 'real autobiography'.[12] It was widely viewed as penetrating beyond the documentary flatness and the pieties of wartime service memoirs. Emphasis on the inscription of an authentic self within the disciplined mind and body of the uniformed subject reflected a preoccupation with the fate of subjectivity in relation to the social and symbolic masses of wartime. These efforts to locate the self are at once pitched against and deformed by the discourses which subordinated the claims of the individual to those of state policy.

Writing about aviation and the RAF had given rise to contradictory figures of the airman as both individualist and disciplinary subject of technology. These figures are the heroes of seemingly opposed

---

[10] Storm Jameson, letter to Richard Hillary, 30 June 1942, RHP, file 6.

[11] Storm Jameson, *The End of This War* (1941), quoted in Martin Ceadel, *Pacifism in Britain 1914–1945: The Defining of a Faith* (Oxford: Clarendon Press, 1980), 297.

[12] John Strachey, 'The New Men', review of Richard Hillary, *The Last Enemy*, *The Spectator*, 169/5,950 (10 July 1942), 44; Michael Newman, *John Strachey* (Manchester: Manchester University Press, 1989), 82.

narratives of the Second World War. The story of the individual's definition through combat, or of his resistance to regimentation, remains crucial to the reproduction of bellicose ideals and of the sublimity of the soldier, who, like Yeats's Irish airman, tests his self-sufficiency against the forces that can destroy his body. This narrative type is at odds with the story of the incorporation of individuals divided by identity and affiliation into a cohesive social enterprise. It is the latter narrative that has been established, in national post-war culture, as the hegemonic pattern of the British experience of the war. Class difference and individualism were the prime themes of this holistic rhetoric in wartime writing; gender and race were, and remain, too deeply troubling to the ideologies underpinning the mobilization of society to risk suggesting that such identities were conditional on the experience of war itself. *The Last Enemy* is a meeting point of individualist and collectivist narratives which, while often opposed for heuristic and propaganda purposes, in practice interpenetrated. The way this conflation was read, and rewritten, raises issues which are fundamental to our understanding of wartime culture.

The Last Enemy makes disfigurement legible, not least to Hillary himself, as a sign of the weightiness of war's ends. The wound is given a voice which pain lacks, but it is a voice that transfers the reality of pain to an unsubstantiated political goal. But viewed as a reintegration of an identity that war has made discontinuous (the solitary survivor is divided from his past), autobiography 'deprives and disfigures to the precise extent that it restores'.[13] *The Last Enemy* represents 'a young man's struggle to identify and tame the self at a point in history when self seemed liable either to extinction or to protective and disfiguring self-promotion'.[14] In extinguishing one self to promote another, the book made selfhood provisional on the forms of its inscription: 'I just don't believe what I wrote in that book—sometimes I do', Hillary wrote to his lover, Mary Booker, in April 1942.[15]

The sincerity of the conversion is threatened by its conventionality as a topos of war experience, translating loss into fulfilment, miming

[13] Paul de Man, 'Autobiography as De-facement', *Modern Language Notes*, 94/5 (Dec. 1979), 930.
[14] Andrew Motion, review of Michael Burn, *Mary and Richard*, *Times Literary Supplement*, 4,439 (29 April–5 May 1988), 466.
[15] Michael Burn, *Mary and Richard, The Story of Richard Hillary and Mary Booker* (André Deutsch, 1988), 85–6.

a Churchillian suspension of closure (the end of the beginning, not the beginning of the end). The pseudonymous 'Gun Buster', who applied the rhetoric of comic-book heroics and understatement to the writing of instant history, encoded the wounds of an earlier campaign as the grounds of the meaning of future struggle. In *Battle Dress*, an officer wounded at Dunkirk—'Years of good comradeship smashed in a second'—rescues an air-raid victim: 'She was dead. But the Captain had come to life again'; 'he had not come to the end. Only to another beginning . . .'[16] At once, the earlier casualty is regenerated, and the function of the freshly broken body as a signifier of survival is metonymically guaranteed. To similar rhetorical effect, Anton Walbrook, in *Dangerous Moonlight* (US title *Suicide Squadron*), played a Polish pilot who loses his memory after ramming a Luftwaffe bomber to revenge a friend's death. The route to the restoration of identity is memorial pianism (the film introduced Richard Addinsel's *Warsaw Concerto*): from defeat springs wholeness.

In the context of Pease's 'better world' and other idealizations of the war as socio-economic project of national renewal, *The Last Enemy's* reconstructed personality is no more than a personality *of* reconstruction, a rationalization which addresses the facticity of violence to the future. Hillary's coding of his and others' wounds is not an isolated, authorial invention, but is continuous with wartime patterns of signifying violence. His rapprochement with 'their war' (with its legitimizing credos, ' "our island fortress" . . . "making the world safe for democracy" ') involves the translation of a material disfiguration into an emotion (206). Elaine Scarry reminds us that 'the record of war survives in the bodies, both alive and buried, of the people who were hurt there'.[17] But Hillary's conclusion turns this record to new account. The end of the self's resistance is also the point at which the body is reduced to a sign for the abstract goals of the war.

Paul de Man has written that the master trope of autobiography is prosopopoeia, 'by which one's name . . . is made as intelligible as a face'.[18] In Hillary's case, autobiography stood in for a face which could be all too intelligible as a trace of violence, and as a consequence culturally unreadable as a sign of the war. With Macmillan

---

[16] 'Gun Buster', 'Active Service', *Battle Dress* (Hodder and Stoughton, 1941), 251–5.
[17] Elaine Scarry, *The Body in Pain: The Making and Unmaking of the World* (New York: Oxford University Press, 1985), 113.
[18] De Man, 'Autobiography as De-facement', 926.

interested in his draft of the book's opening, Hillary was interviewed by Duff Cooper at the MOI and dispatched on a lecture tour to the United States in June 1941.[19] But the Embassy in Washington cancelled all public appearances, judging it a psychological error to employ a scarred and crippled airman in the public relations exercise to persuade America to come into the war.[20] Hillary the war hero threatened to undo the propaganda effort because his appearance in public reversed the economy of symbols whereby the reality of wounds was translated onto abstract or as-yet-to-be-realized goals.[21] He was allowed to make four anonymous broadcasts of material destined for *The Last Enemy*, and completed the book in America, where it was published as *Falling Through Space* in the Spring of 1942.[22] *The Last Enemy* was, then, a transmissible figure for a face that spoke too plainly of the inadmissible cost of war.

The Last Enemy's alleged deformation of its author's self is bound up both with the cloaking of the disfigurement of bodies in combat, and with the disfiguring regimentation of individuals which is carried through into the mobilization and representation of the collective war effort. Hillary sat for the painter Eric Kennington, who had illustrated *Seven Pillars of Wisdom* (privately published in 1926) and who leant the unpublished airforce journals, *The Mint*, to Hillary: 'Like T. E. Lawrence he wanted a portrait, primarily to help him learn himself, and stared at it surprised, saying "I've got a face". '[23] But Hillary's scalpel-sculpted lips and eyelids are not a mark of individual history or identity alongside the artist's series of commissioned portraits of RAF personnel, with their stark emphasis of bone and sinew. Kennington's 'decisive foursquare individual style is peculiarly adapted for the portrayal of a Service of Team-Individualist types, with the varied and far-flung interests of the practical, technical, business-like modern fighting man,' opined Sir Ronald Storrs, former Imperial administrator ('the most brilliant Englishman in the Near East' according to Lawrence in *Seven Pillars of Wisdom*), MOI lecturer and instant historian (in the *Quarterly*

---

[19] Lovat Dickson, *Richard Hillary* (Macmillan, 1950), 122–3.

[20] Michael Burn, *Mary and Richard*, 25.

[21] For what America saw during the war, see George H. Roeder Jr., *The Censored War: American Visual Experience During World War Two* (New Haven: Yale University Press, 1993).

[22] Typescripts of the broadcasts are in the RHP, File 4.

[23] Eric Kennington quoted in Eric Linklater, 'Richard Hillary', *The Art of Adventure* (Macmillan 1947), 95.

History of the War), and later chair of the English Association.[24] The synthetic ideal of this official encomium, which echoes Hillary's vision of 'a new race of Englishmen arising out of this war ... a harmonious synthesis of the governing class and the great rest of England', suggests the extent of the ideological work that could be accomplished with the ambivalent figure of the airman, a model of both the ideal self and the ideal state.[25] Hillary's scars do not affirm his autonomy as duellist, but incorporate him into the nation, an imaginary body, via a portraiture which affirms a type. Kennington's second painting of Hillary, 'Heart of England', makes this reduction almost too explicit. An airman with bandaged hands and face appears to lay a single rose on East Anglia, as if the fens were the surface of an ops. room map table, an image which recalls the Ditchley Portrait (*c*.1592), Marcus Gheeraert the Younger's full-length portrait of Elizabeth I posed on a map of England. This articulation of concealments which are normally perceptually disjunct—the bandaged wound and the abstract representation of violence on the strategic map—is an emblem of the national enterprise which in its exhorbitance comes close to laying bare its constituent rhetorical components.

THE LEGENDS OF RICHARD HILLARY

To fight without faith is to fight with grace,
The self reconstructed, the false heart repaired.

Herbert Read.[26]

In the summer of 1942, Atlantic shipping losses approached their wartime peak; Axis armies threatened the Middle East in their advances on the Nile delta and through the Ukraine; Allied plans for opening a second front in Europe were deferred long into the future. But propagandists sought to exploit Hillary's signature to figure the

[24] Eric Kennington, *Drawing the R.A.F.: A Book of Portraits* (Oxford University Press, 1942), 30; T. E. Lawrence, *Seven Pillars of Wisdom: A Triumph* (1926. Jonathan Cape, 1935), 57. See also H. E. Bates, introduction to *War Pictures by British Artists*, no. 3, R.A.F. (Oxford University Press, 1942), 6.

[25] Hillary, *The Last Enemy*, 174–5.

[26] Herbert Read, 'To a Conscript of 1940', in M. J. Tambimuttu, *Poetry in Wartime* (Faber, 1942), 122.

earlier crisis of 1940 as a moment of rebirth. He was commissioned to write for the RAF's journal, and to address a Foyle's literary luncheon on the subject of intellectuals and Nazism. W. J. Turner, editor of the 'Britain in Pictures' series, in which established authors celebrated the continuity of the national cultural tradition, asked him to write 'Britain in the Air'.[27] Alberto Cavalcanti, who took over Grierson's GPO Film Unit, creating features which promoted the discipline of the un-uniformed British subject in direct resistance to the Wehrmacht (battles which Britain's garrisoned army could not fight in Europe), sought unsuccessfully to film *The Last Enemy*.[28] However Hillary did script a short, *Those in Peril*, based on his recovery by the Margate lifeboat: the protagonist, prevented from serving in the RAF by his poor eyesight, ceases to envy 'the boys with wings' when he finds a role in an Air-Sea Rescue unit.[29] This scenario recasts the plot of *The Last Enemy*—Hillary's progress from rescued to rescuer—by deleting the injured body as a catalyst for revaluation: it is at once a more schematic presentation of patriotic sacrifice, and a dissociation from his record of the self's desperate and destructive attachments. As Hillary's self-figuring became public property, he found that in writing himself into the war he had not resolved but exacerbated the burden of symbolic conscription to the national enterprise.[30]

The Last Enemy, because its narrative circularity held two versions of the airman hero in an unstable relation, read two ways at once: it was a document of self-dedication to the collective, and a testament of resistance to constraints on self-determination. Elizabeth Bowen saw Hillary's scrutiny of selfhood as a cultural bulwark against the war's destruction of the personal life:

I *have* met people who (in most cases with relief) have suspended their sense of identity for the duration, and are content to try to approximate to what they believe to be a general type. For such people, the war was at least a

[27] W. J. Turner, letter to Richard Hillary, 3 July 1942, RHP, file 6.

[28] He produced *The Foreman Went to France* (1942), from a J. B. Priestley story, and directed *Went the Day Well?* (1942), an adaptation of Graham Greene's propaganda tale 'The Lieutenant Died Last', written for the US market.

[29] Ealing Studios' promotional leaflet; The *Sunday Times* observed that Hillary's involvement guaranteed that 'the film will avoid the lower depths of imbecility'. Cuttings in RHP, file 4. The motif of sight and insight is given a darker treatment in H. E. Bates's air-sea rescue novella *The Cruise of the Breadwinner* (1946).

[30] In an unpublished TS story 'Fighter Pilot' (RHP, file 4), a 'universally disliked' airman transcends his egotism by guiding his burning plane into the Thames, rather than bale out over London.

means to by-pass personal problems. But for natures of Mr. Hillary's type, war, though it might shift the area of the personal problem, made it more, rather than less, acute.[31]

But V. S. Pritchett rejected the view that the book represented the victory of individual consciousness over the conscience of the collective. He noted that Hillary 'unhappily conveys the impression that he likes the spectacle of himself believing, and not that he believes'. Pritchett's review pre-empted the interpretation of Hillary's death as a rewriting or fulfilment of *The Last Enemy*:

Suspended above the hospital bed like some horrifying and conscious chrysalis in his mask, his coloured eye-pads, his bandages and his tannic varnish, the burned man hangs waiting to be reborn into a new life. The technical ingenuity, on which modern man relies in life, appears to play the part once taken by moral resources in moments of disaster. A man may be so curious about his own case that curiosity itself may sustain him.[32]

That self-consciousness would come to represent not a dissociation from war's imperatives, but a fatal process whereby the quest for self-knowledge was distorted by wartime ideologies and symbols.

Arguably the most important contribution to the posthumous re-imagining of Richard Hillary was by a refugee from Nazism. Arthur Koestler, a Hungarian Jew, had resigned from the Communist Party in 1938 after rediscovering Zionism (*Darkness at Noon* (1940) exposed the Moscow show trials). *Scum of the Earth* (1941), his first book in English, narrated his escape from occupied Europe, after internment in France *before* the Nazi invasion, via Casablanca. Interned for a month in Pentonville prison, he served in the Pioneer Corps, was commissioned to (but did not) write a pamphlet on the Gestapo for Orwell's Searchlight series, and subsequently worked for the MOI Films Unit and the BBC.[33] According to Koestler's ostensibly demystifying memorial essay 'The Birth of a Myth' (May 1943) Hillary was not in any conventional sense a casualty of war, but of the desperate search for a creed to fight for. While it was literally true that the enemy did not bring about Hillary's death—he was killed, along with his navigator, learning, against medical advice, to fly

---

[31] Elizabeth Bowen, 'A Man and the War', review of Richard Hillary, *The Last Enemy*, *The Tatler and Bystander*, 165/2,141 (8 July 1942), 54.

[32] V. S. Pritchett, 'Shot Down in Flames', review of Richard Hillary, *The Last Enemy*, *The New Statesman and Nation*, 24/593 (4 July 1942), 12.

[33] David Cesarani, *Arthur Koestler: The Homeless Mind* (William Heinemann, 1998), 148, 178.

twin-engined night-fighters—Koestler's inference is significant for its emphasis on the destructive effects of the symbols that mediate violence. What made Hillary a symbol—and he was not the legendary material of an 'ace' but a broken, grounded airman—was a lack which was not personal but social and ideological. The impact of this theory can be traced in the writings of critics of the war, and of servicemen who, in Michael Walzer's words, did not 'regard the struggle against the evil of Nazism as their primary purpose'.[34] *The Last Enemy* was viewed by Koestler as a provisional but ultimately deterministic rationalization. The terms in which Hillary sought to define himself could not be transcended because they were coincident with a social process which consumes the individuals which it promotes as symbols of the emptiness of ideology. Koestler replaces Pritchett's metaphor of the chrysalis (derived from MacIndoe's burns unit regimen) with the trope of crystallization: Hillary is 'petrified' into legend or symbol.[35] This image of flesh turned to stone, like the idea of Hillary dying to discover his epitaph, defies the common-sense logic that the memorial recalls the soldier's deeds. For here, the (blank) memorial becomes the cause of his death. Koestler's reading of Hillary's life and death catalysed reflections on the place of the individual in the war because it made partially explicit a signifying process which it also renewed, the flight of the mind from the broken body to symbols and ideals which redeemed violence in a political language.

Voted the best article of 1943 by *Horizon* readers, the essay is a palimpsestic supplement to *The Last Enemy*, drawing on (and silently modifying) Hillary's correspondence in an emergency restoration which echoes the dead man's attempt to define the survivor's responsibility: 'In times of war the dead recede quicker and myths form faster' (227). This is a pregnant apprehension of the way the traces of violence come to bear meaning, and one which promises to make the symbolic dimension of warfare perceptible. Hillary struggled not so much with selfhood as with the 'expectations of his Time'. Koestler granted him awareness that his life and death were symbolic, but this only confirms him as an impotent witness to the formation of the legend that required his own destruction—'the core the captive of the crystal, closing in around it to fulfil its predestined pattern' (229).

---

[34] Michael Walzer, 'World War II: Why Was This War Different?', *Philosophy and Public Affairs*, 1/1 (Fall 1971), 10.   [35] Koestler, 'The Birth of a Myth', 227.

By likening Hillary's instinct, which lures him back to flying, to a 'diffuse emotion latent in the social medium which strives for expression', Koestler suggested that the individual was powerless against conscription to a culture's eagerness for symbols which point beyond the facts of war. Like a microbe which 'penetrate[s] the blood-stream and burn[s] him out, in order to preserve the symbolic shell', the rage for meaning becomes inseparable from the means of extinction (227 and 229). Eric Linklater would write that Hillary was 'a national possession, an exemplar of his age, a symbol of its reverdissement'.[36] The lack of an English idiom for this idea of a growing green again echoes Hillary's halting efforts to verbalize his new-found purpose. The myth of palingenesis ('a "new birth" occurring after a period of perceived decadence'), which is the core of Fascist ideology, is also too green in the conclusion to *The Last Enemy*, too idealistic to bear much scrutiny.[37] But symbols, like those Richard Hillary was written into, make ideas less vulnerable to the counter-claim of 'my one and only body'.[38]

Hillary's reflections on the self-image he had created in *The Last Enemy* are adduced by Koestler as evidence that his last chapter was 'helpless stammering', a gesture at the significance of his life which he could not sustain: 'he had to die in search of his own epitaph'.[39] Repelled by the press's '"Knights of the Air"' ideal, which revived the rhetoric of 1916, Hillary recorded that he had written his book

in the hope that the next generation might realize that while stupid, we were not that stupid, that we could remember only too well that all this has been seen in the last war, but that in spite of that and not because of it, we still thought this one worth fighting (230).

But the 'tongue-in-the-cheek patriotism . . . [of] the heretic crusader' was conformist, 'as typical for the mental climate of this war as the stoning of the dachshunds for the last' (231). Scepticism about the war's purpose—embarrassment at 'big words and slogans', fighting 'rather *in spite of* than *because of* something'—doesn't arrest wartime culture's legitimation of destruction. It supplies, in the form of a 'Holy Grail', a justification which is even less tangible, and hence less open to rational thought (230 and 243). The quotation from

[36] Eric Linklater, 'The Undefeated, no. 9: Richard Hillary', TS script for Home Service broadcast, 21 March 1948, 40. RHP, file 6.

[37] Roger Griffin, *The Nature of Fascism* (Routledge, 1993), 32–6.

[38] Dylan Thomas to Glyn Jones (11 Sept. 1939), *The Collected Letters*, ed. Paul Ferris (1985. Paladin, 1987), 408.   [39] Koestler, 'The Birth of a Myth', 230.

Hillary's letter citing Koestler's own theories about wartime myth-making is crucial to the essay's power of generalization from the 'stammering' of *The Last Enemy* to the discursive regimes of the militarized state. Life is lived on the trivial plane which artists try to view from the tragic or absolute plane, but the physical danger of war places people at the intersection of the two. Adaptation typically involves an assimilation of the tragic to the trivial: in Hillary's words, people ' "elaborate conventions and formulae—e.g. R.A.F. slang and understatement" ' (238). As Koestler views it, promotion from the trivial to the tragic 'transforms undergraduates into heroes, psychology into mythology, a thousand conditioned reflexes into the Battle of Britain'. The metaphor seems to yield an opposition between culture's 'Pompeii-effect', its petrifaction of violence into dignified forms, and the bathetic effects of ironic service registers and idioms (238). But Koestler regarded Hillary's understatement as an 'intellectual camouflage' which disguised the search for a 'redeeming emotion', 'a credo, neither sentimental, vulgar nor archaic, whose words one could say without embarrassment' (243).

The servicemen who wrote to *Horizon* to 'amplify' this account of Hillary's state of mind certainly did not register the way Koestler, whose credentials as an anti-Nazi were substantial, had opened the way for a critique of scepticism. Lt. Michael Howard, awaiting embarkation for the Mediterranean, preferred the title 'agnostic crusaders' to Koestler's 'heretic', because the latter was too positive:

We are not fighting for democracy—many are temperamentally anti-democratic. We are not even sure that we are fighting for the external verities, as our fathers were—and are—so magnificently certain. Our standards of battle are banners without marks.

The Last Enemy had given expression to the inarticulate feelings of a generation, 'a desperate ignorance, and absurd faith in spite of it'.[40] In the same number of *Horizon*, a young Royal Artillery officer, Eversley Belfield, granted Koestler's 'myth of the Lost Generation' the status of fact, in a passionate diagnosis (following F. R. Leavis and I. A. Richards) of introspection and self-destructive frustration, the latter due to 'the overpowering vulgarity of the Press, the radio, advertising and the like instruments of propaganda that overwhelm the nerves of the mind by their persistence and universality'.[41]

[40] Michael Howard, letter to *Horizon*, 7/42 (June 1943), 430–1.
[41] Koestler, 'The Birth of a Myth', 243; Eversley M. G. Belfield, letter to *Horizon*, 7/42 (June 1943), 432.

However the painter Keith Vaughan, serving as Koestler had done, in the Pioneer Corps, but as a conscientious objector not an 'alien', recognized that the article gave authority to the myths it sought to analyse. Although, like Belfield, he was 'deeply influenced by the life of Lawrence', Vaughan questioned the meaning of the example of Aircraftsman Shaw's submission to something bigger than himself (which reprised Lawrence's 'slavery' to the ideal of freedom during the Arab revolt: 'By our own act we were drained of morality, of volition, of responsibility, like dead leaves in the wind.') The importance of *The Mint* to Hillary's return to flying was as a 'sentimental confirmation of a decision which he would in any case have taken'.[42]

In 1943, Koestler published *Arrival and Departure*, which drew on the report of the Jewish Labour *Bund* concerning ghetto liquidations in Poland and systematic gassings of Jews at Chelmno.[43] The novel reprises the analysis of Hillary in the figure of a wounded pilot with an 'artificial face', who has been attached to the Embassy of a neutral country because, 'he has become a barbarity to look at'.[44] Peter Slavek, the refugee hero of the novel, awaits passage to the country at war with his torturers, where he wants to join the fight, though suspecting he will—like Koestler—end up digging ditches. Slavek too incorporates aspects of Koestler's interpretation of Hillary: he is a 'fossil in the crystal of frozen time'; his memories of torture return as paralysis and delirium, during which he mimes flying a plane and being shot down (59). He has '"all the best qualities of his generation: their balance of scepticism and devotion, their unsentimental self-sacrifice"'; his crisis is a '"plunge into some mythological well"', and a desire for martyrdom (68). But, read alongside the essay, Peter's statelessness represents a potential which Hillary's self-projection as unwilling national symbol denied him: Peter 'had abandoned the fraternity of the dead, and the fraternity of the living had not yet received him' (133).

The novel ends with his parachuting into enemy territory:

There was no one to tell him whether he had succeeded or failed, and no scale to measure the value of his deeds. All he could hope for was that his

[42] Keith Vaughan, *Journal and Drawings 1939–1965* (Alan Ross, 1966), 56–7; T. E. Lawrence, *Seven Pillars*, 29.

[43] Cesarani, *Arthur Koestler*, 202. For the contexts and implications of press reporting of the *Bund* report in 1942, see Tony Kushner, *The Holocaust and the Liberal Imagination* (Oxford: Blackwell, 1994), 135.

[44] Arthur Koestler, *Arrival and Departure* (Jonathan Cape, 1943), 131.

departure might help to bring forth that event of which one is allowed to speak only at certain moments; and this was not one of them (188).

This muteness contrasts with Hillary's 'stammering', deferring any rhetoric of the 'event' (with its linkage of personal and national destinies). Understatement and liberating altitude coalesce in a motif of action freed from the pressure of the discourses which hedge it round. But as with the elision of the death of Hillary's navigator, this heroic poise before landfall (and with it the tangible dangers facing the undercover agent) draws on a compensatory myth. The airman's autonomy remains a potent figure of transcendence. But the fatalism of this motif of 'departure' contrasts with the idealism of H. E. Bates's description of the airman as 'one of the faces of those who fight wars they do not make and for whom flying and life are one: the faces of those who should be watched, the faces of the young—not the young who die, but of the young who are shot down and live—of the young who are at the beginning of things'.[45] Koestler drafted a sequel, in which, after landfall, Slavek learns about the reality of the Nazi programme of extermination (theorized in *Arrival and Departure* (141–4) with an imaginary map of a biologically re-engineered Europe). Returned to England, his attempt to organize a rescue mission is blocked by his CO, 'after all, we have a war on our hands'.[46] In Bates's stories about Bomber Command, the omission of the purpose of flying over Germany is disguised by the miming of such service understatement. Whether viewed as inarticulacy or stammering, this discourse was part of the obstacle to Koestler's attempt to write the reality of occupied Europe into Britain's cultural representation of the war.

Koestler's reading of Hillary and his book was not uncontested. Hillary's family attempted to regain control over the son's reputation, but the ensuing struggle, in which Koestler was closely involved, effectively thwarted the publication of counter-statements. A committee to organize a Richard Hillary Trust Fund was set up soon after the publication of 'The Birth of a Myth', in the summer of 1943, the proceeds from a projected memoir, with other royalties, to provide a prize for young authors. Koestler resigned when Lovat Dickson, Hillary's editor at Macmillan, urged postponement until a larger post-war printing could boost sales of *The Last Enemy* when interest in war books might be expected to decline.

[45] 'Flying Officer X' [H. E. Bates], 'The Beginning of Things', *How Sleep the Brave and Other Stories* (Jonathan Cape, 1943), 59.   [46] Cesarani, *Arthur Koestler*, 212–13.

The original idea had been to publish Koestler's and Linklater's articles, the latter a memoir written for a limited edition of *The Last Enemy*, together with Hillary's letters to his lover Mary Booker.[47] Michael Hillary, Richard's father, wanted two separate volumes, and was unhappy with Koestler's article—'it is manifestly untrue and its conclusions are obviously wrong'—preferring Linklater's more discursive typescript memoir, 'The Numbered Days', which had concluded that 'the cynic affirmed his faith in human purpose'.[48]

Mary Booker wrote in May 1944 to the novelist Phyllis Bottome, a second cousin of Peter Pease, asking her to take on a project which had foundered.[49] Bottome was known for a love story set in Nazi Germany, *The Mortal Storm* (1937, as a Penguin Special) and a novel of the Blitz, *London Pride* (1941), which ended with a vision of 'the city spiritualised'.[50] She felt that both Koestler and Linklater had been grudging of Hillary's courage; she had told Hillary that *The Last Enemy* proved that he had given what Peter would have given.[51] The fictionalised life she proposed never materialized, and in the absence of an authorized memoir (Dickson's biography did not appear until 1950), Koestler's circulated alongside more conventional elegies:

> Death the last enemy? No, self was that.
> His brave book proved it. It was self he killed.[52]

Hillary's reputation even extended to Germany: in *Oflag* VII B Kennington's 'Heart of England' inspired A. C. Rawlings to write a memorial (but in Colditz, Michael Burn, who would write about Hillary's relationship with his future wife, Mary Booker, did not hear of him). Christabel Bielenberg was lent a copy of *The Last Enemy*, valued for its 'understatement' in relation to the 'blown up rubbish' of Nazi print culture, by Adam von Trott zu Solz (subsequently executed for his part in the July 1944 plot against Hitler).[53]

---

[47] Eric Linklater, letter to Michael and Edwyna Hillary, 30 Dec. 1943, RHP, file 8.

[48] Michael Hillary, letter to Lovat Dickson, 2 May 1944, RHP, file 8; Eric Linklater, TS 'The Numbered Days', p. 62, RHP, file 9.

[49] Mary Booker, letter to Phyllis Bottome, 26 May 1944, RHP, file 8.

[50] Jenny Hartley, *Millions Like Us: British Women's Fiction of the Second World War* (Virago, 1997), 27.

[51] Phyllis Bottome, letter to Mary Booker, 29 May 1944, RHP, file 8; letter to Richard Hillary, 31 July 1942, RHP, file 6.

[52] M. H. Noel-Paton, 'The Last Enemy (To the Memory of Fl. Lt. Richard Hillary, R.A.F.V.R.)', *Blackwood's Magazine*, 1,530 (April 1943), 293.

[53] A. C. Rawlings, 'Ave atque vale', RHP, file 6. Christabel Bielenberg, *The Past is Myself* (Chatto and Windus, 1968), 139, 146. She doesn't elaborate on the book she took by mistake, Eric Knight's upbeat novel of the 'People's War', *This Above All* (1941).

In Jocelyn Brooke's *The Passing of a Hero*, Phipps, a belle-lettriste employed at the MOI, is asked to write a memorial volume for Denzil Pryce-Foulger, student novelist, Mosleyite fellow-traveller, wartime broadcaster on the arts and casualty in the Normandy landings: 'The thing would be to build up a sort of Pryce-Foulger legend—like Richard Hillary or Anthony Knebworth.' But the debunking narrator reckons Pryce-Foulger gave little scope for the 'mythopoeic faculty'.[54] Hillary did, and still does. Sebastian Faulks, not the only novelist to achieve celebrity in the 1990s with fiction about the Great War, warmed up the biographical record to cast the pilot as a 'fatal Englishman', in a triptych completed by two dissolutes, naive-painter Christopher Wood and Cold-War pawn Jeremy Wolfenden.[55] Koestler, in attempting to analyse the formation of a symbol, helped to incubate one: if his essay found Hillary's war aims adolescent, many of its readers were prepared to believe that the war could be fought on those terms.

'ROMANCE OF THE AIR—WAR'S LAST BEAUTY PARLOUR'[56]

Aviation became a decisive tactical and strategic weapon in the Second World War. But aeronautical technology had long fascinated the popular and literary imaginations. Well before the formation of the RFC in 1912, and the establishment of the 'ace' as a new kind of national hero in the middle of the Great War, a literature of future aerial warfare had created a 'general climate of "air-mindedness"'.[57] Aviation was, alternately, affirmative or barbarically destructive of what it was to be human. Contradictions in the imagining of flight, and in the representation of the RAF as a symbol of individualist or, conversely, totalitarian political values, are both a context and product of the Hillary legend. In narrating the replacement of an aesthetics of flight with an awareness of the consequences of strategic bombing, *The Last Enemy* links the symbolic and strategic histories

---

54 Jocelyn Brooke, *The Passing of a Hero* (The Bodley Head, 1953), 155.

55 Sebastian Faulks, *The Fatal Englishman: Three Short Lives* (Hutchinson, 1996).

56 E. M. Forster in a letter to Christopher Isherwood, quoted in Valentine Cunningham, *British Writers of the Thirties* (Oxford: Oxford University Press, 1988), 202.

57 Michael Paris, *Winged Warfare: The Literature and Theory of Aerial Warfare in Britain 1859–1917* (Manchester: Manchester University Press, 1992), 17.

of the 'awful prestige of a new and much advertised form of warfare'.[58]

The aerial subjugation of whole armies and populations had been advocated in fictional texts long before the Great War. Count Rostopchin rallied Moscow with broadsheets describing 'the balloons that were to destroy the French' in *War and Peace*.[59] H. G. Wells narrated an attack on New York by German dirigibles in *The War in the Air* (1908), and the destruction of civilization in *The Shape of Things to Come* (1933). But such prognoses were outnumbered by visions of the positive revolutionary potential of flight. T. E. Lawrence wrote in the 1920s that 'the conquest of the air is the first duty of our generation. . . . By our handling of this, the one big new thing, will our time be judged'.[60] Judgement, when it came, would be influenced by the indiscriminacy of aerial attack but, between the wars, flight was celebrated for restoring humanity to warfare.[61]

The conventionality of Hillary's figure of the airman as duellist is evident from comparison with Cecil Lewis' RFC memoir, *Sagittarius Rising* (1936), which itself drew on nineteenth- and early twentieth-century conventions for describing terrestrial combat:

> To be alone, to have your life in your own hands, to use your own skill, single-handed, against the enemy. It was like the lists of the Middle Ages, the only sphere in modern warfare where a man saw his adversary and faced him in mortal combat, the only sphere where there was still chivalry and honour. If you won, it was your own bravery and skill; if you lost, it was because you had met a better man.[62]

Aviation reinvented the glamour of war. The official history of the 1914–18 air war, written by Oxford's Professor of English, Sir Walter Raleigh, drew on reminiscence to supplement incomplete Air Ministry records, emphasizing personal heroics.[63] 'Was there ever such a company of heroes as that Air Force [the RFC] of ours?', asked a book published during the Battle of Britain.[64] Yeats's Irish Airman

---

[58] John Mair, *Never Come Back* (Gollancz, 1941), 216.

[59] Leo Tolstoy, *War and Peace*, trans Louise and Aylmer Maude (1868–9, trans 1922–3. Oxford: Oxford University Press, 1991), 891.

[60] T. E. Lawrence, *The Mint* (Jonathan Cape, 1955), 181.

[61] During and after the Gulf War, the US and Iraq contested the outcome of the use of 'smart' guided weapons in the same terms.

[62] Cecil Lewis, *Sagittarius Rising* (Peter Davies, 1936), 45.

[63] Paris, *Winged Warfare*, 4–6.

[64] J. M. Spaight, *The Sky's the Limit: A Study of British Air Power* (Hodder and Stoughton, 1940), 17.

pursued a 'lonely impulse of delight', immune from adversarial politics; Robert Gregory, 'Our Sidney' and another non-combatant casualty, remade war as a human accomplishment.[65] Richard Hillary, dubbed 'the new Sir Philip Sidney', represented a similar reorientation of war to civil and aesthetic virtues.[66] But the technology which Cecil Lewis constructed in terms of chivalric decorum, in contrast to the 'murder' going on below, was murderous to those not privileged to escape the mud for the empyrean.[67] 'It is recognised as one of the most triumphant assertions of man's mastery over his biped handicap', wrote Wyndham Lewis; but as a target of straffing he knew all about 'aeronautical caddishness'.[68]

The tactical and technological distinction between aerial combat and air-to-ground massacre, between fighter and bomber, Churchill's the few and the many, would only fully make its mark on literary representations of flight in the wake of strategic bombing (despite the literature of the terror of bombing from Spain).[69] In 1936, Cecil Lewis imagined an air battle over London, but confined to duelling pilots.[70] *Fighter Pilot*, an account of flying Hurricanes before the fall of France, innocently arrogates the bomber threat as a vehicle of contempt in a fantasy (not unlike Sassoon's vindictive 'Blighters') that 'a few bombs' will wake English cricketers from their 'smug insular contentedness' (a similar thought had concluded Orwell's *Homage to Catalonia*).[71] Guy Gibson, constructed as a national hero by the Air Ministry in the wake of Operation Chastise (the Dambusters raid), would write, in a book sponsored by the RAF, of the low losses of aircraft over Northern Italy, and comment: 'whatever damage our bombs did, it was certainly a good portent of the future of civil aviation and the complete reliability of British aircraft'.[72]

---

[65] W. B. Yeats, 'An Irish Airman Foresees his Death' and 'In Memory of Major Robert Gregory', *Collected Poems* (Macmillan, 1982), 148–52.

[66] Robert Pitman, 'Did This Hero Crash His Plane On Purpose?', *Sunday Express*, 5 May 1957, RHP, file 11.

[67] Cecil Lewis, *Sagittarius Rising*, 45. Great War writers' use of figural altitude, for instance Owen's 'The Show' and the opening of Henri Barbusse's novel *Under Fire: The Story of a Squad*, trans W. Fitzwater Wray (Dent, 1917), contributed to the aeroplane's purchase on the imagination.

[68] Wyndham Lewis, *Blasting and Bombardiering* (Eyre and Spottiswoode, 1937), 164.

[69] See Valentine Cunningham (ed.), *The Penguin Book of Spanish Civil War Verse* (Harmondsworth: Penguin, 1980), 157–71.   [70] Cecil Lewis, *Sagittarius Rising*, 46.

[71] [Paul Richey], *Fighter Pilot* (Batsford, 1941), 121.

[72] Guy Gibson, *Enemy Coast Ahead* (Michael Joseph, 1946), 211; see Richard Morris, *Guy Gibson* (1994. Harmondsworth: Penguin, 1995), 221–8.

Thus, while wartime experience complicated the perception of the aeroplane, the potency of what Laurence Goldstein calls the 'technological sublime' remained substantially intact.[73] Indeed, it gained a new dimension in terms of the relationship of man and machine. Images of the assimilation of disparate individuals to a corporate discipline (associated with the bomber crew, rather than the fighter squadron) could function as a blueprint of national unity. But this incorporation was also conceived as having a dehumanizing, even sinister potential, as a subjection to technology and the machinery of regimentation, and the creation of proto-totalitarian ideologies.

AVIATION AND NATIONAL IDEOLOGY: 'A NEW RACE OF ENGLISHMEN'

The Last Enemy, commemorating one 'lost generation', describes another being 'incubated' on RAF stations. Although Hillary had not yet read Lawrence's book, this is the RAF of *The Mint*. For both men, joining the RAF was a project of self-construction, but Lawrence was dismantling a former self: wilful submission to dehumanizing drill was a disowning of a legendary identity. *The Mint*'s inventory of service regimentation—'"our mob's on fatigue for the duration"'—anticipates Foucault's analysis of perpetual penality, in which punishment is a reduplicated imposition of the discipline which '"makes" individuals' into tractable components of a technology.[74] Lawrence offered himself as fodder to basic training in a bizarre expiation, 'wondering if my authority . . . deflowered myself and those under me'.[75] These descriptions refer to Lawrence's training at Uxbridge in 1922. Shortly afterwards, the publication of his identity forced him to leave the service. The appendix of *The Mint* records his return to the RAF at Cranwell, and comes closer to Hillary's projection of a 'new race'. Service as a technician 'teaches a man to live largely on little. We belong to a big thing, which will exist for ever and ever in unnumbered generations of standard airmen, like ourselves'.[76]

[73] Laurence Goldstein, *The Flying Machine and Modern Literature* (Macmillan, 1986), 68.

[74] T. E. Lawrence, *The Mint*, 81; Michel Foucault, *Discipline and Punish: The Birth of the Prison* (Allen Lane, 1977), 170.

[75] T. E. Lawrence, *The Mint*, 104.   [76] Ibid. 205.

In Hillary's other published writings about the RAF, unconstrained by the disciplines of autobiography, individualist and collective definitions are often blurred. In distinguishing the RAF as possessing a sensibility, not a mentality, he personified the institution and represented its members as mere replicants, stamped with an institutional personality. However he denied that the man is produced by the institution: 'pilots forming the Air Force inevitably remain human beings within that organization, as the soldiers within the Army and the sailors within the Navy never can'.[77] In his Foyle's lecture, he assured his audience that the pilot was too well oriented in his field to 'go Fascist'.[78] The necessity for this reassurance lies in the troubling rhetorical and symbolic adjacency of Hillary's 'new race' and Nazi race-policy, represented in Koestler's *Arrival and Departure* as an experiment to 'breed a new species of homo sapiens'.[79]

Throughout the 1930s, flying and Fascism had been closely connected in both literary and popular culture. Auden associated *The Orators* with Fascist ideals: 'My name on the title-page seems a pseudonym for someone else, someone talented but near the border of sanity, who might well, in a year or two, become a Nazi.'[80] Lindberg's relationship with Goering and the Luftwaffe was well publicized.[81] Griffiths notes that 'many of the same young men who expressed sympathy for German aspirations . . . were later to be among the first to come forward to join the Auxiliary Air Force and the RAFVR'.[82]

Rex Warner's allegory of totalitarianism, *The Aerodrome* (1941) is, like Hillary's and Lawrence's books, a narrative of desire for the machine and for submissive incorporation into a race of overmen. Warner's airmen exhibit a brutal 'irresponsibility' to 'anything which was outside their own organization', invading and occupying the neighbouring village and supplanting conventional authority.[83] The charismatic Air Vice Marshall propounds an anti-sentimental

---

[77] Richard Hillary, 'The Pilot and Peace', *The Royal Air Force Journal*, 19 (July 1942), 16, RHP, file 4.

[78] Richard Hillary, 'Where Do We Go From Here?', *John O'London's Weekly*, 48/1,194 (20 Nov. 1942), 62.

[79] Koestler, *Arrival*, 144.

[80] Quoted in John Fuller, *W. H. Auden: A Commentary* (Faber, 1998), 88.

[81] Modris Eksteins, *Rites of Spring: The Great War and the Birth of the Modern Age* (Bantam Press, 1989), 322-3.

[82] Richard Griffiths, *Fellow Travellers of the Right: British Enthusiasts for Nazi Germany 1933-39* (1980. Oxford: Oxford University Press, 1983), 140.

[83] Rex Warner, *The Aerodrome: A Love Story* (The Bodley Head, 1941), 81.

bond of discipline, revoking ties of tradition and paternity to form 'a new and a more adequate race of men' (206). It is a superiority incarnated in altitude. From the air 'those inhabitants of the earth who had never risen above it, never submitted their lives to a discipline like ours', appear 'defenceless and ridiculous' (247–8).

The self-sufficiency of 'an organization manifestly entitled by its own discipline' to arrogate authority is, however, undone by its excesses. The sublimity of powered flight becomes a tyranny, in the shape of fly-by-wire technologies which will eliminate the pilot's residual scope for initiative at the controls of his plane (214–15). Nature, in the seasonal existence of men who work on the surface of the earth, is resurgent as the basis of resistance to the mechanization of the individual, an organicist motif also to be found in the mystical nationalism of Antoine de Saint-Exupéry's *Flight to Arras* (1942). The Air Vice Marshall's will to power is revealed as an eruption of the private into the political sphere, 'not self-effacement but a change of identity', paralleling the case of Lawrence (333).

In *The Aerodrome*, discipline, both political and technological, is the foundation of totalitarianism: Wells had prophesied that airpower made war 'a matter of apparatus, of special training. . . . It had become undemocratic'.[84] Wartime representations of the RAF simultaneously deny and assert these visions. The cultivated indiscipline of the officer-pilot is at once anti-authoritarian and elitist, a sign of a refusal to obey that could only arise from a thoroughly formalized and rule-bound sub-culture (similar contradictions surface in writing by POWs). Biggles, in his Second World War incarnation, flies with 'officers who do not take kindly to discipline', but for Ronald Adam's RFC ace MacMurray, return to the (renamed) service involves learning that it was no longer a 'freelance job'.[85] This duality charges Arthur Gwynn-Browne's *Gone for a Burton* (1945) with a political resonance that is otherwise absent from its populist treatment of war aims. Alone among the crew of his crashed bomber, Kim is determined to evade capture. He wants to continue the fight, not for his country 'which had left him rotting in its slums', but for the RAF, 'the agency which had helped him to become a man', an organization which is the antitype of 'drivelling Democracy'.[86] The

[84] H. G. Wells, *The War in the Air* (George Bell and Sons, 1908), 181–2.

[85] Captain W. E. Johns, *Spitfire Parade: Stories of Biggles in War-time* (Oxford University Press, 1940), 11; Ronald Adam ['Blake'], *Readiness at Dawn* (Gollancz, 1941), 20.

[86] Arthur Gwynn-Browne, *Gone for a Burton* (Chatto and Windus, 1945), 24.

community of the RAF comes before politics: '"it isn't a copy of what society is outside"' (336). In Gwynn-Browne's set-piece debate about the post-war world, Kim reacts aggressively to questions about the organization's revolutionary potential; he 'wasn't going to have the RAF dragged in by an outsider' (286). There is 'something indivisible about the RAF' (337). But this is a fugitive vision, as distant as the bombers that the crew hear flying above them while they are missing in France, a product of the bonds created by their enterprise as escapers, when they made their '"own discipline"' (370). Repatriated to a recuperation camp, Kim and Anthony are reduced to the ranks, and find themselves perpetually on fatigues for their resistance to the same supra-personal discipline which they had dreamt-up in their insular response to the conditions of occupied Europe. Reversing the supremacist trajectory of *The Mint*, Gwynn-Browne's airmen end up as juvenile sentimentalists in a service seemingly indifferent to the ideology they have projected onto it. Hillary was also disabused of this vision on re-posting. He returned to Lawrence's starting point, and another symbol of totalitarianism, 'a regimented concentration camp'. This, he told Mary Booker, would have made another *The Mint*, if the lack of privacy had not prevented writing.[87]

The political content of these images of an organization which both suspends and amplifies individuality was not always clear to contemporaries. To Louis MacNeice, the self's subjugation to the machine was an outmoded left-wing ideal:

The Marxist obsession encouraged us to crawl, to pretend ourselves cogs in a machine or part of the pattern in the lino. This pretence of humility was morbid—it was like Colonel Lawrence effacing himself in the Tank Corps. Now, with a war on, we need not be so anxious for self-effacement, we can leave that job to the bombs. This is our time to be arrogant.[88]

This is another statement of Bowen's praise for the self-realizing Hillary: service uniforms readily offered themselves as the masks of an absented selfhood. Keith Vaughan, however, saw these images of the RAF as witness to the appeal of Fascism to the introvert:

The attraction of an organization which enforces a programme of action which is beyond criticism, allowing them just sufficient time as individuals to appreciate their captivity is obvious, but one cannot escape the conclusion that all this is a sickness. The RAF promises just this and so did Fascism in

---

[87] Linklater, *The Art of Adventure*, 93–4.
[88] Louis MacNeice, 'Broken Windows or Thinking Aloud' (1941–2) in *Selected Prose*, 137.

its early days. It is the iron lung for the psychologically rigid. The support that banishes the fear of freedom. It gives pilots their strange, strained, rather hectic dignity, the 'ethereal quality' Hillary called it. It is the reason why so many people are really happier during a war than in peace time. They are given an artificial armour over their soft shells.[89]

This is a precise diagnosis of the metallization of the body which attracts and repels the other airman who made a 'profound impact on [Hillary's] life', Antoine de Saint-Exupéry, the famed author and mail-pilot, who wrote in 1939 of the desire 'to be a completely anonymous serviceman'.[90]

Flight to Arras recounts a reconnaissance sortie flown while France falls to the invading German armies. Saint-Exupéry's privileged spectating of his nation's defeat culminates in a post-debriefing vision of earthbound humility, and the seeds of future freedom in French soil. Hillary came close to the language of Saint-Exupéry's rediscovery of faith—'I shall fight for Man. Against Man's enemies— but against myself as well'—but not to its political ambivalence.[91] *Flight to Arras* is penetrating in its vision of the appropriation of the individual by the mechanisms of war, avoiding 'the wet blanket of understatement', but vague in its concluding registrations of the meaning of defeat, where 'mysticism has sunk into mystification'.[92] Its narrative is, like that of *The Last Enemy*, organized about a trajectory of rehumanization. The airman who views refugees as 'infuriosa wriggling under a microscope' eventually identifies with the peasantry.[93] The route to this conclusion is via the political fact of defeat, and a critical understanding of the mastery of the war machine over man. Like Warner's redundant pilots, and like the debt-repayment of Hillary's flyers, Saint-Exupéry, by strapping in, is yielding his humanity to a machine:

I am attached to the plane by a rubber tube as indispensable as an umbilical cord. The plane is plugged into the circulation of my blood. Organs have been added to my being, and they seem to intervene between me and my heart (20).

[89] Vaughan, *Journal*, 57.
[90] Michael Hillary, TS essay, p. 1, RHP, file 6; Antoine de Saint-Exupéry, *Wartime Writings 1939-1945*, ed. Norah Purcell (1986. Picador, 1988), 19.
[91] Antoine de Saint-Exupéry, *Flight to Arras*, trans. Lewis Galantière (Heinemann, 1942), 157.
[92] Philip Toynbee, 'New Novels', review of Antoine de Saint-Exupéry, *Flight to Arras*, *The New Statesman and Nation*, 24/607 (10 Oct. 1942), 245.
[93] De Saint-Exupéry, *Flight to Arras*, 64.

The airman does not realize himself, but is 'used up' in an accelerated senescence (42). He ceases to possess himself, awaiting war's claim on what is no longer his own:

During the day my body was not mine. Was no longer mine. Any of its members might at any moment be commandeered; its blood might at any moment be drawn off without my acquiescence. For it is another consequence of war that the soldier's body becomes a stock of accessories that are no longer his property. The bailiff arrives and demands a pair of eyes—you yield up the gift of sight. The bailiff arrives and demands a pair of legs—you yield up the gift of movement. The bailiff arrives torch in hand and demands the flesh off your face—and you, having yielded up the gift of smiling and manifesting your friendship for your kind, become a monster (50).

Hillary's defacement resonates here, not as the result of an evanescent myth-making, but as the material consequences of organized violence. Yet such violence, as Koestler and Hillary could see, might be assimilated to the forms by which a society articulates its interests. It is in those forms that Hillary, and those who interpreted his life and work, attempted to construct meanings around the inarticulable fact of wounding, and the as-yet-unrealized goals of war.

The pacifist literary critic John Middleton Murry seized on Koestler's thesis to accuse Hillary of having 'fake[d] the record'.[94] Submission to 'the creed which the public is made happy to believe they professed' was populist self-betrayal (99). In 1940, Murry had warned that 'holding a nation together by turning it into a regiment' would destroy what was ostensibly being defended. His formulation—'for the sake of living to lose the reasons for life'—anticipates Joseph Heller's more pointed irony: '"anything worth dying for . . . is certainly worth living for"'.[95] Murry's essay on Hillary contests the apparent necessity in Churchill's phrase '"fighting for survival"': 'Hillary is the essence of what survives,—the impossibility of life. What Hillary foreknew as an individual, Britain will discover as a nation.'[96] *The Last Enemy* uncritically reproduced the cultural logic of war:

War comes to many, always, as a great simplification of issues too tangled to unravel; but it is largely a false simplification. The moral and spiritual struggle can never be entirely comprehended in the physical, and is much more rarely decided by it than men in the heat of conflict persuade themselves.[97]

---

94 John Middleton Murry, 'Richard Hillary', *The Adelphi*, 20/4 (July–Sept. 1944), 97.

95 John Middleton Murry, *Democracy and War* (Nisbet and Co., 1940), 10, 5; Joseph Heller, *Catch-22* (Jonathan Cape, 1962), 242.

96 Murry, 'Richard Hillary', 101.   97 Murry, *Democracy and War*, 33.

In *The Last Enemy*, the destruction of the 'reasoned arguments' of the pacifist David Rutter by Hitler's aggression—'he knew well enough that it had become a crusade', '"it was no longer a question for personal conscience but for the conscience of civilization"'—prefigures Hillary's owning of his 'honourable' scars (237–8). Although the narrative reveals that the technology which permitted a 'return to war as it ought to be' is really the means to the mass, random killing of civilians, in Murry's reading 'aesthetic reasons' for flying are supplanted by sentimental abstractions (16, 151).

Reviewing H. E. Bates's pseudonymous Air Ministry-commissioned stories, T. C. Worsley observed that understatement was at once the idiom of the time, as far as the RAF was concerned, and 'the sentimental trap set for all post-Hemingway story writing'.[98] It offered no resistance to myth-making: refusal to use big words—political and moral abstractions—did not staunch the mind's flight to such conceptions. Murry, adapting Koestler's formulation to his critique of the strategic bombing campaign against Germany, wrote that Hillary 'had projected himself into . . . a tragedy of understatement . . . of the man who puts meaning into his own life by insisting on a meaning in the deaths of his friends'. The true significance of Hillary's self-examination, betrayed in the very scene of an 'obscenity—the blasting of simple families to death in their homes' which would be redoubled upon 'simple families through the length and breadth of Germany', was that it foretold the masking of barbarity by rationalizations and positive symbols: 'The glory of the fighter-pilot grinds slowly and inexorably down to the shame of Bomber Command.'[99] This perspective is occluded in H. E. Bates's rehearsing of the 'laconic jargon of flight' in his stories of bomber crews: 'expressed in no language but their own', the destructive labour of young British men is a 'good show'.[100]

Koestler speculated that the war would generate a new kind of writing, and a rejection of liberal–individualist ideology:

With the 'bourgeois' novel getting more and more exhausted and insipid as the era which produced it draws to its close, a new type of writer seems to take over from the cultured middle-class humanist: airmen, revolutionaries,

[98] T. C. Worsley, 'Stirling Station', review of H. E. Bates ['Flying Officer X'], *The Greatest People in the World*, *The New Statesman and Nation*, 24/610 (31 Oct. 1942), 295.

[99] Murry, 'Richard Hillary', 99–100.

[100] H. E. Bates, *The Greatest People in the World and Other Stories* (Jonathan Cape, 1942), 55–6.

adventurers, men who live the dangerous life; with a new operative technique of observation, a curious alfresco introspection and an even more curious trend of contemplation, even mysticism, born in the dead centre of the hurricane.[101]

But he helped Hillary's contemporaries perceive him not as a pioneer but as a survival from an earlier age of English heroism, and whose doubts are a source of pathos rather than of critical consciousness.

[101] Koestler, 'The Birth of a Myth', 240.

3

'What targets for a bomb': Spectacle, Reconstruction and the London Blitz

'THE background to this war, corresponding to the Western Front in the last war, is the bombed city.'[1] Spender's correlation, from the distance of 1943, is arguably more obvious in historical retrospect, because urban ruin has become as instantly legible a symbol as the Flanders trenches. Familiar landscapes make war visualizable: they also make it seem inevitable, natural, as if defensive entrenchments and levelled residential districts were not man-made environments. By contextualizing the spatial and temporal implications of Spender's 'background', we can start to understand how such an environment takes hold of the imagination, the way its content is conceived, and the symbolic work performed by its representations.

Air power is crucial in the genealogy of the presiding symbols of Second World War discourses: in the later 1930s it had dominated official and private imaginings about what the next war would be like. Inter-war developments in technology and strategy threatened to transform the spatial and ethical co-ordinates of war, targeting civilians in their distant homes, not soldiers on the designated terrain of the battlefield. Panoramas of urban ruin were being represented publicly and privately long before the first raids on London in September 1940. The interaction of such expectations with the practical experience of air raids is a significant aspect of the Blitz as an organizing figure for the no-longer metaphorical Home Front. The practical problem of housing people who should not, by pre-war calculations, have survived the bombing reveals the scale of the discrepancy between expectation and actuality. But omission of the fate of the built environment is reversed in verbal and pictorial representations of the raids of 1940–1, in which the urban fabric is foregrounded at the expense of human figures. There is a striking parallel

[1] Stephen Spender, introduction to *War Pictures by British Artists*, 2nd ser., no. 4, *Air Raids* (Oxford University Press, 1943), 6.

with the administrative operations of strategic description, one that requires us to ask how representations of the bomb-damage, and the symbols they helped put into circulation, relate to the discursive maintenance of the war effort, and in particular the disappearance of the hurt body.

IMAGINING AERIAL BOMBARDMENT

Turning the Luftwaffe's bombers from the airfields of south-east England onto London postponed Hitler's plans for the invasion of Britain. The attack on the Soviet Union, and declaration of war on the United States after Pearl Harbour in December 1941, effectively ended the threat of Wehrmacht landings. But in September 1940, Britons who could not know this were in the front line of the battle they had long anticipated. Henry Green's novel of the Auxiliary Fire Service, *Caught* (1943), begins with the statement 'When war broke out in September we were told to expect air raids.' This understated evocation of collective anticipations (its form a compressed echo of the soon abandoned second-person narrative voice which opens Flaubert's *Madame Bovary*, and in striking contrast to the apocalyptic rhetoric of Green's pre-Blitz emergency memoir, *Pack My Bag*) immediately complicates the author's legal disclaimer that 'only 1940 in London is real'. The apprehension of that reality owed as much to the preceding decade as it would to contemporary and retrospective myth-making.[2] Graham Greene, looking back from October 1940, wrote of a culture's 'impatience because the violence was delayed'.[3]

The invasion-scare literature of the pre-1914 period, of which Erskine Childers's *The Riddle of the Sands* (1903) is a classic, had been supplanted between the wars by fantasies and prophecies of airborne destruction; gas and germ warfare, and high explosive.[4] The

[2] Henry Green, *Caught* (Hogarth Press, 1943), 5. For the emergent mythology of the air raids, see Angus Calder, *The Myth of the Blitz* (Jonathan Cape, 1991), 1–19; on representations of bombed London in propaganda to America, Nicholas J. Cull, *Selling War: The British Propaganda Campaign Against American "Neutrality" in World War II* (Oxford: Oxford University Press, 1995), 97–125.

[3] Graham Greene, 'At Home', *Collected Essays* (The Bodley Head, 1969), 448.

[4] See Martin Ceadel, 'Popular Fiction and the Next War, 1918–1939', in Frank Gloversmith (ed.), *Class, Culture and Social Change: A New View of the 1930s* (Brighton: Harvester, 1980), 161–84. Childers's novel is all the more emblematic of the genre's relation to military policy development because it centres on the disruption of the planning and preparations for an invasion that remains a speculative possibility.

next-war projections of policy-makers necessarily also inhabited the imaginary. A proposal for an Air Pact 'to outlaw aerial bombing' had made little headway during the 1934–5 rearmament negotiations with Germany.[5] But Stanley Baldwin's statement that 'the bomber will always get through' was an untested hypothesis informed by the priorities of British rearmament policy.[6] Guilio Douhet, the Italian theorist of air power, speculated as early as 1921 that aeroplanes would modify the space of future wars by nullifying the frontier: 'Nothing man can do on the surface of the earth can interfere with a plane in flight, moving freely in the third dimension.'[7] The aeroplane, he argued, was not adaptable for defence, and hence the distinction between soldiers and civilians had been erased. (Disney countered this unhappy prognosis with the cartoon headline 'Dumbombers for Defence' in a wartime movie about overcoming disfigurement).[8] Imaginary projections of aviation strategy changed the way people imagined the space of battle, and what they understood to be the rules of war, well in advance of its tactical application. The Luftwaffe's bombing of the Basque capital Guernica in April 1937 became a concrete reference point both for calculations of the impossibility of civil defence and for popular conceptions of modern militarist atrocity. Picasso's *Guernica*, exhibited in Paris, London, and across the United States in the two years after its composition, points to the contrast between the impact on the pre-war imagination of this tactical exercise of limited air power, and the way in which the strategic bombing of Britain was represented as a triumph of metropolitan resistance to tyranny. Writhing in the confines of an electric-lit room, Picasso's human and animal forms find no counterpart in the vistas of wrecked buildings which typify British wartime art. Moore's tube-dwellers take the solidity of stone, while the resolution on the faces in Edward Baird's group-portrait 'Unidentified Aircraft' (1942, City Gallery, Glasgow) qualifies both the picture's haunting disturbance of perspective and the vulnerable delicacy of its pastiche early-Renaissance cityscape.

With hindsight, Government projections from the late 1930s have the look of alarmist fiction. In 1937 the Committee for Imperial Defence put the toll of a sixty-day air-campaign against Britain at

[5] Richard Lamb, *The Drift to War, 1922–1939* (W. H. Allen, 1989), 112–13.
[6] Quoted in Tom Harrisson, *Living Through the Blitz* (Collins, 1976), 22.
[7] Guilio Douhet, *The Command of the Air*, trans. Dino Ferrari (Faber, 1943), 14.
[8] *Dumbo*, dir. Ben Sharpsteen (US: Walt Disney, 1943).

nearly two million, of whom a third would be killed. A Ministry of Health committee estimated that between one and three million hospital beds would be required, largely for the treatment of a hysterical urban population, and the Home Office planned mass burials and the burning of bodies in lime.[9] In a journal entry for 3 September 1939, clerk and novelist George Beardmore recorded: 'We had all taken *The Shape of Things to Come* too much to heart, also the dire prophecies of scientists, journalists and even politicians of the devastation and disease that would follow the first air raid. We pictured St Paul's in ruins and a hole in the ground where the Houses of Parliament had stood.'[10] Even at this stage damage to buildings was an ambivalent sign for human injury. Officials projected the effects of next-war air offensives on the basis of the Zeppelin and Gotha raids of 1914–18, but also extrapolated from unreliable medico-military and anecdotal evidence. The official history of wartime social provision concluded that the 'apocalyptic prophecies of the nineteen-thirties obscured the humdrum problems of. . .the business of living in cities' after aerial attack.[11]

Inverting Fussell's rule-of-thumb—'every war is ironic because every war is worse than expected'—the kill ratio for high-explosive delivered by air over urban concentrations had been grossly exaggerated.[12] Ritchie Calder would write of an 'extravagant provision for the *dead*'.[13] Government and public opinion generally 'overlooked the magnitude of the problem of people without homes'.[14] The policy of evacuation, which by the outbreak of war was far more advanced than Civil Defence provision, was calculated not simply to save lives but to prevent the outbreak of civil insurrection amongst a population psychologically unhinged by the enemy's airforce. Wartime art's focus on buildings, not bodies, must be related to the negation, in Britain, of apocalyptic projections—the millions of hurt bodies and deranged minds piled up by statisticians and policy-makers—but these imaginings are not so much supplanted by reality

---

[9] Richard M. Titmuss, *Problems of Social Policy* (HMSO and Longmans, Green and Co., 1950), 13.

[10] George Beardmore, *Civilians at War: Journals 1938–1946* (Oxford: Oxford University Press, 1986), 34.   [11] Titmuss, *Problems of Social Policy*, 327.

[12] Paul Fussell, *The Great War and Modern Memory* (Oxford: Oxford University Press, 1977), 7 and *Wartime: Understanding and Behaviour in the Second World War* (Oxford: Oxford University Press, 1989), 3–13.

[13] Ritchie Calder, *The Lesson of London* (Secker and Warburg, 1941), 23.

[14] Titmuss, *Problems of Social Policy*, 328–9.

as reworked into new forms in which violence connoted social cohesion, rather than the destruction of persons, and in which the sensuous apprehension of destructive force made the vulnerable body more, not less, invisible. Dan Billany recognized that the pleasure that could be wrung from the spectacle of air raids displaced concern for human casualties:

What hurt was the knowledge that human beings, with soft flesh like ours, were in the centre of the holocaust. You could see no injury and hear no cries: only the spectacular play of lights and the roll of guns and bombs. The guns were angry, the bombs were angry. They were arrogant, they shouted each other down. It was a mere side issue in their debate, that men and women and children were being briefly shouldered out of life.[15]

The intersection of the redescription of casualties as a side-effect of military force, and the wound's invisibility in the representation of that force, suggests the potentially mutually-reinforcing rhetorical adjacency of aesthetic responses to violence and strategic abstractions.

During the Great War, air raids on Britain had created fear and panic, one death on the mainland for every thousand British corpses in corners of foreign fields, and a new romance of war: air power had the potential to amaze and delight. Katherine Mansfield wrote from Paris about a Zeppelin raid:

the Ultimate Fish. . .passed by, flying high, with fins of silky grey. It is absurd to say romance is dead when things like this happen & the noise it made— almost soothing you know—steady—and clear doo-da-doo-da—like a horn. I longed to go out & follow it.[16]

D. H. Lawrence spiritualized the raiders over London by juxtaposing the transubstantiations of Christianity, art, and war:

there, in the sky, like some god vision, a Zeppelin, and the searchlights catching it, so that it gleamed like a manifestation in the heavens, then losing it, so that only the strange drumming came down out of the sky where the searchlights tangled their feelers. There it was again, high, high, high, tiny, pale, as one might imagine the Holy Ghost far, far above.[17]

Popular reaction, while often hysterical, also encompassed such fascination. Mr Punch celebrated the setting ablaze of a Zeppelin as the

[15] Billany, *The Trap* (Faber, 1950), 86.

[16] Katherine Mansfield, letter to John Middleton Murry, 21 March 1915, *The Collected Letters of Katherine Mansfield*, ed. Vincent O'Sullivan and Margaret Scott, i (Oxford: Clarendon Press, 1984), 159.

[17] D. H. Lawrence, *Kangaroo* (Martin Secker, 1923), 242.

'most thrilling aerial spectacle ever witnessed'.[18] During a raid in John Buchan's *Mr Standfast*, a crowd lurks in the atrium of a Tube station, 'as if they were torn between fear of their lives and interest in the spectacle'.[19] These descriptions reveal how mistaken it is to view the glorification of war in Marinetti's pre-war Futurist manifestos as a political and aesthetic aberration.

Visions of a future which contained the military perfection of such sublime weapons were the earliest impacts of the Second World War on the imagination. They helped create what John Langdon-Davies, drawing on the Spanish experience, claimed to be the most unnerving aspect of strategic bombing, its pre-emptive effects on the mind. If surprise was 'already being used against us' in 1938, it was in part because 'the forces of darkness stealing up in the obscurity of an uncertain future' had already taken shape in people's imaginations.[20] Before the Rotterdam and London raids of 1940, Mass Observation concluded that, whatever the state of official preparations, the image of the bomber was having practical effects: 'the expectation of enemy aeroplanes had already, before the war started, begun to change the social structure of Britain.'[21]

Orwell represented the apocalyptic imagination bathetically in the figure of George Bowling, who believes that war is 'booked for' 1941, and envisages what will happen to the Strand:

No, not all smashed to pieces. Only a little altered, kind of chipped and dirty-looking, the shop-windows almost empty and so dusty that you can't see into them. Down a side street there's an enormous bomb crater and a block of buildings burnt out so that it looks like a hollow tooth.[22]

The world is too late for Bowling's separate peace: the urbanized Lower Binfield of his bucolic nostalgia is rocked by the bombs of Britain's belatedly rearmed airforce. *Nineteen Eighty-Four*—and not just the cratered cityscape of Airstrip One, but also Winston Smith's fantasy of resistance—has its origins in the prophetic mentality personified in Bowling.

---

[18] Quoted in Trevor Wilson, *The Myriad Faces of War* (Cambridge: Polity Press, 1988), 392.

[19] John Buchan, *Mr Standfast* (Hodder and Stoughton, 1919), 188.

[20] John Langdon-Davies, *Air Raid: The Technique of Silent Approach: High Explosive Panic* (Routledge, 1938), 142.

[21] Mass Observation, *War Begins at Home*, ed. Tom Harrisson and Charles Madge (Chatto and Windus, 1940), 43.

[22] George Orwell, *Coming Up for Air* (Gollancz, 1939), 35.

Also published in 1939, Green's *Party Going* and Nevil Shute's *What Happened to the Corbetts* represent different approaches to the literary assimilation of the imaginary flights of next-war thought. The former, begun in 1933, glosses oblique social comedy with a threat that is only beginning to break through into the insulated consciousness of some of its characters. Shute's novel, by contrast, is a technocratic inventory of the projected effects of air raids. It is a domestic version of Wells' *The Shape of Things to Come*, a next-war apocalypse tempered with self-reliance and small-boat seafaring, and a romance set amidst the destruction of both the infrastructure and liberties of modern life. The Corbetts escape their de-civilized south-coast town in a yacht, fleeing not just bombs and epidemics, but the threat of being trapped there by the authorities. Shute's emphasis on the problems of the survivor throws light on the state's intransigence over civil defence: what was being defended from whom? Were citizens being protected from an enemy, or was the state defending itself from its potentially dangerous citizens (who are controlled by the bomb-dropping enemy)? In its emphasis on private resistance and survival the novel runs contrary to subsequent collectivist symbols of the air raids (as does its prefiguration of the focal significance of a national seafaring tradition in the 'little ships' iconography of Dunkirk, for instance in the 1942 Hollywood film *Mrs Miniver*, and Paul Gallico's story *The Snow-Goose* (1941). However the post-war uniform edition brings the novel into line with events under a by-then hegemonic description, reconfiguring it as a premonition of communal unity: '[Shute] foresaw the heroism and humanity with which the English people would react and described this, in most moving terms, before it happened.'[23] This translation of violence into an aspect of national character (known in advance of its instantiation) is indicative of the pace at which crisis is turned into a useable past. A rhetoric which links pasts and futures is a powerful tool for designating the content of the present, the present being precisely where the fact of the injured body might undo the eliminative logic of war.

In Green's *Party Going* the transformations threatened by bombing are figuratively attached to happenings within the precincts of a fog-bound Victoria station. The rail terminus, starting point for so many journeys to war in the 1930s (Auden and Isherwood embarked

---

[23] Nevil Shute, *What Happened to the Corbetts*, uniform edition (Heinemann, 1952), dust wrapper.

for China from this station in 1938), is a scene of social disintegration.[24] Fog paralyses the metropolis, as the bomber, descending
equally unexpectedly, was supposed to do. The shutters that fall between an enervated upper class suspended between Mayfair and the
south of France in the station hotel and commuters caught, as if in an
air raid, between work and home, are the redoubts of a civil defence
of class distinction (which persisted through a war which levelled
buildings but not as many inequalities as people were encouraged, or
wanted, to believe). The rich in their hired suites possess a privileged
altitude with respect to the crushing mass in the concourse, an altitude aligned with the indifference of the enemy bombardier, or Nero
(proverbially indifferent to the burning of Rome) whose portrait
hangs on a bedroom wall. Outside, the crowd in their abandonment
embody their destiny: their mutterings, 'one vast confused hum like
numbers of aeroplanes flying by', include the observation ' "what targets for a bomb" '.[25] In an extended conceit, the entropy of the crowd
anticipates destruction:

They were like ruins in the wet, places that is where life has been, palaces,
abbeys, cathedrals, throne rooms, pantries, cast aside and tumbled down
with no immediate life and with what used to be in them lost rather than hidden now the roof has fallen in.[26]

Translations between the human and the architectonic, figure and
background, would be a dominant device in representations of the
bombing of Britain which redeemed violence as resistance. And in
One of Our Aircraft is Missing (1941) the hum of bombers becomes
a morale-boosting music to the ears of Dutch resistors who delight in
the sight of *Übermenschen* running for cover.

THE SPECTACLE OF METROPOLITAN RUIN

This noble capital, the pride of England and of Europe, I believe no man is so strangely wicked as to desire to see destroyed
by a conflagration. . . . [but] who would have been content
never to have seen London in its glory?

Edmund Burke[27]

[24] The railway journey was transformed figuratively as well as physically in wartime,
into a kind of moving prison or barracks, destination unknown, though reports of rail-
transports of Jews eastwards would be met with scepticism.
[25] Henry Green, *Party Going* (Hogarth Press, 1939), 177–8.   [26] Ibid. 201.
[27] Edmund Burke, *A Philosophical Enquiry into the Origin of our Ideas of the Sublime
and the Beautiful*, ed. Adam Phillips (Oxford: Oxford University Press, 1990), 44.

Zeljko Sikic, president of Dubrovnik Council [during the Croatian War of 1991–2], was amazed by the Western intelligentsia's indifference to human suffering and obsessive concern for 'heritage': 'Just because the medieval quarter still stands, are the Serbian attacks acceptable? I suppose if the centre of London was flattened you would say, "Oh, that doesn't matter, just as long as the Tower is in one piece." '

Mark Almond[28]

Spectacle and anticipatory projection are related as instances of the play of appearance and reality. John Strachey, who left the Communist Party over its Moscow-determined opposition to an 'imperialist war', wrote that:

the reality is never as bad as the fantasy: never as terrifying, never as shattering. That is why the raids, when they came, were such a genuine relief to so many people. But there is another side to that. The reality is seldom as interesting, as rich, as exciting, as satisfying, as the fantasy, either.[29]

The notion that violence was a relief had both psychological and ideological aspects. Strachey's narrative of Civil Defence stresses the morale-boosting side-effects of bombing which bind the vulnerable individual into a new community.[30] This is on one level a corrective to strategists' fantasies of the remote-subjugation of the population, which would lead to a massive investment of productive capacity in the area-bombing of Germany. But Strachey's vision is also an exercise in redescription. The assimilation of the effects of violence to ideals of consensual state governance, so that they become a component of nation building, is a remarkable cultural production.

Pre-war writing on the bomber threat had emphasized division. But Blitz-culture stressed communal harmony as the bombs rained down, issuing images of social ritual, from Moore's Tube drawings to the unlikely scenario of family readings from Clemence Dane's *The Shelter Book: a gathering of Tales, Poems, Essays, Notes and Notions. . . for use in Shelters, Tubes, Basements and Cellars in*

[28] Mark Almond, *Europe's Backyard War: The War in the Balkans* (William Heinemann, 1994), 391 n. 13.
[29] John Strachey, *Post D: Some Experiences of an Air Raid Warden* (Gollancz, 1941), 67–8.
[30] The community of the targeted replaces the idealized solidarity of the proletariat. Strachey dissociated himself from CPGB policy as late as the invasion of Norway, see Kevin Morgan, *Against Fascism and War: Ruptures and Continuities in British Communist Politics, 1935–41* (Manchester: Manchester University Press, 1989), 119–20.

War-time (published 12 December 1940).[31] The way in which the violence 'brought home' to civilians is made homely, even as homes in
their millions are damaged, has a corollary in the representation of
the air raids as an aesthetic spectacle of urban ruin. But to interpret
representations of the awe-inspiring qualities of destruction as contributing to national survival in a technological contest, and, simultaneously, sponsoring a radical interpretation of that contest's
possible outcome in progressive social change, may be to underesti-
mate the implications of the convergence of an ideology of spectacle
and the legitimation of state violence.

The anarchist art theorist Herbert Read, taking a detour from
Bank to Piccadilly during the 17 April 1941 'great raid', was moved to
contemplate a revolution in taste, reconstruction 'in a new style': the
present crisis would speed up experiment in the arts. Destruction
freed the aesthetic from bureaucratic apparatuses: 'all institutions,
institutes, associations and federations had become so many empty
forms, structures with their windows blown out, their walls cracked,
their reports and memoranda a heap of sodden ashes.'[32] 'There is
something of release in the destruction of the greatest monuments',
noted Spender.[33] Louis MacNeice believed that the Luftwaffe had
'broken the end wall' of the 1930s' cul-de-sac.[34] Henry Green wrote
to Rosamund Lehmann that 'these times are an absolute gift to the
writer. Everything is breaking up'.[35] The idea that war is an agent in
the evolution of art is in tension with the widely remarked frustration of aesthetic activity by war. Art produced as a conscious effort
to draw inspiration from the upheavals of the war years, for instance,
the 'prophetic surrealism' of the New Apocalypse—Read's anarch-
ism influenced J. F. Hendry's programme in the anthology *The White
Horseman* (1941)—and the New Romanticism (Alex Comfort's and
Robert Graecan's anthology *Lyra* of 1942 was prefaced by Read),
has survived no better than more mainstream wartime writing.[36]

---

[31] Information supplied by the curator of the Longman archive, Reading University
Library. Clemence Dane [Winifred Ashton, 1888–1965] had written a novel about a future
Fascist dictatorship in Britain, *The Arrogant History of White Ben* (1939).
[32] Herbert Read, 'Art in an Electric Atmosphere', *Horizon*, 3/17 (May 1941), 309.
[33] Spender, *Air Raids*, 7.
[34] MacNeice, *Selected Prose*, 139.
[35] Quoted in Rod Mengham, 'Reading "The Lull"', *Twentieth-Century Literature*,
29/4 (Winter 1983), 457.
[36] A. T. Tolley, *The Poetry of the Forties* (Manchester: Manchester University Press,
1985), 101–127.

Discourses of social reconstruction are, it would seem from the stories by which Britain's war is remembered, the legitimate form of the bellicist credo that war produces cultural and political health. Nevertheless, aesthetic conventions and effects also had a significant role in wartime culture's representation of the war to its participants. The constructions placed on violence contributed to the formation of behaviour and understanding: 'corpses were quite all right so long as one had an official relationship with them', or, one might add, one of artistic detachment.[37] The aesthetic framing of violence is an unofficial form of the heavily coded response, an aspect of what Jay Winter has called 'the propaganda of private enterprise', not state management of opinion but a culture's ubiquitous 'sanitization' of war, which makes war thinkable.[38] Contrary to Freud's claim in 'Why War?' that 'the aesthetic ignominies of warfare play almost as large a part in. . .repugnance as war's atrocities', war's delight of the senses veiled atrocity, or rendered it apprehensible.[39]

'The moment the look dominates, the body loses its materiality.'[40] The power of the spectacle of violence to drive out thoughts of soft flesh has its literary apotheosis in the compulsion which, in James Hanley's novel *No Directions*, drives the painter Clem Stevens from a basement shelter, oblivious to the 'great shuddering arse' of a man who is dying in the doorway, to view a 'city rocked with outrageous power'.[41] Jean-François Lyotard has written of the sublimity of 'all great historical upheavals', which are 'the formless and figureless in historical human nature'.[42] But the characterization of the disaster as that which exceeds figuration omits persons, and is also figureless in the sense of the spectator's withdrawal or detachment. The representational fiat by which wartime spectacle is dis-figured, evacuated of human content, is fittingly represented in Clem's entrancement by

[37] Strachey, *Post D*, 92.

[38] Jay M. Winter, 'Imaginings of War: Some Cultural Supports of the Institution of War', in Robert A. Hinde (ed.), *The Institution of War* (Macmillan, 1991), 155.

[39] Sigmund Freud, 'Why War?', in Leon Bramson and George W. Goethals (eds.), *War: Studies from Psychology, Sociology and Anthropology* (New York: Basic Books, 1968), 79. Contrast William James, quoted in John Fraser, *Violence and the Arts* (Cambridge: Cambridge University Press, 1974), 105: the horrors of war 'make the fascination'.

[40] Luce Irigaray, quoted in Griselda Pollock, *Vision and Difference: Femininity, Feminism and Histories of Art* (Routledge, 1988), 50.

[41] James Hanley, *No Directions* (Faber, 1943), 139.

[42] Jean-François Lyotard, 'The Sign of History', in Derek Attridge, Geoff Bennington, and Robert Young (eds.), *Post-Structuralism and the Question of History* (Cambridge: Cambridge University Press, 1987), 174.

destructive force which animates the merely mineral: 'Life had come to iron, steel, to stone.'[43]

Stuart Sillars's argument for an ethically more positive view of wartime art implies that war determined its own representation, namely a rediscovery of the sublime in response to the 'surreal elements' of the bombing.[44] Art of the 1940s was not a programmatic return to Burke but an instinctive coming to terms with 'terrifying yet aesthetically uplifting' violence: 'The Sublime was part of reality for city-dwellers.'[45] Violence is ordered through the correlation of mind and broken matter: 'the blitz offered an external correlative to the familiar state of inner turmoil: external and internal worlds came together to produce a curious and unwonted harmony.'[46] However, the source of this harmony, as of the sense of community which figures so frequently in evocations of the Blitz, remains unclear: is it in the experience of violence itself or in its conceptualization?

The psychologically-uplifting and politically-reconstructive mode of the sublime which Sillars derives from the correlation of a new environment and an emergent community can be reassessed in relation to conceptions of aesthetic apprehension which, because they are 'referred wholly to the Subject', and contribute nothing to knowledge, dovetail less easily with utopian collectivity.[47] Kant's description of the apprehension of the beautiful as a 'subjective harmonizing of the imagination and the understanding', without external determination, locates both the site and source of harmonization where they cannot be adduced as social resistance.[48] A 'non-referential pseudo-cognition which . . . is agreeably free of a certain material constraint' is less evidently the origin of duty than of pleasure.[49] Discriminating between the sublime and the beautiful in wartime Britain is neither an attempt to secure metaphysical categories, nor to read off the mental states of participants from their representations. What is significant is the kind and degree of reflexiveness with which pleasurable and admonitory perceptions were used to describe and interpret war.

In the *Critique of Judgement* Kant cited war as an activity which indeed properly elicited feelings of the sublime: judgement gives its

---

[43] James Hanley, *No Directions*, 140.
[44] Stuart Sillars, *British Romantic Art and the Second World War* (Macmillan, 1991), 83.   [45] Ibid. 83, 97.   [46] Ibid. 96.
[47] Immanuel Kant, 'Critique of Aesthetic Judgement', *Critique of Judgement* (1928 and 1952. Oxford: Clarendon Press, 1991), part i, 41–2.   [48] Ibid. part i, 86.
[49] Terry Eagleton, *The Ideology of the Aesthetic* (Oxford: Blackwell, 1990), 85.

verdict to the general, not the statesman: 'Even where civilization has reached a high pitch there remains this special reverence for the soldier.'[50] The sublime transcends the material facts of war, but this depends on the way war is conceptualized. War is sublime only where it is 'conducted with order and a sacred respect for the rights of civilians'. However, not only is this qualification theoretical, but it is contradicted by the incompatibility of sublimity and peace, in which a debasing self-interest prevails.[51] Furthermore, even where war is identified with barbarism, it can be redeemed as a precondition of justice, 'a deep-seated, maybe far-seeing, attempt on the part of supreme wisdom, if not to found, yet to prepare the way for a rule of law governing the freedom of states, and bring about their unity in a system established on a moral basis.'[52] In the moral co-ordination of the nation in wartime, the idea of the sublimity of war functions as a detour from the facts of violence. Broadcasting on 19 May 1940, as German forces overran France, Churchill spoke of 'one of the most awe-striking periods' of French and British history, 'beyond doubt the most sublime', a perspective to be understood in relation to the premier's favoured trope of the future historian's detachment.[53]

Perpetual Peace, Kant's case for abolishing war, published five years after the *Critique* in 1795, revalued sublimity in relation to violence. In autocratic societies, the head of state 'can . . . decide on war, without any significant reason . . . and unconcernedly leave it to the diplomatic corps (who are always ready for such purposes) to justify the war for the sake of propriety'. Under a republican constitution, however, citizens would not consent to hostilities because 'this would mean calling down on themselves all the miseries of war'.[54] Reason, 'as the highest legislative moral power, absolutely condemns war as a test of rights and sets up peace as an immediate duty'.[55] This duty raises self-interest over the blandishments of war's publicity-corps.

In writing about air-raids, the demarcation between positive and negative pleasures of aesthetic perception is often insecure, and so

[50] Kant, *Critique of Judgement*, part i, 112.

[51] Ibid. part i, 112–13; 'Longinus', 'On Sublimity' in D. A. Russell and M. Winterbottom (ed.), *Ancient Literary Criticism* (Oxford: Clarendon Press, 1972), 502, explains the decline of sublimity in literature in terms of 'the unlimited war which lays hold of our desires' in time of peace.

[52] Kant, 'Critique of Teleological Judgement', *Critique of Judgement*, part ii, 96.

[53] Churchill, *War Speeches*, i. 184.

[54] Immanuel Kant, *Political Writings*, ed. Hans Reiss, second edition (1970. Cambridge: Cambridge University Press, 1991), 100.   [55] Ibid. 104.

too is the link between the spectacle of violence and sublimity's admonitions to 'complacent subject-centredness'.[56] Thomas De Quincey, advocating the amoral apprehension of violence, acknowledged an interval of compassion prior to the crowd's seduction by the aesthetic impact of the Drury Lane fire of 1809: 'after we have paid our tribute of regret to the affair considered as a calamity, inevitably, and without restraint, we go on to consider it as a stage spectacle.'[57] Louis MacNeice found himself 'half appalled' and 'half enlivened' by a 'fantasy of destruction'. In the face of 'a spectacle . . . on a scale which I had never come across', the deaths of Londoners 'were another matter', but a matter about which it was considerably more difficult to be articulate.[58] In Waugh's *Put Out More Flags* (1942), Basil Seal baits Poppet Green, a talentless bohemian paralysed by the sound of the sirens, with the Blitz's gift of a broken-up world: '"You know I should have thought an air raid was just the thing for a surréaliste; it ought to give you plenty of compositions— limbs and things lying about in odd places you know."'[59] Keith Douglas would produce *tableaux vivants* of human meat on North African battlefields, but such images are very unusual in representations of the Home Front. Working for Kenneth Clark's War Artists Advisory Committee in the East End of London, Graham Sutherland mistook the spillage from butchers' shops for bits of an undetected corpse. He could imagine wrecked bodies, but not depict them: bedding blown into the street 'looked more like a body than a mattress', a transformation which reverses the modelling of the figures in Henry Moore's sketches of London Tube-dwellers, whose apparently kapok-stuffed limbs and torsos suggest refugees' bundles.[60]

For many writers the spectacle of the Blitz was underwritten by the fantasy of a city emptied of human life, like eighteenth-century landscapes denuded of the agricultural poor. Ruins were a restoration of a pre-modern world, enunciating residual, not progressive, ideologies. Back in April 1939, Greene, trying to sell a book of reportage on

[56] Eagleton, *Ideology of the Aesthetic*, 89.

[57] Thomas De Quincey, 1854 'Postscript' to 'On Murder Considered as one of the Fine Arts', *The Collected Writings of Thomas De Quincey*, ed. D. Masson (A. C. Black, 1897), xiii. 72.

[58] MacNeice, 'The Morning After the Blitz' (May 1941), *Selected Prose*, 118.

[59] Evelyn Waugh, *Put Out More Flags* (Chapman and Hall, 1942), 39.

[60] Graham Sutherland, 'Images Wrought from Destruction' (1971), in *Sutherland: The War Drawings* (Imperial War Museum, 1982), 2; Henry Moore, *Shelter Sketch-Book* (Editions Poetry London, 1945).

a future bombed London, wrote to Ben Huebsch: 'It will be a very queer city indeed, down to Victorian size in population. An empty Piccadilly, what a dream!'[61] In an unfinished wartime novel Barbara Pym noted an archaeological felicity granted to urban space by air raids: 'Maida Vale is wide and *noble*, I always think, in spite of the decaying grandeur of some of the houses. Now, with ruins from the bombing here and there, the nobility seemed accentuated, as if the ruins were those of ancient Greece or Rome.'[62]

The classical world reappeared in the midst of modernity at the moment modern technology threatened to end civilization. Vera Brittain referred to damaged London in 1940 as 'The Ruins of Troy'.[63] H. D. imaginatively connected the tombs of Karnak with contemporary wreckage:

> there, as here, ruin opens
> the tomb, the temple; enter,
> there as here, there are no doors . . .[64]

John Lehmann's version of this archaeological fancy concerned an abandoned London which would be 'a more extraordinary sight than eighteenth-century Rome as one sees it in the old prints of Piranesi'.[65] These visions recall Robert Rosenblum's remarks on neo-classical historicism: 'On the one hand, the greatly publicized ruins of Greece and Rome could stimulate a retrospective nostalgia for a lost, irretrievable past; and, on the other, a prospective Utopianism that would heroically attempt to reconstruct these remote glories in the service of modern history.'[66] In the wartime culture of the ruin, reconstructionist Utopianism and nostalgia, though they might be ideologically opposed, stemmed from the same redescriptive motives.

Perhaps the best known of the spatio-temporal transformations of bombed London is Bowen's story 'Mysterious Kôr' (*Penguin New Writing*, 1944). Pepita evacuates London imaginatively: '"I don't know how other girls manage: I always think about Kôr"', the

---

[61] Quoted in Norman Sherry, *The Life of Graham Greene: 1939–1955* (Jonathan Cape, 1994), 9.
[62] Barbara Pym, 'So Very Secret', *Civil to Strangers and Other Writings* (Macmillan, 1987), 297.
[63] Vera Brittain, *England's Hour* (Macmillan, 1940), chapter title.
[64] H. D., *The Walls Do Not Fall* (Oxford University Press, 1944), 7.
[65] John Lehmann, *I Am My Brother* (Longmans, Green and Co., 1960), 131.
[66] Robert Rosenblum, *Transformations in Late Eighteenth Century Art* (1967. Princeton: Princeton University Press, 1969), 112.

'completely forsaken city' that she recreated from Rider Haggard's *She* (1887).[67] She suppresses the unbearable facts of her vulnerability by excluding the contingent and human: '"How can anyone think about people if they've got any heart?"' She and her soldier lover are homeless in the blackout, not bombed out but crowded out of 'buildings strained with battened-down human life'.[68] The moonlight which defeats the blackout seems to collaborate in her fantasy by dissolving stragglers from the Underground into invisibility, like Eliot's punningly 'disfigured street' in *Little Gidding*.[69] Ruins perceived as spectacle are less obviously a spur to collective identifications than a subject-centring compensation.

Pepita's imaginative therapy suggests how visions of an antique London were also the mind's flight from violence against persons: identity is shored up by an aesthetic apprehension which unearths delight or continuity while excluding war's human calamities. Bowen felt that the imagination must dominate its objects or be extinguished, but she also recognized detachment as self-deformation. In 'Sunday Afternoon', published in Robert Herring's *Life and Letters Today* (July 1941), history's implacable invasions are not only remote (from the safety of Ireland) but inconceivable:

'The bombing?' said Henry. 'Yes. But as it does not connect with the rest of life, it is difficult, you know, to know what one feels. One's feelings seem to have no language for anything so preposterous.'[70]

The aesthetic problem and the problem of the personal life are elided: '"this outrage is *not* important. There is no place for it in human experience; it apparently cannot make a place of its own. It will have no literature"'.[71] Henry's denial represents not only a species of political and ethical neutrality (part of Bowen's war work was reporting to London on such Irish 'conversations') but also the imagination's flight from crisis. Art, Bowen wrote, using an architectonic image swollen with contemporary connotations, 'puts up a buttress' against 'shapelessness, lack of meaning, and being without

---

[67] Bowen, *The Demon Lover and Other Stories* (Jonathan Cape, 1945), 175.

[68] Ibid. 176, 173.

[69] T. S. Eliot, *Four Quartets* (Faber, 1944), 40. Eliot had written 'dismantled', before alighting on the phrase that condenses ruin and the invisibility of the human, see Helen Gardner, *The Composition of 'Four Quartets'* (Faber, 1978), 195–6. Maud Ellmann, *The Poetics of Impersonality: T. S. Eliot and Ezra Pound* (Brighton: Harvester, 1987), 126, notes the pun in 'dismantled'.

[70] Bowen, *The Demon Lover* (1945), 19.   [71] Ibid.

direction'.[72] But aesthetic consolations were not merely a private matter; as a vehicle of the rhetoric of omission they ramified in the public conduct of the war.

In 'Summer Night', another of Bowen's Irish stories, '"war's an awful illumination"', revealing that '"we don't live. . . . can no longer express ourselves"', not something external to culture but that culture's most exacting test.[73] But the visual spectacle of a blacked-out world lit up by violence, so often the point of departure for imaginative and stylistic reverie, negates both diagnoses. Louis MacNeice described a night sky turned into an art-work, a 'backcloth for opera or ballet, a sumptuous Oriental orange-print mottled with bursts of black'.[74] Rose Macaulay could 'say nothing for this horrid scene, except that, aesthetically, it has a kind of lurid and infernal beauty'.[75] Conventions of omission outlasted the war. Lawrence Durrell, echoing Saint Loups's and M. de Charlus's descriptions of Parisian Zeppelin raids in Proust's *Le temps retrouvé* (1927), would later write of Alexandria beautified by the 'mere saturnalia of a war', a perspective which contrasts strongly with the 'Alexandrian way of death . . . a decomposition in greys and greens' which he described in 1944.[76] The spectacle is all: 'There was no room for human beings or thought of them under this vast umbrella of coloured death.'[77]

The urban landscape was turned into a literal no-man's land, the imagination exceeding the exigencies of black-out, evacuation, and shelters by depopulating the city.[78] Vera Brittain made the comparison to contend that the present conflict was 'less a struggle between men, than a conflict between methods of technical production'.[79] Visions of a dehumanized city are in part determined by a tradition of anti-urban representations which gained an extra dimension with the threat of strategic bombing. The English Association's *England: An Anthology* posited an 'unceasing reaction against urban life' as a marker of Englishness.[80] The urban nemesis, bombed by your own

---

[72] Elizabeth Bowen, Graham Greene, and V. S. Pritchett, *Why Do I Write?* (Percival Marshall, 1948), 24.

[73] Elizabeth Bowen, *Look at All Those Roses: Short Stories* (Gollancz, 1941), 228.

[74] MacNeice, 'The Morning After the Blitz', *Selected Prose*, 118.

[75] Rose Macaulay, *Consolations of the War*, quoted in Arthur Stanley (ed.), *Britain at War: An Anthology* (Eyre and Spottiswoode, 1943), 281.

[76] Lawrence Durrell, *The Alexandria Quartet* (Faber, 1962), 668; letter to Arthur Miller, 8 Feb. 1944, *The Durrell–Miller Letters*, ed. Ian S. MacNiven (Faber, 1988), 160.

[77] Durrell, *Quartet*, 669.   [78] Spender, *Air Raids*, 6.

[79] Brittain, *England's Hour*, p. xi.

[80] The English Association, *England: An Anthology* (Macmillan, 1944), p. vi.

side, in *Coming up for Air* had earlier been the fantasy of Orwell's
Gordon Comstock in *Keep the Aspidistra Flying*.[81] John Betjeman
hailed the bomber as a salvation from urbanization: 'Come, friendly
bombs, and fall on Slough!'[82] During the war, the fragmentation of
urban space was redeemed nostalgically in the description of metropolitan districts as villages and hamlets.[83]

J. M. Richards's *The Bombed Buildings of Britain* (1942) is the
most painstaking examination of urban destruction from the period.
Others would go further than this 'Record of Architectural Casualties' to transfer life to inanimate forms: Vera Brittain wrote in 1940 of
'architectural wounds', and Barbara Nixon described bombed
homes as 'lacerated creatures patched up with sticking plaster', but
no other text than Richards's lingers so longingly on the damage.[84]
His inventory of 'casualties' consists of hundreds of captioned
photographs preserving the sudden and temporary phenomenon of
urban ruin.[85] Reconstruction and renovation are regretted; bombed
buildings lose 'their vivid spectacular character' in the process of
tidying-up.[86] Richards echoes De Quincey's amoralism when he argues that the preservation of ruins is not a moral enterprise (as, for
instance, an admonitory memorial to war's destructiveness, such as
the shells of cathedrals in Berlin and Coventry) but desirable 'for the
sake of the intensely evocative atmosphere'.[87]

While popular architectural discourse was preoccupied with
welfare-motivated reconstruction, *Bombed Buildings* underlined
the Blitz's aesthetic remodelling of Britain's cities.[88] The destruction of the North Bastion of the Tower of London (post-1842) was

[81] George Orwell, *Keep the Aspidistra Flying* (Gollancz, 1936), 24–5, 30, 111, 297.

[82] John Betjeman, 'Slough', *Continual Dew: A Little Book of Bourgeois Verse* (John Murray, 1937), 4.

[83] Mollie Panter-Downes, *London War Notes 1939–1945*, ed. William Shawn (Long-mans, 1972), 100, 108. See also Robert Henrey, *A Village in Piccadilly* (Dent, 1942). See MacNeice *Selected Prose*, 101, on the Tube station supplanting the village hall, but note that Hollywood moved Mrs Miniver from Chelsea to a rural village.

[84] Brittain, *England's Hour*, 137; Barbara Nixon, *Raiders Overhead* (Lindsay Drum-mond, 1943), 37.

[85] The urban heritage was a subject popular with wartime publishers, see e.g. John Betjeman's *Vintage London* (1942) and *English Cities and Small Towns* (1943).

[86] J. M. Richards (ed.), *The Bombed Buildings of Britain: A Record of Architectural Casualties: 1940–1941* (The Architectural Press, 1942), 2. Compare T. J. Clark, *The Painting of Modern Life: Paris in the Art of Manet and his Followers* (Thames and Hudson, 1985), 37, on the 'picturesque of demolition' which emerged during Baron Haussmann's mid-nineteenth-century remodelling of Paris, which 'could make the city look sublime for a moment'. [87] Richards, *Bombed Buildings*, 2.

[88] See e.g. Mass Observation, *An Enquiry into People's Homes* (John Murray, 1943).

welcomed as the excision of a structure of 'no architectural consequence'. Air raids had another satisfying by-product in the reve-
lation of normally hidden details of a building's structure and
fabrication: ruin is not loss but rediscovery. Above all, the effects of
violence were worth preserving for their own new and surprising
aesthetic. The Ruskinian tones belie the fact that Richards does not
relate the destruction to the builders, occupants, or users of these
buildings:

> The architecture of destruction not only possesses an aesthetic peculiar to
> itself, it contrives its effects out of its own range of raw materials. Among the
> most familiar are the scarified surface of blasted walls, the chalky substance
> of calcined masonry, the surprising sagging contours of once rigid girders
> and the clear siena colouring of burnt-out brick buildings, their rugged
> cross-walls receding plane by plane, on sunny mornings in the City. More-
> over, the aesthetic of destruction bears no relationship to any architectural
> merit the building may have possessed in life. In death merit is of a different
> order, and some of the most dramatic and evocative ruins have flowered sud-
> denly out of a structure no one would have looked at twice.[89]

These felicitous perceptions of violence (along with the conceit of
a quasi-democratic architectural heroism, echoing People's War
rhetoric) reinforce unmindfulness of human injury and home-
lessness. Wanda Ostrowska's paintings were promoted in terms of
a comparable anthropomorphization of stone: the survivor of
Warsaw in 1939 'felt with these stones, as though indeed they had
breathed and lived'.[90] The BBC commissioned a series of features
under the title 'The Stones Cry Out'.[91] The substitution is repeated,
with another twist to the dematerialization of the body, in Peter
Quennell's commentary to photographs by Cecil Beaton: 'the qualities of the *ego* are of far tougher substance than the brickwork of a
city church.'[92]

Graham Sutherland's memories of 1940 indicate a facility for tran-
scribing violence within the parameters of art. Falling glass recalls
Debussy, the movements of a steel lift shaft in the wreckage of a
building 'suggested a wounded tiger in a painting by Delacroix': 'The
City was more exciting than anywhere else mainly because the

[89] Richards, *Bombed Buildings*, 56, 3.
[90] Viola G. Garvin, *London's Glory: Twenty Paintings of the City's Ruins by Wanda Ostrowska* (George Allen and Unwin, 1945), 6, 16.
[91] Barbara Coulton, *Louis MacNeice in the BBC* (Faber, 1980), 52, 204.
[92] Cecil Beaton, *Time Exposure* (Batsford, 1941), 126.

buildings were bigger, and the variety of ways in which they fell more interesting.' The East End also offered visual delights: 'great—surprisingly wide—perspectives of destruction seeming to recede into infinity and. . . windowless blocks . . . like sightless eyes'. There, but as if in an afterthought, he notes 'one did think of the hurt to people'.[93] MacNeice also perceived London divided aesthetically as well as politically, the West End wreckage 'exhilarating', the East End 'heart breaking'.[94]

Stephen Spender, writing in 1943, registered the varieties of these translations between mineral and animal, Sutherland animating the inert allegorically, Moore heroically fossilizing the living:

There is an unearthly glory about Graham Sutherland's study of Devastation in an East End Street; and his pictures of twisted girders have something in them of twisted humanity. . . . Henry Moore's figures of people sleeping in the Underground shelters have acquired something of the quality of stone buildings. We feel that these people are the guardians and even the foundations of the streets above them.[95]

But these substitutions of London's fabric for its people threaten, by their congruence to strategic abstractions, to contradict Moore's statement that the Tube-dwellers 'humanized everything I had been doing'.[96] An anonymous contemporary critic qualified the observation that Sutherland's figures 'withdraw from the human plane almost to. . .the frontiers of the surreal', by insisting that the artist 'never abandons the human scene for the realms of pure abstraction'.[97] But the human form enters Sutherland's wartime work as late as the tin miners sequence of 1942: his records of bomb damage in Wales, then London, foreground the violent rending of architectural structure, and paralleling Richards, celebrate newly animate formations of inert material. The visceral rather than mechanical forms in 'Machinery fallen through floor of city factory' (1941) may suggest altered flesh, but the human is an absence.[98]

---

[93] Sutherland, 'Images Wrought from Destruction', 1–2.
[94] MacNeice, 'London Letter (5): Reflections from the Dome of St Paul's' (July 1941), *Selected Prose*, 131–32.
[95] Spender, *Air Raids*, 7.
[96] Quoted in Robert Hewison, *Under Siege: Literary Life in London 1939–1945* (Weidenfeld and Nicolson, 1977), 152.
[97] 'Art Critic', 'War Artists and the War', *PNW* 16 (March 1943), 116.
[98] Roberto Tassi, *Sutherland: The Wartime Drawings* (Sotheby Parke Bernet, 1980), cat. no. 27, p. 46.

RENAISSANCE LONDON

Representations of the Blitz promoted metropolitan hegemony: 'London became a world capital. . .an emblem of freedom and culture.'[99] Reporting of the Blitz was an important dimension of diplomatic and propaganda efforts to counteract American isolationism, but at home the emphasis created resentment. Provincial towns, according to Ritchie Calder, 'appeared to be jealous of London's bombs!' (he dedicated his London book to 'The People of the Provinces').[100] William Sansom noted 'the proud and tetchy fight for the possession of scars'.[101] London dominated perceptions of contemporary reality—'The basic story was scripted, and could now be transferred *en bloc* to any other city'—and the capital usurped the countryside's role as 'symbol of things English'.[102] The effects are visible in the genre of travel writing, revising both its scope and rationale. H. V. Morton's account of 1939 journeys was already outmoded when it was issued in 1942, its conclusion poising a pre-Blitz, post-Dunkirk England between a future generation's perception of 'the most dramatic and adventurous incident in the whole of England's history', and a future social historian's conclusion that 'we to-day are in a more secluded backwater than our ancestors in the Napoleonic period'.[103]

Vera Brittain's ambition to produce an updated 'wartime variety' of Priestley's *English Journey* (1934) was thwarted by travel restrictions, but she made a virtue of this, convinced that London was the site of 'dramatic events' on which 'the world's eyes concentrated'. Retracing Priestley's itinerary would have generated impressions which 'differ little from similar impressions in peace-time'.[104] The title of *England's Hour*, temporal not geographical, unified a population through a moment of adversity centred on the capital. London was the new front where 'mothers in their homes, run risks comparable to those of the fighting soldier in the first Great War'. If the Zeppelin raids had ' "brought it home to us" ', this second Great War

---

[99] Alan Ross, *The Forties: A Period Piece* (Weidenfeld and Nicolson, 1950), n.p.
[100] Ritchie Calder, *The Lesson of London*, 108.
[101] William Sansom, *Westminster in War* (Faber, 1947), 24; see also Harrisson, *Living Through the Blitz*, 150–51, for Mass-Observation's reporting on popular dissatisfaction with the low media profile of provincial air raids.
[102] Angus Calder, *The Myth of the Blitz*, 128; Sansom, *Westminster*, 9.
[103] H. V. Morton, *I Saw Two Englands* (Methuen, 1942), 287, 289.
[104] Brittain, *England's Hour*, p. ix; *Testament of Experience*, 262–3.

was to take place in the home, and in particular the homes of Londoners.[105] Brittain's *Testament of Youth* (1933) described the exciting, then alarming impact of Zeppelin raids on the imagination, and subsequently, the bloody aftermath of an attack on London.[106] But that book's argument, aligned with the redefinition of nationhood in Great War soldiers' writing, was to deny that the war had been brought home to the civilian population.[107] This view is revised in her travels through London in the autumn of 1940 (with the book's dedicatee, Storm Jameson); noting the 'peculiar resemblance between damaged houses robbed of their roofs and ravaged trees deprived of their branches', walking the streets is figured as a return to post-Armistice Flanders.[108]

'Whatever touches London touches the world', wrote A. C. Ward, beginning another essentially metropolitan tour of wartime Britain. Mapping literary history onto 'an unidentifiable landscape' was one way of re-enforcing cultural bearings, and also of aestheticizing the 'caprices of high explosive'.[109] A toppled 'but otherwise uninjured' statue of Milton, 'the first wartime casualty', speaks to the nation from one of Ward's plates: 'O spirit . . . what in me is dark / Illumine, what is low raise and support.'[110] MacNeice scripted 'Dr Johnson Takes It' for the BBC on the survival of the St Clement Danes statue of Samuel Johnson. It is against this romancing of destruction as a symbol of a transhistorical Englishness that Ruthven Todd addressed his poem 'These are Facts' (1941). The heritage industry that emerged to annotate the effects of bombing on England's built-culture was, to Todd, part of the most insidious propaganda activity, the rhetoric that makes corpses disappear and builds ideologically-freighted edifices in their place: 'People are more than places, more than pride; / A million photographs record the works of Wren.'[111]

The bombing changed the urban landscape, but not only physically; representations of the Blitz as event or, equally, as environment, resulted in revisions of both the concept and of the iconography of

[105] Brittain, *England's Hour*, pp. xi, 117.
[106] Vera Brittain, *Testament of Youth: An Autobiographical Study of the Years 1900–1925* (Gollancz, 1933), 157, 261, 365–6.
[107] Ibid. 429–30 and *Testament of Experience*, 278.
[108] Brittain, *England's Hour*, 275.
[109] A. C. Ward, *A Literary Journey Through Wartime Britain* (New York: Oxford University Press, 1943), 4, 8–9. Arthur S. G. Butler's *Recording Ruin* (Constable, 1942) turned official damage inspection into a kind of travel writing.
[110] Ward, 10 and plate facing p. 12.
[111] Ruthven Todd, *Until Now: Poems* (Fortune Press, 1943), 52.

the city. Office workers photographed in *Picture Post* crunched shattered glass underfoot, as if testing the reality of the destruction, but, as the caption tells us, they had been prepared for this transformation of the everyday: 'The Morning After: City Workers come Back into a Changed World. Coming up in the Tube they read of the raid. Coming out of the Tube, they see its effects.'[112] Movement between suburb and centre is a passage between worlds (a familiar motif for initiation into war which we will re-encounter in writings about the war in the desert). The bombing exacerbates a contrast— ideologically and aesthetically encoded in early twentieth-century garden suburbs and in the failure of inter-war town planning— between the unregenerate man-made centre, and the suburbs with their gardens and pastiche vernacular, symbols of rural or English values.[113] But the image of Tube travellers also evokes the phenomenon of Tube dwellers, the question of whose willingness to resurface raised a wholly different perspective on the physical and moral structure of London under attack, the fear of social breakdown.

Before the war, the lack of organized provision for protecting urban populations was the theme of a Communist Party campaign (J. B. S. Haldane contributed *A.R.P.*, addressed to 'the sort of man and woman who is going to be killed if Britain is raided again from the air').[114] The Government only reconsidered its intransigence over deep shelters, and the use of existing structures like the Underground, because of the threat of a propaganda defeat (communists were vigorously anti-war at this stage).[115] Ironically these same contested shelters, denied to the public in the first weeks of the raids, would become an emblem in the myth of the city under siege, part of an inherently conservative revision of the city as a coherent system of social relations.[116] The Communist Party of Great Britain (CPGB) was the first to redefine the bomber threat in the class terms which would underpin the legend of levelling, but one of the earliest trade histories of the Blitz presented its campaign as 'a deliberate attempt

---

[112] *Picture Post*, 11/5 (3 May 1941), 10.

[113] See Kenneth Frampton, *Modern Architecture: A Critical History*, rev. edn. (Thames and Hudson, 1985), 28, and Peter Hall, *Cities of Tomorrow* (Oxford: Blackwell, 1990), 87–112, for the ideology of garden suburbs.

[114] J. B. S. Haldane, *A.R.P.* (Gollancz, 1938), 7.

[115] Henry Green, 'Firefighting', *Texas Quarterly*, 3/4 (Winter 1960), 106.

[116] Ritchie Calder, *The Lesson of London*, 94–7, described the reversal of Tory policy as the triumph of Labour politicians Morrison and Wilkinson, and of the People's War debate.

to undermine the morale of the people'.[117] The Underground shelters are retrospectively deemed 'a science fiction novel in action' in Bryher's memoir *The Days of Mars*, but she does not make it clear whether this is because, architecturally, Underground stations resemble futuristic space stations or, in the spirit of the genre, this other world beneath the streets was a socio-political experiment.[118] But Henry Moore, struck by the fit between this new environment and his own aesthetic—'I had never seen so many reclining figures and even the train tunnels seemed to be like the holes in my sculpture'—did not stay underground to complete his sketches: 'It would have been like drawing in the hold of a slave ship'.[119]

The evacuation of inner-city populations into economically and culturally more prosperous regions, reversing the journeys of Engels, Mayhew, Booth, and Orwell, demonstrated to middle-class England 'how deplorable is the standard of life and civilization among the urban proletariat'.[120] No contemporary treatment is as ambitious as William Golding's 1954 evacuation parable, *Lord of the Flies*. In wartime evacuee-fiction, class comedy reasserts traditional class politics—a Londoner searching for a Fish and Chip shop thinking rural England is Battersea Park.[121] The mysterious urban origin of the irreclaimable Connollys is one of many wartime opportunities exploited by Basil Seal in *Put Out More Flags* (1942).[122] Joyce Cary's *Charley is my Darling* (1941) is more subtle: the shaving of the evacuee-hero's head for lice imprints the projections of class prejudice, changing him 'from a respectable-looking young citizen in a brown suit, to something between the convict of history and the kind of street Arab represented in old comic papers'.[123]

The Luftwaffe was credited not only with healing the social divisions that defence measures revealed, but with clearing slums and spurring the modernization of Britain's housing stock. 'The writs are being served by the bombers' wrote Ritchie Calder, who observed

[117] Constantine Fitz Gibbon, *The Blitz* (Allan Wingate, 1957), 15–16.

[118] Bryher [Winifred Ellerman], *The Days of Mars: A Memoir 1940–1946* (Calder and Boyars, 1972), 18. See Philip John Davies (ed.), *Science Fiction, Social Conflict and War* (Manchester: Manchester University Press, 1990), 1–7.

[119] Quoted in Alan Ross, *Colours of War: War Art 1939–45* (Jonathan Cape, 1983), 37.

[120] Harold Nicolson, *Diaries and Letters*, ed. Nigel Nicolson, 3 vols. (Collins, 1968), ii, 33. See Ruth Inglis, *The Children's War: Evacuation 1939–1945* (Collins, 1989), 8, 34, 85–8.

[121] Kitty Barne, *Visitors from London* (Dent, 1940), 65–6; see also Richmal Crompton, *William and the Evacuees* (George Newnes, 1940), 9–43.

[122] Waugh, *Put Out More Flags*, 94–6, 105.

[123] Joyce Cary, *Charley is my Darling* (Michael Joseph, 1940), 13.

that the ruins were 'symbolic of the catastrophic End of an Age' of inequality.[124] A 1942 pamphlet superimposed the legend 'WHAT IS THE FUTURE TO BE?' on photographs of bomb damage, implying that the victory of planning was a primary war objective.[125] Bombers were also envisaged as a moral scourge: Graham Greene extrapolated the anti-urban and anti-suburban rhetoric of *Brighton Rock* (1938) to condemn the squalor of a provincial England that 'demanded violence'.[126] Connolly provided the metropolitan complement in a cleansing of the accumulated 'fear and hypocrisy' of Kensington, Bayswater and Chelsea: 'had it not been for the bombers, the houses would have ignited one day of their own accord by spontaneous combustion.'[127] In fact, rather than fantasy, the patchwork destruction of inner cities, 'moth-eaten but, with famous exceptions like Plymouth and Coventry, inadequately cleared by the blitz', determined the indirection of post-war planning, despite post-war optimism that 'these devastated areas may be replanned on more convenient lines'.[128] The folk-judgement on centralized planning, and its 'totalitarian' modernism (debased Le Corbusian-slab tower-blocks), has no truck with wartime substitutions: the destruction of Britain's cities initiated by Goering was completed by the town planners.[129]

Voluntarism and the hierarchical network of civil defence contributed to the idea of a collective reorganization of city space.[130] MacNeice argued that this collectivity was a spontaneous rationalization of urban life, not a coercive regimentation, or even an expedient reaction: 'London since the Blitz has become more comprehensible. . . . a visible and tangible symbol of freedom; it has not been centralised, organised, rationalised, dehumanised into a streamlined ad. for the cult of the State.'[131] Nigel Balchin's novel

---

[124] Ritchie Calder, *Start Planning Britain Now*, 7; *The Lesson of London*, 125.

[125] Ralph Tubbs, *Living in Cities* (Harmondsworth: Penguin, 1942), 5.

[126] Greene, *Collected Essays*, 448.

[127] Cyril Connolly, 'Writers and Society, 1940-3', *The Condemned Playground: Essays 1927-1944* (Routledge, 1945), 272

[128] Lionel Esher, *A Broken Wave: The Rebuilding of England 1940-1980* (Allen Lane, 1981), 43; C. H. Holden and W. G. Holford, *The City of London: A Record of Destruction and Survival* (The Architectural Press, 1951), see 184-230.

[129] See Miles Glendinning and Stefan Muthesius, *Tower Block: Modern Public Housing in England, Scotland, Wales and Northern Ireland* (New Haven: Yale University Press, 1994) and Junichi Hasegawa, *Replanning the Blitzed City Centre* (Buckingham: Open University Press, 1992).

[130] See Spender, *Citizens in War—and After* (George Harrap, 1945), 16-17 and HMSO, *Front Line 1940-41* (HMSO, 1942), 136-59.

[131] Louis MacNeice, 'The Way We Live Now—IV', *PNW* 5 (April, 1941), 13-14.

Darkness Falls from the Air (1942) contests this reading, embodying the themes of division and unity in its air-raid settings, a luxury shelter in the West End and a Rest Centre on Commercial Road. Going against the grain of the rhetoric of levelling, the novel represents ' "a rich man's war" ' which exacerbates economic differentials. The industrialists with whom the hero Bill Sarratt works strenuously resist state control (a shadow factory scheme to reduce the disruption of production by air-raids) which they view as a means of 'using the war to bring about Socialism'.[132] The rich get richer all the more quickly in a risk-free 'costs plus' economy, and can invest to avoid danger: Willie Hubbard's property dealing makes him the owner of the most luxurious shelter in London. Shelter is a commodity, one that Sarratt and his wife Marcia are able to rent, moving into a hotel during the worst of the raids for the security of its reinforced steel structure. Their expensive furlough from home is one of the ways in which Sarratt and Marcia cast themselves as tourists in the Blitz. Their involvement in the ideally corporate efforts of civil defence is opportunistic: Marcia's work in the East End is motivated as marital therapy.

The book's climax, in which Sarratt journeys from West to East in the wake of a heavy raid, explores the ambiguous ramifications of the cleaving of London in the Blitz.[133] The city is an impassable labyrinth, its districts isolated by detours, UXBs (unexploded bombs), craters and cordons, but it is at the same time welded into homogeneity by the apparent ubiquity of destruction. The extremes of urban wealth and poverty appear to be unified through their incorporation in a new urban experience: 'London dooth mourne, Lambith is quite forlorne' wrote Thomas Nashe in the comedy from which Balchin derives a title that conceals more ironies than its misquotation of darkness for brightness (following Stephen Dedalus's misremembering in Joyce's *A Portrait*).[134] Buckingham Palace was hit, and the King visited the East End: 'by dint of a few ill-chosen

---

[132] Nigel Balchin, *Darkness Falls from the Air* (Collins, 1942), 202, 58.

[133] The inflectional forms of two Old English verbs, signifying respectively to divide or part, and to adhere or remain faithful to, have converged: Freud's meditations on 'unheimlich' (familiar/unfamiliar), 'The Uncanny', trans. Alix Strachey, *Collected Papers*, iv (Hogarth Press, 1925), 368–407 and Derrida's on '*pharmakon*' (poison/remedy), *Dissemination*, trans. Barbara Johnson (Athlone Press, 1981), are formally and thematically of some relevance to the question of the unstable meanings attributed to air raids.

[134] Thomas Nashe, 'Summers Last Will and Testament', *The Works of Thomas Nashe*, ed. R. B. McKerrow, 5 vols. (Oxford: Blackwell, 1966), iii. 283 and 292; James Joyce, *A Portrait of the Artist as a Young Man*, ed. Richard Ellmann (Jonathan Cape, 1968), 237–8.

bombs, the Luftwaffe had managed to weld the people of London more strongly together than ever before. They became one body of people exposed in their front line.'[135] But when Sarratt finds the body of his wife buried beneath the bombed Rest Centre, this heroic petrifaction is undone: 'I thought it was a lump of concrete at first and then I saw that it was Marcia's head covered in white dust.'[136]

Balchin wasn't the first to notice the tension between flesh and stone in Nashe's poem. Empson observed:

In 'Dust hath closed Helen's eye' one must think of Helen in part as an undecaying corpse or a statue; it is *dust* from outside which settles on her eyelids, and shows that it is long since they have been opened; only in the background, as a truth which could not otherwise be faced, is it suggested that the *dust* is generated from her own corruption.[137]

The 'overpowering sense of London's organic power' described by Bowen (in an image of the 'new channels' of traffic through a remapped city), epitomizes the effects of discourse about the Blitz in relation to 'truth which could not otherwise be faced'.[138] London became a hero of the war, a hero of a narrative in which violence was turned back against it perpetrators in the form of stony resistance.

BUILDINGS AND PERSONS

> I see war (or should I say I feel war?) more as a territory than as a page of history.
>
>   Elizabeth Bowen[139]

In Hanley's *No Directions*, a drunken sailor mistakes a street full of broken glass for a sea of ice. H. D. imagined herself aboard a liner, in an effort to tame the movements of the building in which she lay.[140] From another London flat, Inez Holden described the 'atmosphere of

---

135 Sansom, *Westminster*, 40–1.
136 Balchin, *Darkness Falls from the Air*, 240. Compare the description of a prole's hand, severed in a rocket attack, as a 'plaster cast' in George Orwell, *Nineteen Eighty-Four*, ed. Peter Davison (Oxford: Clarendon Press, 1984), 229.
137 William Empson, *Seven Types of Ambiguity* (Chatto and Windus, 1930), 34–5.
138 Elizabeth Bowen, *The Heat of the Day* (Jonathan Cape, 1949), 86.
139 Bowen, *The Demon Lover* (1952), 217.
140 H. D., *The Gift* [written 1941–3] (Virago, 1984), 133.

shipwreck at sea by night' during a raid.[141] Contemporaries adduced
further relations between transformed spaces and the continuity of
personal identity, drawing on both the expressive and the protective
functions of the built environment: 'the room' is 'an enlargement of
the body', and a boundary around the self 'preventing undifferenti-
ated contact with the world'.[142] Domestic interiors are a figure for
personal autonomy:

control of a single body is normally not shared. I do not find that my decision to walk across the room comes into conflict with some alien decision
that my body will stay sitting down. If I did, this body might start to seem
less like home territory, and more like territory that I was disputing with
someone else.[143]

'The house thrusts aside all contingencies,' writes Bachelard, 'its
councils of continuity are unceasing. Without it, man would be a dispersed being.'[144] The Blitz shouted-down this council. Apocalyptic
or sublime metropolitan panoramas took up and often transvalued
the conventions of 'a deeply pessimistic projection of the city'; the
pathos of domestic destruction drew on another convention of
nineteenth-century fiction, the opposition between anonymity in
the urban labyrinth and self-definition among the possessions that
personalize the private interior.[145]

In the fiction of Elizabeth Bowen houses are places of affiliation, but
where belonging and privacy turn into surveillance and correction,
from Danielstown, ultimately razed by Irish Republicans in *The Last
September* to Holme Dean in *The Heat of the Day*, an architectonic
'intelligence service'.[146] In wartime, these animistic conceits ramified in ways the author was not always in a position to command:
suddenly houses lost the solidity that had made them both the bulwark of humanity, and inhuman. Bowen's remark of 1944—'walls
went down; and we felt, if not knew, each other'—is double-edged:
society is an invasion, an engulfing. That her fictions represented a

[141] Inez Holden, *It was Different at the Time* (John Lane, 1943), 71.
[142] Elaine Scarry, *The Body in Pain: The Making and Unmaking of the World* (New York: Oxford University Press, 1985), 38.
[143] Jonathan Glover, *I: The Philosophy and Psychology of Personal Identity* (1988. Harmondsworth: Penguin, 1989), 76.
[144] Gaston Bachelard, *The Poetics of Space* (Boston, Mass.: Beacon Press, 1969), 7.
[145] Raymond Williams, *The Country and the City* (Chatto and Windus, 1973), 275–6.
[146] Elizabeth Bowen, *The Last September* (Constable, 1929), 5, 238; *Heat*, 247–8.

comparable eruption into the private sphere was not necessarily a compensation:

Each time I sat down to write a story I opened a door; and the pressure against the other side of that door must have been very great, for things—ideas, images, emotions—came through with force and rapidity, sometimes violence.[147]

The windows of Bowen's house of fiction were blacked-out: the territory of war would not, she thought, permit the artistic imagination to impress it with form.

Even in the most conventional images of violently-opened houses, a transgressive vision invades private spaces: 'Blast is an odd thing: it is just as likely to have the air of an embarrassing dream as of man's serious vengeance on man, landing you naked in the street or exposing you in your bed or on your lavatory seat to the neighbours' gaze.'[148] In a direct hit, no house could guarantee a man against his body parts being dispersed about the street, but the survivors in Greene's war-fiction—Bendix, 'miraculously' preserved by a blown-in front door in *The End of the Affair*, and Roe in *The Ministry of Fear*, who is saved in the moment his would-be poisoner across the tea-table is disintegrated—are by no means statistically exceptional. There *were* more damaged houses to be seen than damaged bodies. However, when William Sansom recalls that 'the unscathed mirror or picture hanging exposed on the wall became platitudinous', we are reminded that gazing at 'freaks' acquired its own conventions and standards.[149] For Julian Maclaren-Ross, spotting Graham Greene staring at a bombed-out house, the first surmise is 'he might be writing something about London in the air raids'.[150] MacNeice's 'familiar spectacle of the broken doll's house' was already a literary convention: 'like looking into a doll's house', reflects Orwell's George Bowling on a bombed Lower Binfield street.[151] Apologias concerning the imagination's surrender before the enormity of violence disguise the ubiquity, in private and public discourses, of the figurative and conceptual containment of war's destructiveness.

For firemen, like Sansom and Henry Green, alertness to the dynamics of damaged structures was a matter of survival. But Sansom's

[147] Bowen, *The Demon Lover* (1952), 216, 218.
[148] Graham Greene, *The Ministry of Fear* (Heinemann, 1943), 21.
[149] Sansom, *Westminster*, 13.
[150] Julian Maclaren-Ross, *Memoirs of the Forties* (Alan Ross, 1965), 100.
[151] MacNeice, *Selected Prose*, 120; Orwell, *Coming up for Air*, 271.

wartime writing is pitched squarely within the schemes of perception that underpin the legendary Blitz: violence is apprehensible as an aesthetic challenge when it is targeted against the built environment, redescribed as heroic victimization when it is targeted at persons. Art, he argued, cannot contain or transcribe violence:

The pace has become too violent, machines move too fast for the nerves' perception, the din outsounds the ear, movements and winds and lights strike with such a giant impact that this can scarcely be perceived and even then never, neither in the symbols of language nor in the tones of paint, be recorded.[152]

But it was as a fireman that he began to write stories, and the best of them, in an idiosyncratic writing to the moment, are aimed at overcoming the unrepresentableness of the violent sublime. 'The Wall' (written on a day's leave, 2 April 1941) employs narrative deceleration to pinpoint the instant of percussion.[153] The device depends on a division of the subject of the story, reintroducing a detached observer at the 'core of the violent act itself': 'the short story is for the eye (if the mind's eye)', noted Bowen.[154] In Henry Green's *Caught*, the hero's memory of the raids is supplemented and corrected by a parenthetic commentary. Neither work can achieve the harmonization of inner and outer claimed for the wartime sublime; the division of cognitive work is a sign of a flight from violence as well as a realisation that trying to put it into words puts violence to flight. The outer eye in 'The Wall', arrested by danger, acquires a photographic impartiality to sensation but is also the organ of a transfiguring gaze. A burning warehouse, one moment indistinguishable from any other 'Victorian atrocity happily on fire', is now registered in every detail of symmetry and texture, suffused by the colours of flame which, bulging from the brickwork that frames it, take on tactile, bodily attributes which herald the wall's imminent and catastrophic movement.[155] Gradually, occluding the moonlight to a faint crack, the wall becomes the shutter closing off the scene imprinted on the fireman's brain by hyper-sensitive 'new eyes'. It is left to a deeper consciousness to perceive the movement hidden from the 'surface senses' which remain unruffled in their sifting of marginal detail:

[152] William Sansom, 'A Fireman's Journal', in Stefan Schimanski and Henry Treece (eds.), *Leaves in the Storm: A Book of Diaries* (Lindsay Drummond, 1947), 41–2.
[153] William Sansom, *The Birth of a Story* (Chatto and Windus, and Hogarth Press, 1972), 9; Notebook, Berg Collection.
[154] Elizabeth Bowen, introduction to *The Stories of William Sansom* (Hogarth Press, 1963), 8.   [155] William Sansom, *Fireman Flower* (Hogarth Press, 1944), 110.

'I had leisure to remark many things' (109 and 111). The difficulty of eluding a pre-structured grasp of violence is suggested at the end of Sansom's story by its resolution with a comic-strip convention. It is not that it could not have happened like this, but that when the story's subject is literally saved by form—*nothing* ('one of those symmetrical, oblong window spaces') falls on the place where he is standing—what comes to mind are those conventions, like the opened but undamaged room, which colonized the registration of wartime violence (111).

For a writer with reservations about the possibility of representing violence, Sansom showed a remarkable facility in making it the occasion of discursive performance. Many of these ideas did not get beyond his notebooks, a sign not just of authorial scruple, but also of the competitiveness of the market for descriptions of the Blitz. His papers contain drafts of radio-drama scripts and features, film scenarios, jottings for stories, and an essay on the making of Humphrey Jennings's feature-length AFS documentary, *Fires Were Started* (1943), in which Sansom acted. What unites these various writings is the mediation of experience in terms of the limitations of artistic media. While pictorial artists could 'straightway formulate their impressions' of the primary impact of the bombing, the writer's response was less immediate, less direct.[156] So the possibilities for communicating what this 'world' was like lay in the disparity between documentary images and the unnameable actuality of aerial bombardment.

This gap was manifest in the making of *Fires Were Started*, in which firemen and firewomen played 'themselves', but with their roles bizarrely reversed, for Jennings employed them to start fires. Men who had come through the fire-fighting unscathed were burned working behind the scenes as incendiaries. But these wounds were never seen in the cinema. Acting was more authentically boring than service in the AFS, a 'blank-minded, eternally on-the-wait non-experience', only enlivened during 'the actual moments of shooting'.[157] The analogy between film-making and war experience reflects a figurative convention, what Fussell called 'Theater of War', for intervening in the play of appearance and reality.[158] But here it

---

[156] William Sansom, 'The Great City Fire, 1940', TS (carbon) of film scenario, Berg Collection, 1.

[157] William Sansom, 'Fires Were Started', holograph draft of essay in 'Uppsala' Notebook, Berg Collection, 6.   [158] Fussell, *The Great War*, 191–230.

opens the way to reflection on the relationship between image and its production history. The process of creating an illusion, even one famous for its documentary style (though it originated as a training film), turns in on itself, and illuminates what cannot be incorporated into the representation: real firemen re-enacted an incendiary attack, but the real dangers of this illusion remained invisible.[159]

In 'Building Alive', set in the V-weapon attacks of 1944, Sansom's narration of topographical and architectonic strangeness still rests on a theatrical trope. The 'absolutely reasonless' indiscriminacy of the rocket-bombs (when piloted planes were believed to target bombs with great accuracy) seems to make deciphering the life of buildings a futile task. Houses are literally animated in the story: 'The wall, like a rubber wall in a Disney cartoon, sprang out at my eyes, bulging round'. Unlike Richards, privileged by bombing to see what had lain hidden since construction, Sansom's narrator relies on intuition and imagination to grasp the dynamics of structure (typic-ally conflating bodies and things, for the body has become a thing): 'Walking in such houses, the walls and floors are forgotten; the mind pictures only the vivid inner framework of beams and supports, where they might run and how, under stress, they might behave; the house is perceived as a skeleton.' A nearby blast threatens to bury the narrator, but the cracked house acquires temporary rigidity: the ap-parently stable house opposite collapses on fellow-firemen with the stretcher-case he has helped to extricate. The ironic miracle of sur-vival casts aside contemplation of the dead: the spectacle of the ma-terial phenomenon, the life of the inanimate, deflects the narrator's thoughts: 'A new growth was sprouting everywhere, sprouting like the naked plumbing, as if these leaden entrails were the worm at the core of a birth, struggling to emerge, thrusting everything else aside.'[160] At the core of violence is a myth of renewal.

STORIES OF THE BLITZ: ELIZABETH BOWEN AND HENRY GREEN

Published in 1949, the history and historical contexts of *The Heat of the Day* suggest the war's frustration of artistic activity. With five

---

[159] Roger Manvell, *Films and the Second World War* (Dent, 1974), 358 n. 6.
[160] William Sansom, 'Building Alive', *Horizon*, 13/73 (Jan. 1946), 40, 38. See Mervyn Peake, *The Rhyme of the Flying Bomb* (Dent, 1962), 1.

chapters written, composition was interrupted by the V-weapon attacks on south-east England in 1944.[161] The espionage plot, which
affiliates the novel with the culture of a post-war era when expedient
class and geopolitical alliances had given way to domestic and international paranoia, seems to add to the legendary distance of the
wartime setting. *Heat*, however, is not so much a retrospective
reconfiguration of the past as a reflexive treatment of the constructions through which crisis is inhabited as a historic present, and of
their partial determination of the shape that the history of those
events will take.

The novel dramatizes personalities which, threatened by the disciplines and dislocations in public and private life, are buttressed by
imaginative investment in both propaganda and in the fissures that
destruction creates in the social fabric. The relationship between
Stella Rodney and Robert Kelway is the perpetuation of the 'exhilaration of kindred spirits' amidst destruction, a species of shelter solidarity. The 'demolition' of a moment, by a bomb that falls nearby,
initiates 'deferrings' that are kind to the illusions of 'romantic
love'.[162] The threat of violence is overcome by the imaginary consoli-
dation of personality in an illusion; 'one bought the poetic sense of
it with the sense of death' (85). But because their first words are
drowned out, questions remain unasked, constituting a 'lost clue'
that only surfaces as the lonely spy-catcher Harrison insinuates himself into their pact of innocence (91). The lovers are not, as Stella
believes, out of the war, nor can they be part of some holistic bond it
makes possible, because Robert is 'passing stuff across' (183). His
betrayal of the country is a betrayal of their relationship too, as
things not said come to threaten rather than stabilize the affair. The
war breaks in because, rather than inspite of, Robert's contempt for
it, as Stella recognizes in him a version of Harrison (266).

An 'onlooker' in the attack on London, Stella has the sense of
being 'on furlough from her own life' (89); the garrison society of the
bombed city is one in which she and Robert become 'transfixed' by
the 'extraordinary battle in the sky' (91), and lodged in a 'hermetic
world', a 'habitat' (85). As their experience coalesces into a 'common
memory', their individual actions are relegated to 'simulacra of behaviour' (94). Stella's affair is a parallel, not as Sinfield would have it
a contrast, to the situation of Louie Lewis, whose promiscuous

---

[161] Victoria Glendinning, *Elizabeth Bowen: Portrait of a Writer* (Weidenfeld and
Nicolson, 1977), 149.   [162] Bowen, *The Heat of the Day*, 91, 95.

flirtations in the absence of her soldier-husband are a compensation for the props war has knocked from under her. Connie, a Civil Defence worker and dedicated news pundit, rescues Louie from this self-destructive waist-down individualism and conscripts her, emotionally, to the collective war effort. Starting in the middle of the war narrated by the papers, Louie has difficulties understanding its strategic dimensions, but is soon addicted to the stories that 'make the war seem human', and which proffer her surrogate identities:

Dark and rare were the days when she failed to find on the inside page of her paper an address to or else account of herself. Was she not a worker, a soldier's lonely wife, a war orphan, a pedestrian, a Londoner, a home and animal-lover, a thinking democrat, a movie-goer, a woman of Britain, a letter-writer, a fuel-saver and a housewife? (146).

The triumph of symbol over reality naturalizes contradictory identities, and turns conflict into civility: ' "People to be friendly, that's what the war's for, isn't it?" ' (231). Likewise, Stella persists in her affair, until Harrison's tale (seemingly 'out of a thriller') forces recognition, because she is acclimatized to indirection and obliquity; she had 'lived at the edge of a clique of war. . .commanding a sort of language in which nothing need be ever exactly said' (183, 164). Both she and Louie inhabit fictions which, rather than affirming identity, disperse it across the range of imaginary and symbolic constructions of wartime necessity, a 'common memory' which turns individuals into 'simulacra'.

That these wartime identities are not foundational is evident from her son Roderick's reaction to Robert's treachery: ' "The other way round, he might have got a V.C., quite likely?" ' (288). In 1941, *Picture Post* captioned a photograph of a park crowd: 'England: Where it is Still No Crime to Lie on the Grass, to Speak One's Mind, to Wear Clothes Instead of Uniforms.'[163] Louie has swallowed a similar line that ' "Germans. . . . swallow anything they are told" ' while the war ' "makes us think" ' (148). Bowen's novel, which begins in Regent's Park, describes a wartime environment in which speech is evaded, or duplicitous, or the parroting of official opinion, and in which the opportunities for determining one's own identity are not so much a bulwark against uniformity as an alternative route from autonomy. Domestic spaces, instead of reinforcing the boundaries of selfhood, are the novel's index of the deformation of personality.

---

[163] 'What we are fighting for', *Picture Post*, 8/2 (13 July 1940), 33.

Having given up her house at the beginning of the war, Stella occupies a rented flat which signifies her personality 'unexceptionably but wrongly' (22). Roderick cannot rediscover his old self there because it looks more like 'a story' than a home (44). The Army is 'out to obliterate' him; Stella does not fear his death so much as an irreparable 'dissolution inside his life' (45–6). When he first appears he is between lives; his body can still 'copy . . . unsoldierly . . . spontaneity', but his posture is a physical aspiration 'to fill out the bulky concavities of . . . khaki' (45, 48). Louie's flat is a constant reminder of her insignificance. Holme Dean, the family home of Robert Kelway, is the novel's totalization of the built environment's power to mould, and to atrophy, the identities of inhabitants. Bowen proposes a spatial aetiology of treachery. Holme Dean is a 'man-eating house' designed to 'appease middle-class ladies'; a house in which the women granted the father a 'fiction of dominance' which disguised 'indignities . . . burned deeply into the son's mind' (248–49). Passageways are a labyrinth fraught with the danger of inadvertent encounters. The upper storeys are packed with 'repressions, doubts, fears, subterfuges and fibs'. The shadow of surveillance falls on private spaces, where family members are not themselves, but dedicated to rehearsing for public performance 'the required expression of having nothing to hide' (247).

When Stella confronts Robert, they no longer inhabit a privately constituted realm amidst ruin (in a sketch from 1944 Bowen described calico-covered window frames which 'sealed up' a 'timeless era' of 'absolute dislocation').[164] Now they are 'creatures of history' (187). Stella's coming into knowledge about Robert's spying is succeeded by news of Montgomery's Alamein offensive, '"the war turning"' (171). This chiasmus—the collapse of her illusion of a romantic separate peace juxtaposed with a new outer narrative of military success—suggests that survival rather than victory is as much as can be hoped for in the private sphere. Her recognition that Robert might be an actor in their 'confederacy of love' is marked by a moment in which she has a vision of the world which does not include herself (166, 170). Counterpointing the personal investment in the demolished moment out of which the 'resistance-fantasies' of the affair emerge, the displacement of self involved in this objective perspective is associated with a sober understanding that hollows the

---

[164] Elizabeth Bowen, 'Calico Windows', in Andrew Sinclair (ed.), *The War Decade: An Anthology of the 1940s* (Hamish Hamilton, 1989), 263.

fictive victory of romance over contingency.[165] At the novel's end Stella is a 'vagrant' in another flat during the V-weapon attacks eighteen months later: '"The more wars there are. . .the more we shall learn how to be survivors"' (307). Back in 1940, the dereliction of the space of private life was potentially redeemable in the compensations of human contact: 'The wall between the living and the living became less solid as the wall between the living and the dead thinned' (87). The repetition of London's bombardment at a time when war is 'uncontainable' ('being global meant it ran off the edges of the maps') signals an exhaustion of the imagination's capacity to re-designate the scene of destruction as the territory of fulfilment (298).

Bowen's fiction, and her commentary on its composition, envisage the private self suspended between the stress of the demolition of its material extension and of its own deformation. The formal requirements of the novel she would complete after the war were incompatible with the 'relentless exclusions' of wartime consciousness and the destruction of 'solid things' which left people 'disembodied'. This disembodiment cut two ways; as a therapeutic analogue of strategic redescription, and as 'egotism'. The image of the collapse of the wall between the living and the dead is one that shows, in its architectonic formulation, that stress did not, for Bowen, result in a morale of community, but in self-affirming, and obsessive attachments, object-ive correlatives of private life in the form of an 'object or image or place or love or fragment of memory' with which the destiny of the self 'seemed to be identified, and by which the destiny seemed to be assured'.[166]

Henry Green's contemporaneous fiction is also concerned with the compensations and risks of delusory identities (*Loving*, published in 1945, presents the war as a referentially-fluid alibi in the machinations of servants and mistresses in a country house in neutral Eire.) Green mediates these concerns through the symbolic properties of space and narrative. Michael North notes that the end of *Caught* 'enunciates. . .one of the common themes of British writing about the war: the disconcerting tendency toward instant fictionalization of overwhelming experiences'.[167] The present is fictive, or un-realized, because characters are cut off from their past by the alien

---

[165] Bowen, *The Demon Lover* (1945), 221.   [166] Ibid. 220.

[167] Michael North, *Henry Green and the Writing of His Generation* (Charlottesville: University of Virginia Press, 1984), 117.

identities war forces on them. They become caricatures in their
service roles, apprehending themselves through memories which are
not their own. In 'Mr Jonas' and 'A Rescue' disorientation amidst
violence goes unredeemed by uplifting emotions.[168] *Caught*, by contrast, approaches violence obliquely, in terms of expectation and
memory, and its characters are undone by an imaginative dependence
on public emotion and myth, rather than emancipated by them.

The raids which put an end to the firemen's suspended life of 'endlessly waiting' are not narrated directly, but refracted through the
struggle of Richard Roe to recover his experience.[169] Recuperating
from 'nervous debility' at the family estate, where sister-in-law Dy
brings up his son Christopher, Roe feels compelled to narrate crisis,
despite her therapeutic concern 'to keep his mind vacant'.[170] But he
is also aware that ' "one's imagination is so literary" ', and that in recollection ' "everything seems unreal" ' (174). Parenthetic narratorial
commentary insists 'It had not been like that at all' (176).

In the 1943 story 'The Lull', it only takes the arrival of a stranger
to start the firemen of 1942 'talking back' to the attacks of 1940, 'to
justify the waiting life they lived at present, without fires'.[171] As in
Caught, characters' access to the past is qualified as 'disremembering', a tendency Green had earlier registered in *Pack My Bag* when re-
counting the morbidity of his wartime schooldays in anticipation of
the next war.[172] In three different temporalities—expectation, aftermath, and nostalgia—air raids are a fugitive ground of meaning that
can only be grasped as figure. Imagined or experienced, they shadow
the past and the future as an event against which identity is measured.
Roe's conclusion that the raid in which he is blooded ' "was almost
like an explanation of the whole of our life in the war" ' points to
conflations of fact and value in the apprehension of the event.[173]

Caught embodies different modes of representation and their
mutual interference, a strategy which dramatizes the interaction of
aesthetic and ideological apprehensions of the Blitz. The opacity
of Green's writing is crucial to the re-creation of material and symbolic environments. It makes redundant, or inoperative, distinctions
between psychological referents and the matrix of significance

---

[168] 'Mr Jonas', *Folios of New Writing*, 3 (Spring 1941), 11–17, and 'A Rescue', *PNW* 4
(March 1941), 88–93.
[169] Green, 'Firefighting', 117.   [170] Green, *Caught*, 172, 174.
[171] Henry Green, 'The Lull', *New Writing and Daylight* (Summer 1943), 16.
[172] Henry Green, *Pack My Bag* (Hogarth Press, 1940), 78.
[173] Green, *Caught*, 180.

constituted by style. In fiction 'there is no distinguishing an epistemic from an ontological difference'; *Caught* makes this a principle of construction.[174] The effect of indeterminacy is to show narrative or depiction to be an '*instance* of the human mind', and to reveal how closely identity's confirmation in aesthetic perception is allied to its cancellation in the redescription of injury.[175] Roe's narrative fails Dy's expectations, fed by 'wonderful things' in the papers, because it does not 'catch her imagination' (183, 179). His efforts to involve her are directed not at instancing how '"extraordinary"' the scene was, but the '"extraordinary"' difficulty of accessing it, which he compares to trying to reconstruct the circumstances of his son's abduction, 'even to the firelight on the walls' of the room from which the police recovered him (174). But this detail is itself part of an earlier parenthetic supplement to a story Roe knows only from Dy, a story told 'so brokenly, so interrupted by her imagination' that it gave him 'no picture at all' (17).

At the beginning of *Pack My Bag*, the threat of death prompts a premature taking stock of 'how one changed from boy to man'.[176] *Caught* is the 'not directly personal' version of this theme which Green had not expected to survive to write. It is worked out in Roe's relationship with his son, and further refracted by the links that obtain at a figurative level between the father's efforts to evoke the son's experience of abduction and, later, his experience of the raids. The stained glass windows of the toyshop from which Christopher was snatched depict maritime trading scenes which herald the luminosity of the raids on the docks. They are also linked to Roe's childhood terror high above the glass-stained flagstones of Tewkesbury Abbey, a fear that makes him piss himself during pre-war training on escape ladders.

War's first impact is regimented inactivity which, having displaced the values of pre-war life, seems a casting back to schooldays, and the tyranny of authority. Roe's narrative of the raids is primarily grounded on the question of this authority; the breakdown of the chain of command, from despised regulars to auxiliaries, is his measure of the sublimity of the fires in the docks. Isolation adrift of authority is rationalized as the virtue of disobedience, a form of

---

[174] Gregory Currie, *The Nature of Fiction* (Cambridge: Cambridge University Press 1990), 91.
[175] See Frederic Jameson, *The Political Unconscious: Narrative as a Socially Symbolic Act* (Methuen, 1981), 13.   [176] Green, *Pack My Bag*, 5.

self-reliance or independence which Roe takes to be a possibility '"you only get in war"' (182). His initiation in the world of fire is an emancipation: '"After twelve months there we suddenly were, men again, or for the first time"' (191).

This story of heroism is counterpointed by Roe's consciousness that memory and imagination make his experience of violence unreal. In turn, that scepticism is modified not only by a conviction that the event can provide an explanation, but also that it reveals the limit of understanding: '"the point about a blitz is this, there's always something you can't describe, and it's not the blitz alone that's true of. Ever since it happened I feel I've been trying to express all sorts of things"' (179–80). Dy rejects this appeal to the incomprehensibility of the sublime: to her the fog of action is nature's anaesthetic, or the result of concussion. Struck, however, by the more vivid details of his description, she insists on the veracity of destruction's sensuous imprint: '"the real thing is the picture you carry in your eye afterwards. . . . It can't be what you can't remember"' (179). This version of the spectacle of violence is embodied in the parenthetic supplement to Roe's story, a supplement whose emphasis on visual pleasure, and the desertedness of the scene, aligns it with the aesthetics of destruction's spectacle. Bowen observed, *a propos* childhood, that the 'aesthetic is nothing but a return to images that will allow nothing to take their place'.[177] The child Bowen 'saw Kôr before [she] saw London': if the metropolis was Kôr with roofs on, that return of the unforgotten might seem inevitable when London's roofs came off.[178] The aesthetic is hence a mode of omission. Connected stylistically with Roe's memory of childhood, the parenthetic representation of the Blitz in *Caught* doesn't assert what is supplanted by Roe's narrative of initiation, it embodies a further imaginary flight from actuality. His war experience is not so much devalued as situated between values, suspended between descriptions. One description involves Roe's reconstitution, severed from the personal sphere of his past, as a consenting wartime subject, consenting above all to the ideology which translates the scene of destruction into one of affirmation. Like Louie Lewis, Roe's identity is parasitic on wartime's version of individuality:

[177] Elizabeth Bowen, 'Out of a Book', *Orion*, 3 (Autumn, 1946), 14.

[178] Elizabeth Bowen, 'Rider Haggard: *She*' (1947) in *The Mulberry Tree: Writings of Elizabeth Bowen*, ed. Hermione Lee (New York: Harcourt Brace Jovanovich, 1986), 249.

When they are written, the most fascinating chapters in the history of this war will be those describing the exploits of individuals. The double job of assembling the material from which historians will write and reporting these exploits to the world of this generation has been undertaken by the newspapers and magazines of to-day.[179]

The other descriptive mode is the subject-centring apprehension of violence as spectacle, the supplemented content of Roe's dis-remembered experience. The novel's weaving of these descriptions into an undecidable notation of the Blitz does not generate a critical counterpoint between them but points to their convergence as re-descriptive discourses.

Sebastian Knowles, reading the flames of *Little Gidding* 'as symbolic reinterpretations of the Blitz, attempts to aestheticize and thus in some way to anaesthetize an unbearable reality', judges Eliot's 'aes-theticizing of the Luftwaffe' to be a 'mistake, but . . . a necessary error'.[180] The error springs from a 'desperate need to make sense of the Blitz' on the part of Eliot's public. However, as with Sillars's analysis, this attribution of aesthetic harmonization to the necessity of an historical moment really works to occlude the relations of real-ity and symbol. What is obscured is the extent to which the event was produced by the representations which singled it out.

Strachey's explanation of how anticipation made the raids a relief points to war's internal linkage of the material and the abstract which makes an event visible by casting its component acts of lethal wounding into invisibility. The name given to the period of the raids helped to constitute a singular, national experience of legendary pro-portions. The first syllable of *Blitzkrieg*, the Nazis' lightning war (a tactic drawing on new technologies in weapons and propaganda to break the enemy's morale) was swiftly assimilated into English, its meaning reversed. The Blitz—not lightning victory but enduring resistance—rooted stories and symbols in a localized event, and countermanded the contradictions in public and private responses to the nine-month Luftwaffe campaign against cities across the British Isles. Ritchie Calder wrote that 'the Nazis coined the word "Coventrated" ', as if the neologism was a by-product of the burning

---

[179] Allan A. Michie and Walter Graebner (eds.), *Their Finest Hour: The War in the First Person* (London: George Allen and Unwin, 1940), 9.
[180] Sebastian D. G. Knowles, *A Purgatorial Flame: Seven British Writers in the Second World War* (Philadelphia: University of Pennsylvania Press, 1990), 112, 130.

of the Midlands city, but its referent was both too parochial and too shattering to compete with the symbols of the London Blitz.[181] George Orwell, following the linguistic trends of the war, noted: 'The word "blitz" now used everywhere to mean any kind of attack on anything. Cf "strafe" in the last war. "Blitz" is not yet used as a verb, a development I am expecting.'[182] In fact, days before the 7 September raid that initiated the assault on London, the *Daily Sketch* was already returning linguistic violence to sender: 'We "blitz" hun planes in weekend raids.'[183] But the syllable's use to designate agency was far less important than its substantive signification of a passive resistance. The reality of the raids was redescribed in the aggregation of a blitzed community, an undefeatable civilian colossus. Lacking precise historical and geographical definition, the raids have coalesced under description as a singular event. 'It is generally admitted that "It's not nearly as bad as 1940",' wrote Inez Holden about the V-weapons of 1944: 'Already the Battle of Britain has become a legend for those who were in it, and a myth for those who missed it.'[184] 'What days! what days!' says Alastair Sim's Dr Montgomery in Sidney Gilliat's film *Waterloo Road* (1944), recalling an urban campaign waged and won by civilians. Elizabeth Bowen would also emphasize the fictive element in recent history: 'That autumn of 1940 was to appear, by two autumns later, apocryphal, more far away than peace.'[185]

The process set in train by wartime representations has not diminished in its capacity to configure selectively the meanings of violence, as Thomas Myers has pointed out:

The London blitz and the Dresden fire bombing may be similar technological practices, but contentions of a larger relationship between them as twentieth-century tragedy are most often inadmissible historical readings in the closely guarded national archive of means and ends.[186]

One differential in the early 1940s, was industrial output. The Allies dropped twenty times more bombs on Germany than fell on Britain ('America's answer! Production' read a 1942 US poster).[187] The

---

[181] Ritchie Calder, *The Lesson of London*, 123.

[182] George Orwell, diary entry for 2 Jan. 1941, *CEJL* ii. 381.

[183] *The Oxford English Dictionary*.

[184] Inez Holden, 'Summer Journal', in Schimanski and Treece (eds.), *Leaves in the Storm*, 245.   [185] Bowen, *The Heat of the Day*, 87.

[186] Thomas Myers, *Walking Point: American Narratives of Vietnam* (New York: Oxford University Press, 1988), 12.

[187] Alan Milward, *War, Economy and Society: 1939–1945* (Harmondsworth: Penguin, 1987), 303; Wendy Caplan (ed.), *Designing Modernity: The Arts of Reform and Persuasion 1885–1945* (Thames and Hudson, 1995), 346.

number of Bomber Command personnel killed in targeting this overwhelming material superiority was almost equal to the total of Britons killed by the Luftwaffe and by V-weapons. Wartime thinking largely succeeded in compartmentalizing these perspectives. The bombing of Britain produced morale, the bombing of Germany, an economically costly deployment of scarce resources, was sure to destroy it. (This double-think reached its apogee in the deployment of US air-power in the Middle East and Europe at the end of the century, a policy contingent on the representation of war as a reality duel which can be won without unintended or friendly casualties.) The disappearance or transfiguration of the lethally-injured body in representations of the Blitz was fundamental to wartime perceptions of strategic air power. Bombing's impacts were translated into the spheres of ideology and psychology. The new urban landscapes of war, whether represented in aestheticizing descriptions of a romantically ruined London or in policy-confirming interpretations of aerial photographs of wrecked German cities, were figureless. At the moment strategic air power brought war into the homes of populations, its destructive force was lifted away from the bodies it broke up and invested in sublime conceptions. Engendering unity in Britain's socially stratified cities, 'the power of the air', with the unstinting deployment of technology that kept the recipient of violence at an invisible distance of 30,000 feet, also transformed the junior service, at least in the minds of its advocates, into 'the force that can give us victory'.[188]

[188] Lord Trenchard, quoted in Winston S. Churchill, *The Second World War*, 6 vols. (Cassell, 1948–54), iv. 495–7.

4

Side Show or Second Front?: The Legibility of Battle in North Africa

THE SPACE OF BATTLE

WHAT, asked von Clausewitz, 'is the signification of a combat'? Conceived absolutely, combat is a 'miniature picture of the whole War' (the local application of the violence of which war is the multiplication).[1] Fabrizio, in Stendhal's *La Chartreuse de Parme*, lacks this perspective after Waterloo: 'Have I really taken part in a battle?'[2] He cannot aggregate bodily movements into a Clausewitzian whole in which 'all the powers of each party unite in one great volume and all results in one great shock of these masses'. But lethal wounding events become, on this account, the spoil or waste or residue when war is conceptualized: 'we should . . . look upon small combats at first only as necessary loss, like the shavings of a carpenter's plane.'[3]

The analysis of war in Victor Hugo's *Les Miserables* translates the absolutes of theory into the 'daylight of history'. Hugo cites an abstraction—'To form a clear idea of the Battle of Waterloo we have only to draw a capital A'—only to reject it. In 'the fog of war', 'geometry is misleading, only the tempest is true. . . . No narrator, be he never so conscientious, can fix the exact shape of that ugly cloud that is called battle.'[4] The signification of combat is a question of visibility, and of legibility. The strategist strives to perceive a structure, viewing combat in its relations to 'other parts of the great whole', whereas the narrator recognizes 'a stage in every battle when it degenerates into hand-to-hand combat, dissolves in fragments'.[5] The

[1] Carl von Clausewitz, *On War*, ed. Michael Howard and Peter Paret (Princeton: Princeton University Press, 1976), 316.
[2] Stendhal, *The Charterhouse of Parma*, trans. Margaret Shaw (1839, trans. 1958. Harmondsworth, Penguin, 1988), 77.   [3] Clausewitz, *On War*, 316.
[4] Victor Hugo, *Les Miserables*, trans. Norman Denny, 2 vols. (1862, trans. 1976. Harmondsworth, Penguin, 1980), i. 287, 291.
[5] Clausewitz, *On War*, 316; Hugo, *Les Miserables*, 291.

art of the strategist is to resist the fragmenting of his representation (in theory, the true picture, because it alone guarantees the objective of combat). But the novelist deliberately surrenders the structure which makes Waterloo the letter A in the rhetoric of battle history, seeking to represent what is illegible or fogged. In *War and Peace* the rationalizing vision of the geometer of historical forces is persistently confounded by the course of events (Tolstoy's ideal of historical inquiry is a calculus differentiating 'the infinitesimally small elements by which the masses are moved').[6] Tolstoy reconfigures the pyramid of the command structure: the strategist at its apex is out of the picture, not the sole possessor of it.[7]

It is a commonplace that the modern literature of war holds an oppositional relationship to the reified abstractions of the discourses which administer the larger movements of conflicts between states. Literature becomes war's secret history, bringing to light a truth of war which is always vulnerable to suppression, theoretical idealization or amnesia. That this is often perceived to be a twentieth-century cultural phenomenon has much to do with developments in the way war was conceptualized and imagined between the campaigns of Napoleon and the Great War. Discourses of progress, biology and race, nationalism, psychology, industrialization, and urbanization lay behind perceptions of war as by turns irrational and a civilizing end in itself. The competition between strategic rationalizations and registrations of war's meaninglessness (its autonomy, its excess over human intentions, its unrepresentability) may seem to have been decided, granting epistemological authority to the latter. But such an account is not immune to the implications of its own theoretical underpinning in the conviction that war eludes the forms of rational or artistic discourse. The greater the temptation to stress the irrationality of war, the greater the need for reflection on the signification of combat, and how the meanings of slaughter are construed.

Oppositions between the abstract and the concrete, the absolute and the contingent, the military mass and the militarized civilian, are heuristic rather than metaphysical. The meaning of battle is not located at one or other pole, but is produced in the shuttling of discourse between them, and in relationships between the verbal or iconographic and the material. Whether battle can be represented in

---

6 Leo Tolstoy, *War and Peace*, trans. Louise and Aylmer Maude (1868–9, trans. 1922–3. Oxford: Oxford University Press, 1991), 879–81.

7 Isaiah Berlin, *Russian Thinkers* (1978. Harmondsworth: Penguin, 1994), 34.

any absolute or authoritative sense is best addressed when we have considered how battle is enacted through representation, and can assess whether this question is coherently formulated.

Contemporary writing about Britain's North African war reveals that the signification of combat is correlated to the genres of discourse which depict it. But these activities of depicting combat's content of injuring—whether the writer be war correspondent, intelligence officer, novelist, diarist, or official historian—should not be thought of as external to war, for they are directly or indirectly bound up with the possibility of injury's signification in relation to larger objectives. The figures of synecdochic articulation and legibility which characterized retrospective theoretical and novelistic writing on Napoleon's campaigns are to be found in a number of these genres, along with further indications that the representation of battle draws on a range of historical and cultural precedents which complicate the impact of new military technology. But it is in the activity of imagining combat's spatiality and its geopolitical contexts that its signification is most explicitly revealed to be a function of the discourses which configure it.

The Mediterranean was the only arena in which British ground forces could operate against Hitler's armies between the extrication of the British Expeditionary Force from Dunkirk in June 1940 and the Normandy landings of June 1944. Until the invasion of Sicily and Italy in the summer of 1943, Britain's land war was conducted across the barren North African littoral. This strategic commitment was sustained in the face of both American and Soviet pressure to open a Second Front in northern Europe (an option deferred for logistical and political reasons). Writing in 1942, war-correspondent Alexander Clifford grafted the Libyan campaigns of the winter of 1941–2 onto grand strategy with a richly ambivalent image: 'a single water-tight front in itself it became the left wing of the biggest single front the world has known.'[8] The desert war acquired a significance its isolation denied it by being hinged to the Soviet counter-offensives. But Clifford's geographical figure is an East–West view of Europe (reversing the West–East gradient of the Atlantic and Central European worldview) and this, together with the traditional inferiority of the left flank, counteracts the aggrandisement of what was elsewhere viewed as a side-show. A. D. Divine's description of the

---

[8] Alexander Clifford, '*Crusader*' (George Harrap, 1942), 5.

Algerian landing beaches of Operation Torch (November 1942) as 'the margin of the second front' is another double-edged example of an aggregation of local engagements into a larger and coherent whole.[9] Both need to be set against Soviet suspicions that the Western Allies were dragging their heels, letting Hitler wear his armies out on Russians and Russia (though it should be noted that the North African theatre drew *Luftflotte* 2 from the Eastern Front, and a significant number of submarines from the Atlantic).[10] The large contingents of Indian and Dominion troops, at a time when the Japanese threatened the subcontinent and Australia, were further contradictions in representing this theatre of war as a sign of Britain's military contribution to the defeat of Nazism.

Remoteness from the Continental battlefields on which the defeat of Hitler would have to be achieved facilitated the formation of a distinct set of desert war motifs, which make this an apt context for investigating the ways in which combat signifies. The desert environment, because it appeared a blank, was readily overlaid with interpretations. In this context, the fact that a battlefield is symbolically constructed is all the more apparent. But because it lacked inherent features, the desert would not take the imprint of the military presence: the mapping of force onto shifting sands had a provisionality which highlights the way the execution of violence is dependent on modes of verbal and iconic registration to ground its outcomes.

Britain claimed the right to secure imperial communications but Egypt was ostensibly a sovereign state, and did not declare war on Germany until April 1945.[11] Soldiers and expatriate civilians, outsiders to the collective meanings of the Home Front, defended the empire in a country that remained ambivalent in its allegiance—'one more compromise the English hadn't found'—and where economic and political conditions travestied the goals of a 'fight for democracy'.[12] However, in contemporary fiction, local political conditions are readily overwritten with Home Front ideology. Ideals of instrumental community are the mainstay of Gerald Kersh's *Faces in a Dusty Picture* (1944); John Brophy's *Immortal Sergeant* (1942) centres on the individual's enfranchisement as team player.

---

[9] A. D. Divine, *Road to Tunis* (Collins, 1944), 13.

[10] Gerhard L. Weinberg, *A World at Arms: A Global History of World War II* (Cambridge: Cambridge University Press, 1994), 233.

[11] Peter Mansfield (ed.), *The Middle East: A Political and Economic Survey*, fifth edition (Oxford: Oxford University Press, 1980), 204–5, 207.

[12] Dan Davin, *For the Rest of Our Lives* (Nicholson and Watson, 1947), 50, 161.

Writers were also marooned in the Middle East—'"English exiles. England's reply to Dr. Goebbels"'—and marginality was again inflected as a compensation.[13] 'Created in the midst of war, flourishing in the rear of a combat area', the little magazines like *Oasis* took titles which declared a rearguard action against the imperatives of war and of mainstream literary culture.[14] *Salamander* alluded to cultural rebirth from the ashes of world conflict: despite its geopolitical isolation, John Cromer called it 'a microcosm of world literature'.[15] *Personal Landscape*, edited by Laurence Durrell, Bernard Spencer and Robin Fedden, 'expressed our wish to emphasize the importance of personal life and values when the current of all thought and feeling around us set strongly in the channels of war, and when it was growing ever more difficult to exist outside the "war effort"'.[16] Olivia Manning argued that poets in the Middle East, Durrell's 'castaways', were not subject to the 'inbreeding' of writing in England.[17] This romancing of expatriate wartime culture is amplified in the post-war writing of participants, like Olivia Manning and Lawrence Durrell, and in popular cultural history.[18] But the extent to which exteriority could be used as a lever on wartime ideology was limited. For Manning's heroine, Harriet Pringle, isolation equates with unreality: '"It was almost a relief when the air-raid siren sounded. I felt at once that I knew my way around."'[19] This lack indicates both the dominance of Home-Front experience in retrospective memorialization, and the way, in wartime, it displaced other ways of understanding total war. Harriet comments that '"We know nothing about war-time England"', the

---

[13] Ibid. 141.

[14] Keith Bullen and John Cromer (eds.), *Salamander: A Miscellany of Poetry* (George Allen and Unwin, 1947), 13.

[15] Ibid.

[16] Robin Fedden, *Personal Landscape* (Turret Books, 1966), n.p.

[17] Olivia Manning, 'Poets in Exile', *Horizon*, 10/58 (Oct. 1944), 270–9, and Lawrence Durrell, introduction to Victor Selwyn *et al.* (eds.), *Return to Oasis* (Shepheard Walwyn and Editions Poetry London, 1980), p. xxiii. See A. T. Tolley, *The Poetry of the Forties* (Manchester: Manchester University Press, 1985), 230–6.

[18] See also Artemis Cooper, *Cairo in the War: 1939–1945* (Hamish Hamilton, 1989), 149–60. The moment of this exile has attracted a proportionately high level of academic attention, see Roger Bowen, '*Many Histories Deep': The Personal Landscape Poets in Egypt, 1940–1945* (Madison, NJ: Fairleigh Dickinson University Press, 1995) and Jonathan Bolton, *Personal Landscapes: British Poets in Egypt during the Second World War* (Macmillan, 1997).

[19] Olivia Manning, *Friends and Heroes* (1965) in *The Balkan Trilogy* (1960–5. Harmondsworth: Penguin, 1986), 679.

war's significant centre: ' "I want to go back and see for myself. I want to be in the midst of it." '[20]

Tropes of isolation and marginality sustained the idea of the desert as a battlefield possessing unprecedented transparency or legibility. Correlli Barnett, scourge of the Montgomery legend (its hero is lifted clear of the historical matrix of long-term strategic necessities) nevertheless joins in conceiving the desert campaigns of 1940–3 mythically: 'unique in history', 'war in its purest form', 'fought like a polo game on an empty arena', a utopian recovery of war as an ethically uncomplex contest of arms.[21] Despite his critique of the seductions of charismatic leadership, the amateurism and eccentric dress codes of Douglas's mechanized cavalrymen lurk behind Barnett's chivalric formulations. The urban–industrial scenarios of trench war and strategic bombing are displaced by what is considered, without irony, as a clear field for the play of military force and intelligence, uncomplicated by the (political) problems of occupation, or the 'side-effects' of civilian death. Rommel called it war in 'its most advanced form'.[22]

'The Desert dominated the British press and radio to the disservice of other, less glamorous and indeed more important campaigns.'[23] Once stylized in this way, the conflict was readily assimilable to culture, like the chivalric duels of the Battle of Britain, part of 'British folk-memory, a source of legend, endlessly rewritten as both history and fiction.'[24] But the legibility of the desert war was, and remains, conditional on its repeated reinscription. This process is in turn dependent on the battlefields themselves being perceived as empty of signs ('You must leave the desert as you would hope to find it'), and erasing those that the armies left behind them—tracks, litter, bodies, graves.[25] Thus conceived, the unchartered space of the desert reversed the domination of environment over the war writer: George Fraser concluded that 'mobile warfare, more than trench warfare, permits a certain control and detachment'.[26]

---

[20] Olivia Manning, *The Battle Lost and Won* (1978) in *The Levant Trilogy* (1977–80. Harmondsworth: Penguin, 1985), 355.

[21] Correlli Barnett, *The Desert Generals* (William Kimber, 1960), 21.

[22] Erwin Rommel, 'Rules of Desert Warfare', in Gérard Chaliand (ed.), *The Art of War in World History* (Berkeley: University of California Press, 1994), 957.

[23] Correlli Barnett, *Britain and Her Army 1509–1970* (Allen Lane, 1970), 439.

[24] Ibid.

[25] Regulation quoted by Cecil Beaton, *Near East* (Batsford, 1943), 40.

[26] G. S. Fraser, *Vision and Rhetoric: Studies in Modern Poetry* (Faber, 1959), 142.

The attribution of legibility to the desert battlefields was reinforced by figures of containment and exclusion. Cecil Beaton, covering the desert war for the MOI, needed a pass to enter 'the fraternity inside the barriers of the desert' (literally through a barbed-wire entrance), a fraternity as distinct as that inhabiting the excluded space of the prison camp.[27] This space was both alien and adjacent. Douglas wrote that 'by a day's travelling you reach a new world': Lawrence Durrell, reinforcing the symbolic border from the civilian side, collapsed the separation to an hour's drive.[28] Crossing this frontier could be as disorienting as it would be for American soldiers, commuting by helicopter 'between first world suburbia and third world death' in Vietnam: for Douglas 'two absolutely different worlds co-exist'.[29] This distinction structures his vision of the extremity of war's alterations to the body, whether invoked as the strangeness of 'having walked through the looking-glass', or the bathos of the soldier as tourist,

> a man with no head
> has a packet of chocolate and a souvenir of Tripoli.[30]

The legendary dimension of the desert battlefields can be analysed as 'representational space', a codified space which is 'directly *lived* through its associated images and symbols'.[31] Whereas Barnett's 'legendary' inscriptions of the desert battlefields, like the nature/culture opposition in much Great War poetry, are grounded in notions of a natural, prior space, the Marxist philosopher Henri Lefebvre's theory of the social production of space negates 'the idea that empty space is prior to whatever ends up filling it' (15). Social space is produced by dialectical interaction or spatial practice, and is determined by hegemonic representations of space (scientific, urbanist, technocratic, and we might add strategic). Lefebvre uses the term 'representational space' to designate that space which is lived by inhabitants or users: 'This is the dominated—and hence passively

[27] Beaton, *Near East*, 40.
[28] Douglas, 'Cairo Jag', *Complete Poems*, 97; Durrell in Selwyn *et al.* (eds.), p. xxiii.
[29] William Shawcross, quoted by Alasdair Spark, 'Flight Controls: The Social History of the Helicopter as a Symbol of Vietnam', in Jeffrey Walsh and James Aulich (eds.), *Vietnam Images: War and Representation* (Macmillan, 1989), 98; Geoffrey Hill, '"I in Another Place": Homage to Keith Douglas', *Stand*, 6/4, (1964), 9.
[30] Douglas, *Alamein to Zem Zem* (Editions Poetry London, 1946), 8; *Complete Poems*, 97.
[31] Henri Lefebvre, *The Production of Space* (1974. Oxford: Blackwell, 1991), 39.

experienced—space which the imagination seeks to change and appropriate' (39). Textual spaces do not overthrow represented space, they are further hypostatizations, a denial of space as practice: 'Any attempt to use such codes [those of literary texts] as a means of deciphering social space must surely reduce that space itself to the status of a *message*, and the inhabiting of it to the status of a *reading*' (7). But they may function as dialectical reinscriptions, which is one way of understanding the relations of the readings of the space of battle that arise from the competing perspectives of the soldier-subject and the administrative apparatus (intelligence, logistics, strategy) of the General Staff.

Literary texts intervene in the production of representational space to negate the concepts with which the space of the battlefield is constructed as an abstract arena where outcomes are produced. The social space of battle is articulated by command and class hierarchies, and labour demarcations, particularly the labour of injuring and being injured, which are located at one end of the command structure. As representational space, the battlefield is granted structure by textual systems; contemporaneously as orders, intelligence, truces or surrenders, retrospectively as treaties or history. Barnett writes that 'the oddest thing about the dream world of propaganda is its influence on the real world of battle', but this determination only seems odd when that real world is abstracted from social practice and symbolization.[32]

Geographical isolation on the far side of the Mediterranean had its compensations in the resonances of the region's past: as Fedden noted 'the exile everywhere walks on the dead and their deposits. . . . The dead of countless generations, packed like sardines, stuff the earth. It bursts with corpses.'[33] G. S. Fraser distinguished 'crisis-ridden' English verse from 'the poetry of Cairo, which is calm, conscious of the long perspectives of eastern Mediterranean culture'.[34] But Fedden's Eliotesque remains bear little resemblance to the 'meat in a hole' which, for Keith Douglas, was the only residue of 'an organism / not capable of resurrection'.[35] Douglas's depictions of

[32] Barnett, *The Desert Generals*, 185.

[33] Robin Fedden *et al.* (eds.), *Personal Landscape: An Anthology of Exile* (Editions Poetry London, 1945), 9.

[34] Quoted in Bernard Bergonzi, 'Poetry of the Desert War: British Poets in Egypt 1940–1945', in Vereen Bell and Laurence Lerner (eds.), *On Modern Poetry: Essays Presented to Donald Davie* (Nashville: Vanderbilt University Press, 1988), 17.

[35] Douglas, 'Dead Men', *Complete Poems*, 96.

persons turned into meat eschew speculations that mystify combat's destructiveness as heroic oblivion, registering instead the precarious fact of his own survival. As Eric Leed has suggested, 'for those enmeshed in it, the event had become a "text", the correct reading of which was a matter of life and death'.[36]

The capacity of the work of this unsentimental 'militarist' to generate the possibility of a critique of strategic redescription is perhaps surprising, given the fact that his favoured tropes for the dead parallel the mode of the architectonic spectacle in writing about the Blitz.[37] Douglas's prose and poetry of battle delineates a potentially critical representational space by juxtaposing the material and ideological co-ordinates of that space; damaged flesh and bellicist idealism. The poet Hamish Henderson remarked that the conflict seemed to be 'between the "the dead, the innocent"—that eternally wronged proletariat of levelling death in which all the fallen are comrades—and ourselves, the living'.[38] Here, levelling is not a socially desirable side-effect of the war, but its essential content. Ted Hughes has described war as Douglas's 'ideal subject, the burning away of all human pretensions in the ray cast by death'.[39]

The writing of the New Zealander Dan Davin is in marked contrast. In a region whose archaeology records ancient wars, his historiographic perception of imperial and military repetition sets up a counterpoint with the ideals of radical politics. He unpacks the representational spaces and ideological contexts of killing and dying. Where Douglas's writing is ultimately subjective in its fashioning of a space in which the supremacy and vulnerability of the observer is played out, Davin's has a dialogic dimension, embodying the competition between discourses which encode lethal injury. Both writers, however, contest designations of the desert as an empty arena for the ideal (theoretical) play of abstracted military force, and their techniques for describing the desert as battlefield reveal this to be a space dominated by the language of strategic description.

[36] Eric Leed, *No Man's Land: Combat and Identity in World War I* (Cambridge: Cambridge University Press, 1979), 35, following Paul Ricoeur, 'The Model of the Text: Meaningful Action Considered as a Text', *New Literary History*, 5/1 (Autumn 1973), 91–120: the rules of text-interpretation are paradigmatic for interpretation in the social sciences, because action in its social dimension is fundamentally symbolic.

[37] See Douglas, 'An Untitled Autobiographical Story', *Miscellany*, 13.

[38] Hamish Henderson, *Elegies for the Dead in Cyrenaica* (John Lehmann, 1948), 11–12.

[39] Keith Douglas, *Selected Poems*, ed. Ted Hughes (Faber, 1964), 13.

KEITH DOUGLAS'S ANATOMY OF WAR

'Poetry is like a man,' wrote the undergraduate Douglas, 'whom thinking you know all his movements and appearance you will presently come upon in such a posture that for a moment you can hardly believe it a position of the limbs you know'.[40] His writing about battle is marked by a fascination with the appearance of altered flesh: combat signifies through high explosive's choreography of the human body. In *Alamein to Zem Zem*, his prose 'anatomy' of the push West along the Mediterranean after Montgomery's break-out from El Alamein in November 1942, 'the battlefield is the simple, central stage of the war: it is there that the interesting things happen'.[41] But the echo of Clausewitz's 'element of the thing itself' is not a corrective to abstraction, it is an exclusion of political consider-ations. The other 'end' of the war, the outcome sought by Govern-ments and 'great and rich men' who are 'using us to get it', does not 'excite a poet or a painter or a doctor' (7). This odd kinship points to the juxtaposition between verbal surfaces and deep somatic places in Douglas's work: the dust-blanched corpse in 'Vergissmeinnicht' is visualized as a textual 'skin' and an eviscerated volume ('burst stom-ach like a cave') which demand to be read and physically probed. The story 'Death of a Horse' (*Lilliput*, July 1944) describes a military lesson on the nature of a 'horse's insides': the broken animal is 'stretched out into a diagram', the knacker's man cutting where the veterinary major has marked its coat with chalk.[42] This story looks at first like an example of Fussell's 'literature of chickenshit', expos-ing the 'behaviour that makes military life worse than it need be': Simon, forced to watch a preview of battle's transformation of life into meat faints at the 'wreck' and 'stench' of the horse and the 'hor-rible casualness' of the vet's voice.[43] But a 'horrible casualness' is one of the chief effects of Douglas's writing from the desert. 'Little Red Mouth' is another attempt at a magazine story: a corpse arrested in a 'pose' signifying pain is framed by a bookish irony and a properly stammering reaction, 'trembling with horror, stunned into involun-tary speech'.[44] If Douglas concluded that commercial fiction must

[40] Douglas, 'On the Nature of Poetry' (1940), *Miscellany*, 44.
[41] A suggested title for the book was 'Anatomy of Battle or Anatomy of a Battle', ibid. 147; *Alamein*, 7.   [42] Douglas, *Miscellany*, 138.
[43] Paul Fussell, *Wartime: Understanding and Behaviour in the Second World War* (Oxford: Oxford University Press, 1989), 80–3; Douglas, *Miscellany*, 139.
[44] Douglas, *Miscellany*, 141.

inscribe a point of view which turns in fear or disgust from damaged flesh, there is nothing involuntary about his scrutiny of the dead in the writings that posthumously made his name. These texts are pathological, not pathetic, dedicated to presenting morbid and abnormal bodily conditions rather than to exciting feelings of pity or sadness.

Douglas joined up at the outbreak of war, and ran away from a staff job (ironically as a camouflage instructor) to take part in the offensive that would eventually drive Rommel out of North Africa. An autobiographical story written when he was 12 years old begins, 'As a child he was a militarist'; in September 1939 he promised his Oxford tutor, Edmund Blunden, some 'long-distance essays' on Shakespeare and Chaucer viewed through training manuals and the idiom of English Cavalry Officers.[45] But distance was anathema: 'long range poetry inspired by shocking news items' (an example would be Cecil Day Lewis's 'Lidice', about German reprisals for the assassination of Heydrich) was not war poetry.[46] 'Lyrical and abstract forms' were 'bullshitting' irrelevancies, like propaganda, which stood between him and his subject: 'I never tried to write about war (that is battles and things, not London can Take it) . . . until I had experienced it.'[47] Catching up with the front, Douglas 'had seen the whole arrangement of the Army, almost too large to appreciate, as a body would look to a germ riding in its bloodstream' (9). Appreciation connotes a sympathetic and positive valuation on the basis of an exercise of sensibility and discrimination.[48] But the word also denotes military judgement of the intelligence picture, an appraisal of the strengths of friend and foe (a further sense is a rise in exchange value).[49] Douglas eschews both a habituated 'normal sensibility' and a strategic exchange of the quick for victory: he immerses himself in the body fluids of the Clausewitzian colossus, which are the vital fluids of men. 'Your talk of regrouping', he told Hall, 'sounds to me . . . like the military excuse of a defeated general. There is never much need to regroup. Let your impulses drive you forward.'[50]

---

[45] Ibid. 13, 40.   [46] 'Poets in this War', ibid. 120.

[47] Letter to J. C. Hall (10 August 1943), ibid. 127–8.

[48] 'Normal sensibility is a tissue of what has been conscious theory made habitual . . . conscious theory may make an addition to sensibility . . . [and make] a reader feel stronger about his appreciations', William Empson, *Seven Types of Ambiguity* (Chatto and Windus, 1930), 254.

[49] 'Lord Cork [Admiral of the Fleet] presented his preliminary appreciation, based of course on a purely military study of the problem', Winston S. Churchill, *The Second World War*, 6 vols. (Cassell, 1948–54), i. 416.   [50] Douglas, *Miscellany*, 128.

Montgomery's charge out of Egypt was an opportunity for 'experiences worth writing of', and Douglas was thrilled by the momentum of the chase.[51] It was as if battle alone tempted him out of his 'careful absence of expectation' ('for me it is simply a case of fighting *against* the Nazi regime' he wrote to Blunden in the Spring of 1944, stressing his dissociation from a fight for something called England).[52] The ends of battle were not ideological but a return to and rereading of the spoil of war.

Loot is one of the most important things—and it is the thing that makes all the exhilaration in fighting. And, believe it or not, our utmost thought at the end of battle was loot. By that you must not understand—as I believe you do—pillaging or corpse robbing. But simply rummaging in the glorious bran tub provided by any battlefield.[53]

Liable to be misunderstood as a species of dishonourable conduct (in literary critical terms, a too-cool detachment), his descriptions of battle deny redeeming abstractions, and long-distance outcomes:

it was all over. We had made it. We stood here on the safe side of it, like swimmers. And Guy, lying under the flowers in Enfidaville cemetery, Piccadilly Jim, buried miles behind us, Tom, and all the others, back to the first casualties, during Rommel's attempt to break through to Alexandria; they didn't make it, but it's over for them too.

And to-morrow, we said, we'll get into every vehicle we can find, and go out over the whole ground we beat them on, and bring in more loot than we've ever seen.[54]

Douglas is the flâneur of battle, immersing himself in its crowds (literal and spectral); like Walter Benjamin's Baudelaire he went in search of 'rhyme-booty'.[55]

Writing and looting often overlap in Douglas's North African texts, suggesting an adjacency of the imagination's will to dominate the external world, and the professional killer's 'content' at the 'sorcery' which turns the victim into a sign of his own survival.[56] 'Vergissmeinnicht' is about rifling the possessions of a dead German, and appropriates a foreign intimacy as its title (as the Eighth Army highjacked 'Lili Marlene').[57] A version of the opening of *Alamein to*

---

[51] Ibid. 119.   [52] Ibid. 127, 152-3.

[53] Letter to Jocelyn Baber, ibid. 153-4.   [54] Douglas, *Alamein*, 141.

[55] Walter Benjamin, *Charles Baudelaire: A Lyric Poet in the Era of High Capitalism*, trans. Harry Zohn (New Left Books, 1983), 80.

[56] Douglas, 'Vergissmeinnicht' and 'How to Kill', *Complete Poems*, 111-12.

[57] Sung to the same tune, 'The Dive Bomber's Song' shares the poem's scenario: 'Poor Marlene's boy-friend will / Never see Marlene'. See Martin Page (ed.), *'Kiss me*

Zem Zem was drafted in an Italian exercise book picked up some-where on the battlefield.[58] His reading during operations was also a matter of seizing on what came to hand, including the 19-year-old David Gascoyne's *A Short Survey of Surrealism* (1935), a text which affirms Cecil Beaton's suggestion that the surrealists anticipated the desert battlefield.[59] In the 'ready-made' lay the aesthetic potential of war-spoil and unmade bodies. Gascoyne's belief that surrealism abolished the boundary between the '*real* world' and 'a world to which entrance had generally been supposed . . . to be the sole privil-ege of poets' is echoed by Douglas's 'through the looking-glass' de-scription of his escape from the mundane art of camouflage training to the 'end of the war' that could 'excite a poet'.[60] His account of the 'illogical' world of battle is no more an '"involuntary produc-tion"' than Gascoyne's poems in *Man's Life is this Meat*, an equa-tion to which Douglas gave genuine resonance.[61] Critical dissent about *Alamein to Zem Zem*—a broadly mimetic 'struggle . . . with linguistic and poetic paradigms', or, equally confusedly, 'a little self-consciously, an "unliterary" book'—witnesses the narrative's unsettling blend of contingency and contrivance. The 'rarefied choreography' of normative battlefield description is undone by the interplay of surprise and control.[62] Douglas's movements across the field of battle are interrupted both by the insistence with which altered bodies present themselves to perception, and with which the imagination plays on these alterations.

Douglas's sense of the contemporary poet's belatedness was coun-tered by his opinion that the mechanized soldier had an advantage of perspective 'over the infantrymen, and over all the soldiers and gen-erals of earlier wars'.[63] But *Alamein to Zem Zem* registers the irony that while technology makes possible radically new perspectives

Goodnight, Sergeant Major': The Songs and Ballads of World War II (Hart-Davis, MacGibbon, 1973), 87.

[58] Douglas, BL Add. MS 60586, 3r.

[59] Beaton, *Near East*, 57. Beaton's photographs recontextualize damaged equipment: a tailplane becomes a sphinx by Picasso (plate facing 58).

[60] David Gascoyne, *A Short Survey of Surrealism* (Cobden-Sanderson, 1935), pp. ix–x; Douglas, *Alamein*, 7–8. See also Charles Cruickshank, *Deception in World War II* (1979. Oxford: Oxford University Press, 1981), 19–33.

[61] Douglas, *Alamein*, 8; see André Breton, 'The Automatic Message', *What is Surrealism?: Selected Writings*, ed. Franklin Rosemont (Pluto, 1978), 98.

[62] William Scammell, *Keith Douglas: A Study* (Faber, 1988), 43; Vernon Scannell, *Not Without Glory: Poets of the Second World War* (Woburn Press, 1976) 31; Scarry, *The Body in Pain*, 70.   [63] Douglas, *Alamein*, 97.

on battle, they are assimilated to euphemistic or chivalric codes. Listening in on wireless traffic between tanks places 'before his mind's eye the panorama of the battle', a viewpoint denied to the trench-soldier of 1914-18, except in imaginary prototypes of the Audenesque airman–diagnostician in Barbusse, Owen, and Sorley. The language in which this panorama is articulated is conventional, a mixture of 'voice procedure' (the Army's verbal drill for describing situations) and a cavalry argot whose idioms are 'as stereotyped as in the most ceremonious exchanges of courtesies': there are 'things which are not said'. These messages are heard with greater equanimity than the 'radiophonic Babel of the war, messages of death', picked up contemporaneously by Primo Levi in his Turin physics lab.[64] Douglas's writing is at once paralleled by and dissociated from this camouflaged register, a 'mysterious symbolic language in some ways like that of a wildly experimental school of poets'.[65] The modulation from '"veiled talk"' ('The horse 'as fallen') to the coolness of his own gloss, 'he is bleeding to death', corresponds with Piette's suggestion that Douglas's militarist mind was 'trained to make such moves', but its visceral fascinations destabilize the camouflaging of war as a game.[66]

The gap between the facts of violence and their transcendence in the behaviour and understatement of cavalrymen ('stupidity and chivalry') both attracts and repels. The officer in 'Sportsmen', 'unfortunately killed by an 88' ('"It's most unfair—they've shot my foot off"'), is called Peter, Douglas's pseudonym in the typescript of *Alamein* (he had used the pseudonym Peter Hatred in *The Cherwell* in 1940).[67] Because his narrative is confined to war's interior, the juxtaposition of the horrors of the battlefield, and the breathtakingly improbable conventions to which that reality is suborned, is not subject to a normative interpretation. By contrast, in Robin Maugham's Crusader-campaign novel, *Come To Dust* (1945), which tells how battle's nightmarish aspects correct naive enthusiasms, ideological and stylistic contradictions are apparently resolved by disembodied 'voices' which enjoin the wounded narrator to 'forget the dead' and orientate himself to the outside of war.[68] There is no

---

[64] Ibid.; Primo Levi, *The Periodic Table*, trans. Raymond Rosenthal (1975, trans. 1985. Sphere, 1986), 55.   [65] Douglas, *Alamein*, 97.
[66] Ibid. 97, 101; Adam Piette, *Imagination at War* (Macmillan, 1995), 30.
[67] Douglas, *Complete Poems*, 99, 110; *Miscellany*, 57.
[68] Robin Maugham, *Come to Dust* (Chapman and Hall, 1945), 190.

horror in *Alamein to Zem Zem*; action is plotted as farce not awful disorientation. Motifs of the waste of war—a cardboard topee on a grave signifies 'there is some junk buried here'—are juxtaposed with figures of war as a parody of peace, the dead likened to 'trippers taken ill' (72 and 44). Douglas's writing extrapolates redescriptive conventions but the injured body remains in view. Although he did not evacuate the battlefield of human figures, as writers did in describing bombed London, the fascination with ruptured surfaces makes for a vision which is more disturbingly superficial.

Because he was under 21, Douglas couldn't drive the car he'd hired to collect his belongings from Merton College Oxford when war interrupted his degree: 'At 19 however I'm quite old enough to be allowed to be used in keeping the country safe for other road-users.'[69] Having reached his majority, he wrote Blunden from Egypt:

I had an accident last time I was in Cairo and killed an Arab—He did the usual chicken-crossing-the road stunt. . . . It is curious how doll-like a broken up body looks, in spite of blood. A pity its not so odourless as a doll.[70]

The voice of militarist-imperialist superiority—the victim crossed 'at the double'—is no less offensive because it is imitated (Julian Maclaren-Ross's 'A Bit of a Smash in Madras' appeared in *Horizon* in June 1940).[71] There is no evidence of the existential questioning that dignifies killing an Arab in Camus's contemporaneous *L'Étranger* (1942) as Douglas concludes he is 'exonerated but somewhat shaken'. His figurative repertoire, and the effect of indifference, is extant before El Alamein. The lack of moral resonance in Douglas's callowly worldly aside to his tutor may give us pause to inquire why, in a different context, that lack can go so easily unnoticed. In a story by the much reprinted 'Gun Buster', surrendering troops are run over and the 'battle-cry of the squadron'—'"Blood on the tracks"'—can never again be 'a mere figure of speech'. The Troop Commander, 'overcome by the horror', supplements his orders to advance with exonerations—'"It can't be helped . . . It was nobody's fault"'—but recovers the discipline of command, repressing an inner voice of moral conscience.[72] The story enunciates the battlefield as an arena which redefines human ethical relations: the momentary

[69] Douglas, letter to Blunden (11 September 1939), *Miscellany*, 40–41.
[70] Douglas, letter to Blunden (1 March 1942), ibid., 88–9.
[71] *Horizon*, I/6 (June 1940), 434–55.
[72] 'Gun Buster', *Zero Hours* (Hodder and Stoughton, 1942), 9, 18.

appearance of repulsion and regret serves to underline the necessity and seriousness of this represented space. It is the absence of this division between inner voice and the voice of command that destabilizes the represented space of the battlefield in Douglas's images of it. The corollary of indifference is a scene of carnage which is not made respectable by the restitutive drama of conscience's retreat in the face of military necessity. In Douglas's unlyrical 'réportage', figures of speech and the strange appearance of the dead are interanimated, in representations that negate both pieties and profounder meditations on the rationalization of violence.[73]

The first corpse identified in *Alamein to Zem Zem* is an anticipatory projection; an arm gingerly extended into a trench makes contact not with flesh but with discarded bedding (22). Subsequently, when Douglas's tank crushes a manned parapet, and he sees his 'first dead man', it is a soldier killed in earlier fighting, the first of a number of casualties whose dismemberment does not bare broken flesh, as if explosive had an 'instinct for decency', wrapping-up what is torn (25). The accidents of appearance extends to tanks (the noun verbally camouflaged Great War armoured vehicles as water cisterns), which are softened or made fleshly by the baggage carried on their hulls. These are motifs of the randomness of destruction and survival: standing near a tank which explodes, Douglas is not hit by hot metal but 'wrapped from head to foot in blankets' (113). Battle is a material and semiotic environment which the soldier must learn to decode, the writer to re-encode, for even the dead invite different kinds of misrecognition. One corpse, showing no signs of violence, has a literary precedent in Rimbaud's 'Le Dormeur du Val', which Douglas had translated at Oxford for *Augury*.[74] An expression of agony, rather than of peace, makes him think a body is still alive (another misleading sign of pain). This 'cleverly posed waxwork' is juxtaposed with administrative maskings of violence.[75] It is not a surprise (the 'Dormeur', on the other hand, seemed to have 'come there silently and taken up his position since our arrival'): rather it is the intended side-effect of a military plan, in pursuance of which 'these casualties had been more easily fulfilled than the condition of taking the objectives' (29, 40).

Those objectives are never articulated with grand strategy. *Alamein to Zem Zem* moves rapidly forward in space, but Douglas is

---

[73] Douglas, *Miscellany*, 121.   [74] Douglas, *Complete Poems*, 57–8.
[75] Douglas, *Alamein*, 41.

prone to linger, and retrace his path. The book's supplementary conclusion represents the exhaustion of that movement, and bodes a circling back, which receives a different interpretation in the self-reflexive 'Vergissmeinnicht'. Douglas's wounding is as important in the structure of the memoir as had been Richard Hillary's to the rhetoric of *The Last Enemy*. Injury is ironically made the consequence of an overly ingenious reading of his environment ('I had come to expect such things to be cunningly hidden'), and it is described in the terms, both surreal and misprising, which Douglas used for the 'curious dead'. Massive force is registered as stasis, as he is suspended, 'standing, numbed', by the first explosion (117–18). The signs of violence—a multiply punctured body—are reconfigured by the art of the Medical Officer: with dressings, eye-patch, remnants of uniform and scorched moustache—and ready to produce a 'traditional grin'—Douglas is an 'artistic whole'. This description of injury as an aesthetic transformation turns Douglas into an object of perception, putting him theatrically 'in the picture'. Living up to appearances—the wounded Douglas looks about in vain for 'someone from the Army Film and Photographic Unit' (120)—coincides figuratively with the cumulative effect of his descriptions of the dead. There may no logic to the chances of survival, but the rules of visual engagement with the battlefield transcend matters of life and death. Douglas's mode of depicting broken bodies parallels, in its grisly offhandedness, the disfiguring gaze of the commander, or indeed of the Army Film Unit director of 'that mediocre film "Desert Victory"', which 'gave no idea where most of [its] "action" pictures were taken', privileged to dispose units of force in a representational space (10).

The curious aspect of the dead is the evidence of an aesthetic perception which competes with other maskings of violence, especially heroic codes. Descriptions of dead bodies counterpoint personal and class romances of battle. On one level, they prefigure the wounding of the narrator, which ended the earliest draft of the book. The narrative's continuation onwards in a dilatory fashion, to victory, introduces another A–Z logic, not that of individual initiation in battle, but of the campaign's apparently relentless progress. The autobiographical frame, and an emphasis on war as a waste, is contrasted with an historical frame: the conclusion, from a strategic and political point of view, is ironic and deflating, a boast about future looting. Substituting the aesthetic for the political, Douglas's memoir displaces ideologically-, and psychologically-motivated redescription with an alternative omission. However, the forms of his representation of battle raise questions about monolithic strategic depictions which map injuring events as blows given and received by an abstract colossus. His writing vaunts a dispassion that mimes the indifference to the human subject explicit in the military-political determination of the space of battle. 'Actors waiting in the wings of Europe', in one of Douglas's last poems, are not however metonymically incorporated into the strategic colossus but people 'swallowed . . . / into the stomach of war'.[76]

Censorship impinged directly and indirectly on the representation of battle as a space created by those who use it, or are used in it (Douglas's diary was illegal). The solicitor's report on the (now lost) typescript recommended changes to the text on four counts: defamation, defence regulations, military law, and official secrecy. Description of military muddle 'might be deemed to give rise to alarm and despondency'; reference to looting was 'unfortunate, because [looting] is contrary to International Law'.[77] The account of supposedly coded radio traffic which organized the battlefield as a cricket match or foxhunt (the trope of war as sport intended here to disguise injuring-intentions from the enemy) might aid Axis forces: 'the fact that the information may already be known to the enemy is immaterial' (BBC correspondent Godfrey Talbot did succeed in publishing a transcription of military radio traffic).[78] The criticism of *Desert Victory* was a 'dangerous' accusation of public deception.[79] Alun Lewis, who was never to see combat (a telling idiom), had described the choreographed tank manoeuvres (a rationalization of the tactical space of battle) as 'the most thrilling and convincing and sobering film I've seen of war'.[80] Douglas himself was in a sealed transit camp, awaiting the Normandy invasion, when the report was submitted, and thus was not responsible for any action taken on its recommendations.[81] By the time of publication in 1946 some

---

[76] Douglas, *Complete Poems*, 117.   [77] Douglas, BL Add. MS 53773, 160r.

[78] Douglas, *Alamein*, 97–101; BL Add. MS 53773, 160r; Godfrey Talbot, *Speaking from the Desert* (Hutchinson, 1944), 60,.

[79] Douglas, *Alamein*, 10; BL Add. MS 53773, 160r.

[80] Alun Lewis (25 May 1943), *Letters to my Wife*, ed. Gweno Lewis (Bridgend: Seren Books, 1989), 352.

[81] Desmond Graham, *Keith Douglas 1920–1944: A Biography* (Oxford: Oxford University Press, 1974), 250; introduction to Keith Douglas, *Alamein to Zem Zem*, ed. Desmond Graham (Oxford: Oxford University Press, 1979), 12–13.

regulations under the Emergency Powers (Defence) Act (1939) had been revoked (others remained in place until 1959).[82]

The form of the posthumously published book, with its supplement of poems like Blunden's *Undertones of War*, was not determined by its author (Douglas thought his publisher Tambimuttu had agreed to a separate volume of poetry).[83] Critics have largely ignored this, interpreting the different media of ink drawing, prose and verse as part of a genetic, compositional process from engagement to aesthetic detachment: the poet 'attacked a certain incident . . . from various angles and in different forms'.[84] But Douglas's pencil sketches are not preliminary representations: he continued to rework them, and he prepared further illustrations for his poems on his return to England (at Tambimuttu's request), and for his narrative in March 1944.[85] The case for an art of depths is advanced by Edna Longley: Douglas's eye 'does not so much look from alternative angles, as aim at progressive penetration'.[86] Provisional would be a better term for Douglas's anatomic vision which distinguishes battle's component acts and products but does not weld them into an organic, naturalizing whole.

DAN DAVIN: INTELLIGENCE, INSUBORDINATION, AND HISTORY

Douglas's insistence on war art being posterior to experience is one of many registrations of the ethic of participation that defines the rhetoric, and the reception, of writing about the Great War: where historians give only 'certain aspects of . . . strategy and tactics . . . The nearest contacts with truth are the accounts of eye-witnesses to incidents from which a general picture can be built up'.[87] It recurs in Davin's *For the Rest of Our Lives* as the soldier's sense of superiority

---

[82] See Neil Stammers, *Civil Liberties in Britain During the 2nd World War: A Political Study* (Croom Helm, 1983), 217–18.

[83] For instance, two of the line drawings (*Alamein*, 41, 48) were rotated by the printer, turning Douglas's level ground into a slope, see BL Add. MS 53775 A.

[84] A. Banerjee, 'Keith Douglas and the Dead Soldier: An Artistic Confrontation', *The Literary Half-Yearly*, 15/1 (Jan. 1974), 91.

[85] Douglas, BL Add. MS 53775A; Graham, *Keith Douglas*, 231–2, 238.

[86] Edna Longley, *Poetry in the Wars* (Newcastle upon Tyne: Bloodaxe, 1986), 105.

[87] Guy Chapman (ed.), *Vain Glory: A Miscellany of the Great War* (Cassell, 1937), p. vii.

to war's 'audience'—correspondents who can 'have a look then go away again'.[88] Yet the officer protagonists of this novel are themselves, as often as not, excluded from the affirming bond of combat by staff postings, and employed in the description of injuring and death in war. Davin, wounded on Crete in 1941, served subsequently at GHQ, at one time sharing an office with Enoch Powell whose war verse was obsessed with the guilt of the survivor.[89] Vietnam journalist Michael Herr, distancing himself from a supine, jargon-swallowing Press Corps, noted that they got all the facts but 'never found a way to report meaningfully about death, which of course was really what it was all about'.[90] Davin's novel addresses the mutually reinforcing ideologies which redesignate and mask violence along the command structure—from the 'orgasm' of destruction to the abstractions of global strategy—and the way they intersect with the political causes which are seen to legitimate the targeting of violence against persons.

The inscription of dialogically related perspectives is the most significant device in Davin's fictionalization of the war, in which he served with the Second New Zealand Division in Greece, Crete, North Africa, and Italy. His subsequent commission, in 1947, as an official New Zealand military historian brings into play a further dimension to the problem of the multiple significations of the space of battle. But Davin had already addressed these questions about the war's means and aims in the novel he had written in 1944–5. He is ostensibly apologetic about the relationship of his fiction to the collective historical record to which he contributed.[91] Yet, in describing the disparity between the 'objective' reconstructions of historians and the incomplete knowledge of agents, he makes a strong case for the role of the narrative imagination in recovering wartime experience. 1944 saw the publication of von Neumann's and Morgenstern's *Theory of Games and Economic Behaviour*, which revealed how

---

[88] Davin, *Lives*, 96.

[89] Keith Ovenden, *A Fighting Withdrawal: The Life of Dan Davin: Writer, Soldier, Poet* (Oxford: Oxford University Press, 1996), 152; Enoch Powell, *Dancer's End and The Wedding Gift* (The Falcon Press, 1951).

[90] Michael Herr, *Dispatches* (1977. Picador, 1978), 173.

[91] See Davin, *Lives*, 5–6; preface to Dan Davin, *Crete*, Official History of New Zealand in the Second World War 1939–1945 (Wellington: War Historical Branch, Department of Internal Affairs, 1953), pp. vii–viii; introduction to Dan Davin, *The Salamander and the Fire: Collected War Stories* (Oxford: Oxford University Press, 1986), pp. vii–xvi; and introduction to Dan Davin (ed.), *Short Stories from the Second World War* (Oxford: Oxford University Press, 1982), pp. vii–xiv.

'*agents* make a fundamental difference to the complexity of the world'.[92] For Davin, manipulation of point of view, stratified by grammatical person, register and rank, could create narratives 'inward with events' and agency.[93] These devices also functioned as a mode of insubordination: the route by which the battle for Crete entered the official record involved an inversion of the executive and epistemological hierarchy of the command structure, 'a very junior and ignorant subaltern' judging men who were his superiors in the field.[94]

The writing of war fiction and war history created a conflict of loyalties (New Zealanders expected blame to be apportioned for the deaths of countrymen in the military disaster on Crete).[95] The 'historian's scruples' meant that imaginative narratives had to have 'a genuine historical framework'.[96] But 'privilege[d]' access to documentation of military operations (including General Freyberg's personal archive) might clash with the memories of fellow combatants, living and dead. Davin sought a compromise between objective and subjective points of view, a fidelity to the conditions in which judgements and actions took place which would restore the determinants of individual behaviour. The phrase with which he identifies these contexts—'truth of the facts'—is ambivalent, pointing both to a duty to the conventions of official history and to what is lost to hindsight.[97] The closure achieved in retrospection erases the contexts of past actions: 'consequences which seem to us inevitable because we know they took place were, even for those who then predicted them correctly, uncertainties of an inscrutable future'.[98] These contexts are, perhaps, imaginatively recuperable as the limits of understanding in a moment of a present crisis (a clash of interests or signs which is irreducible to 'facts and events'[99]), but this would be achieved at the cost of the interpretations that constitute the narrative of the campaign considered holistically. 'Action', writes John Keegan, 'is essentially destructive of all institutional studies': it confounds the

---

[92] Daniel C. Dennett, *Darwin's Dangerous Idea: Evolution and the Meanings of Life* (1995. Harmondsworth: Penguin, 1996), 252.

[93] Davin, *Salamander*, p. xiv.   [94] Davin, *Crete*, p. vii.

[95] Ovenden, *A Fighting Withdrawal*, 244.   [96] Davin, *Salamander*, p. xiv.

[97] See Paul Ricoeur, *History and Truth* (Evanston Ill.: Northwestern University Press, 1965), 27, on the 'historian's struggle to find a nomenclature that will allow him both to identify and to specify; this is why historical language is necessarily *equivocal*'.

[98] Davin, *Crete*, pp. vii–viii.

[99] Pierre Bourdieu, *Homo Academicus* (Cambridge: Polity, 1990), 160.

doctrines and the structures with which the military historian is concerned.[100]

Describing the German invasion of Crete in May 1941, Davin
eschewed the convention of battalion-level description. His account
would be 'intelligible' only if its form reflected the poor communica-
tion between the Companies of 22 Battalion, a factor which prevented its operation as a unit.[101] The convention of massing forces
under description (along the lines of military command structures)
had to give way to a more fine-grained description, employing
smaller units. This wariness about abstraction and convention is evident when Davin handles judgement. The category of facts, we have
seen, is problematic, nowhere more so than when the global reconstruction of the historian contradicts the interpretations with reference to which an agent behaves. The facts include both the actual
dispositions of animate and inanimate matériel, and beliefs, fears,
and self-deceptions about those dispositions. 'Many explanations in
History and the social sciences . . .', writes Geoffrey Hawthorn,
'turn not on causal connections between states of affairs . . . but on
the relevant agents' own practical reasoning . . . They are conditional, subjunctive hypotheticals, a matter of counterfactual judgement.'[102] *Post factum* analysis shows that withdrawal from positions
near the Maleme airfield was an overly pessimistic reaction; because
it prevented a counter-attack, it contributed substantially to the
eventual loss of the island. Davin, however, qualifies this view with a
psychological perspective, reintroducing human fallibility as a context of action, rather than as a yardstick of assessment. The com-
manding officer's judgement of the strength of his forces was
demonstrably incorrect, but this 'picture' constituted part of the environment to which he reacted. The battlefield's illegibility does not
stop its being read: it is full of signs that may be misinterpreted (self-
deception), or which are designedly misleading (the enemy's decep-
tions). The subjective or engaged context of the commander's
agency, although it may not have corresponded to an objective view,
and cannot be represented by it, should be invoked. In reconstructing
this picture, Davin's register shifts towards sympathetic and novelistic characterization (though, as an official historian, his gloss could

[100] John Keegan, *The Face of Battle* (Jonathan Cape, 1976), 29.
[101] Davin, *Crete*, 99.
[102] Geoffrey Hawthorn, *Plausible Worlds: Possibility and Understanding in History and the Social Sciences* (Cambridge: Cambridge University Press, 1991), 15.

also be read as a bureaucratic exculpation): 'exhausted in mind and body, he saw his situation in a blacker light than the facts warranted'.[103] Such epistemological limitations are crucial components in communicating what constituted a battle (as opposed to the meanings it accrued in a strategic or historical narrative):

> at each crisis of the battle each commander could defend the decision he took in the light of what he knew at the time; and that is basically a stronger position than that of us who criticise the decisions in the light of what we know now and support other possible courses of action in the light of what we shall never know.[104]

'To restore to the past its lost uncertainties,' wrote Hugh Trevor-Roper, before the forgery of Hitler's diaries, 'requires an effort of imagination.'[105]

The restorations attempted in *Crete* can be traced back to the treatment of problems of judgement in *Lives*, and, further, to the representation of the command structure as a network of contradictory perspectives on, and interpretations of, violence against persons, a network which generates the meanings of battle. Spender noted, in his autobiography, the development of a functional attitude amongst firefighters: 'the war no longer seemed a conflict between Germany and Britain, but simply an inter-relationship of jobs within a system.'[106] *Lives* promotes this matrix to the status of an epistemological and administrative structure which connects the work of warfare with political causes. The fog of war is reconceived as an information network, which the characters traverse in successive postings. Permitting them to 'usurp positions arbitrarily and in a fashion not legitimate to the historian', Davin addresses the problem of war's legibility from inside military structures, foregrounding limitations of judgement and interpretation.[107]

The detachment that comes with elevation in the command echelon, and distance from the front turns out to be disorientating. As Frank Fahey acquires a strategic picture his anxiety about the consequences of earlier actions and decisions in the field grows, as does the guilt of the outsider to the camaraderie of front-line troops.

---

[103] Davin, *Crete*, 116.   [104] Ibid. 463.

[105] H. R. Trevor-Roper, 'History and Imagination', in Hugh Lloyd-Jones, Valerie Pearl, and Blair Worden (eds.), *History and Imagination: Essays in Honour of H. R. Trevor-Roper* (Duckworth, 1981), 365.

[106] Stephen Spender, *World Within World* (Hamish Hamilton, 1951), 267.

[107] Davin, *Lives*, 6.

Suspended between experience and knowledge, his situation is emblematic of the gap between actuality and description, the injured body and the meanings it bears. Davin, unlike Douglas, makes politics the thematic core of his fiction (though not of *Crete*); conceptions of the outside of war (its causes, goals, and outcomes) qualify actions in its interior. The idea that war clarifies political antagonisms—'With the last enemy they would forfeit simple judgements and tangle again in peace-time's subtle mesh'—is opposed by revaluations of the distinction between war and peace, a distinction which operates ideologically to deny 'the other war that flowed on under the crust of peace' (183, 380).

Davin's handling of issues of historical representation reveals the processes by which violence is recovered as discursive order. Fahey's training as an historian, which makes him alert to alternatives, handicaps him as a field officer. While others instinctively reach 'irreversible decisions', never looking back, his will is 'weighed down with the possibilities his imagination suggested', which retrospectively 'harass' him: his redeployment as a 'soldier of bumph' gives further rein to these imaginings (54, 198). Studying the Mediterranean theatre of war—'as little amenable to the New Order as to the pax Romana'—is an atomized, academic task, further alienating him from the fraternal compensations of crisis (53). The few thousand yards between the front-line and the rear stands for the relation between action and its textual representation: an officer should not 'stay so long on the staff that figures got more meaning than men' (102). Tony Brandon, back in command of a Company, reflects that on the staff 'your responsibility was for what you thought and wrote. Here it was for what you did. There you were almost a civil servant. Here you were almost the father of a family' (322). Strategic administration reduces the quick to tabulated abstractions, 'divisions [counted] in fractions of an integer'; whereas camaraderie and the 'orgasm[ic]' high pitch of threatened existence yield value amidst carnage (256, 324).

The relationship between staff and front-line duties is an analogue of the historian's alienation from the specificity and otherness of past actions, and a microcosm of the relationship of the outside and inside of war. This heuristic possibility is enlarged upon by an alternation of points of view on combat. Brandon, convinced that without armoured support two NZ battalions are exposed to devastating counter-attack, acknowledges nevertheless that the General responsible for disposing forces has 'a better view of the whole thing' (110). That relatively Olympian and abstracted comprehension derives from an imaginative displacement or transference; intelligence reports are written from the German point of view and the enemy becomes 'the hero of our fictions' (296). Clausewitz's scepticism about the possibility of universal doctrines for the conduct of war was directed at the higher echelons: subjective factors affected command decisions but rules of action could be formulated in the tactical sphere because it was determined by physical, material, and technical factors.[108] But a thoroughgoing application of the principle that the 'nature of war is fighting' reverses this gradient: 'the soldier's view . . . will be much more complicated that the commander's'. While the latter's environment is 'comparatively stable' (especially conceptually—'large, intellectually manageable blocks of human beings'), the soldier fights in a 'wildly unstable physical and emotional environment'.[109] The distinction between the tactical and the strategic is itself dependent on the conceptual and rhetorical conventions that structure the battlefield as a text to be interpreted. Higher order pictures are a translation of violent chaos into discursive order, and that order is an object of desire throughout the command structure, from the infantryman upwards: 'This tactics is all very well, but a bloke misses his bit of strategy, even without the armchair.'[110]

These representational spaces of battle are dialectical terms in a debate about the means and ends of war, and its meanings for persons and states, which is sustained privately and publicly by Davin's committed, intellectual protagonists. Tom O'Dwyer, veteran of Spain, his father killed in the Irish Civil War, feigns neutrality only to evade capture (he plays dead): he sees the German who stands over his 'grave' as a machine, 'adaptable to any ideal's purpose', and like himself, one of the 'miserable proletariat who make the news' (129, 148). But if the Intelligence staff who supply that news are relatively immune to the crisis that makes the killer 'forget his cause' in the contentment of violence perpetrated, the apparatus that provides their understanding is not: ' "Beforehand you can get her all teed up and afterwards you can know all about it. But now, it's hopeless. . . . We know we've got the bloody ridge but. . . . It may be history already by now, Jerry history" ' (314).

---

[108] Azar Gat, *The Origins of Military Thought: From the Enlightenment to Clausewitz* (Oxford: Clarendon Press, 1989), 196.

[109] Keegan, *The Face of Battle*, 47.   [110] Davin, *Lives*, 114.

Crete seeks to make good that kind of lacuna, deliberately isolating the 'baffling and controversial' events of 20 May to 1 June 1941 from larger contexts, in order to gain 'command of the evidence'.[111] *For The Rest of Our Lives* admits no such containment, and opens up both causal and consequential horizons. The three focalizing characters are witnesses to past failures of democracy, and to the legacy of imperialism. Although confronting Rommel in a 'Gentlemen *versus* players' contest that careers to and fro across uninhabited territory, their attention remains fixed on the Soviet Front, which alone is on a 'scale worthy of the issues'.[112] The multi-perspectival registration of battle's shape and significance provides a framework for more ambitious consideration of the political and historical contexts of the war. Just as combat's meaning is not confined to the place of injuring, but is repeatedly re-encoded as it is transmitted along a network of more abstract conceptualizations, so the war is not a bounded, autonomous enterprise, but a structure of action through which political change is promoted and resisted. The North African theatre is often viewed as a side issue, a belated flourish for outmoded ideologies. But even the radical O'Dwyer is caught up in the dominant rhetoric of this anachronistically represented space, perceiving a landscape 'where no irrelevancy obscured the cause' as 'a fit arena for freedom at last to gore down fascism' (99). The absence of political co-ordinates is ironically the guarantee of the linkage of seemingly peripheral Mediterranean operations to the battle between the forces of revolution and reaction across Eastern Europe.

This relationship is given a very different treatment in Evelyn Waugh's *Sword of Honour* trilogy, a critique of the ideological consequence of resistance to Fascism. A late arrival on Crete with the Commando relief force—he was brought in on the *Abdiel*, which evacuated the wounded Davin—Waugh defensively rationalized his own military conduct in an illegal diary, which contains the germ of Guy Crouchback's disillusionment with Ivor Claire's desertion.[113] The shambolic evacuation symbolizes the treachery of the alliance with Stalin, Britain's 'blundering into dishonour'.[114] The debacle is also represented as the discrepancy between the blandishments of a

---

[111] Davin, *Crete*, p. vii.   [112] Davin, *Lives*, 8, 59, 148.

[113] Evelyn Waugh, *The Diaries of Evelyn Waugh*, ed. Michael Davie (Weidenfeld and Nicolson, 1976), 509; Martin Stannard, *Evelyn Waugh: No Abiding City 1939–1966* (Dent, 1992), 38.

[114] Evelyn Waugh, *The Sword of Honour Trilogy* (Harmondsworth: Penguin, 1987), 383.

future regimental history—'further encouragement was given to the hard-pressed garrison'—and the shameless desperation of men awaiting evacuation.[115] The evasions and vacuity of the putative official narrative function as a yardstick for the political acuity Waugh claims for his fiction. Puns on 'in the picture', the Army's way of saying you know where you are and what you are doing, underline Waugh's contention that military activity is an illusion fostered by military language.[116]

Davin's novel is no less sceptical about the gloss that such descriptions place on the political efficacy of organized violence; the war will last '"for the rest of our lives"'[117] The Marxist novelist Jack Lindsay's *Beyond Terror* (1943) also pointed to the contradictions of a war in defence of a democracy which had amounted to 'means test, bugs, slums, hoodlums'. But its conclusion, affirming fighting 'with an awareness of the issues', gives way to the quasi-Paterian private consummation of life lived at 'that centre' of violence, a consummation which is independent of the reality of the 'after-struggle and achievement' of political ideals.[118] Davin's characters are less compromising in their understanding of what war will achieve, and of the cost it involves; the novel returns almost obsessively to contradictions and will not resolve them. It is where the book fails as a dramatization of war—the action regularly stalled by the protagonists' cerebral lectures—that it is most insightful about the structure of war. O'Dwyer's Comintern logic ('"You get freedom at the end of a fight; not during it"') is pitched against Brandon's Orwellian left-individualism ('"my personal war aim, the right to be wrong"').[119] The Catholic Fahey perceives his own voluntary courage as a line of least resistance, a betrayal of both his faith and his ethical socialism (182-3). The relation of the individual to the war is not decided, either by the necessity of historical process or by competing conceptions of the integrity of the self. Nor can a more conventionally heroic act, when O'Dwyer baffles the blast of a mine with his body, resolve the contradictions of killing or dying for a state's self-description. The fate of the bodies of individuals is conditional on

[115] Ibid. 325.

[116] In November 1939, Waugh, *Diaries*, 448-9, wrote witheringly: 'They are saying, "The generals learned their lesson in the last war. There are going to be no wholesale slaughters." I ask, how is victory possible except by wholesale slaughters?'

[117] Davin, *Lives*, 397.

[118] Jack Lindsay, *Beyond Terror: A Novel of the Battle of Crete* (Andrew Dakers, 1943), 162, 311.   [119] Davin, *Lives*, 164, 178.

the fugitive meanings generated by the military's higher echelons. Interpreting communiqués from the Pacific, Frank struggles with ambiguity and indirection, reducing 'reticences, corruptions and abbreviations to intelligibility', and expanding on 'cryptic laconism' (213). With Rommel threatening the Nile cities the Allied war effort gives the appearance of a 'house of index cards', power on paper (208). The textual determinants of the administrative perspective on conflict are paralleled in the memorial reinscription of the pain experienced by combatants. Memory softens experience—'fear and anxiety and haste and exhaustion . . . would be recalled only as excitement'—and pain becomes invisible in public restorations of war's nobility and rationality at some future date 'when wounds and death would reassemble about themselves their heroic overtones and hide the bursting droop of bowels' (124). The environment itself attests to the mutability of war's dematerialized bodily content. Sand preserves 'at the wind's whim some record of the battle', though an Ozymandian ironic permanence is evident in the wreckage of vehicles and the classic iconography of the desert grave, a 'rough cairn of stones . . . an upended rifle, a helmet' (123, 329). But these signs are duplicitous. Over the grave of one of his men, Brandon reflects that there was 'nothing to show that these same emblems stood for all that was alien to his nature, violence, intolerance, and death, until in the end he had taken up against them with their own weapons' (329–30). The memorial speaks to the future, but not of what is past.

'The memory of war is already beginning to pass away,' wrote the novelist Douglas Grant in 1948, 'and we must be reminded to honour those upon whose bravery our safety depended. The maps, biographies, and monographs are mere formalities, and we would wave them aside to read the true historians of our time.'[120] Davin, by working through the implications of this distinction, captured the transience of bodily effort and suffering as it is relayed through the textual and iconographic forms of military intelligence. The true historian required insights into both dimensions of war. L. P. Hartley, in a broadcast review of *Lives*, said that to 'criticise the book . . . for incompleteness of vision its to criticise war itself'.[121] But to excuse the

---

[120] Douglas Grant, 'War and the Writer', *Penguin Parade*, 2nd ser. 3 (Harmondsworth: Penguin, 1948), 68. His combat novel *The Fuel of the Fire* (Cresset Press, 1950) is striking for its handling of the disjunctive identity of the militarised civilian in relation to historical time and private memory.

[121] Quoted in Ovenden, *A Fighting Withdrawal*, 221.

novel as a casualty of war is to miss the way that its failure to digest its arguments (its anatomy of war's semiotic sinews) is also its success. *Lives* transgresses what for Hartley appears a limit of discourse about war, namely 'to criticise war itself', by enunciating its component symbolic as well as material acts. Incompleteness of vision is a charge frequently weighed against wartime writing by those who take hindsight to be an unalloyed benefit (Douglas amongst them). But in their several approaches to representing the war in North Africa and the Mediterranean, Douglas and Davin, the poet and the historian, converged on a significant appreciation of the conditions of the vision permitted to participants in battle. It was not simply a matter of where you stood geographically, temporally, or hierarchically. However much one was in the picture, those pictures, or more accurately the discourses which underpinned their construction, were determinants of social reality.

5

War Aims and Outcomes

PEOPLE'S WAR, PEOPLE'S PEACE

THE culture of wartime Britain seems to invite interpretation by analogy, the Blitz an 'objective correlative' for mental states, 'the private imagination' and domestic Britain 'similarly invaded, dismantled and displaced'.[1] Wartime discourse was itself rife with relational figures, notably 'the seductive analogy between what could be done in war and therefore what could be done in peace'.[2] 'If you could produce planes you could produce houses', declared Paul Rotha's documentary *The Land of Promise* (1945).[3] But taking these equivalences as heuristic guides it is possible to overlook the way analogy functioned as substitution.

War aims are among the most potent, but also unstable, substitutions of all. Pious or idealizing wish-lists, they justify killing and acquire seriousness and solemnity from the fact that killing is going on. War aims draw attention away from the activities of injuring which occur in war's interior, but they can also be substituted for one another (as justifications of the Second World War have been revised between 1939 and the present). The emergence of domestic as opposed to international war aims is one basis of the influential story that Britain's war was about social reconstruction. The relationship between Home Front and global war was played out in the discursive elaboration and containment of war aims. Specifying war aims remained a problem for government and intellectuals, but not even the Prime Minister could put an end to the speculative conversation over what the war's violence might be exchanged for.

Broadcasting on 1 October 1939, Churchill, then First Lord of the Admiralty, identified the purpose of the war as the defence of the

---

[1] Stuart Sillars, *British Romantic Art and the Second World War* (Macmillan, 1991), 15; Adam Piette, *Imagination at War* (Macmillan, 1995), 7.

[2] Corelli Barnett, *The Audit of War: The Illusion and Reality of Britain as a Great Nation* (Macmillan, 1986), 49.

[3] Nicholas Pronay in K.R.M. Short (ed.), *Film and Radio Propaganda in World War II* (Croom Helm, 1983), 67–8.

principle of sovereignty: 'To redeem Europe from the perpetual and recurring fear of German aggression, and enable the peoples of Europe to preserve their independence and their liberties.'[4] Although keen to imagine how later generations would narrate the present struggle, Churchill was reluctant to commit his administration to post-war policy or expenditure: 'Let those who say they do not know what they are fighting for stop fighting and they will see.'[5] Isaiah Berlin, echoing Churchill's cadences, observed that Churchill saved the future by interpreting the present in terms of a vision of the past.[6] As Prime Minister, he suppressed the MOI War Aims Committee's views on maintaining wartime controls for the post-war redistribution of wealth, arguing that vague aims would disappoint people, precise ones compromise future policy.[7] It was Roosevelt, president of the still non-belligerent United States, who pressed for a statement of Britain's international war aims in the form of the Atlantic Charter, a document of persuasion which became the basis for the United Nations Declaration of 1942 (its signatories were declaring war on Germany). But if Churchill was a reluctant inventor of war aims, this only created a vacuum others rushed to fill.

It was a commonplace that fighting Hitler was changing Britain and Britons. If they were not becoming more like the enemy, they felt they were less like their old selves. The economist Alan Milward notes that 'the strategic aim of defence against an enemy is not served if the demands on the economy change society and the political system so much that it is no longer the same as the one originally to be defended'.[8] But a significant fraction of the makers of wartime print, radiophonic, and cinematic culture interpreted the exigencies of Total War, as they were played out through British institutions, as an opportunity for change. War aims were reconceived as the accomplishment of social reconstruction: 'The new Britain is the country we are fighting for.'[9] That many could envisage social progress only by an 'extrapolation of the character of a society in wartime' was a

---

[4] Quoted in Asa Briggs, *War of Words* (Oxford: Oxford University Press, 1970), 118.

[5] Quoted in Kevin Jeffreys (ed.), *War and Reform: British Politics During the Second World War* (Manchester: Manchester University Press, 1994), 90.

[6] Isaiah Berlin, 'Winston Churchill in 1940', *Personal Impressions* (Hogarth Press, 1980), 16.

[7] Harold Nicolson, *Diaries and Letters*, ed. Nigel Nicolson, 3 vols. (Collins, 1966–8), ii. 139.

[8] Alan Milward, *War, Economy and Society: 1939–1945* (1977. Harmondsworth: Penguin, 1987), 21.   [9] Quoted in Barnett, *Audit*, 22

matter of regret to Michael Oakeshott in 1949, for its unity was artificial, its purpose narrow, and its guidance blind.[10] Nevertheless, the perception of social change, and the interpretation of perceived or imagined change as the justification of the war, were of far-reaching consequence.

A 'People's War', fought by and for the masses, always had a conditional component, namely the unrealized connection between means and ends, those who paid and those who were to gain, and this was not lost on contemporaries (who, like Churchill, might remember the broken promises to veterans of the Lloyd George administration). Distrust of the meanings grafted onto mass participation originated in wartime reaction: 'now every government uproots and enslaves its own people *during* a war. . . . This is total war.'[11] Scepticism about the People's War as a socio-political description is now normal: the concept was 'constructed . . . for patriotic purposes'.[12] But, ironically, the People's War gained rather than lost historical authority when used as the title of Calder's 1969 debunking of 'mythical versions of the war', in particular the idea that society was swept 'on to a new course'.[13] Twenty years on, and armed with 'post-structuralist' suspicion about the narratives which had, despite his intentions, been read as 'confirming the Myth', Calder sought to correct misreadings. In *The Myth of the Blitz* he argued that fictive or pre-scripted apprehensions of the war diverted attention from the necessity of radical social change (the Left's version of the war would 'encapsulate a moment of conservatism as a moment of revolution'). Furthermore, the legend of Britain standing alone compromised the nation's understanding of its relation to the movements of twentieth-century history.[14] More recently, Calder has concluded that talk in the 1940s of wartime social revolution 'seems ludicrously inappropriate' in hindsight.[15] Historians are now aware that sources for a 'wartime consensus' are part of the consensus-creating process,

[10] Michael Oakeshott, 'The Universities', in *The Voice of Liberal Learning*, ed. Timothy Fuller (New Haven: Yale University Press, 1989), 116.

[11] Osbert Sitwell, 'Letter to My Son', *Horizon*, 7/39 (March 1943), 170.

[12] Harold Smith (ed.), *Britain and the Second World War: A Social History* (Manchester: Manchester University Press, 1996), 2.

[13] Angus Calder, *The People's War: Britain 1939–1945* (Jonathan Cape, 1969), 15, 17.

[14] Angus Calder, The *Myth of the Blitz* (Jonathan Cape, 1991), 1, 15.

[15] Angus Calder, in I.C.B. Dear (ed.), *The Oxford Companion to the Second World War* (Oxford: Oxford University Press, 1995), 1137.

'agencies for promoting a certain frame of citizen mind'.[16] If a
'"people's war" was first called for by name in *Tribune* on 31 May
1940', it was already being touted within a week of the outbreak of
war in an MOI memorandum to the Home Office on 'The Preservation of Civilian Morale':

> The people should be told this is a civilians' war, or a People's War, and
> therefore that they are to be taken into the Government's confidence as never
> before. . . . But what is truth? We must adopt a pragmatic definition. It is
> what is believed to be the truth. A lie that is put across becomes the truth and
> may, therefore, be justified. The difficulty is to keep up lying. . . . It is simpler
> to tell the truth and, if a sufficient emergency arises, to tell one big, thump-
> ing lie that will then be believed.[17]

Rallying to a People's War meant consenting to increasingly centralized social and economic direction, not to the revolutionary overthrow of authority. For Ambrose Silk, in *Put Out More Flags*, the
phrases 'people's war, total war' were just alternative verbal categories in others' conversations about the kind of war it was going
to be: 'war of nerves, war of propaganda, war of defence in depth,
war of movement . . .'[18] To Waugh, a People's War was anathema.
Charles Ryder makes his callow subaltern Hooper the figure of the
coming age: 'whenever I read some public utterance proclaiming
what Youth demanded in the Future and what the world owed to
Youth, I would test these general statements by substituting
"Hooper". . . . "Hooper Rallies", . . . "International Hooper Co-
operation".' Achieving this future, Waugh darkly and melodramat-
ically hints, involves learning 'a thing or two', like eugenic policies,
from Hitler.[19] Germans had originated one kind of total war, war of
'complete ruthlessness'.[20] In *Put Out More Flags*, a bespectacled girl
from the LSE believes in the combination of sanctionless conflict and
insurrectionary populism, 'a People's Total War'.[21] In fact the two

[16] Jose Harris, 'War and Social History: Britain and the Home Front during the Second
World War', *Contemporary European History*, 1/1 (March 1992), 20.

[17] D. R. Costello, '"Searchlight Books" and the quest for a "People's War", 1941–1942',
Journal of Contemporary History, 24 (1989), 274 n. 3; Ian McLaine, *Ministry of Morale:
Home Front Morale and the Ministry of Information in World War II* (George Allen and
Unwin, 1979), 28.

[18] Evelyn Waugh, *Put Out More Flags* (Chapman and Hall, 1942), 86.

[19] Evelyn Waugh, *Brideshead Revisited: The Sacred and Profane Memories of Captain
Charles Ryder* (Chapman and Hall, 1945), 13, 8.

[20] Robert Graves and Alan Hodge, *The Long Week-End: A Social History of Great
Britain, 1918–1939* (Faber, 1940), 13.   [21] Waugh, *Flags*, 48.

phrases did converge, but in a way that dulled their radical implications. As synonyms, they indicated merely the involvement of the
whole population, omitting reference to what they were doing, or
what was or might be done to them. A complex trading of power between government and populace, and between classes, was simplified
in the utopias and dystopias of planning pastoral, the imaginative
projection of the next world, as compulsive a fantasy in wartime culture as the next war had been in the 1930s.

The Army Bureau of Current Affairs led by W. E. Williams (previ-
ously in charge of the Workers' Education Association (WEA) and
the *Penguin Specials* series) was criticized from the Right because 'the
teaching of war aims . . . had become the indoctrination of peace
aims'.[22] These post-war goals were widely discussed, *Picture Post*
(encouraged with an advantageous paper ration) issuing its 'Plan for
Britain' in January 1941 as 'an essential part of our war aims'.[23] But
as often their content was left vague. *The People's History of the
Second World War* claimed that knowledge of its pages was 'of prime
importance if we would build, not a New Order after Hitler's
pattern, but a happier, brighter world'.[24] The director of the Con-
federation of British Employers grumbled that 'we did not start this
war with Germany in order to improve our social services', but as
Evelyn Waugh's Ian Kilbannock drunkenly reveals, this spin on hostilities was also the white propagandists' conception of victory in the
morale war: '"This is a People's War". . . . "We want heroes of the
people, to or for the people, by, with and from the people".'[25]

Michael Balfour defines propaganda as 'inducing people to leap to
conclusions'.[26] It is one dimension of the verbal substitution of ends
for means, of what violence is said to purchase or substantiate for
violence itself. Peace aims replace war aims not in the wake of the
cessation of hostilities, but in their midst (leaping to conclusions is
structurally integral to the activity of interpreting war as rational
social and political activity). In Britain in the early 1940s these ideals

---

[22] Steven Fielding, Peter Thompson, and Nick Tiratsoo, *'England Arise!': The Labour
Party and Popular Politics in 1940s Britain* (Manchester: Manchester University Press,
1995), 28.   [23] Barnett, *Audit*, 22.

[24] *The People's History of the Second World War: September 1939–December 1940*, ed.
Harold Wheeler (Odham's Press, n.d.), foreword.

[25] Quoted in Nicholas Timmins, *The Five Giants* (1995, Fontana, 1996), 39; Evelyn
Waugh, *The Sword of Honour Trilogy* (1984. Harmodsworth: Penguin, 1987), 271.

[26] Michael Balfour, *Propaganda in War 1939–1945: Organizations, Policies, and Publics
in Britain and Germany* (Routledge & Kegan Paul, 1979), 421.

were bound up with a rhetoric of omission and of the substitution of benign effects for flesh-breaking causes. As hostilities were prolonged, the 'image of the main outline of the war gets a bit blurred and other ideological wars are set up in the mind'.[27] The ideal that warlike behaviour be continued when war had ceased characterized war positively, as a form of social co-existence. Priestley, in *Out of the People*, celebrated a Britain 'being bombed and burned into democracy'.[28]

If popular participation deserved a people's peace, in another sense, the People's War conflated or confused means and ends by making the outcome a projection of that participation. This emphasis on the Home Front (truly a redescriptive one) has usually been interpreted as evidence of the continuation of party politics or of ideological struggles within the agencies of propaganda, but it also reflects non-partisan habits of thought and language in wartime. The impact of these domestic figures for war on the discourse of military behaviour was significant. This is especially evident in relation to the experience of the British Army, garrisoned and unemployed far from city and factory, the sites of heroic civilian resistance and production.

'Exiles in khaki, an army in occupation of their own country.'[29]

Between the wars, the Army was 'a Cinderella of the forces'.[30] Foreign and economic policy (in accordance with military theory) concentrated resources on the modernization of the bomber arm of the Air Force. Planners neglected both the development of armour and a Continental role for the Army. This lowly status was reflected culturally. 'The very last thing he wanted to be in was the infantry. It was a force that invited death and every imaginable kind of discomfort. Post-war literature had left its mark on his outlook.'[31] The unofficial wartime laureate of the cinderella army was Julian

---

[27] Inez Holden, 'Fellow Travellers in a Factory', *Horizon*, 3/14 (Feb. 1941), 121.

[28] Quoted in Angus Calder, *People's War*, 163.

[29] Keith Vaughan, 'Exiles in Khaki', in Denys Val Baker (ed.) *Little Reviews Anthology* (George Allen and Unwin, 1943), 27.

[30] Quoted in Brian Bond, 'The Army Between the Two World Wars', in David Chandler (ed.), *The Oxford Illustrated History of the British Army* (Oxford: Oxford University Press, 1994), 272.

[31] Geoffrey Cotterell, *Then a Soldier* (Eyre and Spottiswoode, 1944), 44.

Maclaren-Ross, who remembered service as his 'Brown Period': browned-off 'Brown Jobs' were perpetually punished for shirking uninterrupted and objectless labour.[32]

After the reversals of 1940 (Norway and Flanders) and 1941 (Greece and Crete) the Army, barring its largely Imperial and Dominion force in North Africa, was confined to garrison duties in Britain and India. The establishment of the Combined Chiefs of Staff after Pearl Harbour prioritized the defeat of Hitler, and the January 1943 Casablanca doctrine of 'unconditional surrender' necessitated a land campaign in Northern Europe (long demanded by the Soviets). But until the summer of 1944, the war against Germany in the west was pursued in the skies, in the Atlantic, around the Mediterranean littoral, and in the factories of Britain and America. After the fall of France, a contemporary Army history noted that 'the term "Home Front", which had long been used figuratively, became a stern reality', a transfer of symbolic capital from military offence to civil defence. 1941–42 'the bulk of the British Army saw no active service of any sort' and its story remained 'uneventful' up to the summer of 1943.[33] A fictional serviceman on leave during the Blitz is told 'it must be funny for a soldier to come home to war', reversing one of the fundamental oppositions in Great War writing, but at the same time updating its theme of frustrated military identities.[34] Robert Graves, one of the generation who had longed for a posting to the Western Front, wrote in late 1941 that 'the British Army has not yet been engaged on a grand scale with the enemy; and despite official reassurances may never be'.[35]

Tom Wintringham's *New Ways of War* were 'guerilla methods' with 'revolutionary implications'.[36] These tactics were the basis of the International Brigade veteran's privately-backed training establishment for the then Local Defence Volunteers (later the Home Guard) formed in May 1940 when Anthony Eden broadcast for recruits.[37] But despite the republican precedents—'near a million British working men now have rifles in their bedrooms and don't in the least wish to give them up'—and the images of civilians taking on the Wehrmacht in films like *Went the Day Well?*, the new way of war

[32] Maclaren-Ross, *Memoirs*, 85. Gunner Edgington, in Spike Milligan, *Mussolini: His Part in My Downfall* (Michael Joseph, 1978), 122, sings 'Its a Brown World without you'.
[33] F. Yeats-Brown and E. W. Sheppard, *Britain at War: The Army* 5 vols. (London: Hutchinson, 1941–7), i. 190; ii. 252; iii. 228.   [34] Cotterell, *Then a Soldier*, 152.
[35] Graves, 'War Poetry in this War', *The Listener*, 26/667 (23 Oct. 1941), 566.
[36] Orwell, *CEJL* ii. 152.   [37] Angus Calder, *People's War*, 138.

was really a prolonged *attente*.[38] Alun Lewis's *Raiders' Dawn* was published in 1942 with the slogan 'The War Poet has arrived at last', but the author's note located him in the 'Home Forces'.[39] In Lewis's stories, frustration at the unconnectedness of military service with either anti-Nazi or pro-democratic ideals is registered in the protest of volunteers at useless regimentation. The hero of 'Flick' has escaped from occupied France, sabotaging German installations *en route*, only to become a 'peace-time soldier'.[40] A Spanish Civil War veteran in 'Private Jones' has to put up with drill and 'talk in the papers about fighting for freedom and decency and our children's futures'.[41] Clive Branson, a real veteran of Spain, wrote from India that '*we want to get on with the job*': the 'people's war against Fascism' was breaking down into enmity between commanders and the troops, just as Sassoon had relocated conflict in Flanders to adversarial relations between staff and private soldiers.[42]

The Great War shadowed Britain's Second World War in other ways, not least in the revived careers of some of its writers (and propagandists). Major Sir John Hay Beith, director of public relations at the War Office, was better known to a literary public as Ian Hay, author in 1915 of *The First Hundred Thousand*.[43] Henry Williamson, who described that book as 'about the battle of Loos but nothing like it', had debunked Hay's vision of the Army's making of men in a bleak narrative of disillusionment and mutilation, *The Patriot's Progress* (1930).[44] Having located the meaning of Dunkirk in a future when the event would 'fall into its true perspective', Hay would draw a firm contrast between the hurried preparations of Kitchener's army and the professional training of the 1940s' infantryman.[45] Graves told Alun Lewis, eager to start an Army paper, to 'be glad the Army has no *Horizon*. The egregious Ian Hay

[38] Orwell, *CEJL* ii. 152.

[39] Michael Shelden, *Friends of Promise: Cyril Connolly and the World of Horizon* (1989. Minerva, 1990), 68.

[40] Alun Lewis, *The Last Inspection* (George Allen and Unwin, 1942), 16–17.

[41] Ibid. 32.

[42] Clive Branson, *British Soldier in India: The Letters of Clive Branson* (The Communist Party, 1945), 12–13.

[43] See Phillip Knightley, *The First Casualty: From the Crimea to Vietnam: The War Correspondent as Hero, Propagandist, and Myth Maker* (New York: Harcourt Brace Jovanovich, 1975), 222.

[44] Henry Williamson, *Love and the Loveless: A Soldier's Tale* (1958. Rev. edn. Panther, 1963), 281.

[45] Ian Hay, 'Foreword: Perspective in Wartime", *The Battle of Flanders 1940* (HMSO, 1941); *Arms and the Men* (HMSO, 1950), 147–8, 158–61.

would edit it, for a certainty.'[46] Henry Williamson, by contrast, remained an outsider, his manifold and contradictory response to Great War violence and policy having evolved into Fascist sympathies. Unlike a number of prominent Britons attracted by the charisma and ideologies of Mussolini, and less frequently, Hitler, Williamson's identifications survived the outbreak of war. Hitler, to whom he compared his other war hero T. E. Lawrence, was 'the only true pacifist in Europe'.[47] In the autobiographical novel-sequence *A Chronicle of Ancient Sunlight* wartime Britian is dramatized in the exclusion and persecution of the veteran Phillip Maddison, arrested under Regulation 18B of the Defence of the Realm Act in *A Solitary War* (1966). Williamson, who had painted the insignia of the British Union of Fascists on the wall of his cottage, was himself questioned during a weekend in the cells of Wells Police Station.[48]

The passage from civilian to uniformed status displaced rites of battle as an archetype of military initiation in Second World War writing. Charles Ryder describes his service as a 'domestic tragedy'.[49] Brideshead is destroyed not by the enemy, but by the British Army (The Brains Trust's C. E. M. Joad complained about military destruction of the countryside, and the threat of war games to English nature is central to two 1944 films, *A Canterbury Tale* and *Tawny Pipit*).[50] Waugh, and Anthony Powell, further cemented the iconography of the frustrated soldier in perpetual training in their post-war novels *Men at Arms* (1952) and *The Valley of Bones* (1964). But Maclaren-Ross's episodes of garrison life in *The Stuff to Give the*

[46] Alun Lewis, *Alun Lewis: A Miscellany of his Writings*, ed. J. Pikoulis (Bridgend: Poetry Wales Press, 1982), 139.

[47] Williamson claimed that Lawrence would have been the hope of European ex-servicemen, restoring 'the spirit of Christmas Day, 1914', quoted in Richard Griffiths, *Fellow Travellers of the Right: British Enthusiasts for Nazi Germany 1933–39* (1980. Oxford: Oxford University Press, 1983), 135–6. The authors of three of the most outspoken attacks on Great War and post-war England from the perspective of the civilian soldier also wrote biographies of Lawrence. Robert Graves was authorized by Lawrence, as an act of charity, to put together *Lawrence and the Arabs* (1927), Richard Aldington wrote the iconoclastic *Lawrence of Arabia* (1955) and Williamson contributed *Genius of Friendship: 'T. E. Lawrence'* (1941). The best-known critic of British and imperial military policy in the Great War, B. H. Liddell Hart, published *'T. E. Lawrence': In Arabia and After* in 1934.

[48] Anne Williamson, *Henry Williamson: Tarka and the Last Romantic* (Stroud: Alan Sutton, 1995), 233, but see A. W. Brian Simpson, *In the Highest Degree Odious: Detention Without Trial in Wartime Britain* (Oxford: Clarendon Press, 1992), 216.

[49] Evelyn Waugh, *Brideshead Revisited* (Chapman and Hall, 1945), 9.

[50] C. E. M. Joad, 'The Face of England: How it has been Ravaged and How it May be Preserved', *Horizon*, 5/29 (May 1942), 335–48.

Troops (1944) are the classic accounts of the conscript's victimization by the military. These stories negate the ideal of the soldier's
transcendence of the everyday, which is made explicit in bellicose accounts of service life like Gerald Kersh's *They Die with Their Boots
Clean* (1941), a narrative structured according to an industrial model
of production—'The Raw Materials', 'The Foundry', 'The Temper-
ing', 'The Finished Product'.[51] Maclaren-Ross's recruits are not
remade in the image of a technocratic institution, like Lawrence's airmen in the later parts of *The Mint*, but are trivially undone by a system whose irrational procedures seem to lack any purpose but their
own manifestation and elaboration, regimes of perpetual penality
that remind us of Foucault's history of the 'docile body'.

Many writers drew analogies between the soldier and the prisoner
or 'undesirable alien'.[52] Experience of the Army contradicted
People's War ideals and was used to challenge its ideology. Although
Lewis argued in his Battalion magazine that 'the army was only a
passing phase and . . . we were still free men under our khaki', in his
story 'It's a Long Way to Go', a school teacher's 'constant active fight
for a better world' is defeated by 'endless waiting'.[53] He transferred
back to teaching with the Brigade Education Staff (the Army Bureau
of Current Affairs, founded in June 1941, used regimental officers)
only to run up against Army attempts 'to silence true patriotic criticism'.[54] Resistance lay in a wartime literary career—a writer could
'get a lot of publicity if . . . victimised'—but the citizen-soldier-
writer's ability to connect what grand strategy and disciplinary tactics put asunder remained conditional.[55]

The identity of the civilian-soldier was a culturally contested
one. Gerald Kersh lambasted 'the intellectual footslogger-faute-
de-mieux' for misrepresenting the 'normal man in strange circumstances'. Effete successors to the revolutionary poets of the trenches
were travestying the hostilities-only soldier as someone who

wants to revolt, snarls at discipline, goes mad, stabs sergeants, deserts, is a
coward, bullies his inferiors, crawls to his N.C.O.s, truckles to his officers,
has a friendly regard for his enemy, fears that he may kill a Beethoven in a

---

[51] Compare T. E. Lawrence's part-titles for *The Mint*: 'The Raw Material', 'In the Mill'
and 'Service'.

[52] See 'A Private', 'War Symposium—iii: Ours Not to Reason Why', *Horizon*, 3/15
(March 1941), 179.

[53] Alun Lewis, *Letters*, 78 (5 Dec. 1940); *Last Inspection*, 56–7.

[54] John Pikoulis, *Alun Lewis: A Life* (Bridgend: Poetry Wales Press, 1984), 120.

[55] Alun Lewis, *Letters*, 118 (10 March 1941).

bayonet-charge, listens to birds singing all day long, commits suicide, and wants to go unwashed.[56]

Maclaren-Ross and Alun Lewis are implicitly included with the editors—Denys Val Baker (*Little Reviews Anthology*), Stefan 'Szymanski' (sic), Tambimuttu (*Poetry London*) and Reginald Moore (*Bugle Blast*, with Jack Aistrop)—arraigned by Kersh for this liberal–bohemian propaganda. At the other extreme was Koestler's 'thoughtful corporal' imagined browsing in the YMCA library or a Smith's bookstall and planning to 'write a short story on army life for *Tribune* or *New Writing*'.[57]

Representations of the literate infantryman reflected educational reforms, the demography of a conscript as opposed to a regular army, and a desire to draw the military into the reconstructionist orbit. The army certainly needed to modernize quickly, but revolution in the forces—'doing away with the predominance of a single class and introducing a less mechanical form of discipline'—was, as Orwell put it in 1939, unthinkable while the aim was to 'stop Hitler'.[58] In *The Life and Death of Colonel Blimp* (1943)—which Churchill attempted to suppress as 'propaganda detrimental to the morale of the Army'—the ruthless means to victory lies in the initiative of subalterns who rescript a military exercise by seizing the institutions of an antediluvian cadre.[59] The Army was perceived as counter-revolutionary, undoing national unity (the cancelling of social difference) by making 'as many officers in a month as the public schools turn out schoolboys by the year'. While classes were 'liquefying and uniting', OCTU (Officer Corps Training Unit) recreated outmoded conceptions of social authority and deference, a divergence that generated class antagonism in the Forces: '*In the "People's Army" of today officership is no longer a responsibility: it is a privilege.*'[60]

This configuration of the residual and emergent ideologies that determined the imagined role of the subaltern captures Alun Lewis's conception of his predicament, marked off but not empowered.

[56] Gerald Kersh, *Clean, Bright and Slightly Oiled* (Heinemann, 1946), 20–1.
[57] Quoted in Bernard Bergonzi, *Wartime and Aftermath: English Literature and its Background 1939–1960* (Oxford: Oxford University Press, 1993), 20.
[58] Orwell, 'Democracy in the British Army', *CEJL*, i. 403–4.
[59] *The Life and Death of Colonel Blimp*, dir. Michael Powell and Emeric Pressburger (1943); Paul Addison, *Churchill on the Home Front 1900–1955* (1992. Pimlico, 1993), 350–1.
[60] Anon., 'War Symposium—v: The Creation of a Class', *Horizon*, 4/21 (Sept. 1941), 170, 167.

Once commissioned he lost more than a perspective: 'now there is no anonymity . . . no privacy now. . . . all my fine ideas for improving the army vanished.'[61] T. E. Lawrence, looking for a subject which was 'smaller' than the Arab Revolt, had persuaded the then Sir Hugh Trenchard to get him into the ranks of the RAF: 'the best place to see a thing from is the ground. It wouldn't "write" from the officer level.'[62] Owen, of course, had written it from that level as an 'improver', a leader of and pleader for his men (Lewis would claim that war 'has become an integral part of his [own] life experience, not a violent thought-slaying wound as it was to Owen').[63] Lewis was after a 'completer understanding of the World War' than that of the poets of the 1914–18 war, but his idea of the obstacles to this may surprise us: 'the problem is, I think, a new one—to be in the Army and to write.'[64] That is, to negotiate the glories and servitude of military life, and their connection to political and private futures, while it was all going on (this determination itself a measure of the frustration of anticipated roles).

In the wake of Dunkirk, 2nd Lt Goronwy Rees, onetime assistant editor at *The Spectator*, and recently posted from a Sandhurst OCTU to Sassoon's and Graves's Royal Welch Fusiliers, usurped the editorial pages of *Horizon*, where Connolly had loftily advised artists to ignore the war. That advice was irresponsible, wrote Rees:

the soldier has the right, in return for his blood and his life and his despair, for the crimes he must take on himself, to ask that those most qualified, by their sensibility, by their more lucid perception of values, by their release from belligerence, should comprehend, analyse, illuminate, commemorate, his sacrifice and his suffering and the horror to which he is condemned, to understand and reveal that even in war he is a human being and not a brute too ignoble for the artist's notice.[65]

The values he 'dimly feels' he is defending are the ones without which art, and *Horizon*, cannot survive, so artists should reciprocate by acting as the voice of soldiers. Most of the sacrifices Rees enumerates were, in his case, anticipatory: he spent his war in Intelligence (he worked on the disastrous Dieppe raid of August 1942, performed to

[61] Alun Lewis, *Letters*, 181 (Dec. 1941).

[62] T. E. Lawrence, *The Letters of T. E. Lawrence*, ed. Malcolm Brown (Oxford: Oxford University Press, 1991), 192, 209.   [63] Alun Lewis, *Miscellany*, 116.

[64] Alun Lewis, *Raiders' Dawn and Other Poems* (George Allen and Unwin, 1942), dust jacket; *Letters*, 101 (21 Jan. 1941).

[65] Goronwy Rees, 'Letter from a Soldier', *Horizon*, 1/7 (July 1940), 468, and see *A Chapter of Accidents* (Chatto & Windus, 1971), 151.

satisfy calls for a Second Front, and on the planning of the Normandy landings). His memoirs are ambivalent about stepping imaginatively into soldiers's boots: intelligence work induced 'an
almost animal sensitivity' to the risks to which others were exposed,
but the detachment of the role meant you could assess the accuracy
of projections, and close files: 'the evidence is before you in the shape
of bodies spreadeagled on beaches or wire.'[66]

Rees's appeal for representation, in particular for an aesthetic redemption of the soldier who bears the guilt of breaking sanctions
against killing which do not apply to the conduct of the state, was
also ambiguous, calling for a recognition of war's brutality and for
its omission in analysis and commemoration: 'not one more squalid
incident in the interminable suicide of humanity, but tragic and terrible birth'.[67] The pacifist Alex Comfort argued that writers should
not take the soldier's view, or they risked colluding with the bureaucratic indifference that determined the soldier's fate on the battlefield:

The writer must come to grips with him [the enemy soldier] factually, unless
he is to adopt the expedient of seeing him only as the soldier sees him, a distant source of indiscriminate missiles—which is a concept of the last war,
not this one. It might almost be wise to take the plunge and write at least
partly in the character of a private in the enemy army.[68]

Many fewer writers took up Comfort's challenge than Rees's. In
'Lance-Jack', when Lewis's persona hears his step as the 'tramp of
heavy boots. . . . drowning the bare and bleeding footfalls of the
beggars and the refugees' he thinks 'Heil Hitler': the effect is to
identify the soldier as a universal scourge.[69] Lewis was co-signatory
of Horizon's 'Why Not War Writers?' in October 1941 which turned
Rees's plea for the writer to integrate and redeem war's costs into a
manifesto for official artists (a bid to legitimize the division between
those who fight and those who write).[70] Creative writers could 'bring
home with a depth and vividness impossible to the writer of a newspaper report or feature article, the significance of what is happening
all about us'; they 'should be used to interpret the war world so
that cultural unity is re-established and the war effort emotionally

---

[66] Rees, Accidents, 156.   [67] Rees, 'Letter', 471.
[68] Alex Comfort, 'On Interpreting the War', Horizon, 5/29 (May 1942), 361.
[69] Alun Lewis, Last Inspection, 79.
[70] For an earlier plan to steer artists into 'safe war jobs', see Lionel Esher, 'The Plot to
Save the Artists', Times Literary Supplement (2 Jan. 1987), 12–13.

co-ordinated'.[71] The equivocation in this pitch, between propaganda and autonomous culture, is evident when compared with the project set out in 1942 by Basil Wright, a veteran of the Documentary Film Movement involved in more than forty MOI films:

> It is today the job of documentary to integrate the immediate war effort with the facts and implications of radical social and economic changes which are part and parcel of it. . . . Our films must be the shock troops of propaganda.[72]

Wariness about the relations of art to propaganda did not prevent writers from serving the agencies of persuasion. In 'Where are the War Poets?', Day Lewis apostrophized vested interests as a 'They' who: 'Borrow our language now and bid | Us to speak up in freedom's cause'; and indeed (having sought and gained military exemption) he worked in Bob Fraser's Publications Division at the MOI alongside exponents of the rhetoric of redescription like Hilary St George Saunders and J. M. Richards, helping to maintain a steady output of official pictorial journalism about the services and major theatres of war.[73] Orwell, at the BBC, provided both strategic summaries and talk about poetry for Indian audiences.

Horizon's manifesto put the non-appearance of war poetry down to hesitancy: writers 'did not see the issues as clearly as they had seen the Spanish Civil War, for example, or the last European war'.[74] To Spender, consensus was confined to the minds of propagandists whose output was full of contradictions: 'A poet who represented the spirit of official England to-day would write verse that was a synthesis of Rupert Brooke's 1914 *Sonnets* and the Anthology *Poems for Spain*.'[75] In the latter volume, Spender had written of the 'considerable part' that poetry had played in the Spanish War, nothing that 'the struggle of the Republicans has seemed a struggle for the conditions without which the writing and reading of poetry are almost impossible'.[76] This equivocal ideal of a poetry that was at once political

---

[71] Arthur Calder-Marshall *et al.*, 'Why Not War Writers?: A Manifesto', *Horizon*, 4/22 (Oct. 1941), 236 and 238.

[72] Quoted by Pronay in Short (ed.), *Film and Radio Propaganda*, 63.

[73] C. Day Lewis, *Word Over All* (Jonathan Cape, 1943), 30; Sean Day-Lewis, *C. Day-Lewis: An English Literary Life* (Weidenfeld and Nicolson, 1980), 124 and 138–9.

[74] Calder-Marshall *et al.*, 'Why Not War Writers?', 236.

[75] Stephen Spender, 'Books and the War—V: The Creative Artist in Our Time', *PNW* 6 (May 1941), 125.

[76] Stephen Spender and John Lehmann (eds.), *Poems for Spain* (Hogarth Press, 1939), 7.

and above politics, a means and an end of war, is, it is to be inferred, untenable once its component terms have been co-opted by the state.

Eliot, broadcasting in 1942, noted with satisfaction that little of what the younger poets were writing 'gives an answer to satisfy the sort of people who ask "where are *our* war poets?"' (my emphasis).[77] The substitution of a possessive pronoun for the newspapers' definite article marks the poet's distrust of 'collective emotion'.[78] Edwin Muir similarly deprecated thinking of poetry 'in public terms, as one thinks of state policy or military policy'.[79] Auden, who wrote in 1939 that 'poetry makes nothing happen', would later amplify his rejection of an instrumental theory of art: 'Orpheus who moved stones is the archetype, not of the poet, but of Goebbels.'[80] Day Lewis's poet can only 'defend the bad against the worse'.[81]

The 1941 manifesto has the look of an expedient and defensive gesture of co-operation but in fact it comes close to revealing the actual role of many writers and artists employed, albeit with fewer fanfares, throughout the agencies of state publicity. In *The Unquiet Grave*, Connolly dismissed talk of unity as the coin that purchased consent to violence:

Fraternity is the State's bribe to the individual; it is the one virtue which can bring courage to members of a materialist society. All State propaganda exalts comradeship for it is this gregarious herd-sense and herd-smell which keeps people from thinking and so reconciles them to the destruction of their private lives. A problem for government writers, or for the war artists in their war cemeteries: how to convert Fraternity into an aesthetic emotion?[82]

Anticipating Anderson's 'imagined community'—'the nation conceived as a deep, horizontal comradeship. . . . that makes it possible . . . for so many millions . . . willingly to die for such limited imaginings'—Connolly nevertheless equates war with the disruption of the private sphere.[83] Karl Miller rightly dubs him 'the supreme civilian'.[84] Fraternity is also the synchronization of national

[77] T. S. Eliot, 'Poetry in Wartime' (Oct. 1942), quoted in Christopher Ricks, *T. S. Eliot and Prejudice* (Faber, 1988), 269.

[78] T. S. Eliot, 'A Note on War Poetry', *The Complete Poems and Plays* (Faber, 1969), 202.

[79] Edwin Muir, 'War Poetry', letter to *The Listener*, 26/667 (23 Oct. 1941), 567.

[80] W. H. Auden, 'In Memory of W. B. Yeats', *The English Auden,: Poems, Essays and Dramatic Writings, 1927–1939*, ed. E. Mendelson (Faber, 1977), 242; 'Squares and Oblongs' in *Poets at Work*, ed. Charles D. Abbott (New York: Harcourt, Brace and Co., 1948), 180.   [81] Day Lewis, *Word Over All*, 30.

[82] Cyril Connolly, *The Unquiet Grave* (Curwen Press, 1944), 28.

[83] Benedict Anderson, *Imagined Communities*, rev. edn. (Verso, 1991), 7.

[84] Karl Miller, *Authors* (1989. Oxford: Oxford University Press, 1990), 170.

consciousness. The 'community in anonymity' made possible by the nineteenth-century novel and newspaper was extended by wartime radio, with the Nine O'Clock News reaching half the population.[85] Patrick Wright has suggested that 'the national past postulates a collective subject': in wartime, this identity was shaped by a shared future horizon and the tendency, encouraged by popular broadcasters like Churchill and Priestley, to view the present as historic.[86]

Lewis's poem 'After Dunkirk' is part of this scripting of the legendary present, transforming victims into agents, and transcending both the '[h]orror of war' and submission to the 'subterfuges of democracy'.[87] 'Making complete all that was misbegotten', Lewis was joining forces with John Masefield—poet of 'adventure and toil by land and sea', celebrant in 1916 of the 'epic moral triumph' of Gallipoli, and now official eulogist of the evacuation of the BEF—to inscribe a redemptive closure on military defeat.[88] These attempts at Connolly's 'aesthetic emotion' of fraternity correlated with the emergent Dunkirk spirit (a key term in the Labour party's reckoning of its post-war electoral chances).[89] Britain accordingly stood alone, its integrity fashioned from defeat and isolation, the fall of France a beginning not an end. Churchill's accession at this moment reinforced a view that the new regime was part of a renewed purpose.[90] *Guilty Men*, which appeared in July 1940, laid all blame for Dunkirk on pre-war politics (on the authority of Churchill himself).[91] Dunkirk was also scripted as heralding the end of the poetic hegemony of the 1930s' 'next-war' doomsters. The novelist Hugh Walpole (who had worked for Beaverbrook's propaganda ministry in the Great War) proclaimed that 'this war has, at one stroke, deprived most of Lehmann's "New Writers" of their contemporaneity. They belong to an earlier age, with their pessimism, their cynicism, their apprehensions, their despair. After Dunkirk new poets were born.'[92]

[85] Anderson, *Imagined Communities*, 25–33; Briggs, *War of Words*, 48.

[86] Patrick Wright, *On Living in an Old Country* (Verso, 1985), 146.

[87] Alun Lewis, *Raiders' Dawn*, 33.

[88] A. P. Wavell, *Other Men's Flowers* (Jonathan Cape, 1944), preface; D. G. Wright, 'The Great War, Government Propaganda and English "Men of Letters" 1914–16', *Literature and History*, 4/7 (Spring 1978), 77; John Masefield, *The Nine Days Wonder* (Heinemann, 1941), 54.   [89] See Fielding, Thompson, and Tiratsoo, '*England Arise!*', 81.

[90] Pikoulis, *Alun Lewis*, 98 argues that Lewis might have signed up in May 1940 in response to the formation of the new National Government that month.

[91] 'Cato', *Guilty Men* (Gollancz, 1940), preface.

[92] Quoted in John Lehmann, *I Am My Brother* (Longmans, Green and Co., 1960), 103; see Peter Buitenhuis, *The Great War of Words* (Batsford, 1989), 137.

Lewis's poem effects an uplifting synchronization of private and public, despite its acknowledgement of the manifold sufferings of war. It begins by invoking the silence of the refugee, but the military test is a 'boon' (both a command and a blessing). In Lewis's prayer (a further sense of boon) Britain's standing alone is both birth and departure, the white wake of the evacuation armada associated with the smile of children. That some are dying, others 'luckier', seems not to deflect the poem's attempt to wrest a conviction that outcomes assuage the pains of war.

H. E. Bates was commissioned in the RAF during the month the *Horizon* manifesto was published, starting his service as war scribe at Uxbridge (where T. E. Lawrence's first airforce career had begun) under the immediate command of novelist and propagandist Hilary Saunders. His department's function was to

show not figures, statistics, bulletins, communiqués and so on to the public, but men, characters, faces. It would dedicate itself to the proposition that figures, if repeated *ad nauseam*, mean nothing, but that a pilot with a pint of beer in his hand and a popsie in bed can illuminate the troubled business of war in a way that will bring war and its participants vividly, excitedly, even painfully alive.[93]

But steering clear of abstractions in an attempt to embody wartime's meanings only redoubled the gap between officially sanctioned description and reality (note the tension between the creative performance, 'painfully alive', and its context of a 'troubled business'). The eavesdropping narrator in the Flying Officer X stories apes aircrew taciturnity ('without heroics, sentimentality, or fuss') in order to shoot the lines that service etiquette suppresses.[94] The form of the short story offered 'limitless fascinating possibilities in the contemporary world of common dislocation', though what interested Bates was the symbolic unification of the fractured realm. The 'social expansion' of his readership into a channel of common experience gave rise, he thought, to collaborative imaginative work—'It is no longer necessary to describe; it is enough to suggest'—but the experience was virtual and symbolically mediated, and a significant precondition of commonality.[95] Lewis, aiming at a 'crystallisation of

[93] H. E. Bates, *The Blossoming World: An Autobiography*, (Michael Joseph, 1971), ii, 180.

[94] Dust jacket of the British Publishers Guild edition of H. E. Bates, *The Greatest People in the World* (Jonathan Cape, 1942).

[95] H. E. Bates, *The Modern Short Story: A Critical Survey* (Thomas Nelson and Sons, 1941), 12 and 24.

the present', risked making his art hostage to symbols and collective emotions that had similar functions and currency.[96] Connolly was sceptical about the value of the imaginative work undertaken by participants or collaborators in the war effort: 'though this war is being fought for culture, the fighting of it will not create that culture.'[97]

But the more pressing matter for Lewis as a writer in the Forces was the question of real, rather than virtual, experience. Elizabeth Bowen's *Tatler* review of his *The Last Inspection* noted its criticism of 'what war does to human life—and worst of all, war before there has been fighting', a judgement that underlines the grasping after significance in the stories which are not about the army without a war but about the Blitz (John Lehmann thought 'They Came' 'unreal and a bit sentimental') and the RAF.[98] Battle-school, Lewis was forced to conclude, was 'as near the real thing as you can go in this unreal trauma that has drugged England's pastoral army in the two years since Dunkirk'. The simulation of action was a surrogate for the imagined transcendence in combat ('the heightened vision | Of life as they saw it in the hour of battle' of 'After Dunkirk') if not for the ends of action: 'your mind grows as tranquil and sensible as your body grows exhausted. Your senses become extraordinarily perceptive.'[99]

Lewis's posting to India at the end of 1942 only relocated the scene of waiting, but it did revise the meaning of Vaughan's army of (no) occupation. India made his acceptance of a military identity more crucial:

> There *is* such a thing as freedom, and in Europe *we are* liberators at the moment. In the East it is less so, alas. Liberty isn't the point at issue, and neither side offers it. That's what makes it so hard to accept. Personally I think it's the pure adventure and enormity of it and the technical military problem that keeps me at it. And the desire for experience and for the scales to fall off completely that I may return and write of it.[100]

In postponing the issue of liberty, he followed government policy to the letter. Churchill, who insisted that the Atlantic Charter did not apply to the empire, would not preside over its 'liquidation' in pursuit of victory.[101] In March 1942, Sir Stafford Cripps's promise of

---

[96] Alun Lewis, *Letters*, 213 (9 May 1942).

[97] 'Comment', *Horizon*, 1/7 (July 1940), 534.   [98] Pikoulis, *Alun Lewis*, 166, 124.

[99] Alun Lewis, *Miscellany*, 152; Evelyn Waugh's Guy Crouchback thinks 'there should be a drug for soldiers . . . to put them to sleep until they were needed' (*Sword of Honour Trilogy*, 257).   [100] Alun Lewis, *Letters*, 393 (9 Sept. 1943).

[101] R. A. C. Parker, *The Second World War: A Short History* (1989. Oxford: Oxford University Press, 1997), 300.

dominion status at the cessation of hostilities had been rejected by the nationalist Congress Party. The 'Quit India' campaign of non-cooperation brought imprisonment of political leaders, riot and its suppression, and reprisals against British troops. Lewis's 'colossal experience' of travelling in India went into the story 'The Orange Grove', in which an army driver with a better-world vision of collective farms (he has served in Palestine) is murdered.[102] The issues were not black and white, although Gandhi spoke then of the necessity of the 'complete separation' of the British and the Indians (Lewis a year later wrote he '*could* be happy in India' only if they were friends).[103] Jinnah, leader of India's Muslims, called for further divisions (freedom equals partition). Subhas Chandra Bose, a pre-war challenger for the leadership of Congress, waited over the border with the Indian National Army, formed from the 60,000 prisoners taken by the Japanese at Singapore, while his followers in India carried out sabotage and terrorism against the British Army.[104] The reconstructionist discourse in Lewis's English writing was displaced by the language of struggle and triumph, though the 'terrible struggles' were internal: 'Quit India, the silly fools. How can we? India is part of the world. It's the world we can't quit.'[105]

In 'The Raid', the first action after three years' training is the arrest of a cinema bomber. The terrorist's killing of three soldiers 'for my country' spells out not just the contradictions in a political creed but also its lack of purchase on reality (84). In 'The Earth is a Syllable', the wounded officer's failures—'the little meetings he'd tried to run, debates around a hurricane lamp on the FUTURE, talks he'd carefully put together on RECONSTRUCTION'—are aggregated with the schemes and the thrills of training as 'queer consolations' (88). Detached from the political and social co-ordinates of Europe, Lewis's investment in surrogates for war becomes more metaphysical. His wife Gweno wrote to him about Koestler's essay on Hillary, a distinctly mythopoeic deconstruction of a contemporary warrior myth. He replied that it was 'twaddle . . . about him being wilfully led to his fascinating death!'[106] Next day he insisted that she had read

---

[102] Quoted in Pikoulis, *Alun Lewis*, 202; Alun Lewis, *In the Green Tree* (George Allen and Unwin, 1948), 114–15.

[103] Stanley Wolpert, *A New History of India*, 5th edn. (1977. New York and Oxford: Oxford University Press, 1997), 334–5; Alun Lewis, *Letters*, 341 (9 May 1943).

[104] Wolpert, *New History of India*, 331–7.

[105] Alun Lewis, *Green Tree*, 87.   [106] Alun Lewis, *Letters*, 353 (25 May 1943).

him wrongly by bringing up Hillary: 'death doesn't fascinate me half as powerfully as life.'[107] He tells her he is busy, healthy: training troops to swim creeks, visiting Bombay to see the 'thrilling . . . and sobering' *Desert Victory* (the Army Film Unit's Alamein feature) and revising a story to enter for the *Horizon* prize (which Koestler will win with his Hillary essay).

The story was 'Ward "O" 3 (b)', a meditation on death, adventure, and betrayal which Lewis wrote while recuperating from an operation on his jaw, injured playing soccer. Anaesthesia is death's surrogate: 'I don't think I need any further experience of leaving this life,' he joked to Gweno, '. . . it was very like I believe, what does happen'.[108] Of the quartet awaiting medical boards in the story, two, like Lewis, hold temporary commissions. Both have been tempted by death—the obliteration of pain—but Moncrieff's life has, if anything, been narrowed by this trauma: death is to be feared, India is loathsome, 'talking about reconstruction' at home is to be despised.[109] In his superficial concern for self Moncrieff breaches the soldier's 'etiquette' of unconcern but Weston wants to be 'going in where you left off'. The fatal casualty of 'The Earth is a Syllable' was afraid he would die in Burma: Lewis imagined him going into the darkness of the jungle ('dark and soft like a mass of congealed blood'), not armoured for a 'schoolboy thrill', and not in Burma, but slipping 'under the hill' to put an end to the guilt of separation from his wife and to the pain of his wounds.[110] Weston similarly confronts the wilderness, but his story's resolution is given a strategic gloss: 'he felt glad to-night, feeling some small salient gained when for many reasons the men whom he was with were losing ground along the whole front to the darkness that there is.'[111] Weston has been cut clear of the war in Europe by the belated news that his French lover got away to America. He will not recapitulate his escape at Dunkirk: 'I want to have a look at Burma. *And I don't want to see England.*'[112] The difference between these desires is brought out by the way a memory of a tank that 'surged softly forward, grunting peacefully and bellying over a slope so sweet and easy' in 'The Earth is a Syllable' is turned into Weston's fear that he will 'never see a Valentine lift her belly over a bund and go grunting like a wild boar at—well, whoever

[107] Ibid. 354 (26 May 1943).   [108] Ibid. 301 (1 Feb. 1943).
[109] Alun Lewis, 'Ward "O" 3 (b)', *PNW* 18 (July–Sept. 1943), 39.
[110] Lewis, *Green Tree*, 87, 90.   [111] Lewis, 'Ward "O" 3 (b)', 48.
[112] Ibid. 39.

happens to be there. I got used to the idea of the Germans. I suppose the Japs will do.'[113]

Like other forces members of *Horizon's* readership, Lewis could not help comparing himself to the dead Hillary:

he did many things I foresee myself doing—insouciance to danger, melo-dramatic personal relationships in the interludes of dying—even the serious thought of life & people is melodramatic in so far as Death prompts it & dramatises life—that is, puts it on a stage and spotlights it.[114]

In Betty Miller's comic novel of garrison life, *On the Side of the Angels* (1945), the war is not drama but 'masquerade': 'when armistice is declared—the khaki will vanish, we'll be clothed in humble civilian tatters again' (132). Claudia falls for a conventionally heroic commando, Captain Herriott, who turns out to be a bank manager and a 'Town councillor and part-time A.R.P. official in a small county town which has never known a blitz . . . prominent member of the local Home Guard . . . dissatisfied with fake attacks on a fake enemy'.[115] Investments in the imaginary dimension of war are a con-sequence of enervating regimentation:

The discipline of military life . . . being an imposed discipline, to be accepted whole and without question, . . . seemed to permit, in compensa-tion, the relaxation of those personal standards, self-imposed and self-maintained, by which, up to now, as a private citizen, he had chosen to live.[116]

The 'mythic attraction that war holds for both sexes' is one reason why symbols can take as strong a hold on the imagination as the material events of the battlefield, especially when the latter can only be imagined.[117]

Lewis's wartime oeuvre is a literature of seemingly perpetual mobilization, and of leaving home (a desertion and an adventure) for a war that did not materialize. The identification with Edward Thomas in Lewis's signature poem about the social dislocation of garrison life, 'All Day it has Rained . . .' (*Horizon*, January 1941), underlines the status of the militarized poet as patient not agent.

[113] Lewis, *Green Tree*, 88; 'Ward "O" 3 (b)', 41.
[114] Lewis, letter to Dick Mills, 17 Oct. 1943, quoted in Pikoulis, *Alun Lewis*, 236.
[115] Betty Miller, *On the Side of the Angels* (Robert Hale, 1945), 234.
[116] Ibid. 104.
[117] Helen M. Cooper, Adrienne Auslander Munich, and Susan Merrill Squier (eds.), *Arms and the Woman: War, Gender and Literary Representation* (Chapel Hill: University of North Carolina Press, 1989), 16.

Thomas's poetry was wartime work, half of it written between enlistment in July 1915 and embarkation for France in January 1917. Neither man lived to write about battle experienced. Lewis, unlike Thomas, squared up to writing about living in the Army, but what mattered was always evading his attempts to realize it, whether it was the unsettling promise of life recreated in the mêlée of mass-regimentation or in the face of death. Death was 'a voice in [Thomas]', according to Lewis, but in his own verse that voice, in a war which Patrick Gardiner described as 'an affair of training and practice, necessary enough but not likely to release the spring that produces poetry', sometimes strikes us as forced.[118] The story 'Grenadier' eavesdrops on soldiers' confessions: 'There is no air of confidence or reticence about it; they might be talking about someone else, despite the use of the first person; and indeed they are, I believe, talking about their *lost* selves, the selves they signed away.'[119] The sentimentality of wartime popular culture, which translated everyday sacrifices into melodramas of doomed romance, understated heroism and better patriotic selves threatened the grounding timbres of sincerity that Lewis sought in narratives and lyrics concerned with the private citizen-soldier. His work sustains a seriousness that G. S. Fletcher found lacking in soldiers' verse, the worst of which was 'a translation . . . of the current *clichés* of English individualism, always indignant, always inconsistent, and never with its finger on the spot.'[120] But the abiding intuitions of the best stories, sensed also in passages of his poetry, reside uncertainly behind the 'talking about someone else', himself, left behind or not yet caught up with.

OUT OF BATTLE

Lewis's war ended with his death (some speculate his suicide) on the eve of what, at his own request, might have been his first contact with the enemy (as Battalion Intelligence Officer he would not normally

---

[118] Lewis, review of *The Trumpet and Other Poems* by Edward Thomas, *Horizon*, 3/13 (Jan. 1941), 80; Patrick Gardiner, 'The Pity of it Iago . . .', *Poetry London X* (1944), 261.

[119] Lewis, 'Grenadier', in Jack Aistrop and Reginald Moore (eds.), *Bugle Blast: An Anthology from the Services*, 2nd ser. (1944), 163.

[120] G. S. Fraser, 'Recent Verse: London and Cairo', *Poetry London X* (1944), 216.

accompany a patrol).[121] Dan Billany's war ended twice, when he was captured in North Africa, and when he was killed during the confused interregnum after the Italian Armistice. His exclusion from hostilities, which is not analogous to the garrison soldier's, is of crucial significance to the form and the meanings of the novel he wrote in Italian Prisoner of War camps between late 1942 and early 1944 (it was published posthumously in 1950). *The Trap* is indignant about many aspects of the war, not least about the bad faith involved in describing war in terms of positive social projects. It reflects Hamish Henderson's contention that the 'levelling' which war produces is not the egalitarian collectivism of 'this band of brothers', exemplified by the excision of distinctions of degree in the roll of honour after Agincourt in Olivier's film of *Henry V*, but the 'proletariat of levelling death in which *all the fallen* are comrades' (my emphasis).[122] Billany's disgust with 'war emotions', and the book's demystification of militarist ideologies and delusions are strongly correlated with expulsion from a military role and identity. The narrator Lt Michael Carr gains a transvaluing perspective on battle when he watches his own men being killed *from the wrong side* as they advance on the German troops who have captured him.

The Trap addresses ideals of social reform in a story of unremitting oppression, not via the facts nor myths of wartime collectivity. The family of Carr's future wife Elizabeth struggle to make a home in the inter-war years, only to have it 'broken open to all the world' in an air raid.[123] The Blitz is not a unifying metropolitan experience heralding a new social order, but a continuation of proletarian subjection. The Pascoes are the antithesis of the lower-middle class Gibbonses in Noel Coward's play *This Happy Breed* (written in the spring of 1939, staged in 1943, and filmed by David Lean in 1944) who were, according to the film's publicity, the 'kind who survive wars, zeppelins, Heinkels, the Kaiser, strikes, political upheavals, despairs, jubilations, the same as you'.[124] The fraction of the Pascoe

[121] John Pikoulis, *Alun Lewis: A Life*, 2nd, rev. edn. (Bridgend: Seren Press, 1992), 235, 232.

[122] Hamish Henderson, *Elegies for the Dead in Cyrenaica* (John Lehmann, 1948), 12. Olivier's screenplay cuts, for example, the disguised Henry's claim to Bates that the King's 'affections are higher mounted' (Shakespeare, *Henry V*, 4.1.103-4, 211), and the phrase 'none else of name' from the roll of English dead (4.8.103, 257).

[123] Dan Billany, *The Trap* (Faber, 1950), 163.

[124] Anthony Aldgate and Jeffrey Richards, *Britain Can Take It: The British Cinema in the Second World War*, 2nd edn. (Edinburgh: Edinburgh University Press, 1994), 210-11.

family which survives bombing is victimized by a Dickensian welfare bureaucracy: ' "It's to be hoped the Government is fighting Hitler as hard as it's fighting us".'[125] Billany interprets this petty tyranny in a way that recalls Kant's model of belligerent autocracy:

our Boy Scouts stand up in voluble indignation and blame Hitler, and Hitler blames them, and both sides take good care not to look at the bodies. But they may, for they can be confident that, on whatever side the blame finally stays, those bodies won't get up and walk again (176).

This passage bears the hallmarks of intemperate Sassoonian satire: it is at once a determinedly perverse way of reading the war but from the perspective of the conscripted subject a compelling one. The trope of war as play is essentially unstable, masking and unmasking by turns: the 'Boy Scout' mentality that administers war is also one of its most potent mystifications, facilitating a conspiracy 'not to look at the bodies'. Carr's anger, directed in the first half of the book against social injustice, reasserts itself on the last page, from behind barbed wire, in an explicit rebuttal of the discourses that seamlessly legitimate the human cost of war in terms of political goals:

The war-emotions are frivolous. A grown man cannot take them seriously. The war is as ridiculous as Sweeney Todd, the Demon Barber. It is not re-lated to the true feelings of real people. Only the sufferings are real. The causes for which we suffer are contemptible and ridiculous (380).

This denial of the necessity of the war, and of its redemption in im-agined futures, is in part determined by Carr's exclusion from it: the POW's perspective on hostilities is a refusal of collective emotions. Capture is a form of disenchantment which results not in passivity but in the violent expulsion or abjection of the militarized identity. The narrative context of this jeremiad is significant, for it comes after an extended narrative of combat, during which that oppositional voice has not been heard. *The Trap* might appear to be a rerun of the Great War novel of disillusionment.

But Billany's narrative frame is at odds with the plotting of a pro-gressive awakening to truth realized in the knowledge acquired in combat and capture. The book opens with the receipt of a letter in an unexplained location, a proleptic reference that makes sense only with Carr's imprisonment (a similar device is employed in Alexander Baron's striking novel about the costs of the Normandy bridgehead,

---

[125] Billany, *Trap*, 169.

From the City, From the Plough (1948), and in *The Last Enemy*). The pre-war narrative is consonant with a perspective conditioned by imprisonment, but the overseas phase suppresses that knowledge, deferring revelations in the manner of the *Bildungsroman*.

After the Pascoes are bombed out, Carr is posted overseas, an event symbolic of society's indifference to the unadapted (many of the draft are being punished for their poor army records) and of the army's usurpation of the self. He is 'imprisoned in [his] own dumbed body, in its khaki that could only be removed for sleeping' (175). Where Alun Lewis imagined soldiers become 'poets when they say Goodbye',[126] Billany sees parting couples choreographed by propaganda:

The situation seemed grotesquely like a play, or an old silent film about the last war. I the young officer, tall, straight, British and determined: clean-shaven, and wearing beautiful barathea and gleaming buttons: with peaked cap, gloves and cane. Elizabeth, the girl-wife, a Mary Pickford role. . . . It was acting an old, dated melodrama, it was the Soldier's Farewell as on the cheap prints: it was not the real, beating life in us that brought us to the station-platform to act these parts. Our very grief was not our own. (185–6)

Personal feelings are displaced by the simulacra of collective behaviour which interpellate Louie in Bowen's *The Heat of the Day*.

The defiance with which the period of Carr's home service and training are represented weakens in proportion to the bonding of men on active service. Once his platoon is transplanted to the militarized space of the Libyan front, commentary on class division in the army and the chronic economic disparities of Egyptian society gives way to a detailed and a non-digressive narrative of the actions of Carr and his men. The battlefield is described hermetically, the opponents who contest it do so apparently outside ideology. The narrowing discursive horizon correlates with the army's usurpation of Carr's reflective capacity and with his isolation from Elizabeth and her family (representatives of his own working-class past) and from the political contradictions of the Home Front.

The 'humanizing' collectivity of the platoon (in which 'lives were common property', and bowels 'our common heritage') reinforces a sense of being 'in the war, not watching from the side', persuading Carr that he has achieved 'perspective', and that he will return a 'better man'.[127] It is, however, captivity which grants Carr the

[126] Alun Lewis, 'On Embarkation', *Ha! Ha! Among the Trumpets: Poems in Transit* (George Allen and Unwin, 1945), 31. [127] Billany, *Trap*, 254–7.

perspective from which he narrates the Pascoes' story, for it undoes the reality with which Carr invests active service. The discrepancy is marked by his eve-of-battle letter to Elizabeth, never dispatched, in which he imagines his death as the result of a deliberate decision, 'having counted the cost and the gain' (278). Like Lewis, Billany plots the make-believe performances of training (which, aggregating platoon-based small-arms practice into divisional manoeuvres and war-games, reinforces the epistemic hierarchy of the command structure) as a gathering proximity to a transcendent reality. This rationale is undone, as it is in so many twentieth-century narratives of combatant disillusionment, when scripted practice gives way to the tactically unscripted chaos of killing, with the additional factor of the narrator's being absented. Combat is newly intelligible from 'six feet of elevation', as Carr finds himself 'in the character of a private in the enemy army' (to recall Alex Comfort's device for avoiding an administrative view of violence) spectating the destruction of his troops in their counter-attack against his surrendered position.

The conclusion that Carr reaches behind barbed wire is such that we are compelled to question it, and to try to explain its stridency. The disintegration of his response to battle is a variant of the opposition of inside and outside which structures the writings of POWs. The circularity of the novel, its last page supplying the context for understanding the first, confirms this generic status. A critique of civil society is voiced from the marginal space of prison, and a critique of military values (including Carr's own vulnerability to 'Boy Scout' mentality, his comic-book-bellicose cry 'Shoot him in the belly') actualized by the difference between being in the war and being out of it (341). The novel's return to the conundrum of its opening (how to give the history of an emotion) is enmeshed within discourses whose function is emotional co-ordination. But prison's exteriority facilitates recognition of war's substitutions of causes for bodies.

WAR AIMS AND WAR EMOTIONS

'We have no other war aim than to destroy Hitlerism, and no elaboration of that simple purpose should be permitted.'[128] The

---

[128] Storm Jameson, citing *The Times* in October 1939, quoted in Jeremy Treglown, 'The *TLS* in the Second World War', in Jeremy Treglown and Bridget Bennett (eds.), *Grub*

object-relations theorist Donald W. Winnicott, writing in 1940, con-
curred. Churchill's unwillingness to speculate about the victories of
the peace avoided delusory assumptions that 'We are good': 'There is
no clear reason why an ability to lead a country to victory should
carry with it an ability to discuss war aims.' Anything beyond a 'fight
for life' required efforts of justification which would ultimately reveal that we are like our enemies in our 'total behaviour', a term with
which Winnicott situated the self-designating democratic subject in
the contexts of historical responsibility, of motivations drawn from
unconscious identification with the enemy, and of gratification from
the collective acting out of 'aggressive or cruel ideas' that threaten to
become conscious.[129] Winnicott's reading of self-promoting war
aims centred on the competing desire for and fear of freedom. The
'preposterous' interventions in the lives of citizens by wartime
government were experienced as relief, and democracy was travestied
in war-aims discourse as 'the State serving the people instead of the
people serving the State' ('Surely the essential thing in democracy is
that the people not only elect but also get rid of the leaders, and take
responsibility for this'). Positive war aims were a redescription of war
as fulfilment: 'By linking freedom with peace and slavery with war
and war effort, we have reached a happy state of affairs, which, however, depends on someone conveniently waging war on us' (216–17).
Winnicott's insistence on 'a military and not a moral victory' re-
deploys Clausewitz's theoretical identification of war with violent
force to define the value of war: 'actual fighting . . . may tend gradually to foster maturity on both sides.' If this conclusion ushers in a
facile redescription of violence (with its echoes of Kant's optimism
about war as reason in the relations of states) the analysis that pre-
cedes it is nevertheless percipient about the way the war was being
fought in words. Neither projections of unadmitted aggression and
deceit onto the enemy, nor smug assumptions of moral superiority,
would win the war. Winning required both 'superiority of fight' and
'calling the bluff to all propaganda' (220).

The language of politics in which war's violence is sanitized and
rationalized is delusional. 'The ordinary individual who is realistic
enough in his domestic world of concrete objects is very apt to think

*Street and the Ivory Tower: Literary Journalism and Literary Scholarship from Fielding to
the Internet* (Oxford: Clarendon Press, 1998), 148.

[129] D. W. Winnicott, 'Discussion of War Aims' in *Home Is Where We Start From*
(Harmondsworth: Penguin, 1986), 210–11.

irrationally as soon as he moves into the political world of personified abstractions.'[130] In the prosecution of war, the functions of
comparable vehicles for abstraction are clear. Alun Lewis's writing in
the Army and in India is shaped not by resistance to the compulsions
of external discipline but by a much more equivocal relationship to
the compensating figures in which political, military, and personal
futures were seductively embodied. Dan Billany's outspoken refusal
of wartime ideologies is grounded in a liminal perspective on the war
which has a concrete basis in prison, whereas Lewis's 'acceptance'
seems to derive from an imaginative habitation of disorienting mar-
gins (between civilian and soldier, home and abroad, life and death).
'Our job is surely to put to the test everything that is thrown at us in
words,' concluded Winnicott.[131] But the ubiquitous dissemination
and invention of war aims made the quest for both intellectual and
emotional immunity to private and public propaganda an exacting
trial. Even the POW experience on which Billany's insights rest
would be colonized, in representations and in practice, by reconstructionist and militarist abstractions.

---

[130] Roger Money-Kyrle, quoted in Jacqueline Rose, *Why War? Psychoanalysis, Politics and the Return to Melanie Klein* (Oxford: Blackwell, 1993), 24.
[131] Winnicott 'Discussion of War Aims', 220.

6

'We're All Prisoners of War'

il est aussi raisonnable de représenter une espèce d'emprisone-
ment par une autre que de représenter n'importe quelle chose
qui existe réellement par quelque chose qui n'existe pas

Albert Camus[1]

'tis as reasonable to represent one kind of imprisonment by another, as it is to represent any thing that really exists, by that
which exists not

Daniel Defoe[2]

METAPHORS OF PRISON AND PRISON
AS METAPHOR

WRITING by and about British prisoners of the European Axis provides a doubly distanced perspective on Britain's war: they were in
Europe, yet excluded from hostilities. It also supplies a context for
assessing the metaphors of imprisonment which were widely employed in the representation of wartime experience in Britain. Prison
writing has long been associated with revaluation: the POW is a
significant figure in reassessments of the meanings of the war. But the
trope of imprisonment also determined apprehensions of the war in
Europe.

Alongside claims about the levelling of distinction and difference,
the war's impact on social structures was interpreted as the subjection of the individual to control, constraint, and coercion. Among
the complaints from the public shelters recorded by the American
correspondent Negley Farson, the phrase ' "We're prisoners of war" '
glossed collective identity as the universal diminution of liberty.[3]

[1] Albert Camus, *La Peste* (Paris: Gallimard, 1947), epigraph.
[2] Daniel Defoe, *Serious Reflections During the Life and Surprising Adventures of
Robinson Crusoe: with his Vision of the Angelick World* (1720. Constable, 1925), p. viii.
[3] Negley Farson, *Bomber's Moon* (Gollancz, 1941), 69.

Tommy Trinder repeats this phrase after his first night's duty in an AFS station in Ealing's 1943 comedy *The Bells Went Down*. In Betty Miller's *On the Side of the Angels*, Claudia's self-dramatizing claim that '"in a sense—we're all prisoners of war"' is countered by her fiancé Andrew's argument that war is a '"general amnesty"' for '"the Prisoners of Peace—the people who've had to live battened down, all their lives"'.[4] Priestley employed penal imagery to condemn a pre-war world in his reconstructionist *Letter to a Returning Serviceman*: 'whole suburbs were like tree-lined concentration camps', and 'to be a young wife was often to be sentenced to a term of solitary confinement'.[5] Conflicting ideas about war's disciplines—as diminishing or supplementing identity—are repeatedly embodied in penal tropes. In 'Mysterious Kôr', the figure of an imprisoning peace had been used to describe the bombed metropolis as a scene of a universal deprivation, 'the war's total of unlived lives'. In her remarks on Richard Hillary, Bowen was critical of identities-for-the-duration: '"war's not just only war; it's years out of people's lives that they've never had before and won't have again"', a kind of penal sentence.[6]

These tropes were not confined to the representation of civil territories or transformed civil institutions. Clive Branson, son of an Indian Army officer, was posted East with the Royal Armoured Corps in 1942, recording 'now I am back as a prisoner of war'.[7] Unlike many who rehearsed this idea, he knew what he was talking about, having spent most of 1938 in one of Franco's concentration camps, but the trope's utility was predicated on its metaphoric not literal signification. Keith Douglas's tank, like Antoine de St-Exupéry's reconnaissance plane, was an enclosed technical space which isolated its inhabitants from each other (cellular distribution) and from the world outside. Climbing into a bomber, Herbert Corby 'shut [him]self in the war'; he subsequently published *Time in a Blue Prison* (1947).[8] The ritual preparations before a sortie were always, potentially, the last actions of the condemned. The gates and barbed wire of the army camp were the portals and walls of prisons, which prevented the conscript's escape back into the civil community. Alun

---

[4] Betty Miller, *On the Side of the Angels* (Robert Hale, 1945), 68–9.

[5] J. B. Priestley, *Letter to a Returning Serviceman* (Home and Van Thal, 1945), 30.

[6] Elizabeth Bowen, *The Demon Lover and Other Stories* (Jonathan Cape, 1945), 189, 187.

[7] Clive Branson, *British Soldier in India: The Letters of Clive Branson*, with an introduction by Harry Pollitt (The Communist Party, 1945), 52.

[8] Herbert Corby, 'Poem', *Hampdens Going Over* (Editions Poetry London, 1945), 21.

Lewis called the scenes of his training 'little Dachau' or 'little Offlag' (sic); OCTU became 'O.G.P.U.' (the Soviet Unified State Political Administration or secret police).[9] Passage in and out of camps was strictly controlled: 'libertymen' were only provisionally and temporarily free, and the infantry were marked-off as inmates by 'the soldier's convict dress' (contemporary images of Officer POW camps could make them seem, by contrast, like holiday camps).[10] Kafka's vision of modernity as a penal matrix lay behind visions of the war as a sentence, like William Sansom's fabular 'The Long Sheet' and Maclaren Ross's 'I had to go Sick'.[11]

Unprecedented government control over the lives of Britons was represented as an exigency of war. In Balchin's *Darkness Falls From the Air*, an industrialist's objection to '"these sweeping things that they do under dictatorships"' is censured with the observation that '"if we don't stop saying that soon we *shall* be in Germany"'.[12] Nevertheless, the idea that, as Louis MacNeice suspected in 1939, we 'must, in order to beat / The enemy, model ourselves upon the enemy'[13] was a troubling contradiction. In Green's repatriation novel *Back* (1946), one subject of Home-Front disciplines wonders '"what we're fighting to finish"'.[14] For pacifist Alex Comfort, Hitler's 'irretrievable victory' would be in persuading 'the English people that the only way to lick Fascism was to imitate it'.[15]

Penal tropes were common in articulating responses to the perceived illiberality of wartime Britain. In addition to the civil and military prison populations, the literally incarcerated included alien internees (concentrated on the Isle of Man) and conscientious objectors who, like composer Michael Tippett, were confined for refusing any kind of war work (though he turned the pages at a Wormwood Scrubbs recital for Benjamin Britten, who was permitted by his tribunal to continue with CEMA concert work).[16] On the Continent, tens of thousands of British servicemen waited for the end of the war

[9] Alun Lewis, *Letters*, 198 (8 March 1942), 209 (28 April 1942); *The Last Inspection* (George Allen and Unwin, 1942), 46.

[10] J. P. W. Mallalieu, *Very Ordinary Seaman* (Gollancz, 1944), 44; Geoffrey Cotterell, *Then a Soldier* (Eyre and Spottiswoode, 1944), 72.

[11] William Sansom, 'The Long Sheet', *Horizon*, 4/22 (Oct. 1941), 276–85.

[12] Nigel Balchin, *Darkness Falls from The Air* (Collins, 1942), 24.

[13] Louis MacNeice, *Autumn Journal* (Faber, 1939), 32.

[14] Henry Green, *Back* (Hogarth Press, 1946), 19.

[15] Alex Comfort, 'Pacifism and the War', in Orwell, *CEJL* ii. 225.

[16] Michael Tippett, *Those Twentieth-century Blues* (Hutchinson, 1991), 145; Humphrey Carpenter, *Benjamin Britten* (Faber, 1992), 176–7.

in POW camps. But Europe was a very different kind of prison for millions of Soviet soldiers, the millions forced to labour in Germany, and the millions transported to death camps in the East.

Keith Vaughan, arrested as a spy when sketching in the late summer of 1940 (after the internment of aliens), prefigures Ioan Davies' account of prison writing as an attempt to control the violent space of the prison cell: inscriptions on the walls of Guildford prison ('meticulous writing, as though as much time as possible must be used up in the writing') were 'the compulsive reiteration of identity' against a space in which 'the binding fluid of your personality is slowly dried out'.[17] Prison writing transcends the cell metaphorically, or it can connect with the outside world by making the prison a model of power and domination. Such writing is subversive—'all prison writing is an expression of . . . reappraisal'—and reimagining other spaces as prisons may well, according to Davies, have the same function.[18] In writing by POWs the POW camp equally functions as a site of reappraisal; the nature of war becomes visible because the prisoner is now, in a sense, external to it. But, as in the case of opposed conceptions of wartime as imprisonment and liberation, writing about the POW experience also promoted bellicose subjectivities.

In Foucault's account of penal institutions, the armies of the eighteenth century are given a key role in 'the birth of meticulous . . . tactics by which the control of bodies and individual forces was exercised within states'.[19] Wartime writers who employed imagery of penal tyranny to describe emotional and material regimentation preempted the weakening of distinctions between disciplinary regimes in Foucault's totalizing thesis. However they did not intuit his genealogy, and 'austere institutions' such as the school and the concentration camp were used interchangeably as symbolic reference points for characterizing military and political authority. The concepts and images of imprisonment so invoked have little to do with the history of actual penal institutions, a point well made by Ken Worpole, who observes of escape books: 'writers in the genre never even saw imprisonment as a particular social condition, with a history and a psychology, and describe prison life as little different from dormitory

---

[17] Keith Vaughan, *Journal and Drawings 1939–1965* (Alan Ross, 1966), 19.
[18] Ioan Davies, *Writers in Prison* (Oxford: Blackwell, 1990), 21.
[19] Michel Foucault, *Discipline and Punish: The Birth of Prison*, trans. Alan Sheridan (Allen Lane, 1977), 168.

life at public school.'[20] The equation of incommensurate totalized regimes—the state at war and the prison or concentration camp—was a significant factor in the shaping and reception of representations of Europe under the Nazis.[21]

The discontinuity between inside prison and outside, which prison writing forges into strategies of political resistance, might mean that prison literature will 'always be appropriated as mere metaphor'.[22] Primo Levi wrote of the way one conception of the prisoner makes another inconceivable:

The concept of escape as a moral obligation is constantly reinforced by romantic literature (remember the Count of Montecristo?), by popular literature, and by the cinema, in which the hero, unjustly (or even justly) imprisoned, always tries to escape, even in the least likely circumstances, the attempt being invariably crowned with success.[23]

Levi despaired that these notions were so deeply rooted as to make his testimony about Auschwitz unbelievable. Stories of escape, for instance the narratives about POW camps which were widely circulated in post-war Britain, had greater authority because of their correspondence to ideals of conduct in prison. Discourses in which domestic disciplines were figured as imprisonment impinged on the wartime reception of information about death camps in Europe. Koestler had to defend 'The Mixed Transport', his 1943 narrative about the systematic murder of 'Useless Jews', against the scepticism that lay behind the question whether it was '"based on fact"' or '"artistic fiction"'.[24] Orwell insisted that Britain had no genuine 'concentration-camp literature' because of a British failure to 'imagine oneself as a victim': 'English disapproval of the Nazi outrages has', he went on, 'been an unreal thing, turned on and off like a tap

[20] Ken Worpole, *Dockers and Detectives: Popular Reading: Popular Writing* (Verso, 1983), 53.

[21] See Tony Kushner, 'The Impact of the Holocaust on British Society and Culture', *Contemporary Record*, 5/2 (Autumn 1991), 351; Bernard Wasserstein, *Britain and the Jews of Europe 1939-1945* (London and Oxford: Institute of Jewish Affairs and Clarendon Press, 1979), 349-352; Richard Bolchover, *British Jewry and the Holocaust* (Cambridge: Cambridge University Press, 1993), 8.

[22] Davies, *Writers in Prison*, 219.

[23] Primo Levi, *If This is a Man* and *The Truce*, trans. Stuart Woolf (1958 and 1963, trans. 1960 and 1965. Sphere, 1987), 386.

[24] Arthur Koestler, 'The Mixed Transport', *Horizon*, 8/46 (Oct. 1943), 244-52, and his reply to scepticism, *Horizon*, 8/48 (Dec. 1943), 433. See also Arthur Koestler, 'On Disbelieving Atrocities', *The Yogi and the Commissar and Other Essays* (Jonathan Cape, 1945), 94-9.

according to political expediency.'[25] Criticism of the collective discipline of Britain's total war disseminated images of victimization to complement those which circulated in representations of the Blitz. This helps to explain the failure of British intellectual culture to transcend parochial horizons: imaginative limitations are a counterweight to the subversive potential of writing from British POW camps in Europe.

'EACH A LITTLE PIECE OF ENGLAND': BRITISH POW-CAMP COMMUNITIES IN EUROPE.[26]

Representations of officer POW camps in Germany and Italy dominate British wartime and post-war consciousness of confinement in occupied Europe: one commentator has argued that in the 1950s the *Offizierlager* were the only aspect of the war understood by the general public.[27] In the immediate post-war decades fiction about the war 'degenerated into jingoism and sentimentality, or dashing tales about the exploits of upper-class officers'; publishers paperbacked escape stories but neglected to popularize other, 'dissenting', texts.[28] It is of some significance for the ways the meanings of the war were articulated in post-war Britain that British troops were not involved in the liberation of the death camps in the East at Auschwitz-Birkenau and Treblinka. Christopher Burney, an English internee who survived Buchenwald, described the arrival of Jews (evacuated from death camps threatened by the Russian advance) in *The Dungeon Democracy* (1945), giving a completely different interpretation of the world that Primo Levi has meticulously described as the 'Grey Zone'.[29] Burney was unable to recognize atrocities for what they were. The moral horror of the 'Grey Zone' was the systematic dehumanization of people, the way the struggle for survival was engineered into the harshest discipline by the Nazi regime. Burney explained this dehumanization not as a product of systematic

[25] Orwell, 'Arthur Koestler', *CEJL*, iii. 235.
[26] *The Captive Heart*, dir. Basil Dearden (1946).
[27] Fraser Harrison, 'Fifties Writing', BBC Radio 3, 11 March 1996.
[28] Andy Croft, *Red Letter Days: British Fiction in the 1930s* (Lawrence and Wishart, 1990), 336. Worpole, *Dockers and Detectives*, 63.
[29] Primo Levi, *The Drowned and the Saved*, trans. Raymond Rosenthal (1986. Michael Joseph, 1988), 22–51.

brutalization, but in racial and cultural terms; 'the prisoners were not British but European'.[30] Reports from repatriated POWs of the 'comradeship, of each man keeping his self-respect and helping the other to do likewise' in British prison-camp communities helped Burney single out the Jews—'more like animals than men'—as contributing to Buchenwald's depravity (66, 89). Inhumanity was not 'a direct offspring of Nazidom', but the expression of a herd mentality (ix). Stories about escaping POWs not only colonized the national memory of the war, they also leant authority to figurative appropriations of the concentration camp, which in turn abetted some facile interpretations of unfamiliar regimes.

British officer POWs were protected by international law, and the disciplines to which they were subjected did not originate solely from their captors (this far, the effects of the distribution of power in the *Offizierlager* were the opposite to those in the 'Grey Zone'). Foucault's prison has 'neither exterior nor gap', but this was not true of British officer POW camps, even in the dimension of the physical, and especially not that of the symbolic.[31] The captured soldier 'remains a member of his own armed forces and is subject to their military discipline'.[32] The captors' authority was incomplete in the sense that, within the limits of the camp, responsibility for organizing time and space devolved onto the inmates: 'All discipline is self-imposed,' observes a character in Eric Williams's *The Tunnel*.[33] This is why the exclusively male society of officer POWs represented in fiction and memoirs, with its escape committees, pragmatic reformulations of sporting codes, amateur theatricals (and female impersonation), elaborate feeding rituals and so on, resembles public school or college life. POWs were a subject people, but they responded to that subjection by creating a culture of their own. The manner in which these camps were inscribed as familiar territory is an important limit on the metaphorical function of figures of the POW.

The POW camps were severe but they were rarely corrective. The guards at Colditz ' "paid very little attention" ' according to the protagonist of Michael Burn's *Yes, Farewell*: ' "We seldom saw them. It's strange . . . the castle was supposed to be a punishment camp." '[34]

[30] Christopher Burney, *The Dungeon Democracy* (Heinemann, 1945), 89.
[31] Foucault, *Discipline*, 236.
[32] P. R. Reid and Maurice Michael, *Prisoner of War* (Hamlyn, 1984), 48.
[33] Eric Williams, *The Tunnel* (Collins, 1951), 109.
[34] Michael Burn, *Yes, Farewell* (Jonathan Cape, 1946), 200.

The function of the camps was not to turn the individual prisoners into adjusted components in the society that was confining them, but to store captured servicemen, to prevent their reintervention in the military struggle: Dan Billany labels a captured British force as 'perishable goods: warehoused at Benghazi'.[35] POWs are logistically costly side-effects of disarming the enemy; hence William Joyce (the Nazis' broadcaster, nicknamed 'Lord Haw-Haw') mocked the besieged garrison at Tobruk as 'the self-supporting prisoners'.[36] Their confinement was otherwise useless, unless they could be employed in productive work. Officer POWs were exempted from labour by the Geneva convention.[37] By late 1944, one-fifth of German labour needs was drawn from occupied territories. British Other Ranks formed a small part of this supplement to Germany's undermobilized work-force, but their experience went largely unrepresented in contemporary and post-war writing about POWs.[38]

Descriptions of POW camps detail various possibilities for negotiating control of the physical and mental spaces produced by administrative and symbolic structures. The perception of capture as a (sometimes welcome) freedom from responsibility, and the countermodel of prison as an opportunity for an imaginative or practical recouping of responsibility, are major themes, which qualify contemporary interpretations of the war as subjection to coercive disciplines. The broader symbolic significance of the space of the prison in POW writing lies in the manipulation of themes of interiority and exteriority, or of agency versus detachment or exclusion. The prisoner was out of the war but, on a personal level, his imprisonment sustained him as a passive participant. This liminal situation can be viewed as an extreme experiential analogue of the mutually-reinforcing dichotomy of discipline and opportunity which resonates through wartime writing.

Representations of the *Offizierlager* reinforce a martial ethos which is everywhere else contradicted by the convergence of policy and technology on the mass-killing of civilians. Inside the wire,

---

[35] Dan Billany, *The Trap*, (Faber, 1950), 367. Compare Arthur Koestler, *Scum of the Earth* (Jonathan Cape, 1941), 138, on the victims of French internment: 'What a find for Himmler's black-clothed men! Three hundred thousand pounds of democratic flesh, all labeled, alive, and only slightly damaged.'

[36] Alexander Clifford, *'Crusader'* (George Harrap, 1942), 59.

[37] Reid and Michael, *Prisoner of War*, 38, 139.

[38] Alan Milward, *War, Economy and Society: 1939–1945* (Harmondsworth: Penguin, 1987), 77, 26, 220.

British military hierarchy and custom were sustained and even exag-gerated: 'men inscribe themselves upon space, immediately covering it with familiar gestures, memories, customs and intentions', as Barthes reminds us.[39] The space of the prison camp was made famil-iar both by private ritual and organized activity. Unofficial produc-tion ranged from elaborate, improvised domestic skills (cooking, utensil making, etc.) to escape, or escapist work: the labours of tunnel construction, disguise manufacture and document forging, as well as literary and artistic creation. J. L. R. Croft and R. A. Axford wrote and published an epistolary fiction *Wychwood Chronicles* (1941), a product of their 'homesickness' which was 'passed by the German censors', and Leslie C. Hunt *The Prisoners' Progress: An Illustrated Diary of the March into Captivity of the Last of the British Army in France—June 1940* (1941).[40] Cultural traffic was bilateral: Benjamin Britten's 'The Ballad of Little Musgrave and Lady Barnard' was composed for a music festival at Eichstätt (*Oflag* VIIB).[41] E. J. Scollay's cartoon series—'Eccentricities of an Ex-POW'—in the manuscript camp magazine *The Quill* (begun in *Oflag* IX in 1941), projects a post-war world in which the only reminders of hostilities are the idiosyncratic domestic skills of the repatriated prisoner.[42]

The camps were island communities prosecuting an innocent and rule-bound campaign of non-co-operation in the midst of enemy ter-ritory. The major American literary response to the Allied bombing of Europe, Kurt Vonnegut's *Slaughterhouse-Five* (1969), was written out of its author's experience as a POW in Dresden. British officer POWs make a cameo appearance, 'dressed half for battle, half for tennis or croquet': 'They were adored by the Germans, who thought they were exactly what Englishmen ought to be. They made war look stylish and reasonable, and fun.'[43] Vonnegut's vignette of a privil-eged and innocent war, sustained in a compound surrounded by starving Russian prisoners, is a brilliant parody of post-war POW

39 Roland Barthes, 'The World as Object', *Selected Writings*, ed. Susan Sontag (1982. Fontana, 1983), 63.
40 J. L. R. Croft and R. A. Axford, *Wychwood Chronicles* (Hutchinson, 1941), preface.
41 Michael White, 'Britten's chorus for a captive audience', *Independent on Sunday*, 10 Nov. 1991.
42 E. G. C. Beckwith (ed.), *Selections from The Quill. A Collection of Prose, Verse and Sketches by Officer Prisoners-of-War in Germany, 1940–1945* (Country Life, 1947), 60, 96, 125, 142, 188, 261, 263.
43 Kurt Vonnegut, *Slaughterhouse-Five* (1969. Vintage, 1991), 68–9.

fiction and memoirs, highlighting the way wartime ideologies and representations contributed to the post-war sanitization of war stories.

The airman evading capture, or the escaping POW, were potential witnesses to events in Europe that went largely unregistered by the majority of Britons: insular perspectives were confronted with new experiences.[44] Even in narratives of escape, the prisoner's access to European realities constitutes the possibility of revisionary inter-pretations of the war rather than a reinforced insularity. Escape and resistance novels like Arthur Gwynn-Browne's *Gone for a Burton* and H. E. Bates's *Fair Stood the Wind for France* dramatize contact with occupied Europeans as a challenge to the ideological and moral presumptions of British airmen. Britons who commute to their work destroying German cities have no way of visualizing the 'other war' fought in cold blood, in the territories over which they return to an unoccupied home.[45] Bates's hero, witness to the violence of life in occupied France, escapes to fight in 'a new way', with 'the clearer anger of a new experience'.[46] However, in both novels, the shock of alien realities is diminished by the narrative's restoration of an insu-lar collectivity, a return to the idealized communities from which the airmen have been missing.

The prisoner's desire to transcend imaginatively what cannot be breached physically is another dimension of the perspective-making claims of prison writing. The theme of prison as a place of recuper-ation, contemplation, and education asserts liberating disciplines, a further appropriation and transformation of its territory. The prison camp was figured as an arena for the making of the self, rather than as a place where persons were corrected or demolished. This self-making took two forms, one concerning the effort to escape physically, the other 'escape of the mind'.[47] These themes bifurcate significantly, and register different perspectives on war. The escape project is often a personal narrative whose end is reintegration with the war effort, a closing of the gap between the excluded prisoner and the warring nation state. Successful escapes were rare, out of 15,000

---

[44] For an example of escapers as sources for a history of occupation 'from below', see Roger Absalom, *A Strange Alliance: Aspects of Escape and Survival in Italy 1943–45* (Florence: Leo S. Olschki Editore, 1991).

[45] Arthur Gwynn-Browne, *Gone for a Burton* (Chatto and Windus, 1945), 77.

[46] H. E. Bates, *Fair Stood the Wind for France* (Michael Joseph, 1944), 163.

[47] Michael Burn, *Farewell to Colditz* (White Lion, 1974), p. ii.

RAF POWs, just 30 escaped back to the UK (those who evaded capture had a greater chance of flight from the Continent).[48] Nevertheless escape-mindedness was widely represented as a continuation of the war effort from within the wire. International convention dictated that escape entailed only a disciplinary punishment.[49] The war that was restaged in miniature within the camps was innocent, or unreal, compared with that from which the POW had been excluded.[50] In a temporal reversal of Hazlitt's judgement on Shakespeare's Henry V—'His adventure on Gadshill was a prelude to the affair of Agincourt, only a bloodless one'—the prison camp was a site for restaging hostilities without violence.[51] Numerous contemporary texts contributed to the domestication of the prison camp. The magazine issued to the families of POWs by the Red Cross displaced the waste of confinement with a barrage of evidence that the camps were sites of physical and spiritual gain; through sport, theatre and music, and education. The reporting of personal parcels, letters home, photographs and art-work, as well as the administration of examinations, forged links across the wire.[52]

Escape-minded pursuit of individual agency in the form of a return to the war, and the post-war oriented educational preparation for 'the battle that looms ahead—the battle of the peace' were often viewed as in competition.[53] According to ex-schoolboy-communist Giles Romilly, co-author with Michael Alexander, of *Privileged Nightmare* (1954), an account of Colditz's well-connected social elite, 'the cult of escape held moral sway': improving your mind for

[48] Aidan Crawley, *Escape From Germany: A History of R.A.F. Escapes During the War* (Collins, 1956), 23, 297–300.   [49] Reid and Michael, *Prisoner of War*, 39.

[50] Prisoners were, however, on occasion deprived of their POW status—Robert Kee dedicated *A Crowd is not Company* (1947) to the memory of fifty men executed after their failed 'Great Escape' from Stalag Luft III. See David Rolf, *Prisoners of the Reich: Germany's Captives 1939–1945* (Coronet, 1989), 110 and Richard Garrett, *P.O.W.: The Uncivil Face of War* (Newton Abbot: David and Charles, 1981), 159–60.

[51] William Hazlitt, *The Characters of Shakespeare's Plays*, in Jonathan Bate (ed.), *The Romantics on Shakespeare* (Harmondsworth: Penguin, 1992), 364.

[52] *The Prisoner of War. The Official Journal of the Prisoner of War Department of the Red Cross and St John War Organization* (May 1942–July 1945). Supplied free to next of kin, the magazine instructed readers how to write letters to a prisoner of war (they should tell him about the 'money you've saved' but not 'the dinner you ate' or the 'vase you broke') and knit socks. Its coverage of camp life is unremittingly upbeat, a feature which it shares with the numerous magazines produced by the prisoners themselves. However there was no cross-fertilization, as censorship rules prevented the distribution of either kind of publication across the wire.

[53] Noel Barber, *Prisoner of War: The Story of British Prisoners Held by the Enemy* (George Harrap, 1944), 41.

post-war responsibilities was regarded as an 'almost treacherous heresy'.[54] Romilly retrospectively suppressed his involvement in running a Marxist study group in Colditz.[55] Individualist escapades, not progressive politics, were the core of post-war narrativization. In John Braine's 1957 novel *Room at the Top*, the prestige of escape, a 'game for officers', is the badge of privilege.[56] The rivalry between the ambitious, self-made Joe Lampton and the wealthy, upper-middle-class Jack Wales is defined by their prison camp experience. Lampton, a prisoner-student supplied with texts from the New Bodleian, observes of the escape-minded Wales:

'It was alright for him to escape. He had a rich daddy to look after him and to buy him an education. He could afford to waste his time. I couldn't. Those three years were the only chance I'd get to be qualified. . . .I was bloody well pleased when I was captured. I wasn't going to be killed trying to escape and I wasn't going to be killed flying again. I didn't like being a prisoner but it was a damned sight better than being dead.'[57]

Lampton's capture is an opportunity to redefine his place in a rigid socio-economic hierarchy, after the war. Prison is revisionary, yet, replicating class structures, it is simultaneously reactionary. Wales's escape makes him the hero of a narrative that he and his class plot for themselves, a narrative that excludes Lampton. War is redefined in these choices, ceasing to be a system in which the individual has a mechanical subservience. As Samuel Hynes has noted:

An individual's war is necessarily a story without a plot, strung along a narrative line that is invented somewhere else by staff officers whom one never sees, or that simply happens, by chance. That narrative must always seem irrational to the junior officers and other ranks who do the particular dying. And rightly so; for war *is* irrational, seen from the inside.[58]

The figure of the escaper, however, is invested with the capacity to liberate himself from inscription in these narratives. Creating his own story, his role was enviable, not least to apologists for the literary imagination like Lord David Cecil: 'A man is admired who escapes from a German prison camp. Why should [the artist] be blamed for

---

[54] Giles Romilly and Michael Alexander, *The Privileged Nightmare* (Weidenfeld and Nicolson, 1954), 86-7.
[55] Burn, *Farewell to Colditz*, p. v.   [56] Garrett, *P.O.W.*, 160.
[57] John Braine, *Room at the Top* (Eyre and Spottiswoode, 1957), 128.
[58] Samuel Hynes, review of Terence O'Brien, *Chasing After Danger*, *Times Literary Supplment*, 4,560 (24-30 Aug. 1990), 900.

escaping out of the dingy, bloodstained prison of contemporary events into the fertile garden of his creative fancy?'[59]

The development of the escape story genre in the immediate post-war period involved a shift from the documentation of daily prison life (Billany's and Dowie's *The Cage* (1949, written by 1943), the bulk of Williams's *Goon in the Block* (1945)) to a preoccupation with individual or small group escape attempts. This change in emphasis was is in part due to the exigencies of the contest between prisoner and captor; contemporary RAF memoirs are also silent about weaponry and tactics.[60] Eric Williams's *Goon in the Block* was in press before Europe was liberated: 'For obvious reasons it has not been possible to tell of the escape, neither are any of the references made to escape strictly true.'[61] The history of RAF escaping was planned in a POW camp, and later commissioned by the Air Ministry Historical Branch 'for the use of the Service'; the text published in 1956 was an abbreviated version. Robert Kee's prison manuscripts were a major source for one chapter.[62] The very existence of escape literature is a kind of security leak.[63] Arthur Koestler declined absolutely to describe his escape from post-invasion France in *Scum of the Earth* because so many details would have to be camouflaged: moreover, up to this point in his narrative, the 'I' was typical; with his escape it ceased to be so.[64]

Goon in the Block—'fact thinly disguised as fiction'—was rewritten as the famous *The Wooden Horse* (1949).[65] Williams's observation that prisoners walk a left-hand circuit round the wire—a form of traffic control—becomes, in *The Wooden Horse*, simply a 'convention', which invites interpretation as an eccentricity signifying British refusal to be dominated in the 'ceaseless war against the enemy'.[66] 'An indomitable spirit rang in their steps', wrote Giles Romilly, once co-editor with his brother (who ran away from Wellington College)

[59] Quoted in Jeremy Treglown and Bridget Bennett (eds.), *Grub Street and The Ivory Tower* (Oxford: Clarendon Press, 1998) 142.

[60] See Guy Gibson, *Enemy Coast Ahead* (Michael Joseph, 1946), 251.

[61] Eric Williams, *Goon in the Block* (Jonathan Cape, 1945), 6.

[62] Crawley, *Escape From Germany*, 7.

[63] P. R. Reid, *The Colditz Story* (Hodder and Stoughton, 1952), 9: 'Escape books are sometimes said to make escaping more difficult for the future . . . they are never criticised for that by the escapers of the Second World War.'

[64] Koestler, *Scum*, 234.

[65] Eric Williams, *The Wooden Horse* (Collins, 1949), preface.

[66] Williams, *Goon*, 47; *Wooden Horse*, 10; *Tunnel*, 109.

of the anti-militarist *Out of Bounds*.[67] Noel Barber corrected the impression that the worst thing about being a POW 'was the feeling of being uselessly out of the war', with the claim of another 'eye-witness', 'we know that our bearing has told on the Germans'.[68] British officers and Other Ranks (a fiction in the name of the People's War: camps were strictly segregated) break into 'Roll out the Barrel' to drown out a German war communiqué in Ealing's *The Captive Heart* (1946). The film was dedicated to men whose 'unbroken spirit is the symbol of a moral victory . . . a war in which no decorations could be given'.[69]

Escape narratives are about the making of men, release from the mass into glamorous autonomy:

Y'know, I enjoyed myself when we were escaping . . . We were really living then. People don't live half the time, y'know . . . I think it's only when you're being hunted that you really live . . . An escaping prisoner is the most privileged person in the world.[70]

This is the polar opposite of Primo Levi's tale of the death camps, a story in which men are unmade by their incarceration, and prevented from narrating. The witness, under constant threat of erasure, having no plot of his own, 'felt overwhelmed by an enormous edifice of violence and menace but could not form for himself a representation of it because his eyes were fastened to the ground by every single minute's need'. Levi's ability to speak of these things is itself a mark of privilege, the privilege of survival which, he felt, falsified his testimony.[71]

The model of prison as an opportunity for intellectual development is potentially radical. Where the escape-minded reformulate the ideological duel of competing states within the space of exclusion, prisoners committed to contemplating their situation in its broadest terms sought escape from ideological confinement. One form this reappraisal could take was a renegotiation of the individual's relationship to the official narratives of the war. Amongst

[67] Giles Romilly, 'Three Sketches from a Prison Camp', *PNW* 26 (1945), 168. For the story of *Out of Bounds*, see Giles and Esmond Romilly, *Out of Bounds: The Education of Giles Romilly and Esmond Romilly* (Hamish Hamilton, 1935), 244–67. Esmond Romilly, who fought in the German XIIth International Brigade in Spain, was shot down in mid-Atlantic in 1942 while serving in the Royal Canadian Air Force (his Spanish escapades had led the War Office to turn him down in 1939).

[68] Barber, *Prisoner of War*, 94, 131.

[69] Dedication to *The Captive Heart*.

[70] Williams, *Wooden Horse*, 252.   [71] Levi, *Drowned*, 6–7.

fictions by prisoners of war, Robert Kee's *A Crowd is not Company* (1947) and *The Impossible Shore* (1949) and Michael Burn's *Yes, Farewell* (1946) relate this project to the idea of escape as access to less parochial frames of reference. Alex Comfort—who in his two novels about Europe and the Nazis, *No Such Liberty* (1941) and *The Power House* (1944), had tried to go beyond these limits—noted that the British writer's effort to represent the war was handicapped by the fact that 'we are an island, isolated from the real Europe, and unable to distinguish it from the dolls' house which our propaganda is making'.[72] Kee and Burn narrate failed attempts at escape which provide insights about the European war on which that reappraisal can go to work, interrogating the meanings of the war. By joining a perspective exterior to the war fought by Britons to intuitions of what the war means in Europe, these novels open up the question of the symbolic and practical determinants on wartime discourse about the war.

CONFINEMENT AND LIBERATION

The wire is the limit both of the prisoner's world and of his continuity in time: the sense of 'ownership' of his former life failed.[73] Bruno Bettelheim, held in a Nazi concentration camp 1938-9, observed that survival was dependent on adaption so extreme as to be a reality exchange. Older prisoners acceded to a radical disjunction in time and selfhood, 'everything that happened to them, even the worst atrocity, was "real" to them'.[74] British POWs, protected by international convention and nourished by the Red Cross (the difference between them and the 'famished . . . unfortunates of Buchenwald and Belsen'), experienced a different mode of this translation out of the world and into the reality of 'the indefiniteness of duration'.[75] After Dunkirk, the Overseas Intelligence Department reported that broadcasting 'is now our only means of addressing a great part of Europe', but these

---

[72] Alex Comfort, 'On Interpreting the War', *Horizon*, 5/29 (May 1942), 359.

[73] Guy Morgan, *Only Ghosts Can Live* (Crosby, Lockwood and Son, 1945), 130.

[74] Bruno Bettelheim, 'Individual and Mass Behaviour in Extreme Situations' (1943), *Surviving and Other Essays* (Thames and Hudson, 1979), 68.

[75] J. E. R. Wood (ed.), *Detour: The Story of Oflag IVC* (The Falcon Press, 1946), 3; *The Captive Heart* (the screenplay was co-written by Guy Morgan).

signals also connoted the unreality of the world beyond the wire: 'For three years the war was just a large scale Radio thriller.'[76]

Clay, the narrator of two novels by Robert Kee, inhabits a spatio-temporally disjunct world, an 'infinite chain of familiar days' (the protagonist's name is a transparent cross-Channel encryption of the author's identity).[77] The literary analogue of the experience of term-less confinement is the chronicle. Like Davin, Kee wrote war history after interpreting the war in fiction: 'artists who re-create life. . . prove the good historians in the end.'[78] His historiographical goal was to restore 'the look of events before later events turned them into history'.[79] The chronicle, drawing on ephemeral sources, restored horizons of ignorance—'no one at the time could ever say exactly what was going to happen next'.[80] Chronicle, lacking 'narrativity', does not produce closure.[81] But the attempt to drive a wedge between the event and its retrospective figuration is a Sisyphean task. In *Scum of the Earth*, Arthur Koestler noted that the fact of his escape, and the goal-directedness of narrative, obstructed his effort to communicate either the 'strange prison rhythm of monotony and excitement', or 'the burning despair' of Europe's internees and concentration camp victims.[82] Kee's relaying of 'the picture which a reader of British and American newspapers and listeners to radio broadcasts might have received as the year unfolded' might circimcumvent certain *post factum* constructions of events, but it cannot so readily reproduce the imaginary and ideological contexts on which those readers and listeners drew in interpreting and evaluating information.[83] There are no innocent appraisals of such information; its significance is a function of the way it can be related to other information and beliefs. A million deaths is front page news; if they are reported in a few column inches on the back page, as the *News Chronicle* carried the Bund report on the extermination of Jews in

---

[76] Briggs, *War of Words*, 229; *The Captive Heart*; Robert Kee, *A Crowd is not Company* (Eyre and Spottiswoode, 1947), 66. See Jeffrey Richards and Dorothy Sheridan (eds.), *Mass-Observation at the Movies* (Routledge and Kegan Paul, 1987), 140, for Mass Observation's 1940 report that the cinema could 'show [the population] the war they cannot see and hardly believe in'.   [77] Kee, *Crowd*, 65.

[78] Robert Kee, 'Mercury on a Fork', *The Listener*, 85/2,186, (18 Feb. 1971), 208.

[79] Robert Kee, *1945: The World We Fought For* (Hamish Hamilton, 1985), p. xxvii.

[80] Robert Kee, *The World We Left Behind: A Chronicle of the Year 1939* (Weidenfeld and Nicolson, 1984), 1.

[81] Hayden White, 'The Value of Narrativity in the Representation of Reality', *Critical Inquiry*, 7/1 (Autumn 1980), 9.

[82] Koestler, *Scum*, 113, 234-5.   [83] Kee, *1945*, p. xxvii.

Poland in June 1942, the veracity of the report is qualified, silently but all the more effectively.[84] Nevertheless, Kee's chronicles resemble the 'live interpretation' of historical re-enactment in the working museums of the late twentieth century (the Imperial War Museum offers a low-tech, participatory 'Blitz Experience') which has 'left any unified view of the national past—liberal radical or Conservative—in tatters. Culturally it is pluralist.'[85] The chronicle also mimes the prisoner-of-war's loss of the contexts with which contemporaries at home interpreted war news. The prison perspective could also complicate a unified view of the war: the absence of certain contexts, or their modification in prisoners' representations of the conditions of their confinement to themselves, made possible different readings of the war.

Turning the contingent into narrative is an act of self-definition, as well as a fundamental operation in the redescription of violence. J. B. Priestley, in 1940, urged the 'correct' way of seeing the war 'as one chapter in a tremendous history, the history of a changing world, the breakdown of one vast system and the building up of another and better one'.[86] Kee's post-war chronicles, respectively a valediction and a salutation, are dependent on boundaries which are the functions of a superimposed narrative order. War's beginning and end are crucial symbols in the interpretation of wartime experience; they are also the junctures at which wartime events must be sutured with broader cultural narratives.[87] The reconstructionist note of *1945: The World We Fought For* is qualified by knowledge of the Cold War and the nuclear threat.[88] Kee's novels explore war's temporality, and the symbolic connections forged between beginnings and ends, in more exacting ways. The POW's experience of the duration of confinement, a microcosm and model of the duration of war, is the basis of a critique of the rhetoric of means and ends.

Capture was represented, conventionally, as the end of an individual's war—for you the war is over. Experiencing a personal end to hostilities, the POW had a different relationship to the temporal frames employed in the rationalization of war. The captive was 'abandoned'; many POW texts are attempts to recover continuity, or

---

[84] Julian Scott, 'The British Press and the Holocaust 1942–1943' (unpub. Ph.D. thesis, University of Leicester, 1994), 263, 270.

[85] Raphael Samuel, *Theatres of Memory: Past and Present in Contemporary Culture* (Verso, 1994), 281. [86] Priestley, *Postscripts*, 36.

[87] See Eric Leed, *No Man's Land: Combat and Identity in World War I* (Cambridge: Cambridge University Press, 1979), p. xi. [88] Kee, *1945*, 354.

rejoin the subject to larger narratives.[89] Writing in La Sauté prison in
Paris in 1943, Jean Genet observed that the difference between the
abandoned and the criminal transforms the prison: 'The great evil of
this war has been its dissolving the hardness of our prisons. . . .
Nothing is more repugnant than an innocent man in prison. He has
done nothing to deserve jail (these are his own words).'[90] Becoming a
POW meant negotiating a new relationship to the collective disciplines of the war effort. The POW existed between 'the feeling of
being uselessly out of the war' and Winnicott's irresponsible fear of
freedom, being 'relieved of all responsibility . . . like going sick when
one was in trouble at school'.[91] The polarization of war as sentence
and as release is reproduced in descriptions of the prison camp:
'When a fighting man is captured he both loses and gains certain
rights and privileges.'[92] The instability of these representations is
witnessed in Kee's fiction by the captive first-person narrator's vacil-
lation between apparently contradictory interpretations of his
predicament. The fluidity of reference of these ideas of freedom and
constraint not only implies the prisoner's imaginative and metaphorical work at transforming his prison, but also the facility with which,
on a wider scale, images of prison contributed to contemporary conceptualizations of the war.

A Crowd is not Company represents Clay's crash-landing in occupied Europe as the transformation of a routine mission into a personal trial, a radical and disorienting complication of military
agency. The airman's duty to evade capture—he is an expensively
trained and scarce component of a military machine—is an extern-
ally enforced autonomy, which puts concepts of autonomy under
stress. John Verney registered the pressure of the escape myths of a
'film-conditioned age': failing to be Ronald Colman, he claimed that
real POWs 'are always glad of an excuse not to try and escape'.[93]
Falling into enemy hands is a release from an unnerving reliance on
self, recalling Keith Vaughan's contention that austere institutions
banish 'the fear of freedom'.[94] But capture simultaneously confounds the 'narrowness of mind' with which 'one has to be equipped

[89] Rolf, Prisoners of the Reich, 50.
[90] Jean Genet, The Miracle of the Rose, trans. Bernard Frechtman (Anthony Blond,
1965), 27.   [91] Quoted in Barber, Prisoner of War, 94; Williams, Goon, 43.
[92] Eric Williams (ed.), The Escapers: A Chronicle of Escape in Many Wars (Eyre and
Spottiswoode, 1953), 15.
[93] John Verney, Going to the Wars: A Journey in Various Directions (Collins, 1955),
206–7.   [94] Vaughan, Journals, 57.

in time of war'.[95] Face to face with the enemy Clay is aware, as if for the first time, that his work as a bomber pilot kills people. In the light of German interpretations of British strategy, he apprehends the inherent contradictions in liberal-democratic war aims: the personal liberties which legitimize his combatant role now seem to him insignificant when compared to the calamities which his work in Bomber Command produces. However the 'mental confusion which awaits defeated men and defeated nations' is only fully confronted in the narrative of liberation in Kee's sequel, *The Impossible Shore*.[96]

Clay's captivity is an alternation between solitude and enforced society. In this context, turning in on the self to escape from the mass is the most accessible liberty. But his imaginative work on the hostile yet soon familiar space of the camp produces equivocal conceptions of the meaning of prison in relation to civil life. As a refuge from 'the stampeding crowd' confinement is a haven. This is one reason why prison life is disjunctive: one cannot take the lessons of prison back to the world because solitude is not to be had elsewhere. However, the camp is also an over-crowded territory. In this sense it is like the world bar one condition, it is escapable. While Clay recognises that physical escape is a fantasy, its cost—limited sentences of solitary confinement—is paradoxically a benefit, the exclusion of massed humanity.[97]

Escape is not straightforwardly an effort to return to the outside, but a complex activity that mimics military conflict. If, as for Dan Billany, capture proves finally that war is a 'stupid' game, it also makes possible the reproduction of war as an innocent game. Escape is 'a schoolboy's dream come true', a cloak-and-dagger sport of secrecy, strategy and invention that is the stuff of 'personal romanticizing'. It is the social complement of the preoccupation with escape into self and solitude. Tunnelling was a way of using up time; would-be escapees dropped out at the last minute. Escape plots generated 'all the ingredients of an exciting life and nothing to pay'.[98] They are literal equivalents of the production of imaginative narrative: Michael Burn observed that writing novels was an alternative escape, but like tunnels, such narratives were rarely brought to completion.[99] The wire of the compound is the margin within which the war is suspended, temporally and in terms of the contest of injuring.

[95] Kee, *Crowd*, 18.   [96] Ibid. 9.

[97] Compare Christopher Burney, *Solitary Confinement* (Clerke and Cockeran, 1952), 152.   [98] Kee, *Crowd*, 75.   [99] Burn, *Yes, Farewell*, 16.

The POW on the run risked a unique encounter with the realities of occupation and totalitarian society. Such encounters were necessarily to be avoided, and the typical escape narrative is centred on the isolated and hopefully invisible efforts of the escapers.[100] Conventional ideas about the escaper's agency in narratives of self-determination underlie the behaviour of the refugee Katherine Lind, in Larkin's *A Girl in Winter* (1947, written in 1945). In deference to her contacts in England, she chooses to tell the events of her journey to Britain 'in a way that freed them of much of their unpleasantness, and made them sound like a series of actions taken of her own will'.[101] In the context of the unified imprisoned mass, escape and its associated ideologies and practices were a means of assuaging the uncertainty caused by the denial of a role in the strategic narrative. Angered by the guards' reiteration of this exclusion, '"For you the war is over"', Clay vows, '"It won't be over for me until it's over for everybody."'[102] This notion of a personal war is a flexible one, signifying both a division of the personality—Michael Burn's protagonist Alan MacLaren is 'escaping in order to escape himself'—and the pitting of self against the enemy in a struggle whose relation to global war takes the form of a simulacrum or metaphor.[103]

A Crowd is not Company can be read as a critical refutation of the ideology which would be firmly established by the escape narratives of Eric Williams and P. R. Reid. In these popular works, escape is both a continuation of global conflict on a local, tactical level, and a form of self-discovery and development. Kee's novels are closer to European traditions of prison writing, notably Koestler's books, which analyse the functions of imprisonment in repressive political regimes. But Kee's narrative owns up to an additional ideological barrier to contact with European realities: 'I wanted to digest the experience. But it changed into a game I was playing at school.'[104] This barrier is in part constituted by the very tropes with which the experience of prison was mitigated and brought under control: but it also reflects the impercipience about occupied Europe amongst British

---

[100] Compare Geoffrey Household's *Rogue Male* (Chatto and Windus, 1939), about a would-be assassin of Hitler (his motives are personal revenge) pursued through the English countryside by Nazi agents.

[101] Philip Larkin, *A Girl in Winter* (Faber, 1947), 230–1.   [102] Kee, *Crowd*, 37.

[103] Burn, *Yes, Farewell*, 37. Both Bettelheim, 'Individual and Mass Behaviour', 52, 68 and Arthur Koestler, *Spanish Testament* (Gollancz, 1937), 289 and *Darkness at Noon*, trans. Daphne Hardy (Jonathan Cape, 1940), 109, make the split consciousness a characteristic of the imprisoned self.   [104] Kee, *Crowd*, 153.

writers determined to find analogues of totalitarian institutions and oppression in their own childhood and wartime experience.

Clay's version of the school-concentration camp analogy transforms the prison camp into an innocent battlefield on which war is enacted as play. Kee's novels do not transcend the effects of these figurative translations, though they do point up their role in the imaginative projection of that world, and by extension the world at large. Like many other texts about POW camps, they are school-minded, an outgrowth of an educational system which valorized suffering, and which by the 1930s had also yielded a system of codes by which the exigencies of political and moral life could be represented in terms of the classroom and dormitory. Graham Greene's anthology *The Old School* is packed with these tropes—in his *It's a Battlefield*, the prison is 'just like a school'—suggesting the extent to which a generation's image of itself against the background of contemporary history was steeped in its memories of an educational system: 'We grow backwards in war time,' observed Evelyn Waugh, who set Guy Crouchback's military training at Kut-al-Imara House Preparatory School.[105] By representing school in terms of totalitarian structures, writers appropriated alien political experience at the same time as they constructed a parochial ideological framework for surveying the European scene. If they looked to Europe, they did so through the filter of British institutions, and the ideologies which their human products embodied. W. H. Auden compared his school to a 'Fascist state' while grammar-school old boy H. E. Bates wrote that the Great War was partly responsible for the fact that he was 'not educated but repressed', only to 'escape' later into a realm of self-fulfilment. Council-school educated Walter Greenwood described how a 'handbell knelled us to imprisonment' (his 1933 novel *Love on the Dole* was eventually filmed in 1941 with a 'New Britain' postscript promising that the unemployed would not be 'forgotten men of peace').[106] Henry Green's likening of Eton to a 'humane concentration camp' represents the colonization of the present by the past:

Once we had escaped and left we never thought we should think of this time again. We never guessed our thoughts would be driven back to it, that we

---

[105] Graham Greene, *It's a Battlefield* (Heinemann, 1934), 17; Evelyn Waugh, letter to Laura Waugh (5 Nov. [1944]), *The Letters of Evelyn Waugh*, ed. Mark Amory (Weidenfeld and Nicolson, 1980), 192.

[106] Graham Greene (ed.), *The Old School: Essays by Divers Hands* (Jonathan Cape, 1934), 17, 27, 33, 77.

might have to die not so long after we came to be old boys, before enough had happened to drive all recollection of it out, if so much is ever forgotten.[107]

Public schoolboys were 'good Storm Troopers', and for the individualist and the deviant there was the constant threat of society's retribution, 'that thunder of feet down the corridor' which left one sitting as 'still as a rabbit wondering if they were coming for one'.[108] If public school made victims, it made victims who were sometimes unable to distinguish the historical and ideological sources of their own suffering from the beliefs which authorized the perpetration of dissimilar acts in circumstances that bear only a banal analogy to the brutalities of British institutions.

In these reconstructions, school comes to pre-empt the worst abuses of power in the adult world; concentration camps, totalitarianism, total discipline. In the process these political institutions are distorted by analogies that falsify their structure, operation and effects. In *Lions and Shadows*, Isherwood was candid about the distortions engendered by these translations:

Thus it was that 'War' dodged the censor and insinuated itself into my book, disguised as 'Rugtonstead,' an English public school. But here we enter upon further complications. I myself had been to a public school. I knew, or had known while I was there, that public-school life wasn't, in any heroic sense, a 'test.' It was a test, if you like, of social flexibility, of a capacity for 'getting on' with one's contemporaries, of slyness, animal cunning, criminal resource—but certainly not of your fundamental 'Manhood' or the reverse. I *had* known all this, did I know it now?[109]

But Osbert Sitwell, bemoaning war as 'the Great Interruption' to a writing career, could conjure away political reality:

Formerly there were only the ordeals of the private and public school to be endured, concentration camps that were certainly vile enough (there I have seen bullying—and in one instance upon a Jew—which would have taxed the ingenuity of German storm-troopers).[110]

As Orwell noted, violence was too remote to be terrifying and writers could 'swallow totalitarianism *because* they have no experience of anything except liberalism'.[111] We are not intended to understand

---

[107] Green, *Pack My Bag*, 93, 128.   [108] Ibid. 97, 101.

[109] Christopher Isherwood, *Lions and Shadows: An Education in the Twenties* (Hogarth Press, 1938), 77.

[110] Osbert Sitwell, 'Letter to My Son', *Horizon*, 7/39 (March 1943) 167–8.

[111] Orwell, 'Inside the Whale', *CEJL* i. 516.

that a school is exactly like a Fascist state or a concentration camp—
Orwell himself qualifies the conditions at his prep. school, St
Cyprians: 'just as bad in an army, and worse, no doubt, in a
prison'[112]—but neither are we intended to see how they are different.
This is crucial in the interpretation of a war which contained acts of
violence which, to the 'liberal imagination'—the term Tony Kushner
borrows to designate the conceptual and experiential framework
determining resistance to knowledge and understanding of the
Holocaust in British culture—are unimaginable or impermissible
predicates of human beings.[113]

The escape-mindedness of much writing about prison operates
similar modes of metaphorical appropriation of prison experience.
This is evident in the efforts of Reid, in the prologue to his first volume on Colditz, to mediate prison life to an armchair audience.
Boyhood reading of First World War escape stories 'urged [him] to
follow the example of their authors'.[114] Reid's allegory of Colditz
domesticates the unfamiliar:

We called Colditz 'the bad boys' camp'. . . . An officer had to pass an entrance exam. before being admitted through its sacred . . . portals. The
qualifying or passing-out test was the performance of at least one escape
from any one of the many 'Prep.-school' camps that were dotted all over
Germany. Naturally, the qualifying escape exam. was not set by the
Germans, nor were 'full marks' a guarantee of entry—in fact, the contrary,
for the hundred per cent. candidate was never available to take up his
vacancy. He was out of bounds and, happily for him, 'expelled' for good![115]

For all its tongue-in-cheek understatement, this is not a merely
rhetorical performance: 'events . . . are not only shaped *post-factum*
in their narration, but . . . were initially determined as they unfolded
by the schematic ways in which they were apprehended, expressed,
and then acted upon'.[116] The ideological salience of these schemes is
witnessed by Arthur Koestler's bitterly satirical use of the school
trope. At the end of *Scum of the Earth* he characterized the British as
'intelligent schoolboys', and he styled his 1942 update on the French

[112] Orwell, 'Such, Such Were the Joys' (written 1947), *CEJL* iv. 348.

[113] See Mark Rawlinson, 'This Other War: British Culture and the Holocaust',
Cambridge Quarterly, 25/1 (1996), 1–25.

[114] Reid, *The Colditz Story*, 17. See A. J. Evans, *The Escaping Club* (John Lane, 1921),
and, for a genealogy of escape reaching back to Genesis, F. Yeats-Brown (ed.), *Escape: A
Book of Escapes of All Kinds* (Eyre and Spottiswoode, 1934), 10: 'We are all escapers'.

[115] Reid *The Colditz Story*, 17–18.

[116] James Young, *Writing and Rewriting the Holocaust: Narrative and the
Consequences of Interpretation* (Bloomington: Indiana University Press, 1988), 5.

internment camps as 'gossip from one's own school'. Koestler insisted on the distinction between a liberal view of the war—sceptical about atrocities—disseminated by the BBC's announcers, and the knowledge of those survivors in and from occupied Europe who 'wear the old school tie in the shape of some scar on the body'.[117] Kee noted the disparity between the war suffered in Europe, and that described on the Home Service, 'as if it was something that was going on in a drawing room'.[118]

Towards the end of *A Crowd is not Company*, Clay descends into passivity at the moment that the structures of confinement break down. Ahead of the Russian armies' advance on Germany, prisoners are evacuated from Silesia in an undisciplined march west. The opposition of prisoner and gaoler can no longer bolster identity; escape from the column would be easy, but the security of the herd exerts a more powerful pull than the potential for autonomous action.[119] Movement does not bring a sense of liberation, but a conviction that release will be in word only. The book ends with an image of confinement as a spatial regress and diminishment, the view through the wrong end of a telescope (this figure also occurs in Burn's *Yes, Farewell* and Billany's and Dowie's *The Cage*). The description applies not to the dominated space of the prison but to a billet crammed with POW-refugees, a microcosm of an irredeemable post-war world: 'there could be no real escape or liberation from this, ever.'[120]

The sequel, *The Impossible Shore*, expands this vision to the displaced victims of occupation and liberation, narrating the experience of release within the frame of two liberations which fail as deliverance, at the book's beginning by the Russians, and by the Americans at its conclusion. ('In a year or two of war', Waugh would write in the 1950s, '"Liberation" would acquire a nasty meaning.')[121] The period between them is a limbo in which the meanings of the end of war are reassessed. The novel opens with a citation of the cliché of capture, 'For us the war was over', a sign of the difference between this end and any end projected from within the stabilized community of the POW camp.[122] Dreams of release are revoked by actuality, a disenchantment Dostoyevsky knew after his Siberian

---

[117] Arthur Koestler, 'Scum of the Earth—1942', *The Yogi and the Commissar*, 85.
[118] Kee, *Crowd*, 243–4.
[119] Compare Pierre on the retreat from Moscow, Tolstoy, *War and Peace* bk. IV, part iii, ch. 12.   [120] Kee, *Crowd*, 252.
[121] Evelyn Waugh, *The Sword of Honour Trilogy* (Harmondsworth: Penguin, 1987), 344.   [122] Robert Kee, *The Impossible Shore* (Eyre and Spottiswoode, 1949), 9.

confinement: 'our dreams and our long divorce from the reality made us think of freedom as somehow freer than real freedom, that is, than it actually is. The convicts had an exaggerated idea of real freedom and that is so natural, so characteristic of every convict.'[123] Liberation by Soviet armour is a violent and frightening return to the world. The longed-for 'life inside one's own control' is negated by disorder; identity is lost in the chaos of what is effectively an occupation.[124] However, the breaching of the camp perimeter broadens perceptual horizons: the narrator begins to see events through the eyes of others. Displaced from the egocentricity of the model-world of the camp, he can view himself objectively, as an individual without significance. That his war is, once again, over is ironic, for Clay has now lost the threads of a narrative, 'caught in something that had neither end nor beginning' (21).

After the enabling conditions of incarceration have been dismantled, the self has no refuge in the status of prisoner. Clay struggles to preserve privacy against humanity's invasions, and as the camp fills with Displaced Persons, the 'self-imposed discipline' of officer POWs is turned into administrative power, exercised on liberated Europeans. British officers fill the vacuum of authority with their own bureaucracy, recreating the illusion of 'normal ordered society' through the recording and distribution of information, and the creation of an emergency civil-service class. The desire for privacy, a room of his own, draws Clay into this managerial cadre as an interrogator of the streams of refugees suspected of containing *Wehrmacht* troops or *Volksturm* amateurs emulating the escapers' craft of disguise and impersonation.

Kee modifies the unstable paradoxes of his earlier volume by revoking the separation between inside and outside the wire, not because Clay has got outside, but because so many people from outside have been brought in. The new inflection of confinement as a kind of escape (from the irrational violence of Europe's liberators) is amplified by Clay's status in the distribution of power. Although this power is gratuitous (Russian policy remains inscrutable and the POWs' future is unclear), it transforms those who wield it. Clay's role as interpreter, not of foreign tongues, but of individuals' stories (about their origins, nationality, and what they have been doing in the war) confronts him with the dilemmas of responsibility that

---

[123] Fyodor Dostoevsky, *The House of the Dead*, trans. Constance Garnett (Dent, 1915), 282.   [124] Kee, *Shore*, 18.

confinement had freed him from. Indifference, assimilated with the
gaze of the powerful, is swift: 'For a moment it was difficult to believe
they were human beings at all. They covered the road and the grass
verge so thickly that they were like insects massed to feed on rotten-
ness' (38–9). Clay recognizes he has learnt that way of seeing from his
German captors (31). The imagery Kee employs, the 'liquid black
crowds', calls to mind the proto-Nazi language and iconography of
the Freikorps (41).[125]

In *A Crowd is not Company*, the pursuit of freedom foundered on
the instability of the boundary of the real and the unreal. In the sequel, and in the context of the indeterminacy of the end of the war,
escape goes through another series of refigurations, all ultimately
found wanting now that a familiar regime is superseded by new
forms of oppression. Walking away into 'the unknown quantity that
the world had now become', Clay is trapped by the military situation
in a liminal realm behind the front (112). The vertiginous freedom of
inhabiting a politically indeterminate territory only makes him
aware of the inevitability of his being caught up again in days
'marked in the normal worldly way by dates and defeats and the complacency of statesmen' (165). Ezra Pound, held at the time of
Germany's surrender in a US Disciplinary Training Centre north of
Pisa, bracketed the end of hostilities with a bowel movement:

[I heard it in the s.h. a suitable place

to hear that the war was over][126]

For Clay, the conjunction of the private and the historical (the end of
an illusion of freedom and the end of war) confirms the prison: 'Now
I was learning what every human being had learnt in his time before
me: that what I had broken through to was only a bigger, more hopeless prison' (201). Alan Moorehead saw 'Germany a prison camp and
all its people prisoners' the day after Victory in Europe.[127] The
Ulyssean project alluded to in Kee's Arnoldian title is beached on a
compulsion to return to the security of the 'real world' on the Allied
side of the Elbe.[128]

---

[125] Klaus Theweleit, *Male Fantasies*, trans. Stephen Conway, Erica Carter, and Chris
Turner, 2 vols. (1977–8. Cambridge: Polity, 1987–9), i. 229–49.
[126] Ezra Pound, Canto LXXVII, *The Cantos* (Faber, 1975), 467.
[127] Alan Moorehead, *Eclipse* (Hamish Hamilton, 1945), 252.
[128] See Matthew Arnold, 'A Summer Night', *The Poems of Matthew Arnold*, ed.
Kenneth Allott (Longmans, 1965), 267–71. *A Crowd is not Company* derives its opposition
of self and crowd from Arnold's 'The Buried Life', *Poems*, 271–5.

The novel ends with two scenes of return that confirm the burden of disillusion that Kee implies must be assumed with freedom. Drivers with the American convoy waiting for POWs at the Elbe puncture Clay's dwindling hope of an exit into autonomy, '"You don't think we came all this way just for you?"'[129] The column of empty lorries is another image of subjugation to the mass as spatial regress, negating the 'false, impossible shore' of the 'soul's horizon'.[130] Later, journeying by train through southern England in the company of the British officers whose regime at Huegeldorf he had escaped, Clay is willing to believe that this return '"really will be the end"'.[131] He has hardened in his conviction that there is no exit to the prison that the world has become, discovering along the way that the real prisoner's escape attempts, despite their mythic potency as autonomous acts, do not break through to that metaphysical prison's outside. His acceptance of a provisional conclusion figures a desire to overcome pessimism (to liberate himself from captivity to an idea which might be the most damaging legacy of his confinement). But it is also a lapse into a kind of conformity now that the disorienting conditions of exile, which provoked reappraisal, have themselves been removed.

The termination of war is represented as no more than a declaration of 'the end', a mere assertion of finality. This confirms the instability of the demarcation of confinement and freedom, war and peace, which Kee's narrative has foregrounded in its persistent figurative transvaluation of such boundaries, and suggests why the book's ending can be neither triumphant nor conclusive. Michael Burn's *Yes, Farewell*, and more particularly Henry Green's *Back*, also linger over these questions about endings, of both war and captivity, and, in the last act of the personal drama of confinement, the juncture between rehabilitation as a new beginning and the fate of the self constructed in prison.

PRISON AND UTOPIANISM

Yes, Farewell, published in 1946, but largely written in Colditz, narrates the forms of moral and intellectual reappraisal which ensue

---

[129] Kee, *Shore*, 247.   [130] Arnold, 'A Summer Night', *Poems*, 270–1.
[131] Kee, *Shore*, 251.

from confinement, linking them to ideals of post-war reconstruction. In the character of Alan MacLaren, 'pitting his free mind against his imprisoned body', Burn configures the relationship between escape in the mind (self-making) and physical escape as an internal division. Confinement is life 'inside a theorem', in which the 'prisoners struggled with themselves'.[132] Sexual desire, an enervating psychological weakness, is cathected to plans to 'get back into the fighting' (8). But these conceptions of freedom, by-products of the imposition of the geometry of prison onto the bodies of inmates ('vertical lines of strain' between the eyes are the imprints of the 'vertical iron bars' of the windows), are destructive of personality (15, 35). Masturbation—MacLaren's hands are instruments of a 'turning in upon himself'—is an analogue of the inwardness of the castle's melancholics (311). The future is reduced to the satisfaction of bodily desire; MacLaren is locked imaginatively into the endemic 'cowardice' of hoping everything outside the prison would remain the same (55). Burn 'even resented the rapid end to the war because [he] had not quite finished [the novel]'.[133] Images associating hands with past and present humiliations—a memory of the awkwardness of sexual initiation ('His hands seemed to have swollen to twice their natural size'), and a portrait showing Hitler standing with 'hands crossed in front of his genitals' that greets his recapture in Munich— underscore the necessity of a different kind of orientation towards the post-war world.[134] Liberation in Yes, Farewell is ultimately defined as an escape from political blindness in a Marxist-inspired critique of liberal individualism.

In Billany's and Dowie's The Cage, the crises of incarceration are to be resolved by metaphorically recasting the prison as a microcosm of a world of solipsists. The revisionary potential of imprisonment is channelled towards transcendence of selfishness: the 'prison of walls and wire' will unhinge the prison of the self. In this moral allegory of prison architecture, with its echoes of the coda of The Waste Land, trust is the key ('A distrustful man is a man in solitary confinement') that can connect the cellular lives of embattled individuals, issuing in an understanding that is figured as surrender—'For us the war was over'—in the contest of egos.[135] Eric Newby presented a very

---

[132] Burn, Yes, Farewell, 8, 15, 83.
[133] Burn, Farewell to Colditz, p. iii.   [134] Burn, Yes, Farewell, 71 and 182.
[135] Dan Billany and David Dowie, The Cage (Longmans, Green and Co., 1949), 34, 157, 190.

different account of the same prison camp, a Fascist orphanage in Northern Italy. The victimization of inmates was not the product of neurosis or Italian authority, but of a caste hierarchy, and a recrudescence of public-school bullying. The policing of the boundary between 'the O.K. people' and the inhabitants of an 'outer darkness', a tyranny deriving from the distribution of power amongst the inmates themselves, contrasts with the description of prisoners' self-discipline as a campaign against their captors in the best-known wartime and post-war POW narratives. Newby abandoned an earlier attempt to write up his diary because of competition from more exciting contemporary accounts of partisans and prison camps, like George Millar's much reprinted *Maquis* (1945) and *Horned Pigeon* (1946): a 'mass walk out' after the Italian Armistice was not exciting enough.[136] Figuring prison as school is here more analytic than compensatory, and as much an analysis of school as of a type of prison.

In Burn's *Yes Farewell*, prison experience becomes a critical perspective on the world from which the prisoner is excluded, but which is nevertheless reproduced inside the prison. Imaginative projections of the prison-castle, and contacts with the conditions of occupied Europe, prompt reflections on the self in its political and social relations. The boundary between the prison and the world outside becomes permeable in the emergence of this critique. When the space of the prison is temporarily enlarged in thespian escapism, staging West End plays which recreate England in the middle of Germany, the effect is to transform not the prison but home. Comedy becomes unintentional satire, exposing 'how meagre was the free life to which all of them were looking forward'.[137] But pessimism about the world also derives from a projection of the prisoner's loss of continuity with it, and from the prison's homeliness. As liberation nears, Jim Irving stages a dream-vision pageant of England's old order (closer in spirit to Woolf's *Between the Acts* than wartime cinematic visions of English history). The dreamer wakes to the 'old dream, almost an obsession now', in which the fantasy of the castle floating through space posits the ubiquity of the conditions of imprisonment (427). Irving personifies the 'alarming forms' of prison thought, rather than its revisionary potential. His life is in suspension, a parenthesis: 'he might have walled himself up' (368). He projects, out of his own

---

[136] Eric Newby, *Love and War in the Apennines* (Hodder and Stoughton, 1971), 7, 37.
[137] Burn, *Yes, Farewell*, 51.

loss, a hopeless post-war world (like Charley Summers in Green's
Back, his lover has died while he is a prisoner). The collapse of personal continuity empties the world. Irving's pageant, and the allegory of imprisonment as a voyage without a compass, is revised in
Burn's poem *The Flying Castle*, which had its origins in a 'waking
nightmare' towards the end of his imprisonment in Colditz and a
new awareness of the necessity of taking up responsibilities again
after having had 'everything settled, however distastefully'.[138] In
both versions, the prisoners are 'travellers on a luxury cruise' like the
European bourgeoisie of Auden's poetry of the early 1930s.[139]
Represented as Irving's fantasy, it is both a registration of the psychological calamities of confinement, and a term in a dialectic of de-
featism and renewal. But published as the author's fiction in 1954
(without reference to the novel) it signalled the revision of the critical
potential of wartime imprisonment, paralleling the process by which
the Second World War was being restaged in POW novels and memoirs of the 1950s as heroic adventure, rather than social revaluation.

   Insular complacency (national and private) and loyalty to the old
political order are symptoms in the novel of pre-war indifference to
European political realities. Bill Franklin's inability to confront the
existence of other regimes of imprisonment in wartime Europe—
'Makes you thank your stars you're British. Christ, what a continent'
—reproduces the myopia of newspaper reports about German concentration camps in the 1930s.[140] As a *Times* correspondent, Burn
had argued his way into Dachau in 1936. MacLaren undergoes a
similar education when an escape attempt brings him into contact
with Europeans fighting a very different war.[141] The escape itself is
'an eccentric holiday' (an innocent version of the flying castle nightmare), and comes to represent an extension of the exile of imprisonment: 'seeing people, whose liberty they had so much envied, as they
were in their disciplined communal life, Alan's desire to be reinstated
in society weakened.'[142] The escaping British POWs are gentlemen
playing a rule-bound game; their motives contrast radically with

---

[138] Michael Burn, *The Flying Castle* (Rupert Hart-Davis, 1954), 10, 7–8. The book was
dedicated to Richard Hillary's parents.
   [139] Burn, *Yes, Farewell*, 152–53. Compare Auden's ship of fools poem 'The month was
April, the year', *The English Auden*, 130–5, and his dream vision 'In the year of my youth
. . .', ed. Lucy S. McDiarmid, *Review of English Studies*, NS, 29/115 (1978), 267–312.
   [140] Burn, *Yes, Farewell*, 314, 228, 203.
   [141] Michael Burn, *The Labyrinth of Europe* (Methuen, 1939) 297–8.
   [142] Burn, *Yes, Farewell*, 129.

those of two absconding Russians, on their way to join Tito's resistance in Yugoslavia. These would-be partisans carry a club, the British are unarmed: 'Alan did not like to say that, if he and Tug were caught, their plan would probably be to consider themselves caught. He had never yet heard of a British escape in which violence was deliberately planned. Death was the certain penalty, and life was still too dear' (166). Escape is codified like a sport: no longer acting on orders and possessing an autonomy denied him as a combatant, the POW weighs up the risks and defines his own precautions.

The contact between Britons and Europeans opens up the conventions of escape narrative to temporary, but nonetheless significant, examination: 'their journey on the Continent had been but an interlude, an exceptional adventure in which their values had been reversed' (386). With their recapture, Burn's escapers are confronted with more sophisticated European perspectives on the war by political prisoners held in the same Munich jail. Tomavich, a Serbian intellectual, mounts an attack on political aloofness: '"What for you has been a mental disturbance to settle in leisure and tranquillity, for us has been an agony"' (192). MacLaren progressively assimilates this position to indict British society. At the outset, according to Tomavich, war is fought for '"self-preservation"', but if it is to bring about a new order, rather than maintain what existed in the past, then the '"first victory is over yourself"' (208 and 251). This analysis is tested in the jail where the POWs' non-political status provides immunity; they alone can hope for survival. The killing of MacLaren's fellow-escapee, while attempting to stop a beating, does not cancel this difference (internalized as a desire to be a victim) but on the contrary, confirms it: 'The times called for something more sustained, more exacting, than the heroic impulse of the moment' (263).

Tomavich envisages prison as a political seminar: MacLaren, when returned to the castle, cultivates his confinement as a liberation from self, not now as a defensive posture with respect to introversion, but as a political programme, integrating the exiled self with a collectivist post-war ideal. The novel ends with the last words of Dostoyevsky's *The House of the Dead* (1861–2), 'New life! Resurrection from the dead!', a citation that enunciates a longed-for personal and collective transformation (432). MacLaren's liberation is identified with the new life of 'Dostoyevski's nation' post-1917, eliding Dostoyevsky's hagiography of the Russian people with MacLaren's perceptions of the heroes of the Soviet war effort.

Personal reconstruction, 'communism meant self-discipline', is the route to social reconstruction (379). This dream of renewal is conditional on redirecting the energies invested in war, reversing the terms of Koestler's essay on Hillary: 'The war had given men back their fellowship in order to confront their death. He wanted the same kind of fellowship in order to confront life' (380).

The optimism of 'yes, farewell', a valediction to the old order, pointed to the re-educative potential of MacLaren's POW experience. But the retitling of the novel as *Farewell to Colditz* in the wake of the television popularization of Reid's Colditz books signalled a change of heart, a goodbye to the war years, not the pre-war era. The 1974 preface urged that the last line of the novel—'If only it could be true for the whole castle, for everyone, now, to-day, all over the world'—should not be understood as pointing to the immanence of reconstruction but as resonating with the disillusion of the post-war era, in particular Burn's own disclaimers about communism.[143] In hindsight Marxism is seen as a defensive and expedient prison diversion, like the digging of tunnels. MacLaren's political education becomes personal resistance to disintegration in prison, rather than a theorized, international resistance to the old order. It possesses only psychological value, and must be rejected simultaneously with prison discipline: 'I might have remained a captive of the ideas, of the intellect, that at Colditz helped to liberate me.'[144]

REHABILITATION AND THE ENDS OF WAR

... the citizen-soldier ... finds himself at the end of a modern war a sharply divided man.[145]

The prisoner takes away something of his captivity, because captivity changes him. In the meantime, the world has changed in his absence (like the conservative politician, he only deludes himself if he believes that a war can be fought to re-establish the reality that was called into

---

[143] See Michael Burn, *Mary and Richard: The Story of Richard Hillary and Mary Booker* (André Deutsch, 1988), 177, for his rejection of 'fashionable dogmatic conclusions'. An approach by the Soviet secret service in Vienna in 1947 provoked a meditation on espionage, see *The Debatable Land: A Study of the Motives of Spies in Two Ages* (Hamish Hamilton, 1970), 7–8.

[144] Burn, *Farewell to Colditz*, p. vi.   [145] Priestley, *Letter*, 3.

question by the disputants' reality claims). Burn spells out the fears of the soon-to-be-liberated who have contrived to preserve a semblance of continuity with the world they were wrenched from: 'They were not confident that they could stand erect, if their inherited props were to be withdrawn.'[146] In Henry Green's *Back* (1946), the theme of return to a world changed or deformed by the socioeconomic imperatives of a crusading war frames an exploration of the distortions produced by the prisoner's inwardness.

Despite the enforced society of the POW camp, 'four years imprisonment with four thousand twirps', Charley Summers is an outcast, a man adrift.[147] He exists out of time, the subject of both exclusion and an interrupted personal narrative. Repatriated before the end of the war, he denies the changes that have occurred during his absence.[148] England is also in a kind of limbo or suspension. It is the summer of the Normandy landings, the event that reconnects Robert Kee's Clay to the war, but which in *Back* sees war disappear over the Channel. War has become a nuisance as those at home orient themselves to its cessation, and personalities-for-the-duration have become weary second nature. 'The war,' as Patrick Hamilton would put it, 'which had begun by making dramatic and drastic demands, which had held up the public in style like a highwayman, had now developed into a petty pilferer, incessantly pilfering.'[149] For Summers, England is unreal because it will not conform to the constructions he places on it. While he persists in this misidentification he is unable to escape the conspiracy or trap that the world has become for him.

The novel opens with Summers visiting the grave of his former lover, Rose, who died the week he was captured. The roses that remind him of his military defeat feed into his compulsive fabrication of a world in which Rose is still, faithlessly, alive, pretending to be a war-widow called Nance Whitmore. Green supplements the vagaries of his protagonist's constructions of reality with obliquities of style and narrative. This, and the novel's chief hermeneutic codes, are intimated in an early passage which, in contrasting prison and liberation, swaps them, so that Summers is seen to be arrested in coming back:

---

[146] Burn, *Yes, Farewell*, 356.   [147] Green, *Back*, 44.

[148] A few thousand sick and wounded POWs were repatriated from German camps before the end of the war. There were two such repatriations before the summer of 1944, see Rolf, *Prisoners of the Reich*, 192–9.

[149] Patrick Hamilton, *The Slaves of Solitude* (Constable, 1947), 101.

The prisoners' camp had flowered with initials, each inmate decorated his bunk with them out there, to let it be known what he taught. Such as 'I.T.' which stood for Inner Temple, at which Marples, this very afternoon perhaps, was still teaching Roman Law. The idea had been to make the clock's hands go round. And now that he'd come, he told himself, all he was after was to turn them back, the fool, only to find roses grown between the minutes and the hours, and so entwined that the hands were stuck.[150]

Inside the camp time is consumed programmatically, initials are a legible itinerary of organized provisions against boredom and stasis; the future is suppressed by using it up. Back in England, everyone's advice is that the key to reintegration lies in the resumption of a sexual or procreative role, an emotional, social, and biological orientation to the future. But Summers falls in on his captive self: 'Prison had made him very pure. His own name for all this was lust' (43). He can no more go back to before the war than he will accept the present; his dilemma concerning the unfaithful woman he has imaginatively exhumed mirrors his involvement with his secretary, Dot Pitter. Rose, once recreated in mistaken recognition, persists for Summers in verbal misconstructions and his censored montage of her old letters. Dot, likewise, is engendered out of unreadable bits of language. The forms and reference numbers of a correspondence with the government department called (with a mixture of authorial obfuscation and punning candour) S.E.C.O., 'bloomed into flesh and blood': she even characterizes herself as a cipher: '"Dot and no comma"' (37, 43). The image of the clock stopped by clutching rose stems recalls the instant in which Summers' exclusion was brought about by 'not noticing the gun beneath the rose', but also points to the 'flowering of four years imprisonment', both in delusion, and in the manner of the text's representation of this incoherent wartime world (5, 44). Summers is arrested or caught in a web of significations which is also one of the chief conditions of this incoherence.

Back is a mannered novel, a baroque embellishment of hints established in Caught, and a foreshadowing of the contrived plotting of Green's late novels Nothing (1950) and Doting (1952). Saturating the narrative with clues that are, seemingly indiscriminately, either too obvious or indecipherable, and which refer us simultaneously to the fictional world of the action, to the historical worlds of the war, and to their representation, Green presents a vision of promiscuous wartime role-play, and an endemic instability or fluidity of reference.

[150] Green, Back, 8–9.

The unrecoverable conditions of knowledge in the text formally prefigure the representation of war as a reality contest in Pynchon's *Gravity's Rainbow* and Heller's *Catch-22*. Roses, homonyms of Rose, and the impenetrable acronyms of wartime bureaucracy, constitute semiotic noise that Summers can only deal with by fictionalizing. His apparently paranoid narrating of a secret history is further obscured by the motivations of other characters and the profligate linguistic cues and red-herrings that constitute the text's opaqueness.

In the England of *Back*, the conditions of war have become normalized as equally opaque structures of management whose inscrutability is a camouflage for self-advancement. Summers' return to his old job makes his boss Corker Mead defensive about the shading into unreality of the wartime socio-economic sphere, in which a general air of the significance of action embedded in discipline substitutes for personality: '"in this war the civilians have had some"' (187). Summers belongs to another war, like the British Expeditionary Force prisoners of 1940 who, in Michael Burn's words, felt like 'survivors from antiquity'.[151] Home Front strategies of self-aggrandizement, which require that Summers is seen as having in some way escaped sacrifice, disguise the illusory significance of Mead's own war; he heads a manufacturing outfit that has no factory, and which is busy with the hush-hush development of a process for hardening steel with bird droppings. The fictionalizing Summers confronts a collective fiction. Arthur Middlewitch, a fellow repatriated POW, falls in with the routine of constructing a surrogate personality and an aura of importance out of secrecy and innuendo, but he turns out to be unemployed. Rose's father Mr Grant, abetted by his wife's amnesia, appears to control his secret past (as father of Nance Whitmore), but the wife has known all along.

Summers' return to work is not stabilizing because the organization of the war effort is itself a riddle. His efforts to keep abreast of office routine parody wartime bureaucracy: the hermetic filing system he invents is an image in miniature of the discrepancy between the official acronymic discourses of war and the reality which it describes and transforms. He perceives maladministration as conspiracy; his conviction that orders are being forged by a competitor is prompted by his concurrent efforts to prove that Rose, the so-called Nance, has disguised her hand. In each case the fantasy derives from,

---

[151] Burn, *Yes, Farewell*, 346.

or is sustained by, the world to which Summers must adjust. Middlewitch's theory about the war making 'brutes out of women' gives Summers an explanation of Rose's change of identity (which as its inventor he alone sees through), namely that she is supporting her sick mother with her immoral earnings.[152] As well as being a prisoner of his adaptation to captivity, Summers is suggestible. The narratives he creates to legitimate his reluctance to adjust to the present are all in some way dependent on the fictions generated by a society at war.

Summers isn't alone in being caught in an adaptation that further complicates the business of living. He is embedded in the misremembering by which Mrs Grant denies the loss of her brother in the Great War: she insists that Summers is the dead man. It is Nance Whitmore who bears the greatest burden, both as the subject of his misrepresentations and as the person who takes responsibility for the novel's sufferers from defective memory, including Mr Grant, her natural father. She is inured to both sacrifice and subjection by her own experience of war, losing her pilot husband of a few weeks, and convinced she is imminently liable to conscription, 'put in uniform and packed off to where the Japs might get at her' (86). Forced to live two lives, she fights her corner: ' "I've a life of my own" ', precisely what Summers has lost contact with in captivity (72–4). His resumption of a life that can unfold in the present, rather than one arrested in the reinvention of the past, is blocked by the difficulty of making the kind of claim Nance can make in the unstable environments of wartime.

The end of *Back* has challenged critics to paraphrase ambiguity. At the moment of the consummation of the relationship between Summers and Nance there is a textual eruption of roses. The lampshade casts rose tints over her flesh, and in a post-coital release of emotion Summers twice expels the syllable ' "Rose" ' (208). As with the end to *The Impossible Shore*, the ultimate yield of the transformative processes of captivity and liberation resists conclusive inscription, for the discursive and the real remain irrecoverably intertwined in a symbol at once private and national.

Green charges the situation of the repatriated POW with a general significance; it is emblematic of wartime's assault on the idyll of personal continuity constructed by memory, and of the discursive

[152] Green, *Back*, 28.

resources with which resistance or survival is undertaken. Like Richard Roe in *Caught*, Summers is a prisoner of his imaginative work on memory. This compulsion to narrate is an attempted bulwark against loss, flux and external enforcement, like the patient with Korsakov's syndrome reported by Oliver Sacks, 'continually creating a world and self, to replace what was continually being forgotten and lost': in Summers' case narration reproduces what it would repulse.[153]

In the very different circumstances of the return from the death camps (different because the regime of extermination was designed to exclude this possibility), Primo Levi found testimony blocked by myth, in particular a myth that figures the end as a healing and forgetting: 'After the disease, health returns; to deliver us from imprisonment "our boys" arrive just in time, the liberators, with waving flags; the soldier returns and again finds his family and peace.' The victim of Auschwitz has no place in this recuperative scheme; liberation is a return to nothing, *and* the beginning of a terrible remembrance.

> In that moment in which they felt they were again becoming men (that is, responsible), the sorrows of men returned: the sorrow of the dispersed or lost family; the universal suffering all around; their own exhaustion, which seemed definitive, no longer curable; the problems of a life to begin all over again amid the rubble, often alone.[154]

This survival and return is incommensurate with the themes of liberation explored in British fictions of the 1940s. But the differences between regimes of confinement are eroded by the use of prison as a figure to comprehend existential and socio-political conditions, and the consequent denial of the realities of prison experience. Writings by and about British POWs, together with the tropes that refer themes of confinement and liberation to less stringent wartime disciplines, were a vehicle of a general appropriation, 'emphasizing the personal heroisms and frequently falsifying them' at the expense of the 'fascinating uniformities, compulsions, mechanisations and masses of this war'.[155] As one of the leading genres of post-war narrative about 1939–45, escape stories contributed to the structuring of the remembered war, a selective, legible and usable past. The

---

[153] Oliver Sacks, *The Man who Mistook his Wife for a Hat* (1985. Pan Books, 1986), 105.   [154] Levi, *Drowned*, 52.

[155] Tom Harrisson, 'War Books', *Horizon*, 4/24 (Dec. 1941), 421.

Continental dimension that POW stories gave to Britain's war meshed with myths of resistance, symptoms in the new Europe of the repression of wartime realities in Fascist Italy and Vichy France. The figure of the prisoner of war constructed in post-war culture was essentially conservative, in both formal and political terms, a bearer of the anti-centralist ideology of officer-class individualism and self-reliance. Wartime writings by prisoners of war, a category in which I have included texts whose publication was delayed into the later 1940s, were less orthodox. Confronted by contradictions between the world before/outside the wire and the world inside, and exploring these as they impacted on the sense of self, writers like Robert Kee and Michael Burn arrived at critically distanced perspectives on Britain's war. To this extent these writings are unrepresentative, the products of alienating circumstances and alienated identities (by contrast with militarised lives in garrison UK). But exteriority or exclusion were temporary and provisional. The process by which the prisoner of war became a symbol of unquestionning defiance was overdetermined by cultural and ideological factors with an ultimately parochial frame of reference.

Conclusion

I HAVE argued that the character of wartime writing was strongly determined by its relations to the discourses with which, in the broadest sense, Britain's war effort was administered. The complexity of those discourses—correlated with the fundamental structure of war but disseminated in myriad daily communiqués and conversations—does not permit the description of wartime culture in terms either of top-down propaganda or of spontaneous consensus. In consequence it is not plausible to ascribe straightforwardly consensual or oppositional meanings to many wartime texts. 'Suspicious and naive readings of the war' are caught up in equal measure in what Adam Piette calls 'war as story', but which we might gloss as the array of redescriptive activities which translated violence into admissible meanings.[1]

A decade ago, Alan Munton wrote that the literature of the war 'has disappeared into an Orwellian memory hole'.[2] There are manifold reasons why this writing is seen to lack the cultural salience acquired by literature of the Great War, amongst which comparison of literary value is by no means the only significant issue. (The cultural values which determine what is read as war literature are crucial in this respect. Scholarship on writing by women and non-combatant men is one field in which the advocacy of apparently ephemeral literature leads to a more fine-grained understanding of the symbolic economy in which attitudes to war, as well as wartime behaviour, are embedded.) The soldier poets of 1914–18, a number of whom reinterpreted their wartime writing in post-war memoirs, invented an image of the futility of war which has been read as distilling both the values of participants and the conflict's historical meaning. This reading, instanced not so much by academic scholarship as by anthologies and school curricula, has become influential because its simplifications are a counsel to liberal morality (the emphasis on soldiers' victimhood, rather than on their commission of violent acts, anticipates the compensations derived from modes of cultural and

---

[1] Adam Piette, *Imagination at War* (Macmillan 1995), 164.
[2] Alan Munton, *English Fiction of the Second World War* (Faber, 1989), 4.

historical explanation focused on the intellectual reparation of oppressed groups). In relation to a war defined as futile by Great War poetry, varieties of the belief that war is not a desirable political instrument are at once harrowingly and agreeably confirmed. The Great War as mediated in its minority literature of protest is a national guilt from which the reading of that literature repeatedly exonerates us. This is the moral equivalent to Adorno's charge that 'the so-called artistic representation of naked bodily pain . . . contains . . . the potentiality of wringing pleasure from it'.[3]

The cultural determination of the usable meanings of the Second World War has been significantly different. But then the war was different, not just in the language of moral and political philosophy, but in relation to the poets' image of the Great War. The killing of persons in the Second World War was justified by linkage to issues which the Great War, as popularly constructed, signally lacked. Far from being more straightforward (a just war in Augustine's vocabulary), the Second World War is as a consequence a more complex cultural phenomenon. This is the case with respect both to the images around which popular memory is organized, and to the moral and political questions with which 1939–45 confronts hegemonic twentieth-century attitudes to war. No aspect of wartime writing has achieved the kind of reception that confirms both its general authority and its usefulness to later generations. This is not just because the Second World War was not narratable simply as the twentieth-century's version of tragedy, namely the disasters of system-failure (the literary legacy of Vietnam in the United States reproduces some of the patterns of British Great War remembrance). It is also due to the regularity with which apparently incommensurable readings of the war have circulated in the political discourse of the last fifty years. The ways in which the Second World War has been made sense of militate against the promotion of its literature to a canon of war writing predicated on the senselessness of war.

Adam Piette, in a richly discriminating and provocative reading of wartime fiction and poetry, suggests that the neglect of this corpus derives from 'some obscure guilt within British culture about its own isolation from the real horrors of the war': 'It has become a stock reaction to books about the war to demand that the enemy's voice be heard, that stories from occupied Europe take centre stage, that a

---

[3] Quoted and translated by Lawrence L. Langer, *The Holocaust and the Literary Imagination* (New Haven: Yale University Press, 1975), 1.

global view be attempted.'[4] Whether or not Piette is right to suggest that Britain's war has become the repressed content of *our* Second World War, and I think that the process is less advanced, and more uneven, than his remarks imply, the meanings of the war have changed over the last fifty years. As a young subaltern facing his and his friends' deaths, the military historian Sir Michael Howard wrote of an 'ignorance of what we are fighting for which no amount of propaganda or religion will enlighten'.[5] But the contradictions with which he then wrestled are lost to the narrative of academic history: 'yet again' in 1939, he argued in his 1977 Trevelyan lectures on the history of opposition to the 'cultural habit' of military conflict, 'the liberal conscience endorsed a national struggle as a just war'.[6]

The justifications of this struggle were far from clear to those who wrote and those who fought. Mass Observation's Tom Harrisson trawled through the first two years' worth of war writing for *Horizon*: 'To judge from most war books, Britain is fighting this war to protect the world against Auden and Picasso, the Jews and any form of collectivism.'[7] According to Koestler, writing in 1943, 'the great majority of the people in this country has still not the faintest idea of what this bogy of fascism means'.[8] *The Plague*, Camus's allegory of the occupation, spells out the meaning of what Koestler calls a 'healthy lack of imagination': 'our townsfolk were like everybody else, wrapped up in themselves; in other words they were humanists; they disbelieved in pestilences. A pestilence isn't a thing made to man's measure; therefore we tell ourselves that pestilence is a mere bogy of the mind, a bad dream that will pass away.'[9] In Britain, what would be called genocide was not a creditable or admissable component of the war.[10] We can gauge this from the way extermination was employed as an imaginary *limit* to the outcome of hostilities. The Home Intelligence Unit reported in 1941 that 'there is at present

4 Piette, *Imagination at War*, 1.

5 Michael Howard, letter to *Horizon*, 7/42 (June 1943), 430.

6 Michael Howard, *War and the Liberal Conscience* (1978. Oxford: Oxford University Press, 1981), 13, 108.

7 Tom Harrisson, 'War Books', *Horizon*, 4/24 (Dec. 1941), 420.

8 Arthur Koestler, 'Knights in Rusty Armour', *The Yogi and the Commissar and Other Essays* (Jonathan Cape, 1945), 102.

9 Ibid. 101; Albert Camus, *The Plague*, trans. Stuart Gilbert (Hamish Hamilton, 1948), 37.

10 The word is introduced in Raphael Lemkin, *Axis Rule in Occupied Europe* (Washington, DC: Carnegie Endowment for International Peace, 1944), 79: 'New conceptions require new terms'.

no evidence that it is possible to defeat the people of Britain by any means other than extermination'.[11] Kenneth Clark, in an internal MOI paper on the implications of the Vansittartist 'Anger Campaign' to encourage identification of the German people with the aggressive policies of their Nazi Fuhrer, asked 'if the Germans really are incorrigible, what can be the outcome of the war? Are we hoping to exterminate 80 million people or to keep them in continual subjection?'[12] This is a reminder we don't need of the difference between the regimes that fought the Second World War. But we do need to be reminded of how this difference was understood in the war years because 'the Second World War has been reinvented': 'in an official Department of Education guide . . . the Allies were fighting to stop Nazi persecution of minorities and to end the Holocaust'.[13] Recent research on wartime media organizations such as Fleet Street and the BBC has advanced our understanding of the interaction of censorship (directed and internalized) and rhetoric in determining Britons' access to information about the war conducted by the Nazis in Europe.[14] This book has sought to unearth the content of wartime understanding, and to show how it was determined by the network of intersecting discourses about the war.

More than anything, the belated discovery of and tardy reckoning with the Holocaust in the English-speaking world has altered the terms on which the war is remembered. This reading of the war, however, has not driven out more parochial symbols of the conflict. Indeed it can be seen to renew them. A high-profile example, which despite its origin in Hollywood has a greater demographic reach in Britain than home-grown memorials like John Boorman's *Hope and Glory* (1987), is the retelling of the war in the movies of Steven Spielberg. The sequence through the comic spectacular *1941* (1979), the comic-book leather-clad Nazis of *Raiders of the Lost Ark* (1981), *Empire of the Sun* (1987, a version of J. G. Ballard's Japanese POW camp memoir), *Always* (1989, a remake of Dalton Trumbo's 1944 propaganda picture *A Guy Named Joe*), *Schindler's List* (1993) and *Saving Private Ryan* (1997), suggests a progressively more sobering

---

[11] Quoted in Jeffrey Richards, 'National Identity in British Wartime Films' in Philip M. Taylor (ed.), *Britain and the Cinema in the Second World War* (Macmillan, 1988), 60.

[12] Ian McLaine, *Ministry of Morale: Home Front Morale and the Ministry of Information in World War II* (George Allen and Unwin, 1979), 156.

[13] Tony Kushner, 'Wrong War, Mate', *Patterns of Prejudice*, 29/2 & 3 (1995), 3.

[14] Richard Breitman, *Official Secrets: What the Nazis Planned, What the British and Americans Knew* (Allen Lane, 1999).

view of the war, especially in the last decade. The two most recent films derive their quasi-documentary authority as witness from a cinematic imitation of the appearance of archival footage (using Hollywood technology to make Hollywood production values disappear). Nevertheless, Spielberg's story is still about individualism and escape. This is not so much homage to the past, as to the past's stories about itself, a recycling and appropriation of some of the stories with which the war was fought. Hollywood, of course, was in on the business of reinventing the war, or rather symbols of the war, from the moment Greer Garson's Mrs Miniver was transplanted to an English village from the West End home of her namesake in the pre-war *Times*.

Nostalgia is a significant motive for what Henry Green called disremembering. Ian McEwan, reflecting on recent fiction about the war (including his own novels *Black Dogs* and *The Innocent*), remarks that 'it was when we were good'.[15] I have sought to analyse the ways in which state-administered violence was constructed as a variety of goods. This has involved bracketing much of the post-war period's re-imagining of the events first given shape in wartime representations. If this inquiry begs the question of how its own form and goals have been determined by a half-century of cultural work on the memory of the Second World War, it is in part because the history of the war's remembrance is yet to be written.

[15] Valentine Cunningham, 'Novel Concerns IV: Battler Britain', BBC Radio 3, 8 Jan. 1998.

Bibliography

(Place of publication is London unless otherwise stated.)

UNPUBLISHED SOURCES

BOOKER, MARY, Letter to Phyllis Bottome, 26 May 1944, RHP, file 8.
BOTTOME, PHYLLIS, Letter to Richard Hillary, 31 July 1942, RHP, file 6.
—— Letter to Mary Booker, 29 May 1944, RHP, file 8.
DOUGLAS, KEITH, BL Add. MS 53775 A and 53775 B (drawings and water colours).
—— BL Add. MS 53774 (draft of *Alamein to Zem Zem* in 1943 desk diary).
—— BL Add. MS 53773 (draft poems and solicitor's report on *Alamein to Zem Zem* typescripts).
—— BL Add. MS 60586 (exercise book with draft of opening of *Alamein to Zem Zem*).
HILLARY, MICHAEL, TS essay, RHP, file 6.
—— Letter to Lovat Dickson, 2 May 1944, RHP, file 8.
HILLARY, RICHARD, Undated TS to Lovat Dickson, RHP, file 3.
—— TS story, 'Fighter Pilot', RHP, file 4.
—— TS story, 'Sea Voyage', RHP, file 4.
JAMESON, STORM, Letter to Richard Hillary, 30 June 1942, RHP, file 6.
LINKLATER, ERIC, TS, 'The Numbered Days', RHP, file 9.
—— 'The Undefeated, no. 9: Richard Hillary', TS script for Home Service broadcast, 21 March 1948, RHP, file 6.
—— Letter to Michael and Edwyna Hillary, 30 Dec. 1943, RHP, file 8.
RAWLINGS, A. C., 'Ave atque vale', RHP, file 6.
SANSOM, WILLIAM, 'The Great City Fire, 1940', TS (carbon) of film scenario, Berg Collection, New York Public Library.
—— 'The Odd World of Fire', TS essay with the author's corrections, Berg Collection, New York Public Library.
—— 'A Tale of Two Fires', TS (carbon), Berg Collection, New York Public Library.
—— 'Fires Were Started', holograph draft of essay in 'Uppsala' Notebook, Berg Collection, New York Public Library.
—— Notebook, containing holograph notes for articles, stories etc., Berg Collection, New York Public Library.
TURNER, W. J., Letter to Richard Hillary, 3 July 1942, RHP, file 6.

FILMS

A Canterbury Tale, dir. Michael Powell and Emeric Pressburger (Rank/Archers, 1944).

The Captive Heart, dir. Basil Dearden (Ealing, 1946).

Dangerous Moonlight, dir. Brian Desmond Hurst (RKO, 1941).

Desert Victory, dir. David MacDonald (MOI/British Army Film Unit, 1943).

Dumbo, dir. Ben Sharpsteen (US: Walt Disney, 1943).

Fires Were Started, dir. Humphrey Jennings (Crown Film Unit, 1943).

The First of the Few, dir. Leslie Howard (Melbourne/British Aviation, 1942).

The Foreman Went to France, dir. Alberto Cavalcanti (Ealing, 1942).

Henry V, dir. Laurence Olivier (Rank/Two Cities, 1944).

In Which We Serve, dir. Noel Coward (Rank/Two Cities, 1942).

The Life and Death of Colonel Blimp, dir. Michael Powell and Emeric Pressburger (GFD/Archers, 1943).

A Matter of Life and Death, dir. Michael Powell and Emeric Pressburger (GFD/Archers, 1946).

Mrs Miniver, dir. William Wyler (US: MGM, 1942).

One of Our Aircraft is Missing, dir. Michael Powell and Emeric Pressburger (British National, 1941).

The Next of Kin, dir. Thorold Dickinson (Ealing, 1942).

Tawny Pipit, dir. Bernard Miles (GFD/Two Cities, 1944).

Went the Day Well?, dir. Alberto Cavalcanti (Ealing, 1942).

PRIMARY SOURCES (INCLUDING WARTIME REVIEWS
AND CRITICISM)

• 'A PRIVATE', 'War Symposium—iii: Ours Not to Reason Why', *Horizon*, 3/15 (March 1941), 176–87.

ADAM, RONALD ['Blake'], *Readiness at Dawn* (Gollancz, 1941).

AISTROP, JACK, and MOORE, REGINALD (eds.), *Bugle Blast: An Anthology from the Services*, second series (1944).

ALDINGTON, RICHARD, *Death of a Hero* (Chatto and Windus, 1929).

• ANON., 'War Symposium—v: The Creation of a Class', *Horizon*, 4/21 (Sept. 1941), 166–72.

ARNOLD, MATTHEW, *The Poems of Matthew Arnold*, ed. Kenneth Allott (Longmans, 1965).

'ART CRITIC', 'War Artists and the War', *PNW* 16 (March 1943), 108–17.

AUDEN, W. H., 'W. H. Auden's "In the year of my youth . . ."', ed. Lucy S. McDiarmid, *Review of English Studies*, NS, 29/115 (1978), 267–312.

—— *The English Auden: Poems, Essays and Dramatic Writings, 1927–1939*, ed. Edward Mendelson (Faber, 1977).

BALCHIN, NIGEL, *Darkness Falls from the Air* (Collins, 1942).

BARBER, NOEL, *Prisoner of War: The Story of British Prisoners Held by the Enemy* (George Harrap, 1944).

⊛ BARBUSSE, HENRI, *Under Fire: The Story of a Squad*, trans W. Fitzwater Wray (Dent, 1917).

BARNE, KITTY, *Visitors from London* (Dent, 1940).

BARON, ALEXANDER, *From the City, From the Plough* (Jonathan Cape, 1948).

BATES, H. E., *The Modern Short Story: A Critical Survey* (Thomas Nelson and Sons, 1941).

—— [as Flying Officer X], *The Greatest People in the World and Other Stories* (Jonathan Cape, 1942).

—— Introduction to *War Pictures by British Artists*, no. 3, R.A.F. (Oxford University Press, 1942).

—— [as Flying Officer X] *How Sleep the Brave and Other Stories* (Jonathan Cape, 1943).

—— *Fair Stood the Wind for France* (Michael Joseph, 1944).

—— *The Cruise of the Breadwinner* (Michael Joseph, 1946).

—— *The Blossoming World: An Autobiography*, vol ii (Michael Joseph, 1971).

❋ BEARDMORE, GEORGE, *Civilians at War: Journals 1938–1946* (Oxford: Oxford University Press, 1986).

BEATON, CECIL, *Time Exposure*, with a commentary and captions by Peter Quennell (Batsford, 1941).

—— *Near East* (Batsford, 1943).

❋ ❋ BECKWITH, E. G. C. (ed.), *Selections from The Quill: A Collection of Prose, Verse and Sketches by Officer Prisoners-of-War in Germany, 1940–1945* (Country Life, 1947).

BELFIELD, EVERSLEY M. G., Letter to *Horizon*, 7/42 (June 1943), 431–3.

BETJEMAN, JOHN, *Continual Dew: A Little Book of Bourgeois Verse* (John Murray, 1937).

BILLANY, DAN, *The Trap* (Faber, 1950).

—— and DOWIE, DAVID, *The Cage* (Longmans, Green and Co., 1949).

BOWEN, ELIZABETH, *The Last September* (Constable, 1929).

—— *Look at All Those Roses: Short Stories* (Gollancz, 1941).

—— 'A Man and the War', review of Richard Hillary, *The Last Enemy*, *The Tatler and Bystander*, 165/2, 141 (8 July 1942), 54–6.

—— 'Calico Windows', in Andrew Sinclair (ed.), *The War Decade: An Anthology of the 1940s* (Hamish Hamilton, 1989), 261–4.

—— *The Demon Lover and Other Stories* (Jonathan Cape, 1945).

—— 'Out of a Book', *Orion*, 3 (Autumn 1946), 10–14.

—— *The Heat of the Day* (Jonathan Cape, 1949).

—— *Collected Impressions* (Longmans, Green and Co., 1950).

—— *The Demon Lover and Other Stories*, uniform edition (Jonathan Cape, 1952).

—— *The Mulberry Tree: Writings of Elizabeth Bowen*, ed. Hermione Lee (New York: Harcourt Brace Jovanovich, 1986).

—— GREENE, GRAHAM, and PRITCHETT, V. S., *Why Do I Write?: An Exchange of Views Between Elizabeth Bowen, Graham Greene and V. S. Pritchett* (Percival Marshall, 1948).

BRAINE, JOHN, *Room at the Top* (Eyre and Spottiswoode, 1957).

BRANSON, CLIVE, *British Soldier in India: The Letters of Clive Branson*, with an introduction by Harry Pollitt (The Communist Party, 1945).

BRITTAIN, VERA, *Testament of Youth: An Autobiographical Study of the Years 1900–1925* (Gollancz, 1933).

—— *England's Hour* (Macmillan, 1940).

—— *Seed of Chaos: What Mass Bombing Really Means* (New Vision, for The Bombing Restriction Committee, 1944).

—— *Testament of Experience: An Autobiographical Study of the Years 1925–1950* (Gollancz, 1957).

BROOKE, JOCELYN, *The Passing of a Hero* (The Bodley Head, 1953).

BRYHER [WINIFRED ELLERMAN], *The Days of Mars: A Memoir 1940–1946* (Calder and Boyars, 1972).

BUCHAN, JOHN, *Mr Standfast* (Hodder and Stoughton, 1919).

BULLEN, KEITH, and CROMER, JOHN, (eds.), *Salamander: A Miscellany of Poetry* (George Allen and Unwin, 1947).

BURN, MICHAEL, *The Labyrinth of Europe* (Methuen, 1939).

—— *Yes, Farewell* (Jonathan Cape, 1946).

—— *The Flying Castle*, illustrated by Richard Macdonald (Rupert Hart-Davis, 1954).

—— *Farewell to Colditz* (White Lion, 1974).

BURNEY, CHRISTOPHER, *The Dungeon Democracy* (Heinemann, 1945).

—— *Solitary Confinement* (Clerke and Cockeran, 1952).

BUTLER, ARTHUR S. G., *Recording Ruin* (Constable, 1942).

CALDER, RITCHIE, *Start Planning Britain Now: A Policy for Reconstruction* (Kegan Paul, 1941).

—— *The Lesson of London* (Secker and Warburg, 1941).

CALDER-MARSHALL, ARTHUR, *et al.*, 'Why Not War Writers?: A Manifesto', *Horizon*, 4/22 (Oct. 1941), 236–9.

CAMUS, ALBERT, *La Peste* (Paris: Gallimard, 1947).

—— *The Plague*, trans. Stuart Gilbert (Hamish Hamilton, 1948).

CARY, JOYCE, *Charley is my Darling* (Michael Joseph, 1940).

'CATO' [Michael Foot, Frank Owen and Peter Howard], *Guilty Men* (Gollancz, 1940).

CHAPMAN, GUY, (ed.), *Vain Glory: A Miscellany of the Great War 1914–1918 written by those who fought it on each side and on all fronts* (Cassell, 1937).

CHURCHILL, WINSTON S., *The War Speeches of Winston Churchill*, ed. Charles Eade, 3 vols. (Cassell, 1951–2).

CHURCHILL, WINSTON S. *The Second World War*, 6 vols. (Cassell, 1948–54)

CLIFFORD, ALEXANDER, '*Crusader*' (George Harrap, 1942).

COMFORT, ALEX, 'On Interpreting the War', *Horizon*, 5/29 (May 1942), 358–62.

CONNOLLY, CYRIL [as 'Palinurus'], *The Unquiet Grave: A Word Cycle by Palinurus* (Curwen Press, 1944).

—— *The Condemned Playground: Essays 1927–1944* (Routledge, 1945).

CORBY, HERBERT, *Hampdens Going Over* (Editions Poetry London, 1945).

COTTERELL, GEOFFREY, *Then a Soldier* (Eyre and Spottiswoode, 1944).

CROFT, J. L. R., and AXFORD, R. A., *Wychwood Chronicles* (Hutchinson, 1941).

CROMPTON, RICHMAL, *William and the Evacuees* (George Newnes, 1940).

CUNNINGHAM, VALENTINE, (ed.), *The Penguin Book of Spanish Civil War Verse* (Harmondsworth: Penguin, 1980).

DAVIN, DAN, *For the Rest of Our Lives* (Nicholson and Watson, 1947).

—— *Crete*, Official History of New Zealand in the Second World War 1939–1945 (Wellington: War History Branch, Department of Internal Affairs, 1953).

—— *The Salamander and the Fire: Collected War Stories* (Oxford: Oxford University Press, 1986).

—— (ed.), *Short Stories from the Second World War* (Oxford: Oxford University Press, 1982).

DAY LEWIS, C., *Word Over All* (Jonathan Cape, 1943).

DE QUINCEY, THOMAS, *The Collected Writings of Thomas De Quincey*, ed. D. Masson, 14 vols. (A. C. Black, 1897).

DEFOE, DANIEL, *Serious Reflections During the Life and Surprising Adventures of Robinson Crusoe: with his Vision of the Angelick World* (1720. Constable, 1925).

DEL, VECCHIO, JOHN, *The 13th Valley* (1982. Sphere, 1988).

DIVINE, A. D., *Road to Tunis* (Collins, 1944).

DOSTOEVSKY, FYODOR, *The Novels of Fyodor Dostoevsky*, trans. Constance Garnett, 12 vols. (1912–20), vol. 5, *The House of the Dead* (Dent, 1915).

DOUGLAS, KEITH, *Alamein to Zem Zem* (Editions Poetry London, 1946).

—— *Selected Poems*, ed. Ted Hughes (Faber, 1964).

—— *Complete Poems*, ed. Desmond Graham (Oxford: Oxford University Press, 1979).

—— *Alamein to Zem Zem*, ed. Desmond Graham (Oxford: Oxford University Press, 1979).

—— *A Prose Miscellany*, ed. Desmond Graham (Manchester: Carcanet, 1985).

DURRELL, LAWRENCE, *The Alexandria Quartet* (Faber, 1962).

—— *The Durrell-Miller Letters*, ed. Ian S. MacNiven (Faber, 1988).

ELIOT, T. S., *Four Quartets* (Faber, 1944).

—— *The Complete Poems and Plays* (Faber, 1969).

ENGLISH ASSOCIATION, THE, *England: An Anthology* (Macmillan, 1944).

EVANS, A. J., *The Escaping Club* (John Lane, 1921).

FARSON, NEGLEY, *Bomber's Moon* (Gollancz, 1941).

FEDDEN, ROBIN, *Personal Landscape* (Turret Books, 1966).

—— *et al.* (eds.), *Personal Landscape: An Anthology of Exile* (Editions Poetry London, 1945).

FRASER, G. S., 'Recent Verse: London and Cairo', *Poetry London X* (1944), 215–19.

GARDINER, PATRICK, 'The Pity of it Iago . . .', *Poetry London X* (1944), 260–1.

GARVIN, VIOLA G., *London's Glory: Twenty Paintings of the City's Ruins by Wanda Ostrowska* (George Allen and Unwin, 1945).

GENET, JEAN, *The Miracle of the Rose*, trans. Bernard Frechtman (Anthony Blond, 1965).

GIBSON, GUY, *Enemy Coast Ahead* (Michael Joseph, 1946).

GRAVES, ROBERT, 'War Poetry in this War', *The Listener*, 26/667 (23 Oct. 1941), 566–7.

—— and HODGE, ALAN, *The Long Week-End: A Social History of Great Britain, 1918–1939* (Faber, 1940).

GREEN, HENRY, *Party Going* (Hogarth Press, 1939).

—— *Pack My Bag* (Hogarth Press, 1940).

—— 'Mr Jonas', *Folios of New Writing*, 3 (Spring 1941), 11–17; reprinted in *PNW* 14 (July–Sept. 1942), 15–20.

—— 'A Rescue', *PNW* 4 (March 1941), 88–93.

—— 'The Lull', *New Writing and Daylight* (Summer 1943), 11–21.

—— *Caught* (Hogarth Press, 1943).

—— *Back* (Hogarth Press, 1946).

—— 'Firefighting' *Texas Quarterly*, 3/4 (Winter 1960).

GREENE, GRAHAM, *It's a Battlefield* (Heinemann, 1934).

—— (ed.), *The Old School: Essays by Divers Hands* (Jonathan Cape, 1934).

—— *The Ministry of Fear* (Heinemann, 1943).

—— *Collected Essays* (The Bodley Head, 1969).

'GUN BUSTER', *Battle Dress* (Hodder and Stoughton, 1941).

—— *Zero Hours* (Hodder and Stoughton, 1942).

GWYNN-BROWNE, ARTHUR, *Gone for a Burton* (Chatto and Windus, 1945).

H. D., *The Walls Do Not Fall* (Oxford University Press, 1944).

—— *The Gift* (Virago, 1984).

HMSO, *Front Line 1940–41* (HMSO, 1942).

HAMILTON, PATRICK, *The Slaves of Solitude* (Constable, 1947).

HANLEY, JAMES, *No Directions* (Faber, 1943).

HARRIS, ROBERT, *Enigma* (Hutchinson, 1995).

HARRISON, TONY, *Selected Poems* (Harmondsworth: Penguin Books, 1984).

—— *The Gaze of the Gorgon* (Newcastle upon Tyne: Bloodaxe, 1992).

HARRISSON, TOM, 'War Books', *Horizon*, 4/24 (Dec. 1941), 416–37.

HAY, IAN, *The Battle of Flanders 1940* (HMSO, 1941).

—— *Arms and the Men* (HMSO, 1950).

HELLER, JOSEPH, *Catch-22* (Jonathan Cape, 1962).

HEMINGWAY, ERNEST, *A Farewell to Arms* (Jonathan Cape, 1929).

HENDERSON, HAMISH, *Elegies for the Dead in Cyrenaica* (John Lehmann, 1948).

HENREY, ROBERT, *A Village in Piccadilly* (Dent, 1942).

HERR, MICHAEL, *Dispatches* (1977. Picador, 1978).

HILLARY, RICHARD, *The Last Enemy* (1942. Macmillan, 1950).

—— 'The Pilot and Peace', *The Royal Air Force Journal*, no. 19 (July 1942).

—— 'Where Do We Go From Here?', *John O'London's Weekly*, 48/1,194 (20 Nov. 1942), 61–2.

HOLDEN, INEZ, 'Fellow Travellers in a Factory', *Horizon*, 3/14 (Feb. 1941), 117–22.

—— *It was Different at the Time* (John Lane, 1943).

HOUSEHOLD, GEOFFREY, *Rogue Male* (Chatto and Windus, 1939).

HOWARD, MICHAEL, Letter to *Horizon*, 7/42 (June 1943), 430–1.

HUGO, VICTOR, *Les Miserables*, trans. Norman Denny, 2 vols. (1862, trans. 1976. Harmondsworth, Penguin, 1980).

HUNT, J. L., and PRINGLE, A. G. (eds.), *Service Slang: A First Selection* (Faber, 1943).

ISHERWOOD, CHRISTOPHER, *Lions and Shadows: An Education in the Twenties* (Hogarth Press, 1938).

JARRELL, RANDALL, *The Complete Poems* (New York: The Noonday Press, 1969).

JOAD, C. E. M., 'The Face of England: How it has been Ravaged and How it May be Preserved', *Horizon*, 5/29 (May 1942), 335–48.

JOHNS, W. E., *Spitfire Parade: Stories of Biggles in War-time* (Oxford University Press, 1940).

JOYCE, JAMES, *A Portrait of the Artist as a Young Man*, ed. Richard Ellmann (Jonathan Cape, 1968).

KAVAN, ANNA, 'The Case of Bill Williams (i)', *Horizon*, 9/50 (Feb. 1944), 96–9.

KEE, ROBERT, *A Crowd is not Company* (Eyre and Spottiswoode, 1947).

—— *The Impossible Shore* (Eyre and Spottiswoode, 1949).

—— 'Mercury on a Fork', *The Listener*, 85/2, 186, (18 Feb. 1971), 207–8.

—— *The World We Left Behind: A Chronicle of the Year 1939* (Weidenfeld and Nicolson, 1984).

—— *1945: The World We Fought For* (Hamish Hamilton, 1985).

KENNINGTON, ERIC, *Drawing the R.A.F.: A Book of Portraits* (Oxford University Press, 1942).

KERSH, GERALD, *Clean, Bright and Slightly Oiled* (Heinemann, 1946).

KING-HALL, STEPHEN, *Total Victory* (Faber, 1941).

KOESTLER, ARTHUR, *Spanish Testament* (Gollancz, 1937).

—— *Darkness at Noon*, trans. Daphne Hardy (Jonathan Cape, 1940).

—— *Scum of the Earth* (Jonathan Cape, 1941).

—— 'The Birth of a Myth: In Memory of Richard Hillary', *Horizon*, 7/40 (April 1943), 227–43.

—— 'The Mixed Transport', *Horizon*, 8/46 (Oct. 1943), 244–52.

—— 'Replies to Some Enquiries', *Horizon*, 8/48 (Dec. 1943), 433.

—— *Arrival and Departure* (Jonathan Cape, 1943).

—— *The Yogi and the Commissar and Other Essays* (Jonathan Cape, 1945).

LARKIN, PHILIP, *A Girl in Winter* (Faber, 1947).

LAWRENCE, D. H., *Kangaroo* (Martin Secker, 1923).

LAWRENCE, T. E., *Seven Pillars of Wisdom: A Triumph* (1926. Jonathan Cape, 1935).

—— *The Mint: A day-book of the R.A.F. Depot between August and December 1922 with later notes by 352087 A/c Ross* (Jonathan Cape, 1955).

—— *The Letters of T. E. Lawrence*, ed. Malcolm Brown (Oxford: Oxford University Press, 1991).

LEHMANN, JOHN, *I Am My Brother* (Longmans, Green and Co., 1960).

LEVI, PRIMO, *If This is a Man* and *The Truce*, trans. Stuart Woolf (1958 and 1963, trans. 1960 and 1965. Sphere, 1987).

—— *The Periodic Table*, trans. Raymond Rosenthal (1975, trans. 1985. Sphere, 1986).

—— *The Drowned and the Saved*, trans. Raymond Rosenthal (1986. Michael Joseph, 1988).

LEWIS, ALUN, review of *The Trumpet and Other Poems* by Edward Thomas, *Horizon*, 3/13 (Jan. 1941), 78–80.

—— *Raiders' Dawn and Other Poems* (George Allen and Unwin, 1942).

—— *The Last Inspection* (George Allen and Unwin, 1942).

—— 'Ward "O" 3 (b)', *PNW* 18 (July–Sept. 1943), 31–48.

—— *Ha! Ha! Among the Trumpets: Poems in Transit* (George Allen and Unwin, 1945).

—— *In the Green Tree* (George Allen and Unwin, 1948).

—— *Alun Lewis: A Miscellany of his Writings*, ed. John Pikoulis (Bridgend: Poetry Wales Press, 1982).

—— *Letters to my Wife*, ed. Gweno Lewis (Bridgend: Seren Books, 1989).

LEWIS, CECIL, *Sagittarius Rising* (Peter Davies, 1936).

LEWIS, WYNDHAM, *Blasting and Bombardiering* (Eyre and Spottiswoode, 1937).

LINDSAY, JACK, *Beyond Terror: A Novel of the Battle of Crete* (Andrew Dakers, 1943).

MACLAREN-ROSS, JULIAN, 'A Bit of A Smash', *Horizon*, 1/6 (June 1940), 434–55.

—— *The Stuff to Give the Troops: Twenty-Five Tales of Army Life* (Jonathan Cape, 1944).

—— *Memoirs of the Forties* (Alan Ross, 1965).

MACNEICE, LOUIS, *Autumn Journal* (Faber, 1939).

—— *Selected Prose of Louis MacNeice*, ed. Alan Heuser (Oxford: Oxford University Press, 1990).

MAIR, JOHN, *Never Come Back* (Gollancz, 1941).

MALLALIEU, J. P. W., *Very Ordinary Seaman* (Gollancz, 1944).

MANNING, OLIVIA, 'Poets in Exile', *Horizon*, 10/58 (Oct. 1944), 270–9.

—— *The Balkan Trilogy* (1960–5. Harmondsworth: Penguin, 1986).

—— *The Levant Trilogy* (1977–80. Harmondsworth: Penguin, 1985).

MANSFIELD, KATHERINE, *The Collected Letters of Katherine Mansfield*, ed. Vincent O'Sullivan and Margaret Scott (Oxford: Clarendon Press, 1984–).

MASEFIELD, JOHN, *The Nine Days Wonder: The Operation Dynamo* (Heinemann, 1941).

• MASS OBSERVATION, *War Begins at Home*, ed. Tom Harrisson and Charles Madge (Chatto and Windus, 1940).

—— *An Enquiry into People's Homes: A Report Prepared by Mass-Observation for The Advertising Service Guild: The Fourth of the 'Change' Wartime Surveys* (John Murray, 1943).

MAUGHAM, ROBIN, *Come to Dust* (Chapman and Hall, 1945).

MICHIE, ALLAN A., and GRAEBNER, WALTER (eds.), *Their Finest Hour: The War in the First Person* (George Allen and Unwin, 1940).

MILLER, BETTY, *On the Side of the Angels* (Robert Hale, 1945).

MILLIGAN, SPIKE, *Mussolini: His Part in My Downfall* (Michael Joseph, 1978).

MONSARRAT, NICHOLAS, *The Cruel Sea* (Cassell, 1951).

• MOORE, HENRY, *Shelter Sketch-Book* (Editions Poetry London, 1945).

MOOREHEAD, ALAN, *Eclipse* (Hamish Hamilton, 1945).

MORGAN, GUY, *Only Ghosts Can Live* (Crosby, Lockwood and Son, 1945).

MORTON, H. V., *I Saw Two Englands: The Record of a Journey Before the War, and After the Outbreak of War, in the Year 1939* (Methuen, 1942).

• MORTON, J. B., 'Introduction', *War Pictures by British Artists*, no. 2, *Blitz* (Oxford University Press, 1942).

• • MUIR, EDWIN, 'War Poetry', letter to *The Listener*, 26/667 (23 Oct. 1941), 567.

• • MURRY, JOHN MIDDLETON, *Democracy and War* (Nisbet and Co., 1940).

—— 'Richard Hillary', *The Adelphi*, 20/4 (July–Sept. 1944), 97–101.

NASHE, THOMAS, *The Works of Thomas Nashe*, ed. R. B. McKerrow, 5 vols. (Oxford: Blackwell, 1966).

NEWBY, ERIC, *Love and War in the Apennines* (Hodder and Stoughton, 1971).

● NICOLSON, HAROLD, *Diaries and Letters*, ed. Nigel Nicolson, 3 vols. (Collins, 1966–8).

NIXON, BARBARA, *Raiders Overhead* (Lindsay Drummond, 1943).

NOEL-PATON, M. H., 'The Last Enemy (To the Memory of Fl. Lt. Richard Hillary, R.A.F.V.R.)', *Blackwood's Magazine*, 1,530 (April 1943), 293.

ORWELL, GEORGE, *Keep the Aspidistra Flying* (Gollancz, 1936).

—— *Coming up for Air* (Gollancz, 1939).

—— *Nineteen Eighty-Four*, ed. Peter Davison (Oxford: Clarendon Press, 1984).

—— *The Collected Essays, Journalism and Letters*, ed. Sonia Orwell and Ian Angus, 4 vols. (Secker and Warburg, 1968).

OWEN, WILFRED, *Collected Letters*, ed. Harold Owen and John Bell (Oxford: Clarendon Press, 1967).

—— *The Complete Poems and Fragments of Wilfred Owen*, ed. Jon Stallworthy, 2 vols. (Chatto and Windus, Hogarth Press, and Oxford University Press, 1983).

● ● PAGE, MARTIN (ed.), *'Kiss me Goodnight, Sergeant Major': The Songs and Ballads of World War II* (Hart-Davis, MacGibbon, 1973).

● PANTER-DOWNES, MOLLIE, *London War Notes 1939–1945*, ed. William Shawn (Longmans, 1972).

● PARTRIDGE, ERIC, (ed.), *A Dictionary of R.A.F Slang* (Michael Joseph, 1945).

● PEAKE, MERVYN, *The Rhyme of the Flying Bomb* (Dent, 1962).

POUND, EZRA, *The Cantos* (Faber, 1975).

POWELL, ENOCH, *Dancer's End and The Wedding Gift* (The Falcon Press, 1951).

● ● PRIESTLEY, J. B., *Postscripts* (Heinemann, 1940).

—— *Letter to a Returning Serviceman* (Home and Van Thal, 1945).

PRITCHETT, V. S., 'Shot Down in Flames', review of Richard Hillary, *The Last Enemy*, *The New Statesman and Nation*, 24/593 (4 July 1942), 12.

PYM, BARBARA, *Civil to Strangers and Other Writings* (Macmillan, 1987).

READ, HERBERT, 'Art in an Electric Atmosphere', *Horizon*, 3/17 (May 1941), 308–13.

REES, GORONWY, 'Letter from a Soldier', *Horizon*, 1/7 (July 1940), 467–71.

—— *A Chapter of Accidents* (Chatto & Windus, 1971).

REID, P. R., *The Colditz Story* (Hodder and Stoughton, 1952).

RICHARDS, J. M. (ed.), *The Bombed Buildings of Britain: A Record of Architectural Casualties: 1940–1941*, with notes by John Summerson (The Architectural Press, 1942).

[RICHEY, PAUL], *Fighter Pilot: A Personal Record of the Campaign in France* (Batsford, 1941).

ROMILLY, GILES, 'Three Sketches from a Prison Camp', *PNW* 26 (1945), 164–75.

—— and ROMILLY, ESMOND, *Out of Bounds: The Education of Giles Romilly and Esmond Romilly* (Hamish Hamilton, 1935).

—— and ALEXANDER, MICHAEL, *The Privileged Nightmare* (Weidenfeld and Nicolson, 1954).

SAINT-EXUPÉRY, ANTOINE DE, *Flight to Arras*, trans. Lewis Galantière (Heinemann, 1942).

—— *Wartime Writings 1939–1945*, trans. Norah Purcell (1986. Picador, 1988).

SANSOM, WILLIAM, 'The Long Sheet', *Horizon*, 4/22 (Oct. 1941), 276–85.

—— *Fireman Flower* (Hogarth Press, 1944).

—— 'Building Alive', *Horizon*, 13/73 (Jan. 1946), 36–40.

—— *Westminster in War* (Faber, 1947).

—— *The Stories of William Sansom* (Hogarth Press, 1963).

—— *The Birth of a Story* (Chatto and Windus, and Hogarth Press, 1972).

SASSOON, SIEGFRIED, *The War Poems*, ed. Rupert Hart-Davis (Faber, 1983).

SCHIMANSKI, STEFAN, and TREECE, HENRY (eds.), *Leaves in the Storm: A Book of Diaries* (Lindsay Drummond, 1947).

SELWYN, VICTOR, DE MAUNAY, ERIK, FLETCHER, IAN, FRASER, G. S., and WALLER, JOHN, (eds.), *Return to Oasis: War Poems and Recollections from the Middle East 1940–1946* (Shepheard Walwyn and Editions Poetry London, 1980).

SHAKESPEARE, WILLIAM, *Henry V*, ed. Gary Taylor (Oxford: Oxford University Press, 1982).

SHUTE, NEVIL, *What Happened to the Corbetts*, uniform edition (Heinemann, 1952).

SITWELL, OSBERT, 'Letter to My Son', *Horizon*, 7/39 (March 1943), 159–77.

SPAIGHT, J. M., *The Sky's the Limit: A Study of British Air Power* (Hodder and Stoughton, 1940).

SPENDER, STEPHEN, 'September Journal', *Horizon*, 1/2 (Feb. 1940), 102–21; 1/3 (March 1940), 211–24; 1/5 (May 1940), 356–63.

—— 'Books and the War—V: The Creative Artist in Our Time', *PNW* 6 (May 1941), 125–37.

—— Introduction to *War Pictures by British Artists*, 2nd ser. no. 4, *Air Raids* (Oxford University Press, 1943).

—— *Citizens in War—and After* (George Harrap, 1945).

—— *World Within World* (Hamish Hamilton, 1951).

—— and LEHMANN, JOHN (eds.), *Poems for Spain* (Hogarth Press, 1939).

STANLEY, ARTHUR (ed.), *Britain at War: An Anthology* (Eyre and Spottiswoode, 1943).

STENDHAL, *The Charterhouse of Parma*, trans. Margaret Shaw (1839, trans. 1958. Harmondsworth, Penguin, 1988).

STRACHEY, JOHN, *Post D: Some Experiences of an Air Raid Warden* (Gollancz, 1941).

—— 'The New Men', review of Richard Hillary, *The Last Enemy*, *The Spectator*, 169/5,950 (10 July 1942), 44.

⊕ SUTHERLAND, GRAHAM, 'Images Wrought From Destruction', *Sutherland: The War Drawings* (Imperial War Museum, 1982), 1–10.

TALBOT, GODFREY, *Speaking from the Desert: A Record of the Eighth Army in Africa* (Hutchinson, 1944).

TAMBIMUTTU, M. J. (ed.), *Poetry in Wartime* (Faber, 1942).

—— 'In Memory of Keith Douglas', *Poetry London* X (Editions Poetry London, 1944).

THOMAS, DYLAN, *The Collected Letters*, ed. Paul Ferris (1985. Paladin, 1987).

TODD, RUTHVEN, *Until Now: Poems* (Fortune Press, 1943).

TOLSTOY, LEO, *War and Peace*, trans. Louise and Aylmer Maude (1868–9, trans. 1922–3. Oxford: Oxford University Press, 1991).

TOYNBEE, PHILIP, 'New Novels', review of Antoine de Saint-Exupéry, *Flight to Arras*, *The New Statesman and Nation*, 24/607 (10 Oct. 1942), 245–6.

TUBBS, RALPH, *Living in Cities* (Harmondsworth: Penguin, 1942).

⊕ VAUGHAN, KEITH, 'Exiles in Khaki', in Denys Val Baker, ed., *Little Reviews Anthology* (George Allen and Unwin, 1943), 18–27.

—— *Journal and Drawings 1939–1965* (Alan Ross, 1966).

VERNEY, JOHN, *Going to the Wars: A Journey in Various Directions* (Collins, 1955).

VONNEGUT, KURT, *Slaughterhouse-Five or The Children's Crusade* (1969. Vintage, 1991).

⊕ WARD, A. C., *A Literary Journey Through Wartime Britain* (New York: Oxford University Press, 1943).

WARNER, REX, *The Aerodrome: A Love Story* (The Bodley Head, 1941).

—— *Why Was I Killed?: A Dramatic Dialogue* (John Lane, 1943).

WAUGH, EVELYN, *Put Out More Flags* (Chapman and Hall, 1942).

—— *Brideshead Revisited: The Sacred and Profane Memories of Captain Charles Ryder* (Chapman and Hall, 1945).

—— *The Sword of Honour Trilogy* (1984. Harmondsworth: Penguin, 1987).

—— *The Diaries of Evelyn Waugh*, ed. Michael Davie (Weidenfeld and Nicolson, 1976).

—— *The Letters of Evelyn Waugh*, ed. Mark Amory (Weidenfeld and Nicolson, 1980).

WAVELL, A. P., (ed.), *Other Men's Flowers* (Jonathan Cape, 1944).

WELLS, H. G., *The War in the Air And Particularly How Mr Bert Smallways Fared While It Lasted* (George Bell and Sons, 1908).

● WHEELER, HAROLD (ed.), *The People's History of the Second World War: September 1939-December 1940* (Odham's Press, n.d.).

WILLIAMS, ERIC, *Goon in the Block* (Jonathan Cape, 1945).

—— *The Wooden Horse* (Collins, 1949).

—— *The Tunnel* (Collins, 1951).

—— (ed.), *The Escapers: A Chronicle of Escape in Many Wars: with Eighteen First-hand Accounts* (Eyre and Spottiswoode, 1953).

WILLIAMSON, HENRY, *The Wet Flanders Plain* (The Beaumont Press, 1929).

—— *A Fox Under my Cloak* (Macdonald, 1955).

—— *Love and the Loveless: A Soldier's Tale* (1958. Rev. ed., Panther, 1963).

WOOD, J. E. R. (ed.), *Detour: The Story of Oflag IVC* (The Falcon Press, 1946).

WOODCOCK, GEORGE, 'The Dark Night of the Intellect', *Now*, NS 2 (1944), 1–4.

WOOLF, VIRGINIA, *The Diary of Virginia Woolf*, ed. Anne Oliver Bell, 5 vols. (Hogarth Press, 1977–84).

YEATS, W. B., *Collected Poems* (Macmillan, 1982).

YEATS-BROWN, F. (ed.), *Escape: A Book of Escapes of All Kinds* (Eyre and Spottiswoode, 1934).

SECONDARY SOURCES

ABBOTT, CHARLES D., ed., *Poets at Work* (New York: Harcourt, Brace and Co., 1948).

ABSALOM, ROGER, *A Strange Alliance: Aspects of Escape and Survival in Italy 1943–45* (Florence: Leo S. Olschki Editore, 1991).

ADDISON, PAUL, *Churchill on the Home Front 1900–1955* (1992. Pimlico, 1993).

● ALDGATE, ANTHONY, and RICHARDS, JEFFREY, *Britain Can Take It: The British Cinema in the Second World War*, 2nd edn. (Edinburgh: Edinburgh University Press, 1994).

ALMOND, MARK, *Europe's Backyard War: The War in the Balkans* (William Heinemann, 1994).

ANDERSON, BENEDICT, *Imagined Communities: Reflections on the Origin and Spread of Nationalism*, rev. edn. (Verso, 1991).

● AUDEN, W. H., *Forewords and Afterwords* (Faber, 1973).

BACHELARD, GASTON, *The Poetics of Space*, trans. Maria Jolas (Boston, Mass.: Beacon Press, 1969).

● BALFOUR, MICHAEL, *Propaganda in War 1939–1945: Organizations, Policies and Publics in Britain and Germany* (Routledge & Kegan Paul, 1979).

BANERJEE, A., 'Keith Douglas and the Dead Soldier: An Artistic Confrontation', *The Literary Half-Yearly*, 15/1 (Jan. 1974), 85–91.

BARNETT, CORRELLI, *The Desert Generals* (William Kimber, 1960).

—— *Britain and Her Army 1509–1970: A Military, Political and Social Survey* (Allen Lane, 1970).

—— *The Audit of War: The Illusion and Reality of Britain as a Great Nation* (Macmillan, 1986).

BARTHES, ROLAND, *Selected Writings*, ed. Susan Sontag (1982. Fontana, 1983).

—— *The Rustle of Language*, trans. Richard Howard (Berkeley and Los Angeles: University of California Press, 1989).

BATE, JONATHAN (ed.), *The Romantics on Shakespeare* (Harmondsworth: Penguin, 1992).

BAUMAN, ZYGMUNT, *Modernity and the Holocaust* (Cambridge: Polity, 1989).

BELL, VEREEN, and LERNER, LAURENCE (eds.), *On Modern Poetry: Essays Presented to Donald Davie* (Nashville: Vanderbilt University Press, 1988).

BENJAMIN, WALTER, *Illuminations*, ed. Hannah Arendt, trans. Harry Zohn (1970. Fontana, 1973).

—— *Charles Baudelaire: A Lyric Poet in the Era of High Capitalism*, trans. Harry Zohn (New Left Books, 1983).

BERGONZI, BERNARD, *Wartime and Aftermath: English Literature and its Background 1939–1960* (Oxford: Oxford University Press, 1993).

BERLIN, ISAIAH, *Personal Impressions* (Hogarth Press, 1980).

—— *Russian Thinkers* (1978. Harmondsworth: Penguin, 1994)

BETTELHEIM, BRUNO, *Surviving and Other Essays* (Thames and Hudson, 1979).

BIELENBERG, CHRISTABEL, *The Past is Myself* (Chatto and Windus, 1968).

BOLCHOVER, RICHARD, *British Jewry and the Holocaust* (Cambridge: Cambridge University Press, 1993).

BOLTON, JONATHAN, *Personal Landscapes: British Poets in Egypt during the Second World War* (Macmillan, 1997).

BOURDIEU, PIERRE, *Homo Academicus*, trans. Peter Collier (1988. Cambridge: Polity, 1990).

BOWEN, ROGER, *'Many Histories Deep': The Personal Landscape Poets in Egypt, 1940–1945* (Madison, NJ: Fairleigh Dickinson University Press, 1995).

BRETON, ANDRÉ, *What is Surrealism?: Selected Writings*, ed. Franklin Rosemont (Pluto, 1978).

BRIGGS, ASA, *War of Words*, vol. iii of *The History of Broadcasting in the United Kingdom* (Oxford: Oxford University Press, 1970).

BROPHY, JOHN, and PARTRIDGE, ERIC (eds.), *Songs and Slang of the British Soldier: 1914–1918* (Scholartis Press, 1930).

BUITENHUIS, PETER, *The Great War of Words: Literature as Propaganda 1914-18 and After* (Batsford, 1989).

BURKE, EDMUND, *A Philosophical Enquiry into the Origin of our Ideas of the Sublime and the Beautiful*, ed. Adam Phillips (Oxford: Oxford University Press, 1990).

BURN, MICHAEL, *The Debatable Land: A Study of the Motives of Spies in Two Ages* (Hamish Hamilton, 1970).

—— *Mary and Richard: The Story of Richard Hillary and Mary Booker* (André Deutsch, 1988).

CALDER, ANGUS, *The People's War: Britain 1939-1945* (Jonathan Cape, 1969).

—— *The Myth of the Blitz* (Jonathan Cape, 1991).

CAPLAN, WENDY (ed.), *Designing Modernity: The Arts of Reform and Persuasion 1885-1945* (Thames and Hudson, 1995).

CARPENTER, HUMPHREY, *Benjamin Britten* (Faber, 1992).

CEADEL, MARTIN, *Pacifism in Britain 1914-1945: The Defining of a Faith* (Oxford: Clarendon Press, 1980).

—— 'Popular Fiction and the Next War, 1918-1939', in Frank Gloversmith (ed.), *Class, Culture and Social Change: A New View of the 1930s* (Brighton: Harvester, 1980).

—— *Thinking About Peace and War* (1987. Oxford: Oxford University Press, 1989).

CESARANI, DAVID, *Arthur Koestler: The Homeless Mind* (William Heinemann, 1998).

CHALIAND, GÉRARD (ed.), *The Art of War in World History: From Antiquity to the Nuclear Age* (Berkeley: University of California Press, 1994).

CHANDLER, DAVID (ed.), *The Oxford Illustrated History of the British Army* (Oxford: Oxford University Press, 1994).

CLARK, IAN, *Waging War: A Philosophical Introduction* (Oxford: Clarendon Press, 1988).

CLARK, T. J., *The Painting of Modern Life: Paris in the Art of Manet and his Followers* (Thames and Hudson, 1985).

CLARKE, PETER, *Hope and Glory: Britain 1900-1990* (Harmondsworth: Allen Lane/The Penguin Press, 1996).

CLAUSEWITZ, CARL VON, *On War*, ed. Michael Howard and Peter Paret (Princeton: Princeton University Press, 1976).

COOPER, ARTEMIS, *Cairo in the War: 1939-1945* (Hamish Hamilton, 1989).

COOPER, HELEN M., MUNICH, ADRIENNE AUSLANDER, and SQUIER, SUSAN MERRILL (eds.), *Arms and the Woman: War, Gender and Literary Representation* (Chapel Hill: University of North Carolina Press, 1989).

COSTELLO, D. R., '"Searchlight Books" and the quest for a "People's War", 1941-1942', *Journal of Contemporary History*, 24 (1989), 257-76.

COULTON, BARBARA, *Louis MacNeice in the BBC* (Faber, 1980).

CRAWLEY, AIDAN, *Escape From Germany: A History of R.A.F. Escapes During the War* (Collins, 1956).

CROFT, ANDY, *Red Letter Days: British Fiction in the 1930s* (Lawrence and Wishart, 1990).

CRUICKSHANK, CHARLES, *Deception in World War II* (1979. Oxford: Oxford University Press, 1981).

CULL, NICHOLAS J., *Selling War: The British Propaganda Campaign Against American "Neutrality" in World War II* (Oxford: Oxford University Press, 1995).

CUNNINGHAM, VALENTINE, *British Writers of the Thirties* (Oxford: Oxford University Press, 1988).

—— 'Novel Concerns IV: Battler Britain', BBC Radio 3, 8 Jan. 1998.

CURRIE, GREGORY, *The Nature of Fiction* (Cambridge: Cambridge University Press, 1990).

DAVIES, IOAN, *Writers in Prison* (Oxford: Blackwell, 1990).

DAVIES, PHILIP JOHN, (ed.), *Science Fiction, Social Conflict and War* (Manchester: Manchester University Press, 1990).

DAY-LEWIS, SEAN, *C. Day-Lewis: An English Literary Life* (Weidenfeld and Nicolson, 1980).

DEAR, I. C. B. (ed.), *The Oxford Companion to the Second World War* (Oxford: Oxford University Press, 1995).

DE MAN, PAUL, 'Autobiography as De-facement', *Modern Language Notes*, 94/5 (Dec. 1979), 919–30.

—— *The Resistance to Theory* (Manchester: Manchester University Press, 1986).

DENNETT, DANIEL, C., *Darwin's Dangerous Idea: Evolution and the Meanings of Life* (1995. Harmondsworth: Penguin, 1996).

DERRIDA, JACQUES, *Dissemination*, trans. Barbara Johnson (Athlone Press, 1981).

DICKSON, LOVAT, *Richard Hillary* (Macmillan, 1950).

DOUHET, GUILIO, *The Command of the Air*, trans. Dino Ferrari (Faber, 1943).

EAGLETON, TERRY, *The Significance of Theory* (Oxford: Blackwell, 1990).

—— *The Ideology of the Aesthetic* (Oxford: Blackwell, 1990).

EKSTEINS, MODRIS, *Rites of Spring: The Great War and the Birth of the Modern Age* (Bantam Press, 1989).

ELLMANN, MAUD, *The Poetics of Impersonality: T. S. Eliot and Ezra Pound* (Brighton: Harvester, 1987).

EMPSON, WILLIAM, *Seven Types of Ambiguity* (Chatto and Windus, 1930).

ESHER, LIONEL, *A Broken Wave: The Rebuilding of England 1940–1980* (Allen Lane, 1981).

226   *Bibliography*

ESHER, LIONEL, 'The Plot to Save the Artists', *Times Literary Supplement* (2 Jan. 1987), 12–13.

FAULKS, SEBASTIAN, *The Fatal Englishman: Three Short Lives* (Hutchinson, 1996).

FIELDING, STEVEN, THOMPSON, PETER, and TIRATSOO, NICK, '*England Arise!': The Labour Party and Popular Politics in 1940s Britain* (Manchester: Manchester University Press, 1995).

FITZ GIBBON, CONSTANTINE, *The Blitz* (Allan Wingate, 1957).

FOUCAULT, MICHEL, *Discipline and Punish: The Birth of the Prison*, trans. Alan Sheridan (Allen Lane, 1977).

—— *The Foucault Reader*, ed. Paul Rabinow (1984. Harmondsworth: Penguin, 1986).

FRAMPTON, KENNETH, *Modern Achitecture: A Critical History*, rev. edn. (Thames and Hudson, 1985).

FRASER, G. S., 'Keith Douglas: A Poet of the Second World War', *The Proceedings of the British Academy*, xlii (British Academy and Oxford University Press, 1956).

—— *Vision and Rhetoric: Studies in Modern Poetry* (Faber, 1959).

FRASER, JOHN, *Violence in the Arts* (Cambridge: Cambridge University Press, 1974).

FREUD, SIGMUND, 'Why War?', in Leon Bramson and George W. Goethals (eds.) *War: Studies from Psychology, Sociology and Anthropology* (1964. New York: Basic Books, rev. edn. 1968), 71–80.

—— 'The Uncanny', trans. Alix Strachey, *Collected Papers*, iv (Hogarth Press, 1925), 368–407.

FULLER, JOHN, *W. H. Auden: A Commentary* (Faber, 1998).

FUSSELL, PAUL, *The Great War and Modern Memory* (1975. Oxford: Oxford University Press, 1977).

—— *Wartime: Understanding and Behaviour in the Second World War* (Oxford: Oxford University Press, 1989).

—— *Killing in Verse and Prose and Other Essays* (Bellew Publishing, 1990).

GARDNER, HELEN, *The Composition of 'Four Quartets'* (Faber, 1978).

GARRETT, RICHARD, *P.O.W.: The Uncivil Face of War* (Newton Abbot: David and Charles, 1981).

GASCOYNE, DAVID, *A Short Survey of Surrealism* (Cobden-Sanderson, 1935).

GAT, AZAR, *The Origins of Military Thought: From the Enlightenment to Clausewitz* (Oxford: Clarendon Press, 1989).

GIDDENS, ANTHONY, *Modernity and Self-Identity: Self and Society in the Late Modern Age* (Cambridge: Polity, 1991).

GILBERT, MARTIN, *Britain and Germany Between the Wars* (Longmans, 1964).

GLENDINNING, MILES, and MUTHESIUS, STEFAN, *Tower Block: Modern Public Housing in England, Scotland, Wales and Northern Ireland* (New Haven: Yale University Press, 1994).

GLENDINNING, VICTORIA, *Elizabeth Bowen: Portrait of a Writer* (Weidenfeld and Nicolson, 1977).

GLOVER, JONATHAN, I: *The Philosophy and Psychology of Personal Identity* (1988. Harmondsworth: Penguin, 1989).

GOLDSTEIN, LAURENCE, *The Flying Machine and Modern Literature* (Macmillan, 1986).

GRAHAM, DESMOND, *Keith Douglas 1920–1944: A Biography* (Oxford: Oxford University Press, 1974).

—— *The Truth of War: Owen, Blunden, and Rosenberg* (Manchester: Carcanet, 1984).

GRANT, DOUGLAS, 'War and the Writer', *Penguin Parade*, 2nd ser. 3 (Harmondsworth: Penguin, 1948), 57–68.

—— *The Fuel of the Fire* (Cresset Press, 1950).

GRIFFIN, ROGER, *The Nature of Fascism* (Routledge, 1993).

GRIFFITHS, RICHARD, *Fellow Travellers of the Right: British Enthusiasts for Nazi Germany 1933–39* (1980. Oxford: Oxford University Press, 1983).

HALDANE, J. B. S., *A.R.P.* (Gollancz, 1938).

HALL, PETER, *Cities of Tomorrow: An Intellectual History of Urban Planning and Design in the Twentieth Century* (Oxford: Blackwell, 1990).

HANCOCK, W. K., and GOWING, M. M., *British War Economy, History of the Second World War*, United Kingdom Civil Series (HMSO and Longmans, Green and Co., 1949).

HANLEY, LYNNE, *Writing War: Fiction, Gender, and Memory* (Amherst, Mass.: University of Massachusetts Press, 1991).

HARRIS, JOSE, 'War and Social History: Britain and the Home Front during the Second World War', *Contemporary European History*, 1/1 (March 1992), 17–35.

HARRISON, FRASER, 'Fifties Writing', BBC Radio 3, 11 March 1996.

HARRISSON, TOM, *Living Through the Blitz* (Collins, 1976).

HARTLEY, JENNY, *Millions Like Us: British Women's Fiction of the Second World War* (Virago, 1997).

HASEGAWA, JUNICHI, *Replanning the Blitzed City Centre: A Comparative Study of Bristol, Coventry and Southampton, 1941–1950* (Buckingham: Open University Press, 1992).

HAWTHORN, GEOFFREY, *Plausible Worlds: Possibility and Understanding in History and the Social Sciences* (Cambridge: Cambridge University Press, 1991).

HEWISON, ROBERT, *Under Siege: Literary Life in London 1939–1945* (Weidenfeld and Nicolson, 1977).

HILEY, NICHOLAS, Review of Stuart Sillars, *Art and Survival in First World War Britain*, *Times Literary Supplement*, 4,459 (16–22 Sept. 1988), 1,023–24.

HILL, GEOFFREY, ' "I in Another Place": Homage to Keith Douglas', *Stand*, 6/4, (1964), 6–13.

HOBSBAWM, ERIC, *Age of Extremes: The Short Twentieth Century 1914–1991* (Michael Joseph, 1994).

HOLDEN, C. H., and HOLFORD, W. G., *The City of London: A Record of Destruction and Survival* (The Architectural Press, 1951).

HOWARD, MICHAEL, *War and the Liberal Conscience* (1978. Oxford: Oxford University Press, 1981).

HYNES, SAMUEL, *A War Imagined: The First World War and English Culture* (Bodley Head, 1990).

—— Review of Terence O'Brien, *Chasing After Danger: A Combat Pilot's War over Europe and the Far East, 1939–1942*, *Times Literary Supplement*, 4,560 (24–30 Aug. 1990), 900.

INGLIS, RUTH, *The Children's War: Evacuation 1939–1945* (Collins, 1989).

JAMESON, FREDERIC, *The Political Unconscious: Narrative as a Socially Symbolic Act* (Methuen, 1981).

JEFFREYS, KEVIN (ed.), *War and Reform: British Politics During the Second World War* (Manchester: Manchester University Press, 1994).

KANT, IMMANUEL, *Political Writings*, ed. Hans Reiss, 2nd edn. (1970. Cambridge: Cambridge University Press, 1991).

—— *Critique of Judgement*, trans. James Creed Meredith (1928 and 1952. Oxford: Clarendon Press, 1991).

KEEGAN, JOHN, *The Face of Battle* (Jonathan Cape, 1976).

KNIGHTLEY, PHILLIP, *The First Casualty: From the Crimea to Vietnam: The War Correspondent as Hero, Propagandist, and Myth Maker* (New York: Harcourt Brace Jovanovich, 1975).

KNOWLES, SEBASTIAN D. G., *A Purgatorial Flame: Seven British Writers in the Second World War* (Philadelphia: University of Pennsylvania Press, 1990).

KUSHNER, TONY, 'The Impact of the Holocaust on British Society and Culture', *Contemporary Record*, 5/2 (Autumn 1991), 349–75.

—— *The Holocaust and the Liberal Imagination* (Oxford: Blackwell, 1994).

—— 'Wrong War, Mate', *Patterns of Prejudice*, 29/2 & 3 (1995), 3–13.

LAMB, RICHARD, *The Drift to War, 1922–1939* (W. H. Allen, 1989).

LANGDON-DAVIES, JOHN, *Air Raid: The Technique of Silent Approach: High Explosive Panic* (Routledge, 1938).

LANGER, LAWRENCE L., *The Holocaust and the Literary Imagination* (New Haven: Yale University Press, 1975).

LEED, ERIC, *No Man's Land: Combat and Identity in World War I* (Cambridge: Cambridge University Press, 1979).

LEFEBVRE, HENRI, *The Production of Space*, trans. Donald Nicholson-Smith (1974. Oxford: Blackwell, 1991).

LEMKIN, RAPHAEL, *Axis Rule in Occupied Europe* (Washington D. C.: Carnegie Endowment for International Peace, 1944).

LIGHT, ALISON, *Forever England: Femininity, Literature and Conservatism Between the Wars* (Routledge, 1991).

LINKLATER, ERIC, *The Art of Adventure* (Macmillan, 1947).

'LONGINUS', 'On Sublimity', in D. A. Russell and M. Winterbottom (eds.), *Ancient Literary Criticism* (Oxford: Clarendon Press, 1972), 462–503.

LONGLEY, EDNA, *Poetry in the Wars* (Newcastle upon Tyne: Bloodaxe, 1986).

LYOTARD, JEAN-FRANÇOIS, 'The Sign of History', in Derek Attridge, Geoff Bennington, and Robert Young (eds.), *Post-Structuralism and the Question of History* (Cambridge: Cambridge University Press, 1987), 162–80.

McGUIGAN, JIM, *Cultural Populism* (Routledge, 1992).

McKIBBIN, ROSS, *Classes and Cultures: England 1918–1951* (Oxford: Oxford University Press, 1998).

McLAINE, IAN, *Ministry of Morale: Home Front Morale and the Ministry of Information in World War II* (George Allen and Unwin, 1979).

MANSFIELD, PETER (ed.), *The Middle East: A Political and Economic Survey*, 5th edn. (Oxford: Oxford University Press, 1980).

MANVELL, ROGER, *Films and the Second World War* (Dent, 1974).

MENGHAM, ROD, 'Reading "The Lull"', *Twentieth-Century Literature*, 29/4 (Winter 1983), 454–64.

MEYERS, JEFFREY, *Hemingway: A Biography* (Macmillan, 1986).

MILLER, KARL, *Authors* (1989. Oxford: Oxford University Press, 1990).

MILWARD, ALAN, *War, Economy and Society: 1939–1945* (1977. Harmondsworth: Penguin, 1987).

MONTGOMERY, FIELD MARSHALL THE VISCOUNT, *Memoirs* (Collins, 1958).

MONK, RAY, *Wittgenstein: The Duty of Genius* (1990. Vintage, 1991).

MORGAN, KEVIN, *Against Fascism and War: Ruptures and Continuities in British Communist Politics, 1935–41* (Manchester: Manchester University Press, 1989).

MORRIS, RICHARD, *Guy Gibson* (1994. Harmondsworth: Penguin, 1995).

MOSSE, G. L., *Fallen Soldiers: Reshaping the Memory of the World Wars* (New York: Oxford University Press, 1990).

MOTION, ANDREW, review of Michael Burn, *Mary and Richard*, *Times Literary Supplement*, 4,439 (29 April–5 May 1988), 466.

MUNTON, ALAN, *English Fiction of the Second World War* (Faber, 1989).

MYERS, THOMAS, *Walking Point: American Narratives of Vietnam* (New York: Oxford University Press, 1988).

NAGEL, THOMAS, *Mortal Questions* (1979. Cambridge: Cambridge University Press, 1991).

—— *The View from Nowhere* (1986. New York: Oxford University Press, 1989).

NEWMAN, MICHAEL, *John Strachey* (Manchester: Manchester University Press, 1989).

NORRIS, CHRISTOPHER, *Uncritical Theory: Postmodernism, Intellectuals and the Gulf War* (Lawrence and Wishart, 1992).

NORTH, MICHAEL, *Henry Green and the Writing of His Generation* (Charlottesville: University of Virginia Press, 1984).

NUSSBAUM, MARTHA, *Poetic Justice: The Literary Imagination and Public Life* (Boston, Mass.: Beacon Press, 1995).

OAKESHOTT, MICHAEL, *The Voice of Liberal Learning*, ed. Timothy Fuller (New Haven: Yale University Press, 1989).

OUDITT, SHARON, *Fighting Forces: Writing Women: Identity and Ideology in the First World War* (Routledge, 1994)

OVENDEN, KEITH, *A Fighting Withdrawal: The Life of Dan Davin: Writer, Soldier, Poet* (Oxford: Oxford University Press, 1996).

The Oxford English Dictionary, 2nd edn. (Oxford: Oxford University Press, 1989).

PARIS, MICHAEL, *Winged Warfare: The Literature and Theory of Aerial Warfare in Britain 1859–1917* (Manchester: Manchester University Press, 1992).

PARKER, R. A. C., *The Second World War: A Short History* (1989. Oxford: Oxford University Press, 1997).

PICK, DANIEL, *War Machine: The Rationalisation of Slaughter in the Modern Age* (New Haven: Yale University Press, 1993).

PIETTE, ADAM, *Imagination at War* (Macmillan, 1995).

PIKOULIS, JOHN, *Alun Lewis: A Life* (Bridgend: Poetry Wales Press, 1984).

—— *Alun Lewis: A Life*, 2nd, rev. edn. (Bridgend: Seren Press, 1992).

PITMAN, ROBERT, 'Did This Hero Crash His Plane On Purpose?', *Sunday Express*, 5 May 1957, RHP, file 11.

POKE, G. J., 'Story of a Hero', *Everybody's Weekly* 28 Sept. 1940, RHP, file 6.

POLLOCK, GRISELDA, *Vision and Difference: Femininity, Feminism and Histories of Art* (Routledge, 1988).

PRENDERGAST, CHRISTOPHER, *Paris and the Nineteenth Century* (Oxford: Blackwell, 1992).

PRONAY, NICHOLAS, and SPRING, D. W. (eds.), *Propaganda, Politics and Film* (Macmillan, 1982).

PROST, ANTOINE, and VINCENT, GÉRARD (eds.), *Riddles of Identity in Modern Times*, trans. Arthur Goldhammer (Cambridge, Mass.: Belknap Press, 1991), vol. v of Philippe Ariès and Georges Duby, eds, *A History of Private Life*.

RAWLINSON, MARK, 'This Other War: British Culture and the Holocaust', *Cambridge Quarterly*, 25/1 (1996), 1–25.

REID, P. R., and MICHAEL, MAURICE, *Prisoner of War* (Hamlyn, 1984).

RICHARDS, JEFFREY, and DOROTHY SHERIDAN (eds.), *Mass-Observation at the Movies* (Routledge and Kegan Paul, 1987).

RICKS, CHRISTOPHER, *T. S. Eliot and Prejudice* (Faber, 1988).

RICOEUR, PAUL, *History and Truth*, trans. Charles A. Kelbley (Evanston, Ill.: Northwestern University Press, 1965).

ROEDER, GEORGE H. JR., *The Censored War: American Visual Experience During World War Two* (New Haven: Yale University Press, 1993).

ROLF, DAVID, *Prisoners of the Reich: Germany's Captives 1939–1945* (Coronet, 1989).

ROSE, JACQUELINE, *Why War?—Psychoanalysis, Politics and the Return to Melanie Klein* (Oxford: Blackwell, 1993).

ROSENBLUM, ROBERT, *Transformations in Late Eighteenth Century Art* (1967. Princeton: Princeton University Press, 1969).

ROSS, ALAN, *The Forties: A Period Piece* (Weidenfeld and Nicolson, 1950).

—— *Colours of War: War Art 1939–45* (Jonathan Cape, 1983).

SACKS, OLIVER, *The Man who Mistook his Wife for a Hat* (1985. Pan Books, 1986).

SAMUEL, RAPHAEL, *Theatres of Memory: Past and Present in Contemporary Culture* (Verso, 1994).

SCAMMELL, WILLIAM, *Keith Douglas: A Study* (Faber, 1988).

SCANNELL, VERNON, *Not Without Glory: Poets of the Second World War* (Woburn Press, 1976).

SCARRY, ELAINE, *The Body in Pain: The Making and Unmaking of the World* (New York: Oxford University Press, 1985)

SCOTT, JULIAN, 'The British Press and the Holocaust 1942–1943' (Unpub. Ph.D. thesis, University of Leicester, 1994).

SEARLE, JOHN, *The Construction of Social Reality* (1995. Harmondsworth: Penguin, 1996).

SHELDEN, MICHAEL, *Friends of Promise: Cyril Connolly and the World of Horizon* (1989. Minerva, 1990).

SHERRY, NORMAN, *The Life of Graham Greene: 1939–1955* (Jonathan Cape, 1994).

SHORT, K. R. M., (ed.), *Film and Radio Propaganda in World War II* (Croom Helm, 1983)

SILLARS, STUART, *British Romantic Art and the Second World War* (Macmillan, 1991).

SIMPSON, A. W. BRIAN, *In the Highest Degree Odious: Detention Without Trial in Wartime Britain* (Oxford: Clarendon Press, 1992).

SINFIELD, ALAN, *Literature, Politics and Culture in Postwar Britain* (Oxford: Blackwell, 1989).

SMITH, HAROLD (ed.), *Britain and the Second World War: A Social History* (Manchester: Manchester University Press, 1996).

STAMMERS, NEIL, *Civil Liberties in Britain During the 2nd World War: A Political Study* (Croom Helm, 1983).

STANNARD, MARTIN, *Evelyn Waugh: No Abiding City 1939–1966* (Dent, 1992).

TASSI, ROBERTO, *Sutherland: The Wartime Drawings*, trans. Julian Andrews (Sotheby Parke Bernet, 1980).

TAYLOR, A. J. P., *English History 1914–1945* (Oxford: Oxford University Press, 1965).

TAYLOR, PHILIP M. (ed.), *Britain and the Cinema in the Second World War* (Macmillan, 1988).

THEWELEIT, KLAUS, *Male Fantasies*, trans. Stephen Conway, Erica Carter, and Chris Turner, 2 vols. (1977–8. Cambridge: Polity, 1987–9).

TIMMINS, NICHOLAS, *The Five Giants: A Biography of the Welfare State* (1995. Fontana, 1996).

TIPPETT, MICHAEL, *Those Twentieth-century Blues* (Hutchinson, 1991).

TITMUSS, RICHARD M., *Problems of Social Policy*, History of the Second World War, United Kingdom Civil Series (HMSO and Longmans, Green and Co., 1950).

TOLLEY, A. T., *The Poetry of the Forties* (Manchester: Manchester University Press, 1985).

TREGLOWN, JEREMY, and BENNETT, BRIDGET (eds.), *Grub Street and the Ivory Tower: Literary Journalism and Literary Scholarship from Fielding to the Internet* (Oxford: Clarendon Press, 1998).

TREVOR-ROPER, H. R., 'History and Imagination', in Hugh Lloyd-Jones, Valerie Pearl, and Blair Worden (eds.), *History and Imagination: Essays in Honour of H. R. Trevor-Roper* (Duckworth, 1981), 356–69.

WALSH, JEFFREY, and AULICH, JAMES (eds.), *Vietnam Images: War and Representation* (Macmillan, 1989).

WALZER, MICHAEL, 'World War II: Why Was This War Different?', *Philosophy and Public Affairs*, 1/1 (Fall 1971), 3–21.

WASSERSTEIN, BERNARD, *Britain and the Jews of Europe 1939–1945* (London and Oxford: Institute of Jewish Affairs and Clarendon Press, 1979).

WEINBERG, GERHARD L., *A World at Arms: A Global History of World War II* (Cambridge: Cambridge University Press, 1994).

WHITE, HAYDEN, 'The Value of Narrativity in the Representation of Reality', *Critical Inquiry*, 7/1 (Autumn 1980), 5–27.

WHITE, MICHAEL, 'Britten's chorus for a captive audience', *Independent on Sunday*, 10 Nov. 1991.

WILLIAMS, RAYMOND, *The Country and the City* (Chatto and Windus, 1973).

WILLIAMSON, ANNE, *Henry Williamson: Tarka and the Last Romantic* (Stroud: Alan Sutton, 1995).

WILMOT, CHESTER, *The Struggle for Europe* (1951. Wordsworth Editions, 1997).

WILSON, TREVOR, *The Myriad Faces of War: Britain and the Great War, 1914-1918* (Cambridge: Polity Press, 1988).

WINNICOTT, D. W., *Home Is Where We Start From* (Harmondsworth: Penguin, 1986).

WINTER, JAY M., 'Imaginings of War: Some Cultural Supports of the Institution of War', in Robert A. Hinde (ed.), *The Institution of War* (Macmillan, 1991).

—— *Sites of Memory, Sites of Mourning: The Great War in European Cultural History* (Cambridge: Cambridge University Press, 1996).

WOLPERT, STANLEY, *A New History of India*, 5th edn. (1977. New York and Oxford: Oxford University Press, 1997).

WOOD, DENIS, *The Power of Maps* (Routledge, 1993).

WORPOLE, KEN, *Dockers and Detectives: Popular Reading: Popular Writing* (Verso, 1983).

WORSLEY, T. C., 'Stirling Station', review of H. E. Bates ['Flying Officer X'], *The Greatest People in the World*, *The New Statesman and Nation*, 24/610 (31 Oct. 1942).

WRIGHT, D. G., 'The Great War, Government Propaganda and English "Men of Letters" 1914-16', *Literature and History*, 4/7 (Spring 1978), 70-100.

WRIGHT, PATRICK, *On Living in an Old Country* (Verso, 1985).

YEATS-BROWN, F., and SHEPPARD, E. W., *Britain at War: The Army*, 5 vols. (Hutchinson, 1941-7).

YEATS, W. B. (ed.), *The Oxford Book of Modern Verse* (Oxford University Press, 1936).

YOUNG, JAMES, *Writing and Rewriting the Holocaust: Narrative and the Consequences of Interpretation* (Bloomington: Indiana University Press, 1988).

ZURBRUGG, NICHOLAS (ed.), *Baudrillard: Art and Artefact* (Sage, 1997).

Index

abstractions 11, 24, 66, 72, 87, 110–11,
    118–19, 121, 127, 129, 131, 134
Adam, Ronald:
    Readiness at Dawn 62
Adinsell, Richard:
    Warsaw Concerto 46
Adorno, Theodor 206
agency 13–14, 17–18, 28, 129–31, 159,
    177–8, 186
airman, the 40–5, 48–9, 51, 55, 57–67, 68,
    123, 155, 176, 184
Air Ministry 11 n. 18, 59
air raids *see* Blitz
    as symbols of resistance 46, 70, 74, 76,
        79, 92–4, 107–9, 144, 161
Aistrop, Jack 149
Aldington, Richard:
    Death of a Hero 28
Alexander, Michael:
    The Privileged Nightmare 177–8
Alexandria 84
Anderson, Benedict 27, 153–4
anonymous serviceman, the 60, 64, 150
anthropomorphization 18, 86
    armies as wrestlers 6, 18–19, 23, 28,
    figure of colossus 28, 120, 127
apocalypse 71, 73–4
Army, British 61, 102, 144–60
    British Expeditionary Force 2, 112, 154,
        201
    as garrison army 49, 145, 156
    Home Forces 146
    OCTU 149–50
Army Bureau of Current Affairs (ABCA)
    22 n. 62, 143, 148
Arnold, Matthew 192–3
Atlantic, Battle of the 29–30
Atlantic Charter 140, 156
Auden, W. H. 8, 42 n. 7, 153, 187, 196, 207
Augury 125
Augustine 206
Auschwitz 171–2, 203
autobiography 40, 44–5, 126
autonomy 37, 55, 101, 106
Auxillary Fire Service (AFS) 69, 96–8,
    104–6, 132

aviation 40
    and the aesthetic 42–3, 57, 59
    bomber aircraft 59, 63, 70, 73, 75, 91
    civil aviation 59
    ethical contrast of fighter and bomber
        tactics 59, 60, 64
    fighter aircraft 39, 59
    representation of military aviation
        44–5, 57–60
    and the sublime 60, 62

Bachelard, Gaston 95
Baird, Edward 70
Baker, Denys Val 149
Balchin, Nigel:
    Darkness Falls from the Air 93–4,
    169
Baldwin, Stanley 70
Balfour, Michael 143
Ballard, J. G. 208
Banerjee, A. 128
Barber, Noel:
    Prisoner of War 177, 180
Barbusse, Henri:
    Under Fire 59 n. 67, 123
Barne, Kitty:
    Visitors from London 91
Barnett, Correlli 115–17, 139
Baron, Alexander:
    From the City, From the Plough 162–3
Barthes, Roland 21, 175
Bates, H. E. 49 n. 29, 55, 66, 155, 187
    Fair Stood the Wind for France 176
    as Flying Officer X 155
battle:
    battlefield 6–7, 23, 68, 110–37, 163
    conventions of battle description 9,
        25–8, 58, 110–12, 123, 127, 130–1,
        134, 136
    legibility of battle 110, 115–8, 125–6,
        131–2
Baudelaire, Charles 121
Baudrillard, Jean 22
Bauman, Zygmunt 17
BBC 1–2, 50, 152
    Home Service 190

Beardmore, George:
  Civilians at War 71
Beaton, Cecil:
  Near East 115–16, 122
  Time Exposure 86
Beaverbrook, Lord 39, 154
Beckwith, E.G.C.:
  Selections from The Quill 175
Beith, Major Sir John Hay 146
  see Hay, Ian
Belfield, Eversley 53–4
Bells Went Down, The 168
Belsen 181
Benghazi 174
Benjamin, Walter 2, 11, 121
Berlin, Isaiah 140
Berlin Olympics 41
Betjeman, John 85
Bettelheim, Bruno 181
Beveridge, Sir William 23
Bielenberg, Christabel 56
Biggles 62
Billany, Dan 5, 72, 161, 174, 185
  The Trap 161–4
Billany, Dan and David Dowie:
  The Cage 179, 190, 194
blackout 83–4
Blitz, the 35, 43–4, 56, 68–109, 124, 156
Blitzkrieg 107
Blunden, Edmund:
  tutor to Keith Douglas 120–1
  Undertones of War 128
body, the 7, 14, 24–30, 52, 120
  and armour 7, 63
  dematerialized 137
  the face 43, 46–7, 54–5, 65, 155
  and the inanimate 26–7, 53, 64–5, 68,
    78–9, 87
  petrifaction 51, 53–4, 79, 86–7, 94,
    155–6
  scars 43, 47–8, 66, 190
  see also wounded body, corpses, the
    dead
bomb shelters 76, 93
Booker, Mary 45, 56
Bose, Subhas Chandra 157
Bottome, Phyllis 56
Bourdieu, Pierre 130
Bowen, Elizabeth 18, 32, 34–5, 49–50,
    106, 156, 168
  The Heat of the Day 94–5, 99–103,
    108, 163
  The Last September 95

'Mysterious Kôr' 82–3, 168
'Summer Night' 84
'Sunday Afternoon' 83
Braine, John:
  Room at the Top 178
Branson, Clive 146, 168
Breton, André 122
Britain, Battle of 23, 39, 42, 53, 108, 115
Britain in Pictures 49
British Union of Fascists 147
Brittain, Vera:
  England's Hour 82, 84–5, 88–9
  Seed of Chaos 28–9
  Testament of Experience 31, 89
  Testament of Youth 89
Britten, Benjamin 169, 175
broadcasting 2, 57, 174, 181
Brooke, Jocelyn:
  The Passing of a Hero 57
Brooke, Rupert 40, 152
Brophy, John:
  Immortal Sergeant 113
Brophy, John and Eric Partridge:
  Songs and Slang of the British Soldier
    10
Bryher:
  Days of Mars 91
Buchan, John:
  Mr Standfast 73
Buchenwald 172–3, 181
Bullen, Keith and John Cromer (eds.):
  Salamander 114
Bund report 182–3
bureaucracy 17–18, 162, 191, 200–1
Burke, Edmund 75
Burma 158
Burn, Michael 56, 204
  Farewell to Colditz 176, 198
  The Flying Castle 196
  The Labyrinth of Europe 36–7
  Yes, Farewell 173, 181, 185, 190, 193–8,
    201
Burney, Christopher:
  The Dungeon Democracy 172–3
  Solitary Confinement 185 n. 97
Butler, Arthur S. G.:
  Recording Ruin 89 n. 109

Cairo 117
Calder, Angus:
  The Myth of the Blitz 141
  The People's War 141
Calder, Ritchie:

The Lesson of London 71, 88, 90 n.
    116, 107–8
    Start Planning Britain Now 91–2
Calder-Marshall, Arthur, *et al.*:
    'Why Not War Writers?' 151–3
camouflage 53, 120, 122–3
Camus, Albert:
    L'Étranger 124
    La Peste 167, 204
Captive Heart, The 172, 180–2
Cary, Joyce:
    Charley is my Darling 91
casualties 26
    anticipated 70–1, 125
    architectural 85, 89
'Cato':
    Guilty Men 154
Cavalcanti, Alberto 49
Ceadel, Martin 9
Cecil, Lord David 178–9
cemeteries 26–7, 137
censorship 127, 175, 177 n. 52
Cesarani, David 54
Chapman, Guy (ed.):
    Vain Glory 128
Childers, Erskine:
    The Riddle of the Sands 69
chivalry 52, 58–9, 115, 123
Churchill, Winston S. 2, 31, 39, 59, 65, 80,
    120 n. 49, 139–40, 149, 154, 156, 165
city, the 68, 73, 81–5, 89–93, 95, 109
    evacuation of human content 78, 82–3
Civil Defence 74–6, 145
civilian soldiers 148, 160
civilians 28, 31, 66, 80, 142, 145
Clark, Ian 20
Clark, Sir Kenneth 81, 208
Clarke, Peter 31
class 33–4, 149
Clausewitz, Carl von 6, 13, 18, 21, 110,
    119, 134
Clifford, Alexander:
    'Crusader' 112
Cold War, the 183
Colditz (Oflag IVC) 36, 56, 173, 177–8,
    189, 193–6, 198
collective, the 15, 19, 30–9, 45, 47, 49,
    60–1, 69, 72, 74, 76, 79, 83, 93, 101,
    113, 144, 153–6, 161–2
Comfort, Alex 77, 164, 169, 181
    'On Interpreting the War' 151
command structures 14, 105, 111, 117,
    129–34, 164

Communist Party 50, 76, 90
concentration camps 36, 44, 63, 168, 171,
    196
    concentration camp literature 171
    and school 170–1, 186–9
Connolly, Cyril 92, 150, 153–4, 156
    The Unquiet Grave 153
conscientious objection 169
conscription 162
    to symbols 41, 43–4, 49, 52
Cooper, Duff 47
Corby, Herbert:
    Hampdens Going Over 168
corpses 7, 81, 117–19, 122, 125–6, 151,
    162
Cotterell, Geoffrey:
    Then a Soldier 144–5
Coultass, Clive 24
Council for Entertainment, Music and the
    Arts (CEMA) 169
Coventry 85, 107–8
Coward, Noel:
    In Which We Serve 24
    This Happy Breed 161
Crete 129–32, 136
Cripps, Sir Stafford 156–7
Croatian War 76
Croft, Andy 34
Croft, J. L. R. and Axford R. A.:
    Wychwood Chronicles 175
Cromer, John 114
Crompton, Richmal:
    William and the Evacuees 91 n. 121
crusade 36, 41, 52
    sceptical crusade 52–3
Currie, Gregory 105

Dachau 36, 196
Dane, Clemence:
    The Shelter Book 76
Dangerous Moonlight 46
Davies, Ioan 170
Davin, Dan 4, 118
    Crete 129–32, 135
    For the Rest of Our Lives 128–9,
    132–38
Day Lewis, Cecil 120
    'Where are the War Poets?' 152–3
dead, the:
    relationships to 40, 42, 51, 54, 66, 78,
    81, 103, 117–26, 130, 198
death camps 171–2, 180
defacement 65

defeat 2, 46, 64
Defence of the Realm Act 128, 147
Defoe, Daniel 167
Del Vecchio:
  The 13th Valley 20 n. 48
De Man, Paul 16, 45–6
demobilization 27
democracy 37, 62, 113, 135, 144, 154
Democratic Order, The 21
De Quincey, Thomas 81, 85
Derrida, Jacques 93 n. 133
desert 113, 115
Desert Victory 126–7, 158
detachment/engagement 8, 13–14, 78, 97,
  115, 128, 131, 151, 191
Dickson, Lovat 55–6
Dieppe Raid 150
discipline 33, 35, 43, 49, 62–3, 149, 159,
  168, 173–4
  disciplined subject 7, 44
disfigurement 45, 47, 54, 78
Displaced Persons 191
Divine, A. D.:
  Road to Tunis 112–3
Dostoyevsky, Fyodor 190–1, 197
Douglas, Keith 4, 81, 115–28, 133, 168
  Alamein to Zem Zem 25, 119, 121–8
  'Death of a Horse' 119
  'How to Kill' 121
  'Little Red Mouth' 119–20
  'Sportsmen' 123
  'Vergissmeinnicht' 6–8, 119, 121, 126
Douhet, Guilio 70
Dresden 108, 175
Dumbo 70
Dunkirk 2, 22, 46, 74, 112, 146, 154, 156,
  158
  as victory 43
Durrell, Lawrence 114, 116
  The Alexandria Quartet 84

Eagle Day 39
Eagleton, Terry 19, 79, 81
Eden, Anthony 145
education 143, 148–9, 176–8, 208
Egypt 113
Eichstätt (Oflag VIIB) 175
El Alamein 102, 119
Eliot, T. S. 153
  Little Gidding 83, 107
  The Waste Land 194
Elizabeth I 48
Ellis, John 1

Ellmann, Maud 83 n. 69
Empson, William 94, 120 n. 48
engagement *see* detachment/engagement
English Association, The 48
  England: An Anthology 84
epitaphs 51–2
escape/escape stories *see* Prisoners of
  War
euphemism 27
evacuation 71, 91, 136, 155
Everybody's Weekly 43
exile 114, 117, 144
extermination 36, 55, 203, 207–8

Farson, Negley:
  Bomber's Moon 167
fascism 34, 52, 61, 147, 169
Faulks, Sebastian 57
Fedden, Robin 114, 117
film 24, 39–40, 46, 49, 70, 71, 74, 75, 98,
  126–7, 158, 161, 184, 187, 208–9
Final Solution, the 17
Fires Were Started 98
First of the Few, The 39
First World War 1, 8–9, 11–12, 52, 72,
  88–9, 146–7, 151–2, 154, 187
  memory of 8, 37, 44, 144, 202, 206
  Western Front 1, 23, 68
  writing of 3, 13, 144–5, 148, 150,
    159–60, 205
Fitz Gibbon, Constantine 90–1
Flaubert, Gustave:
  Madame Bovary 69
Foreman Went to France, The 49 n. 28
Forster, E. M. 57
Foucault, Michel 21–2, 60, 148, 170, 173
France, Fall of 64, 154
Fraser, G. S. 10, 115, 117, 160
freedom 146, 156, 165, 174, 184, 191–3
Freikorps 192
French Revolution 37
Freud, Sigmund 78, 93 n. 133
Freyberg, Lt-General Sir Bernard 130
Fussell, Paul 9, 33–4, 71, 98
  Wartime 11, 119
future *see* time
futurism 73

Gallico, Paul 74
Gallipoli 154
Gandhi, Mohandas K. 157
Gardiner, Patrick 160
Garson, Greer 208

Gascoyne, David:
  A Short Survey of Surrealism 122
Gat, Azar 134
Genet, Jean:
  The Miracle of the Rose 184
Geneva convention 173–4
genocide 37, 207
Gheeraert the Younger, Marcus 48
Gibson, Wing-Commander Guy:
  Enemy Coast Ahead 59
Giddens, Anthony 28
Gilbert, Martin 37
Gilliat, Sidney 108
Glover, Jonathan 95
Goebbels, Josef 114
Goering, Reichsmarschall Hermann 41,
  61, 92
Golding, William:
  Lord of the Flies 91
Goldstein, Laurence 60
GPO Film Unit 49
Graecan, Robert 77
Graham, Desmond 10
Grant, Douglas 137
Graves, Robert 10, 145–7
  'War Poetry in this War' 145
Graves, Robert and Alan Hodge:
  The Long Week-End 142
Green, Henry 77, 96
  Back 169, 193, 199–204
  Caught 69, 97, 103–7
  Loving 103
  'The Lull' 104
  'Mr Jonas' 104
  Pack My Bag 69, 104–5, 187–8
  Party Going 74–5
  'A Rescue' 104
Greene, Graham 49 n. 28, 69, 81–2
  Brighton Rock 93
  The End of the Affair 96
  It's a Battlefield 187
  'The Lieutenant Died Last' 49 n. 28
  The Ministry of Fear 96
  The Old School 187
Greenwood, Walter 187
Gregory, Major Robert 59
Grierson, John 49
Griffin, Roger 52
Griffiths, Richard 61
Guernica 70
Guilty Men 154
Gulf War 22, 27 n. 20, 58 n. 61
'Gun Buster':

  Battle Dress 46
  Zero Hours 124–5
Gwynn-Browne, Arthur:
  Gone for a Burton 62–3, 176

Haggard, Rider 83
Haldane, J. B. S.:
  A. R. P. 90
Hamilton, Patrick:
  The Slaves of Solitude 199
Hancock, W. K. and Gowing, M. M.:
  British War Economy 21
Hanley, James:
  No Directions 78–9, 94
Hanley, Lynne 16
Harris, Jose 30, 142
Harris, Robert 43 n. 8
Harrison, Fraser 172
Harrison, Tony:
  The Gaze of the Gorgon 27 n. 80
Harrisson, Tom:
  'War Books' 203, 207
Hartley, Jenny 24
Hartley, L. P. 137
Hawthorn, Geoffrey 131
Hay, Ian:
  Arms and the Men 146
  The Battle of Flanders 1940 146
  The First Hundred Thousand 146
Hazlitt, William 177
H.D.:
  The Gift 94
  The Walls Do Not Fall 82
Heller, Joseph:
  Catch-22 22, 65, 201
Hemingway, Ernest:
  A Farewell to Arms 41
Henderson, Hamish:
  Elegies for the Dead in Cyrenaica 118,
  161
Hendry, J. F. 77
Henrey, Robert:
  A Village in Piccadilly 85 n. 83
heroism 23, 39–40, 46–7, 49, 51, 53, 55,
  57–9, 74, 86, 94, 106, 118, 126, 136–7,
  203
Herr, Michael:
  Dispatches 129
Herring, Robert 83
Heydrich, Obergruppenführer Reinhard
  120
Hiley, Nicholas 24
Hillary, Michael 56

Hillary, Richard 4, 39–61, 63–7, 126, 157–9, 168, 198
  death of 40, 50–1
  'Fighter Pilot' 49 n. 30
  The Last Enemy 40–53, 55–6, 60, 65–6, 163
  'The Pilot and Peace' 61
  Richard Hillary Trust Fund 55
  'Where Do We Go From Here?' 61
history writing 88, 107, 110–11, 115, 117, 129–34, 137, 182, 207
  chronicle 182
  instant 45–6
  military 25–7, 58, 111, 129–30, 136
  official 71, 179
Hitler, Adolf 2, 39, 41, 56, 147
Holden, Inez:
  'Fellow Travellers in a Factory' 144
  It was Different at the Time 95
  'Summer Journal' 108
Hollywood 208–9
Holocaust, the 189, 208
Home Front 15, 68, 113, 139, 144–5, 163, 201
Home Guard (Local Defence Volunteers) 145, 159
Hope and Glory 208
Horizon 32, 35, 51, 53, 150–3, 158–9
Household, Geoffrey:
  Rogue Male 186 n. 100
houses 71, 89, 95
  see space
  opened houses 95–6, 98–9, 161
Howard, Leslie 39–40
Howard, Sir Michael 53, 207
Hughes, Ted 118
Hugo, Victor 9
  Les Miserables 110
Hunt, J. L. and Pringle, A. G.
  Service Slang 11
Hunt, Leslie C.:
  The Prisoners' Progress 175
Hynes, Samuel 9–11, 178

identity *see* autonomy, personality
  and environment, 95, 102, 194
  frustration of military identity 145–8, 150, 159
  military identity 156
  personal 32, 35, 40–50, 100–3, 181–4, 199–203
  rejection of military identity 162
Imperial War Museum 183

imperialism 124, 135, 156
In Which We Serve 24
India 145–6, 156–8
  Indian troops 113
individual, the 30, 35, 63, 160, 209
  see collective
  and the machine 35, 40, 44, 50, 58, 60–6, 168
  and the mass 8, 15–19, 28–9, 36–7, 44, 60–1
insularity 5, 59, 63, 154, 172, 176, 181, 196, 204, 206
internment 169–70, 172, 189–90
Irigaray, Luce 78
Irish Civil War 95, 134
Isherwood, Christopher:
  Lions and Shadows 188
Italy 112, 192
  armistice 161, 195

James, William 12, 78 n. 39
Jameson, Frederic 105
Jameson, Storm 44, 89, 164
Japan 157, 159, 202
Jarrell, Randall:
  'The Death of the Ball Turret Gunner' 22, 30
Jennings, Humphrey 98
Jews 37, 54, 171, 173, 188, 207
Jinnah, Muhammed Ali 157
Joad, C. E. M.:
  'The Face of England' 147
Johns, W. E. 62
Johnson, Samuel 89
Joyce, James:
  A Portrait of the Artist as a Young Man 93
Joyce, William 174

Kafka, Franz 169
Kant, Immanuel 162
  Critique of Judgement 79–80
  Perpetual Peace 80–1
Kavan, Anna:
  'The Case of Bill Williams' 35
Kee, Robert 179, 204
  A Crowd is Not Company 181–2, 184–7, 190, 192
  The Impossible Shore 181, 190–3, 202
  'Mercury on a Fork' 182
  1945: The World We Fought For 182
  The World We Left Behind 182
Keegan, John 18–19, 25–6, 130–1, 134
Kennington, Eric 47, 56

Drawing the R.A.F. 47–8
Kersh, Gerald:
   Clean, Bright and Slightly Oiled 148–9
   Faces in a Dusty Picture 113
   They Die with Their Boots Clean 148
killing 7, 16, 18–19, 24–6, 42–3, 66, 117,
   136, 185
King-Hall, Stephen:
   Total Victory 23 n. 65
Knebworth, Anthony 57
Knight, Eric:
   This Above All 56 n. 53
Knowles, Sebastian D. G. 107
Koestler, Arthur 50, 149, 186, 189–90, 207
   Arrival and Departure 54–5, 61
   'The Birth of a Myth' 39, 50–4, 65–7,
   157–8, 198
   Darkness at Noon 186 n. 103
   'Knights in Rusty Armour' 207
   'The Mixed Transport' 171
   'On Disbelieving Atrocities' 171 n. 24
   Scum of the Earth 50, 174 n. 35, 179,
   182
   Spanish Testament 186 n. 103
Kushner, Tony 189, 208

Labour Party 154
Langdon-Davies, John:
   Air Raid 73
language *see* war and language
Larkin, Philip:
   A Girl in Winter 186
Lawrence, D. H.:
   Kangaroo 72
Lawrence, T. E. 47, 54, 60, 63, 147–8, 150,
   155
   The Mint 54, 58, 60, 63
   Seven Pillars of Wisdom 47
Leavis, F. R. 53
Leed, Eric 118
Lefebvre, Henri 116–17
Left Book Club 44
Lehmann, John 154, 156
   I Am My Brother 82
Lemkin, Raphael 207
levelling 34, 75, 93, 95, 118, 161, 167
Levi, Primo:
   The Drowned and the Saved 172–3,
   180, 203
   If This is a Man 171
   The Periodic Table 123
Lewis, Alun 4–5, 33, 36–7, 127, 146–51,
   154–60, 163–4, 166, 168–9

'After Dunkirk' 154–6
'All Day it has Rained...' 159
'The Earth is a Syllable' 157–8
'Flick' 146
'Grenadier' 160
'It's a Long Way to Go' 148
'Lance-Jack' 151
'The Orange Grove' 157
'Private Jones' 146
'The Raid' 157
Raiders' Dawn 146
'They Came' 156
'Ward "O" 3(b)' 158–9
Lewis, Cecil:
   Sagittarius Rising 58–9
Lewis, Wyndham:
   Blasting and Bombardiering 59
liberal imagination 189
liberalism 32, 66, 188, 194
liberation 190–1, 194, 197–8, 203
'Lili Marlene' 121
Lindberg, Charles 61
Lindsay, Jack:
   Beyond Terror 136
Linklater, Eric 52, 56
London 69, 75–6, 88–94
'Longinus' 80
Longley, Edna 128
looting 6, 121, 127
Luftwaffe 23, 39, 61, 77, 91, 94, 107, 109
Lyotard, Jean-François 78

Macaulay, Rose 84
McGuigan, Jim 34
McIndoe, Sir Archibald 43, 51
McLaine, Ian 29
Maclaren-Ross, Julian 144–5, 149
   'A Bit of a Smash in Madras' 124
   'I had to go Sick' 169
   Memoirs of the Forties 96, 145
   The Stuff to Give the Troops 147–8
MacNeice, Louis 2, 77, 89, 96
   Autumn Journal 169
   'Broken Windows or Thinking Aloud'
   63
   'London Letter (5)' 87
   'The Morning After the Blitz' 81, 84
   'The Way We Live Now' 92–3
Mair, John:
   Never Come Back 58
Maleme airfield 131
Mallalieu, J. P. W.:
   Very Ordinary Seaman 169

Manning, Olivia:
  The Balkan Trilogy 114
  The Levant Trilogy 114–15
  'Poets in Exile' 114
Mansfield, Katherine 72
Marinetti, Filippo Tommaso 7, 73
Marxism 178, 194, 198
Masefield, John 154
Mass Observation 34, 207
  An Enquiry into People's Homes 85 n.
    88
  War Begins at Home 73
Maugham, Robin:
  Come to Dust 123
Mediterranean 112, 133, 135, 145
Michie, Allan A. and Walter Graebner
  (eds.):
  Their Finest Hour 107
Middle East 114
Millar, George 195
Miller, Betty:
  On the Side of the Angels 159, 168
Miller, Karl 32, 153
Milligan, Spike:
  Mussolini: His Part in My Downfall
    145 n. 32
Milton, John 30, 89
Milward, Alan 140
Ministry of Information (MOI) 10, 28,
  47, 50, 57, 116, 140, 142, 152, 208
  Home Intelligence Unit 207–8
Mitchell, R. J. 39
mobilization 2, 34, 36
Money-Kyrle, Roger 166
Monsarrat, Nicholas:
  The Cruel Sea 29–30
Montgomery, Field Marshall Sir Bernard
  14, 102, 115, 120–1
Moore, Henry 70, 76, 81, 87, 91
Moore, Reginald 149
Moorehead, Alan:
  Eclipse 192
morale 2, 103, 142–3, 149
  see propaganda
Morgan, Guy 181 n. 75
  Only Ghosts Can Live 181
Morton, H. V.:
  I Saw Two Englands 88
Morton, J. B. 10 n. 16
Mosley, Sir Oswald 57
Mosse, G. L. 20
Motion, Andrew 45
Mrs Miniver 74, 209

Muir, Edwin:
  'War Poetry' 153
Munton, Alan 205
Murry, John Middleton:
  Democracy and War 65
  'Richard Hillary' 65–6
music 46, 121, 169
Mussolini, Benito 147
Myers, Thomas 108
myth 51–3, 57, 66, 69, 141

Nagel, Thomas 16–18
narrative archetypes of the war 49–50,
  180, 183–4
Nashe, Thomas 93
National Government 154
national unity 60, 149
  see collective, levelling, reconstruction,
    violence
Navy 61
Nazism 33, 37, 49–50, 172–3, 192, 208
  anti-Nazism 32, 36, 44, 51, 53, 146
  represenations of 37, 41–2
Neumann, John von and Morgenstern,
  Oskar:
  *Theory of Games and Economic
    Behaviour* 129
New Apocalypse 77
New Romanticism 77
Newby, Eric:
  Love and War in the Apennines 194–5
Next of Kin, The 24
next war, the 68–71, 73–5, 154
Nicolson, Sir Harold 140
Niven, David 39–40
Nixon, Barbara:
  Raiders Overhead 85
Noel-Paton, M. H.:
  'The Last Enemy' 56
Normandy landings 127, 162–3, 199
North Africa 6, 48, 112–28, 133–8,
  161–4
North, Michael 103
nuclear war 183
Nussbaum, Martha 17

Oakeshott, Michael 141
Oasis 114
occupied Europe 32, 50, 55, 63, 167, 171,
  186–7, 189, 196–7, 204, 206
  Britain and 32, 55
Olivier, Laurence:
  Henry V 161

Orwell, George 12, 14, 50, 108, 145, 149, 152, 171–2, 188–9
  Coming up for Air 73, 85, 96
  Homage to Catalonia 16, 59
  Keep the Aspidistra Flying 85
  Nineteen Eighty-Four 73, 94 n. 136
Ostrowska, Wanda, 86
Owen, Wilfred 1, 9, 26–7, 42 n. 7, 150
  'Strange Meeting' 6–8, 15, 17

pacifism 66, 147
pain 25, 42, 119, 125, 137
Panter-Downes, Mollie 85 n. 83
Paris, Michael 57
participation 1, 3, 13, 31, 144, 155
Partridge, Eric 10
  A Dictionary of R.A.F. Slang 11 n. 18
patriotism 35, 41, 49, 52, 148, 160
Patton, Paul 22
peace 177
Peace Pledge Union 44
Peake, Mervyn 99 n. 160
Pearl Harbour 69, 145
Penguin New Writing 149
People's Army 149
People's History of the Second World War 143
People's War 5, 31, 86, 90 n. 116, 141–4, 146
Personal Landscape 114
Personality in Wartime 35
personality, wartime 33, 49–50, 101, 106, 168
perspective 122–3, 129–38
  altitude 58–9, 62, 64, 75, 109, 123
  strategic 7, 16–17, 28–9, 68, 72, 111, 118
Picasso, Pablo 207
  Guernica 70
Pick, Daniel 10, 12
pictorial representation 25, 47–8, 56, 70, 76, 81, 91, 128
Picture Post 90, 101, 143
Piette, Adam 20, 123, 139, 205–7
Pioneer Corps 50, 54
planning 40, 92, 143
Poke, G. J. 43
Poland 183
Pound, Ezra:
  Cantos 192
Powell, Anthony:
  The Valley of Bones 147

Powell, Enoch:
  Dancer's End 129
Powell, Michael and Emeric Pressburger:
  A Canterbury Tale 147
  The Life and Death of Colonel Blimp 149
  A Matter of Life and Death 40
  One of Our Aircraft is Missing 75
Prendergast, Christopher 18
press, the 23, 52–3, 90, 101, 105, 107, 115, 182–3, 196
Priestley, J. B. 49 n. 28, 154
  English Journey 88
  Letter to a Returning Serviceman 168, 198
  Out of the People 144
  Postscripts 2, 183
prison 50, 170, 184, 186–7
  as metaphor 168–7, 192–4, 203
Prisoners of War 62, 161–4, 167–204
  escape 175–181, 185–7, 194, 196–7
  escape stories 171–3, 179–80, 185–6, 189, 198, 203, 209
  Russian POWs 175, 197
Pritchett, V. S. 50–1
private life 32–4
propaganda 2–3, 20–1, 31, 34–5, 41, 44, 53, 117, 143–4, 146, 152–3, 165–6, 181, 205
  emotional co-ordination of war effort 80, 151–5, 161
  of private enterprise 78
Proust, Marcel 84
Pym, Barbara:
  'So Very Secret' 82
Pynchon, Thomas:
  Gravity's Rainbow 201

Quennell, Peter 86
Quill, The (Oflag IX) 175

radar 39
RAF 23, 39, 41–2, 44, 47, 49, 57, 60, 66, 144
  Bomber Command 55, 66, 185
  bombing 57–8, 109
  bombing of Germany 28–9, 66, 108–9, 185
  bombing of Italy 59
  and fascism 63
  Oxford University Air Squadron 41
  as political organization 41–2, 54, 61–2, 148

RAF (*cont.*)
  RAFVR 39, 61
  Royal Flying Corps (RFC) 58
Raleigh, Sir Walter 58
Rawlings, A. C. 56
Read, Herbert 48
  'Art in an Electric Atmosphere' 77
rearmament 70, 73, 144
reconstruction 4, 23, 29–30, 34–6, 46,
    77–8, 82, 85, 139–43, 149, 157–8, 183,
    187, 198
  better world 29, 42, 46, 143, 148, 183
  new world order 16, 133, 143
Red Cross 181
  The Prisoner of War 177
redescription *see* violence
Rees, Goronwy:
  A Chapter of Accidents 150–1
  'Letter from a Soldier' 150–1
refugees 50, 54, 64, 81, 151, 155, 190
regeneration 10, 49–50, 52, 78, 151, 154,
    183, 197–8
  new race 48, 61–2
regimentation 30, 36–7, 47, 60, 105, 146,
    148, 159, 170
  nation as regiment 65
  resistance to 31–2, 36, 41, 44, 62, 148
Reid, P. R. 186, 198
  The Colditz Story 189
Remarque, Erich Maria 11
repatriation 63, 199
resistance 32, 70, 73–4, 102
Resistance, the 32
restoration 43, 51, 85, 132, 137
Richards, I. A. 53
Richards, J. M. 99, 152
  The Bombed Buildings of Britain 85–6
Richey, Paul:
  Fighter Pilot 59
Ricoeur, Paul 118 n. 36, 130 n. 97
Rimbaud, Arthur 125
Romilly, Esmond 179–80
Romilly, Giles 177–80
  'Three Sketches from a Prison Camp'
    180
Romilly, Giles and Michael Alexander
  The Privileged Nightmare 177–8
Rommel, Field Marshall Erwin 115, 120–1
Roosevelt, President Franklin D. 140
Rose, Jacqueline 13
Rosenblum, Robert 82
Rotha, Paul 139
ruins 68, 75, 81–3, 85–7, 97–8

Sacks, Oliver 203
Saint-Exupéry, Antoine de 168
  Flight to Arras 62, 64
Salamander 114
Samuel, Raphael 183
Sansom, William 88, 94, 96–9, 169
  'Building Alive' 99
  'The Long Sheet' 169
  'The Wall' 97–8
Sassoon, Siegfried 146
  'Blighters' 59
  'The General' 17
Saunders, Hilary St George 152, 155
Scammell, William 122
Scannell, Vernon 10, 122
Scarry, Elaine:
  The Body in Pain 4, 19–20, 24–9, 46, 95,
    122
Schimanski, Stefan 149
school 173, 186–9, 195
Scolay, E. J. 175
Scott, Julian 182–3
Searle, John 22
Second Front 48, 112, 145, 150
self 185
  see identity, individual
  -determination 185–6
  -effacement 63
  realization of 42, 49
  representation of 36
Shakespeare, William:
  Henry V 17, 39, 161, 177
Shute, Nevil:
  What Happened to the Corbetts 74
Sicily 112
Sidney, Sir Philip 59
Silesia 190
Sillars, Stuart 79, 107, 139
Sim, Alastair 108
Sinfield, Alan 34
Sitwell, Osbert:
  'Letter to My Son' 141, 188
social change 73, 77, 140–4, 152, 161
  see levelling, reconstruction
  revolution 141, 145, 149
socialism 2, 5, 93
Sorley, Charles 122
Soviet Union 23, 48, 69, 112–13, 135,
    191,
space:
  of battle 110–18, 125–6, 134–5
  domestic 100–3
  representational 116–17,

urban 82, 85, 92–3
of war 68, 70
Spaight, J. M 58
Spanish Civil War 16, 59, 134, 146, 152, 168, 180 n. 67
spectacle 72–3, 77–8, 81, 84, 106, 118
Spencer, Bernard 114
Spender, Stephen:
  Air Raids 68, 77, 84, 87
  'Books and the War' 152
  'September Journal' 32
  World Within World 33, 132
Spender, Stephen and John Lehmann (eds.):
  Poems for Spain 152
Spielberg, Steven 208–9
Stalin, Joseph 135
statistics 17, 23, 29–30, 70–1, 133–4, 155
Stendhal 9
  The Charterhouse of Parma 110
Storrs, Sir Ronald 47
Strachey, John 44, 107
  Post D 76, 78
strategy and tactics 14, 23, 134
subjectivity and objectivity, 8–9, 14, 17, 102, 118, 129–31
  see detachment/engagement
surrealism 79, 81, 122
surrender 161, 184
  unconditional surrender 145
survival 29, 43–6, 51, 65, 74, 96, 99, 102, 105, 118, 121, 125–6
survivor's songs 6, 43
Sutherland, Graham 87
  'Images Wrought from Destruction' 81, 86–7

Talbot, Godfrey:
  Speaking from the Desert 127
Tambimuttu, M. J. 128, 149
  'In Memory of Keith Douglas' 3
tanks 7, 25, 134–5, 158, 168
Tawny Pipit 147
Taylor, A. J. P. 1, 3
Thackeray, William Makepeace 9
Theweleit, Klaus 7, 192
Third Reich 8, 22
Thomas, Dylan 52
Thomas, Edward 159–60
Those in Peril 49
time:
  anticipation 68–9, 73, 104, 150
  duration 181–2

future, the 2, 19, 46, 59, 73–4, 80, 88, 130, 137, 140, 142, 146, 150, 154, 157, 200
synchronization of national consciousness 153–4
wartime 3, 33, 35
Tippett, Michael 16
Titmuss, Richard 71
Tito (Josip Broz) 197
Tobruk 174
Todd, Ruthven 89
Tolstoy, Leo 9
  War and Peace 58, 111
Torch, Operation 113
Total War 23, 26, 31, 114, 140–3
totalitarianism 35–6, 57, 61–2, 187–8
  Britain as totalitarian 36, 169
  and the individual 57, 61
Toynbee, Philip 64
travel writing 88
Treblinka 172
Trenchard, Lord 109, 150
Trevor-Roper, Hugh 132
Tribune 142, 149
Trinder, Tommy 168
Trott zu Solz, Adam von 56
Trumbo, Dalton 208
Tubbs, Ralph 92
Turner, W. J. 49

Underground, the 83, 87, 90–1
uniforms 6, 63, 102, 148, 159, 163, 175
United Nations Declaration 140
United States 23, 88, 140

V-weapons 99, 100, 103, 108, 109
Vansittartism 208
Vaughan, Keith 25, 29, 54, 63, 144, 156, 170, 184
Verney, John:
  Going to the Wars 184
victim, the 17, 43, 171–2, 188
Vietnam 116, 129, 206
violence:
  and the aesthetic 77, 83–4, 85–6, 89, 106–7, 126
  consent to 31, 41, 80, 106, 153
  and fantasy 59, 69–70, 76, 81, 92
  fascination with 8, 16, 78, 206
  indiscriminacy of 28, 58, 66, 76, 99, 151
  legitimation of 3–4, 15, 18, 23, 26, 29–30, 52, 77, 129, 162, 165
  mediation of 19, 37–8, 51

violence: *(cont.)*
  and national unity 72, 74, 76, 88, 92
  omission of violence in representation
    of war 27, 84
  rationalization of 19, 41, 51, 66, 111,
    125
  redescription of 4, 19, 24, 27–30, 40, 51,
    71–2, 76, 82, 103, 105, 107–8, 118,
    127, 151–2
  representation of 3, 11–12, 19, 24–30,
    72–3, 77–87, 94–9, 104–9, 110–11,
    115–128
  and the sublime 73, 77–81, 97
  targeting of 17, 109
  transcription of 10, 97
  translations of 8, 16, 24, 27–30, 143–4
Volksturm 191
Vonnegut, Kurt:
  Slaughterhouse-Five 175–6

Walbrook, Anton 46
Walpole, Hugh 154
Walzer, Michael 51
war:
  administration of 7, 17, 24, 39–40, 68,
    111, 117, 132–3, 137, 164, 205, 209
  advocacy of 20
  attitudes to 9, 206
  beginning and end of 121, 144, 161,
    183–5, 190–1 193, 203
  by-products/side effects of 9, 28, 72, 86,
    115, 125
  costs of 30, 47, 136, 150–1
  as duel 18, 42, 48, 58
  and ethics 12, 14, 16–18, 28
  as game 41, 123, 162, 175, 185–6
  glamour of 58, 72, 159
  killing or injuring as central activity of
    11, 13, 18
  material and symbolic dimensions of 2,
    4, 11–12, 14–16, 18–19, 21–2, 35, 51,
    65, 111, 113, 118, 159
  means and ends 3, 8, 13, 14–15, 40, 134,
    143, 153
  and politics 12–13, 15, 24, 133, 135–6
  rationalization of 12–13
  as reality duel 26, 180
  sanitization of 19, 78
  simulation of 156, 164, 185
  as sport 18–19, 41
  structure of 14–15, 20, 24, 26, 74, 136–7
  and technology 9–10, 17, 68, 112
  as waste 110, 121, 124–5

war aims 37, 40, 42, 46, 57, 62, 121, 136,
    139–43, 165–6
  scepticism about 42, 52–3
  peace aims 143
War Artists Advisory Committee 81
war correspondents 88, 112, 129
war and language 10–22
  inarticulacy 41
  muteness/stammering 52, 55, 119
  silence 11–12, 25, 33–4
  slang and service argot 10–11, 42
  understatement 46, 53, 55, 56, 64, 66,
    155
war literature:
  canons of 11, 206
  and ethic of participation 15–16, 128
  literature of disenchantment 9, 16, 44,
    146, 162, 164
  literature of protest 12, 37, 162, 205
  reception of 13–14, 34, 40, 53–4
  value of 38, 44, 77, 205
  war frustrates writing of 77, 99
  war produces 10, 41, 77, 79
  as witness 11
war poet, the 9, 13–14, 146, 152–3
war writers 151–3
Ward, A. C. 89
Warner, Rex:
  The Aerodrome 61–2
  Why Was I Killed? 29–30
Waterloo 110–11
Waterloo Road 108
Watson-Watt, Sir Robert 39
Waugh, Evelyn:
  Brideshead Revisited 142, 147
  Put Out More Flags 81, 91, 142
  The Sword of Honour Trilogy 135–6,
    143, 156 n. 99, 187, 190
Wavell, Field Marshall Sir Archibald:
  Other Men's Flowers 154
Wehrmacht 145, 191
welfare state 31, 34, 143
Wells, H. G. 21
  The Shape of Things to Come 58, 71,
    74
  The War in the Air 58, 62
Went the Day Well? 49 n. 28, 145
White, Hayden 182
Williams, Eric 186
  Goon in the Block 179
  The Tunnel 173
  The Wooden Horse 179–80
Williams, Francis 21 n. 55

Williams, Raymond 95
Williams, W. E. 143
Williamson, Henry 146–7
  A Fox Under my Cloak 8
  Love and the Loveless 146
  The Patriot's Progress 146
  A Solitary War 147
  The Wet Flanders Plain 27
Winnicott, D. W. 165–6, 184
Winter, Jay M. 27, 78
Wintringham, Tom 145
Woodcock, George:
  'The Dark Night of the Intellect' 31
Woolf, Virginia 19
  Between the Acts 195
Worpole, Ken 34, 170–1
Worsley, T. C. 66
wounded body 7–8, 26, 40, 42–3, 98, 126,
  157–8

disappearance of 19–20, 25, 27–30, 49,
  68–9, 72, 107, 109
as sign 26, 43–6, 133
visibility of 24–5, 40, 124
Wright, Basil 152
Wright, Patrick 154
writers and government/the services 33,
  59, 152–3, 155

Yeats, W. B. 45, 58–9
  The Oxford Book of Modern Verse
  9
Yeats-Brown, F. and E. W. Sheppard
  Britain at War: The Army 145
Young, James 189
Yugoslavia 197

Zeppelins 71–2, 84, 89
Zola, Emile 9